AI in Digital Forensics and Cybercrime Investigation:

Methods, Ethics, and Emerging Technologies

Hewa Majeed Zangana
Duhok Polytechnic University, Iraq

Marwan Omar
Illinois Institute of Technology, USA

IGI Global
Scientific Publishing
Publishing Tomorrow's Research Today

Vice President of Editorial — Melissa Wagner
Director of Acquisitions — Mikaela Felty
Director of Book Development — Jocelynn Hessler
Production Manager — Mike Brehm
Cover Design — Jose Rosado

Published in the United States of America by
IGI Global Scientific Publishing
701 East Chocolate Avenue
Hershey, PA, 17033, USA
Tel: 717-533-8845
Fax: 717-533-7115
Website: https://www.igi-global.com E-mail: cust@igi-global.com

Library of Congress Cataloging-in-Publication Data

LCCN 2025036241 (CIP Data Pending)
ISBN13: 9798337365367
Isbn13Softcover: 9798337365374
EISBN13: 9798337365381

British Cataloguing in Publication Data
A Cataloguing in Publication record for this book is available from the British Library.

Table of Contents

Detailed Table of Contents

The increasing complexity and volume of financial data have escalated the challenge of detecting anomalies and fraudulent activities in accounting practices. Artificial Intelligence (AI) offers transformative potential to enhance forensic accounting by automating the identification of irregularities, reducing human error, and improving the efficiency and accuracy of financial investigations. This chapter explores the application of AI techniques—such as machine learning, natural language processing, and anomaly detection algorithms—in forensic accounting to detect financial fraud. It discusses the integration of intelligent systems within accounting frameworks, examines case studies demonstrating successful AI deployment, and addresses ethical considerations and challenges related to data privacy and algorithmic bias. By highlighting emerging technologies and future research directions, this chapter underscores AI's critical role in advancing forensic accounting and strengthening financial crime investigations.

The rapid evolution of malware poses significant challenges for traditional signature-based detection methods, necessitating more intelligent and adaptive approaches. Deep learning, a subset of artificial intelligence, has emerged as a powerful tool in malware classification and behavior analysis. This chapter explores how deep learning techniques, such as convolutional neural networks (CNNs), recurrent neural networks (RNNs), and transformers, are applied to detect, classify, and understand malware in real-time. We discuss various input representations including raw binaries, opcode sequences, and API call graphs, and analyze their impact on model performance. Emphasis is placed on the advantages of deep learning over classical machine learning in handling obfuscated and polymorphic malware. Furthermore, we examine challenges such as dataset imbalance, adversarial attacks, and explainability, and propose possible future directions to improve robustness and transparency in AI-driven malware analysis.

The integration of (AI) into cybercrime investigations has transformed traditional policing, introducing advanced tools for surveillance, pattern recognition, and predictive analytics., they also raise pressing sociological concerns regarding privacy, power asymmetries, and the shifting boundaries of deviance and criminality in digital spaces.This chapter explores how AI-enabled surveillance shapes social control mechanisms and redefines norms in online behavior. Drawing from sociological theories of surveillance, control, and criminalization,the chapter critically examines how automated systems can reinforce existing social inequalities, marginalize certain groups,and amplify biases through algorithmic decision-making.Furthermore, it investigates the implications of AI in reconfiguring the social contract between citizens and the state in the context of digital law enforcement. By analyzing case studies and emerging global trends, the chapter provides a nuanced perspective on the role of AI in both empowering and challenging contemporary cybercrime investigation practices

The integration of nanoscale devices and artificial intelligence (AI) in digital forensics marks a paradigm shift in the capabilities available to investigators combating cybercrime. Nanoscale technologies offer unprecedented precision and efficiency in data acquisition, analysis, and evidence preservation. When combined with AI algorithms, these tools enable automated detection, and real-time threat assessment at the micro and macro levels. This chapter explores the synergistic potential of nanoscale devices and AI in enhancing digital forensic investigations, with a focus on applications such as cyber-physical system forensics, biometric identification, and encrypted data retrieval. While the opportunities are substantial, the convergence of these technologies also introduces new challenges, including data privacy risks, and the potential for abuse by malicious actors. The chapter concludes with an analysis of regulatory gaps, and future trends, emphasizing the need for interdisciplinary frameworks to ensure the responsible deployment of these transformative technologies

The rapid digital transformation of agriculture, powered by the Internet of Things (IoT), artificial intelligence (AI), and precision technologies, has led to the emergence of "Smart Agriculture." While these innovations promise enhanced productivity, sustainability, and resource optimization, they also introduce significant cybersecurity vulnerabilities. Smart agriculture systems, including autonomous machinery, sensor networks, and AI-driven analytics, are increasingly targeted by cybercriminals seeking to disrupt food supply chains, steal sensitive agricultural data, or manipulate decision-making algorithms. This chapter explores the intersection of AI and digital forensics in investigating and mitigating cybercrimes within the agri-tech landscape. It highlights AI's role in proactive threat detection, anomaly monitoring, and evidence collection, while also discussing forensic readiness and challenges related to data integrity, privacy, and ethical governance.

The rapid evolution of artificial intelligence (AI) and autonomous systems is transforming the landscape of digital forensics and cybercrime investigation. This chapter explores the emerging paradigm of autonomous forensic agents and AI-augmented investigators, emphasizing their potential to revolutionize evidence collection, data analysis, and decision-making processes. It delves into the convergence of machine learning, natural language processing, robotics, and cognitive computing to create intelligent agents capable of independently navigating digital environments, identifying anomalies, and assisting human investigators with high precision and efficiency. The chapter also addresses the ethical, legal, and technical challenges that accompany the deployment of such systems, including concerns about bias, accountability, transparency, and interpretability. Drawing from real-world applications, research trends, and interdisciplinary innovations, this forward-looking analysis envisions a future where human expertise is seamlessly integrated with intelligent automation

Preface

INTRODUCTION

In an era marked by exponential technological growth, the convergence of Artificial Intelligence (AI) and digital forensics presents a powerful—and at times provocative—transformation in the fight against cybercrime. This edited volume, *AI in Digital Forensics and Cybercrime Investigation: Methods, Ethics, and Emerging Technologies*, is born out of the urgent need to examine and understand the accelerating impact of AI on forensic science, law enforcement, and the broader digital security landscape.

From machine learning algorithms capable of identifying complex patterns in digital evidence to large language models (LLMs) that can detect and even predict cyber threats, AI is reshaping not only how crimes are investigated, but how digital justice is conceptualized and delivered. In compiling this book, we have sought to bring together leading voices from across disciplines—academia, industry, law enforcement, and policy—to offer both depth and breadth in exploring this multifaceted domain.

This volume provides readers with a dual lens: theoretical foundations that contextualize AI's integration into forensics, and practical insights drawn from real-world applications, case studies, and tool development. Topics include the automation of evidence handling, ethical dilemmas in algorithmic decision-making, the role of AI in legal admissibility of digital evidence, and the implications of AI-driven surveillance. As such, this book is not only a timely exploration of new technologies but also a critical reflection on the responsibilities that accompany them.

Our aim is to support and stimulate research communities at the nexus of AI, cybersecurity, and forensic investigation. We hope this book will encourage meaningful collaboration across technical and legal disciplines, foster innovative research trajectories, and serve as a cornerstone for future scholarship in AI-assisted digital forensics.

This work is intended for a diverse and interdisciplinary audience: academic researchers, graduate students, cybersecurity professionals, forensic investigators, AI developers, legal scholars, and policymakers. Whether you are designing algorithms, enforcing digital law, or debating ethical AI frameworks, we trust that the insights in this volume will be of practical value and intellectual inspiration.

As editors, we are honored to present this collaborative effort and deeply grateful to our contributors for their expertise and commitment to advancing knowledge in this rapidly evolving field. Together, we hope to illuminate the pathways where AI can responsibly and effectively serve the pursuit of digital justice.

ORGANIZATION OF THE BOOK

Chapter 1 opens the volume with a timely investigation into the role of Natural Language Processing (NLP) in deciphering criminal communication across diverse digital platforms. As cybercriminals increasingly exploit unstructured channels like dark web forums, encrypted messaging, and phishing campaigns, this chapter offers a critical look at how NLP techniques—such as named entity recognition and linguistic profiling—support the extraction of actionable intelligence. By integrating NLP within broader machine learning frameworks, the authors illustrate how cyber threat detection can be made more predictive and responsive to emerging adversarial tactics.

Chapter 2 addresses the legal and regulatory terrain that must evolve in parallel with AI-enabled forensic technologies. Focusing on admissibility, accountability, and jurisdictional complexities, the authors dissect the key challenges in harmonizing AI practices with legal norms. They offer comparative insights into international regulatory frameworks, drawing attention to the pressing need for explainability, transparency, and cross-border legal alignment. This chapter serves as a vital guide for policymakers, legal practitioners, and technologists navigating the ethical and judicial frontiers of AI in forensic science.

In Chapter 3, we turn to the power of machine learning in elevating digital forensic capabilities. From anomaly detection to malware classification and digital evidence triage, this chapter provides a robust overview of ML techniques—supervised, unsupervised, and reinforcement learning—and their practical deployments in threat detection. It also thoughtfully engages with the limitations and ethical issues surrounding explainability, data imbalance, and adversarial robustness, encouraging researchers to develop more resilient and trustworthy ML systems for forensic applications.

Chapter 4 introduces the innovative potential of Digital Twin (DT) technology in simulating cybercrime environments. This chapter charts how virtual replicas of digital ecosystems can be used to model attacks, predict adversarial behavior, and test forensic responses in real-time. By combining DTs with AI and machine learning, investigators gain predictive tools that extend beyond reactive methodologies. With compelling case studies and thoughtful exploration of ethical implications, the chapter reveals how digital twins are becoming central to both training and strategic planning in cyber defense.

Chapter 5 explores the evolving intersection of AI and forensic accounting, offering a critical lens into how intelligent systems are redefining financial fraud detection. Through machine learning, NLP, and anomaly detection, this chapter demonstrates how AI can pinpoint irregularities within complex financial data landscapes. Real-world case studies highlight the efficiency gains and risk mitigation made possible by automation. At the same time, the chapter confronts challenges related to algorithmic bias, privacy, and auditability, calling for robust ethical frameworks in financial forensics.

Chapter 6 turns the spotlight on deep learning applications in malware analysis, showcasing the capabilities of CNNs, RNNs, and transformer models in classifying and interpreting malware behavior. By analyzing raw binaries, opcode sequences, and API call graphs, the authors show how deep learning surpasses traditional detection methods, particularly against polymorphic and obfuscated malware. This chapter balances technical rigor with practical insight, also tackling pressing concerns such as dataset bias, explainability, and model vulnerability to adversarial manipulation.

In Chapter 7, the focus shifts to the sociological implications of AI in cybercrime investigations. This critical chapter examines how surveillance technologies reshape social norms, power structures, and notions of criminality in digital spaces. Drawing on sociological theory, it probes the risks of algorithmic bias, social marginalization, and over-policing within AI-driven forensic systems. By linking technology to broader social consequences, the authors challenge readers to consider the ethical and democratic stakes of embedding AI into systems of law enforcement and control.

Chapter 8 introduces a cutting-edge dialogue on the fusion of nanoscale devices and AI in forensic science. These ultra-precise technologies offer powerful tools for biometric identification, encrypted data retrieval, and cyber-physical forensics. Yet, as the chapter astutely observes, they also bring significant risks—ranging from data misuse to privacy erosion. This chapter navigates the dual-use dilemma of emerging technologies, proposing interdisciplinary governance models that balance innovation with ethical oversight.

Chapter 9 expands the forensic lens to the critical field of smart agriculture, where cyberattacks threaten food security and data integrity. As IoT, AI, and robotics become embedded in agricultural systems, so too do vulnerabilities. This chapter examines how AI-driven forensics can be employed to investigate agri-tech cybercrime, enabling anomaly detection, forensic readiness, and digital evidence gathering in rural and high-tech farming environments. It also underscores the urgent need for ethical and secure data practices to protect global food systems.

Chapter 10 envisions a not-so-distant future defined by autonomous forensic agents and AI-augmented investigators. This chapter dives into the convergence of robotics, machine learning, and cognitive computing to support intelligent systems capable of independent evidence discovery and threat analysis. The authors raise important questions around legal accountability, system transparency, and the human-machine partnership in investigative work. By examining real-world prototypes and research trajectories, this chapter positions autonomous agents as the next frontier in digital forensics.

Finally, Chapter 11 closes the volume with a focus on Explainable AI (XAI) in high-stakes forensic settings. The opacity of black-box models presents serious obstacles to trust, legal admissibility, and ethical clarity. This chapter surveys the leading approaches to XAI—ranging from post-hoc explainability to inherently interpretable models—and evaluates their effectiveness in law enforcement and judicial decision-making contexts. Grounded in case studies, it argues for a context-sensitive balance between performance and transparency, ensuring that forensic AI remains accountable to both technical and human standards.

Together, these chapters map the evolving territory of AI in digital forensics, offering both technical depth and ethical reflection. This book invites readers to explore how AI can empower, challenge, and ultimately transform the investigative processes that define cybersecurity and digital justice.

CONCLUSION

As we bring this volume to a close, it is evident that the integration of Artificial Intelligence into digital forensics and cybercrime investigation is not a future possibility—it is a present reality, reshaping the landscape of security, evidence, and justice in profound ways. The chapters in this book collectively illuminate how AI-driven technologies, from natural language processing to deep learning, from autonomous forensic agents to nanoscale devices, are redefining both the capabilities and the contours of forensic investigation in the digital age.

Yet, alongside these innovations arise equally complex legal, ethical, and sociotechnical challenges. Questions of algorithmic accountability, transparency, bias, jurisdiction, and privacy loom large, demanding thoughtful, interdisciplinary responses. We believe that addressing these challenges is not ancillary but central to the responsible advancement of AI in forensics.

This book is both a reflection of current capabilities and a call to action for researchers, practitioners, and policymakers. It encourages continued dialogue across technical, legal, and social domains, and advocates for a forensic future that is not only intelligent, but also just, equitable, and trustworthy.

As editors, we are honored to have curated this collection of work from leading thinkers and innovators across the globe. We hope that this volume serves not only as a reference point for present developments but also as a catalyst for future scholarship, collaboration, and ethical innovation in the evolving nexus of AI and digital forensics.

Chapter 1

Natural Language Processing for Analyzing Criminal Communication and Cyber Threat Intelligence

Hewa Majeed Zangana
https://orcid.org/0000-0001-7909-254X
Duhok Polytechnic University, Iraq

Marwan Omar
https://orcid.org/0009-0000-7534-5490
Illinois Institute of Technology, USA

Ann Rangarajan
https://orcid.org/0009-0006-7179-5404
Illinois Institute of Technology, USA

Basna Mohammed Salih Hasan
Duhok Polytechnic University, Iraq

ABSTRACT

The increasing sophistication of cybercriminal activities necessitates advanced tools for digital forensics and cyber threat intelligence. Natural Language Processing (NLP) has emerged as a pivotal technique for analyzing vast amounts of unstructured text data generated by threat actors across platforms such as dark web forums, social media, encrypted messaging, and phishing emails. This chapter explores the

DOI: 10.4018/979-8-3373-6536-7.ch001

core methodologies and applications of NLP in identifying, interpreting, and predicting criminal communication patterns and cyber threats. It highlights key NLP techniques—such as named entity recognition, sentiment analysis, topic modeling, and linguistic profiling—that facilitate the extraction of actionable insights from malicious communications. Moreover, the chapter discusses the integration of NLP with machine learning and threat intelligence frameworks to improve the detection of emerging threats and adversarial tactics.

INTRODUCTION

The rapid proliferation of digital communication platforms has revolutionized the way individuals interact—but it has also been exploited by malicious actors for criminal and cyberterrorist purposes. As cybercrimes become increasingly sophisticated and covert, digital forensics and cyber threat intelligence (CTI) must evolve to detect, analyze, and mitigate these threats efficiently. Among the most promising tools in this evolving landscape is Natural Language Processing (NLP), which enables automated understanding and interpretation of human language across massive volumes of digital text. NLP has become a crucial component in analyzing communications from dark web forums, social media platforms, phishing emails, and other digital mediums used for illicit activities (Rajendran & Tulasi, 2025; Sufi, 2023a).

Criminal communication is no longer limited to traditional means; rather, it spans encrypted messaging, decentralized platforms, and even the use of emojis and codewords to evade detection (Etaywe et al., 2024). NLP-powered systems can decode such signals using techniques like topic modeling, entity recognition, and sentiment analysis (Sun et al., 2023). For instance, Long Short-Term Memory (LSTM) networks and BERT-based transformers have been applied to capture context and identify intent behind social media communications on darknet forums (Sangher et al., 2024). These models support proactive threat detection by classifying suspicious language patterns and behavioral signals, thus offering real-time insights into emerging threats (Atoum et al., 2025).

Researchers have highlighted how open-source intelligence (OSINT)—extracted from publicly available text—can be harnessed using NLP techniques to detect terrorism-related activities and identify digital footprints of cybercriminals (Chaudhary & Bansal, 2022; Adewopo et al., 2020; Sufi, 2023b). Automated preprocessing and classification methods are now indispensable for filtering relevant threat data from noisy environments like Twitter and Telegram (Johnsen & Franke, 2019). This transition is echoed in contemporary literature emphasizing the automation of cyber threat identification through deep language models (Marinho & Holanda, 2023; Ramírez Sánchez et al., 2021).

Beyond syntactic understanding, NLP has enabled psycholinguistic profiling of online actors, offering behavioral clues that support threat classification and attribution (Etaywe et al., 2024). Coupled with machine learning frameworks trained on terrorism datasets, such approaches are instrumental in enhancing cybersecurity protocols and predictive analytics (Atoum et al., 2025). The integration of synthetic data into LLMs, as explored by Gholami and Omar (2023, 2024), further empowers NLP applications to train on adversarial or underrepresented linguistic domains, strengthening system robustness against obfuscation and deception.

Recent advances in LLM-powered cybersecurity show that NLP is not only limited to surface-level language parsing but can drive deep semantic understanding in threat detection systems (Omar & Zangana, 2025). Techniques explored in the GEADD framework, for instance, leverage GPT-enhanced architectures for zero-day attack prediction (Jones & Omar, 2024). These developments are vital as cybercriminals adopt obfuscation, code-switching, and multilingual strategies to bypass filters and deceive systems (Zangana et al., 2024a).

Concurrently, studies such as those by Huff et al. (2023) and Mohammed et al. (2018) underscore the importance of securing environments where NLP is deployed, especially within sensitive infrastructures like healthcare and wireless sensor networks. The repeal of regulatory safeguards (Nguyen et al., 2018) adds another layer of complexity to ensuring ethical NLP deployments.

With the proliferation of large language models (LLMs) such as GPT and BERT, there's a paradigm shift toward context-aware NLP solutions in CTI. These models have been shown to match or surpass human-level performance in identifying vulnerabilities (Zangana & Omar, 2025; Jones et al., 2023). In the context of quantum-aware cybersecurity, NLP-driven LLMs are being tailored to anticipate threats in quantum-vulnerable ecosystems (Zangana, Mustafa, Li, & Al-Karaki, 2025).

Moreover, the application of NLP in scientific and legal frameworks is gaining traction (Zangana, Omar, & Al-Karaki, 2025a, 2025b), reinforcing the need for interdisciplinary approaches to secure digital ecosystems. NLP is also critical in ensuring ethical AI deployment, particularly in the processing of sensitive STM research and educational data.

In sum, this chapter presents a comprehensive overview of how NLP transforms the landscape of criminal communication analysis and cyber threat intelligence. It highlights its integration with LLMs, machine learning, and OSINT frameworks to enhance threat detection accuracy and foresight. Future sections will explore the technical foundations, ethical dilemmas, case studies, and future directions of NLP in digital forensics and cybersecurity.

BACKGROUND AND RELATED WORK

Natural Language Processing (NLP) has emerged as a transformative technology in the fields of digital forensics and cybercrime investigation. By enabling machines to understand, interpret, and generate human language, NLP facilitates the analysis of large volumes of unstructured text data, such as emails, chat logs, social media posts, dark web forum content, and threat intelligence reports. This capacity is particularly crucial when dealing with cybercriminal activities that rely heavily on textual communication and information dissemination.

Evolution of NLP in Cybersecurity Contexts

The evolution of NLP has been marked by significant shifts from rule-based systems to statistical methods, and more recently to deep learning and transformer-based models such as BERT, RoBERTa, and GPT. In the domain of cybersecurity, earlier NLP systems were used primarily for spam detection and keyword matching in emails. However, the field has matured to encompass sophisticated use cases, including phishing detection, malware documentation analysis, and insider threat prediction.

Modern NLP systems leverage contextual embeddings and fine-tuning on domain-specific corpora to achieve high performance in tasks such as named entity recognition (NER), topic modeling, sentiment analysis, intent detection, and text classification. These capabilities are now central to developing cyber threat intelligence systems that automatically process and interpret communication between threat actors, identify trends and indicators of compromise (IOCs), and map threats to MITRE ATT&CK frameworks.

Criminal Communication in Digital Environments

Criminals increasingly exploit digital platforms for communication, coordination, recruitment, and propaganda. These platforms range from encrypted messaging apps (e.g., Telegram, Signal) to the dark web and social media. Their use of slang, obfuscation, code words, multilingualism, and emojis creates significant challenges for law enforcement and investigators.

Studies have shown that criminal groups often develop their own lexicons or adapt commonly used terms to avoid detection (Pearce et al., 2023). NLP-based techniques such as neural machine translation (NMT), zero-shot learning, and contextual embedding analysis have proven effective in identifying and interpreting these non-standard linguistic patterns.

Several NLP models have been trained on specialized corpora derived from the dark web and cybercrime forums to enhance their ability to decode threat actor communications. For example, researchers like Ameri et al. (2021) and Ferrag et al. (2023) have employed topic modeling techniques (e.g., LDA, BERTopic) to reveal patterns in ransomware negotiation, data breach announcements, and malware sales discussions.

Cyber Threat Intelligence (CTI) Extraction

Cyber threat intelligence (CTI) refers to the collection and analysis of information regarding potential or current cyber threats. NLP plays a crucial role in automating CTI by extracting actionable insights from unstructured text sources. Common NLP techniques used in CTI include:

- **Named Entity Recognition (NER):** to identify indicators such as malware names, IP addresses, URLs, file hashes, and threat actor aliases.
- **Relation Extraction:** to determine relationships among entities (e.g., malware used by a particular group or infrastructure used in an attack).
- **Event Detection:** to pinpoint descriptions of cyber incidents or coordinated campaigns.
- **Sentiment and Emotion Analysis:** to understand the intent and urgency behind communications.

Tools such as MITRE's ATT&CK framework and STIX/TAXII standards have been integrated with NLP pipelines to structure and share threat intelligence effectively (Jiang, 2024; Zangana et al., 2024).

Related Studies and Systems

Several notable systems and studies have demonstrated the efficacy of NLP in this domain. Al-Hawawreh et al. (2023) presented an NLP-based system for detecting cyber threats in real-time social media streams. Gholami and Omar (2024) proposed a multilingual NLP framework for understanding terrorist narratives in online environments, while Happe and Cito (2023) emphasized the integration of LLMs in analyzing insider threat communication within organizations.

Other research efforts, such as those by Guastalla et al. (2023) and Xu et al. (2024), focus on combining NLP with machine learning classifiers and graph-based models to enhance situational awareness in threat intelligence centers. These hybrid approaches allow for better identification of coordinated threat campaigns and enable proactive defense mechanisms.

Challenges in NLP for Cybercrime

Despite significant advances, several challenges persist:

- **Data Scarcity:** High-quality labeled datasets for criminal communication are rare due to ethical, privacy, and legal concerns.
- **Language Complexity:** Use of multiple languages, code-switching, slang, and jargon complicates text analysis.
- **Domain Adaptation:** NLP models trained on general text often struggle to generalize to cybercrime-related contexts without fine-tuning.
- **Adversarial Evasion:** Threat actors deliberately craft text to evade automated detection, posing robustness challenges to NLP systems.

Summary

In summary, NLP has become an indispensable tool in the analysis of criminal communication and the generation of cyber threat intelligence. Its ability to process vast and diverse text sources enhances law enforcement capabilities, intelligence gathering, and proactive threat mitigation. However, continuous innovation and ethical considerations are essential to address the evolving tactics of cybercriminals and ensure responsible use of these technologies.

TYPES OF CRIMINAL COMMUNICATION AND THREAT SOURCES

Understanding the diverse forms of criminal communication and their corresponding threat sources is a critical precursor to deploying Natural Language Processing (NLP) techniques in cyber threat intelligence and digital forensics. Criminals increasingly leverage both surface and hidden communication channels—ranging from social media to encrypted darknet forums—to coordinate, recruit, threaten, or execute cyber and physical crimes. The integration of NLP into this domain demands a comprehensive grasp of how, where, and why such communications occur.

Figure 1 illustrates the estimated distribution of different criminal communication sources based on recent cybersecurity intelligence findings, highlighting the relevance of diverse platforms for NLP-based threat detection.

Figure 1. Sources of criminal communication used in cyber threat intelligence

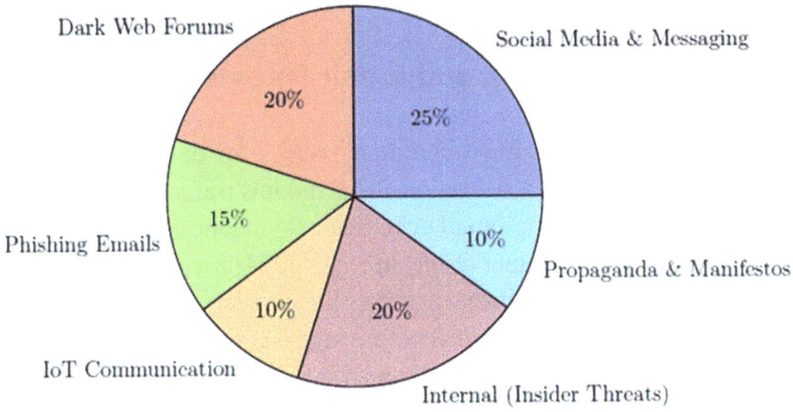

Social Media and Messaging Platforms

Social media platforms such as Twitter, Telegram, WhatsApp, and Facebook are widely exploited by criminals for recruitment, propaganda dissemination, planning illicit operations, and spreading disinformation. NLP-based systems have shown promise in detecting extremist language, hate speech, cyberbullying, and coordination of illegal acts on these platforms (Aghaei et al., 2022; Ameri et al., 2021). These platforms are particularly challenging due to the brevity of messages, informal language, slang, codewords, and multilingual communication.

Alawida et al. (2023) demonstrated how AI-driven approaches, including NLP models, can be effective in analyzing threats from terrorist communications across encrypted chat groups. Similarly, Gupta et al. (2024) outlined the role of deep learning-based NLP tools for monitoring large-scale multilingual data streams from open sources and detecting signals indicative of coordinated attacks.

Dark Web and Encrypted Forums

The dark web hosts a plethora of forums and marketplaces where cybercriminals exchange stolen data, malware, and illicit services. Threat actors often communicate using jargon, obfuscation, and coded language to evade detection. Ferrag et al. (2023) highlight how advanced cryptographic techniques used in these hidden channels pose challenges to traditional surveillance, necessitating intelligent NLP-based parsing and contextual interpretation.

Gholami and Omar (2023, 2024) emphasized the use of transformer-based models for monitoring dark web content and extracting actionable intelligence. These approaches can detect criminal intent and fraud schemes by identifying latent patterns in conversations, product listings, and user behavior.

Phishing, Spear-Phishing, and Email Threats

Emails remain one of the most common vectors for delivering cyberattacks, such as ransomware and data exfiltration. NLP models trained on labeled datasets of phishing and spear-phishing emails can detect syntactic and semantic patterns associated with fraudulent content (Nguyen et al., 2024; Xu et al., 2024). Huff et al. (2023) demonstrated a hybrid approach using NLP and threat intelligence databases to detect zero-day phishing campaigns before significant damage occurs.

The challenge lies in accurately distinguishing malicious communication from legitimate business correspondence, especially when attackers mimic official tone and style. Jin et al. (2024) proposed contextual BERT-based classification models to identify spear-phishing by incorporating organizational metadata and writing style cues.

IoT and Smart Device Communications

The proliferation of Internet of Things (IoT) devices opens new channels for covert communication and data exfiltration. Cybercriminals may hijack smart devices to use them as relays or listening tools. Al-Hawawreh et al. (2023) explored how NLP can be applied to analyze log data and communication protocols of compromised IoT systems, identifying indicators of compromise and malicious command patterns.

Tann et al. (2023) further emphasized that communication among smart devices, though not traditionally linguistic, can be translated into tokenized sequences suitable for NLP analysis to detect anomalies and intrusions.

Insider Threats and Internal Communication

Insider threats represent a unique challenge as malicious actors often operate within legitimate communication frameworks. NLP can be used to monitor and analyze internal communications such as emails, chat logs, and reports to detect behavioral shifts or indicators of sabotage (Jones & Omar, 2024; Ranade et al., 2021). These threats are particularly insidious as they involve actors who are already trusted within the organizational perimeter.

Sultana et al. (2023) leveraged NLP combined with sentiment analysis and behavioral profiling to detect disgruntled employees or those susceptible to manipulation. This proactive detection requires ethical considerations and strict compliance with privacy regulations.

Cyber Threat Intelligence Feeds

Structured and unstructured cyber threat intelligence (CTI) feeds are essential for understanding the evolving landscape of threat actors, tactics, and procedures. NLP is increasingly applied to extract and normalize Indicators of Compromise (IOCs), attacker techniques, and vulnerabilities from CTI reports, blogs, and advisories (Gao, 2023; Guastalla et al., 2023).

Pearce et al. (2023) demonstrated how NLP could enhance situational awareness by clustering semantically similar CTI alerts, facilitating rapid response. Happe and Cito (2023) stressed the importance of ontology-driven NLP systems to categorize and interlink threat information across heterogeneous sources.

Threat Actor Manifestos and Ideological Propaganda

Some threat actors, particularly those involved in acts of terrorism or mass violence, publish manifestos or ideological texts. These documents are often rich in intent-revealing language and ideological cues. NLP tools, particularly topic modeling and semantic analysis, can detect radicalization trends and forecast potential attacks (Georgescu, 2020; Jiang, 2024).

Motlagh et al. (2024) proposed integrating NLP with psychological and linguistic features to detect incitement, targeting, and dehumanization in manifestos. Kereopa-Yorke (2024) also advocated for culturally informed NLP approaches when analyzing indigenous or regional languages involved in extremist content.

Multilingual and Cross-Cultural Threats

Globalization of crime necessitates NLP systems capable of handling multiple languages, dialects, and scripts. Wright et al. (2012) were among the first to advocate for multilingual text analysis for national security purposes. More recent work by Zangana et al. (2024a) addressed language-specific tokenization and semantic mapping, allowing for effective cross-linguistic criminal analysis.

(Omar & Zangana, 2024) also investigated hybrid NLP frameworks that support Arabic, Kurdish, and Persian texts in criminal investigations, highlighting the need for culturally aware and locally relevant models.

NLP TECHNIQUES FOR CRIMINAL COMMUNICATION ANALYSIS

Natural Language Processing (NLP) has become a pivotal technology in analyzing and extracting actionable insights from criminal communication, enabling cyber threat intelligence, digital forensics, and proactive security measures. The complex and evolving nature of criminal discourse—often marked by slang, code words, mixed languages, and obfuscation—requires sophisticated NLP techniques capable of understanding context, intent, and subtle linguistic cues. This section discusses the major NLP techniques applied in criminal communication analysis, supported by the latest research.

To better understand the diverse NLP techniques discussed in this section, the following flowchart visualizes the major NLP processes used in criminal communication analysis—from data collection to intelligence generation.

Figure 2. Flowchart of NLP techniques applied to criminal communication analysis

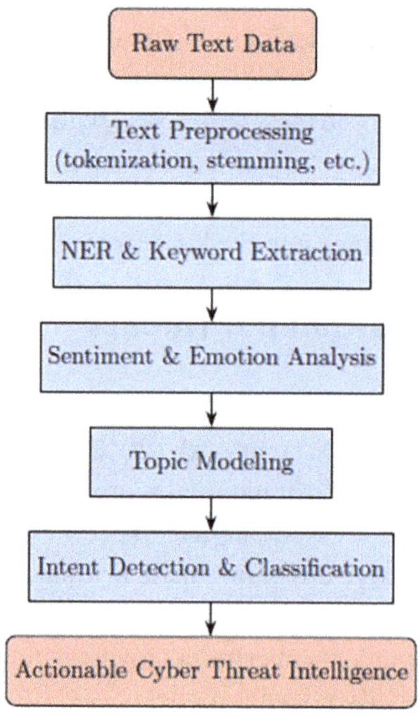

Text Preprocessing and Normalization

Preprocessing is a critical initial step in NLP pipelines to convert raw textual data from social media, emails, dark web forums, or chat logs into structured formats suitable for analysis (Johnsen & Franke, 2019). This includes tokenization, stemming, lemmatization, stop-word removal, and normalization of slang and abbreviations frequently used in criminal communication (Sufi, 2023).

Rajendran and Tulasi (2025) emphasize the importance of domain-specific preprocessing that adapts to the nuances of threat-related texts, including handling emojis, misspellings, and encrypted slang. Preprocessing also helps mitigate noise and improves downstream tasks such as classification or entity recognition.

Keyword Extraction and Named Entity Recognition (NER)

Keyword extraction techniques help identify relevant terms such as names, locations, weapons, dates, and malicious software in criminal texts (Chaudhary & Bansal, 2022). Named Entity Recognition (NER) is particularly vital for recognizing entities related to threat actors and infrastructure within unstructured text sources.

Sangher, Singh, and Pandey (2024) demonstrated the effectiveness of transformer-based models like BERT and LSTM in capturing contextual information to improve NER accuracy, especially when analyzing cyber threat intelligence from darknet forums and social media.

Sentiment and Emotion Analysis

Understanding the emotional tone behind communications provides insights into threat levels and psychological states of actors. Etaywe, Macfarlane, and Alazab (2024) used automated text analysis for psycholinguistic profiling of cyberterrorists, revealing how sentiment analysis combined with linguistic cues can support threat assessment.

Sufi (2023) also highlights the role of sentiment analysis in monitoring social media platforms during conflicts like the Russia–Ukraine cyber war, helping to detect propaganda, misinformation, and incitement.

Topic Modeling and Thematic Analysis

Topic modeling algorithms such as Latent Dirichlet Allocation (LDA) and Non-negative Matrix Factorization (NMF) are employed to uncover hidden thematic structures in large corpora of criminal communications (Sun et al., 2023). This technique assists in categorizing communications into topics like recruitment, attack planning, or fundraising.

Atoum et al. (2025) propose a machine learning framework integrating topic modeling with terrorism datasets, enhancing the identification of emergent threats and thematic trends within textual data.

Text Classification and Intent Detection

Automated classification of texts into categories such as benign, suspicious, or malicious supports scalable monitoring of criminal communication (Sangher et al., 2023). Advanced deep learning models, including Long Short-Term Memory (LSTM) networks and BERT-based transformers, excel in intent identification.

Jones and Omar (2024) introduced the GPT-2 Enhanced Attack Detection and Defense (GEADD) method, a cutting-edge NLP classifier that significantly improves detection of zero-day cyber threats by capturing semantic nuances in threat actor communications.

Anomaly and Adversarial Detection

Criminal communications often contain adversarial content designed to evade detection. Gholami and Omar (2024) explored methods to strengthen deep neural network (DNN) text classifiers against adversarial examples by optimizing training algorithms and data augmentation.

Similarly, Gholami and Omar (2023, 2024) analyzed the use of synthetic data to enhance large language model efficiency, which is crucial for detecting cleverly disguised malicious content within noisy or sparse datasets.

Cross-Lingual and Multilingual Analysis

Criminals operate across language barriers, necessitating NLP models that can process multilingual content. Wright, Dawson Jr, and Omar (2012) underscored the early importance of multilingual cybersecurity analysis, while Zangana and Omar (2025) further advanced frameworks to harness large language models (LLMs) for cross-lingual threat intelligence.

Omar and Zangana (2024, 2025) contributed significant work on adapting BERT and GPT models for languages such as Arabic, Kurdish, and Persian, addressing region-specific criminal communication challenges.

Network and Social Graph Analysis with NLP

Integrating NLP with social network analysis enables tracing communication patterns and identifying central threat actors (Lee, Mujammami, & Kim, 2024). NLP techniques extract conversational content and intent while graph algorithms analyze interactions, enhancing detection of coordinated campaigns.

Rajendran and Tulasi (2025) describe how social media analytics combine NLP with network features to profile threat actors and understand cyber attack trends.

Cyber Threat Intelligence Automation

Automating the mining of cyber threat intelligence (CTI) from unstructured text sources accelerates threat detection and response (Sun et al., 2023). Marinho and Holanda (2023) presented automated frameworks that utilize NLP to extract, classify, and prioritize emerging cyber threats from multiple open sources.

Zangana, Omar, and Al-Karaki (2025) reviewed how LLMs are harnessed to enrich CTI workflows, significantly reducing human analyst workload while improving accuracy and situational awareness.

Ethical and Privacy Considerations in NLP

The deployment of NLP in criminal communication analysis raises ethical challenges around privacy, bias, and misuse (Zangana, Omar, & Al-Karaki, 2025). Ensuring compliance with data protection laws and embedding fairness in model design are crucial to responsible AI in cybersecurity (Zangana, Omar, & Al-Karaki, 2025).

This comprehensive overview underscores how various NLP techniques are synergistically employed to tackle the complexity of criminal communication, enabling more effective cyber threat intelligence and digital forensics.

NLP FOR CYBER THREAT INTELLIGENCE (CTI)

Cyber Threat Intelligence (CTI) has become an essential domain in cybersecurity, focusing on the collection, analysis, and dissemination of information related to potential and actual cyber threats. Natural Language Processing (NLP) has emerged as a powerful tool to enhance CTI by automatically extracting meaningful insights from vast amounts of textual data, including social media, dark web forums, incident reports, and open-source intelligence (OSINT) platforms (Rajendran & Tulasi, 2025; Sun et al., 2023).

The Role of NLP in CTI

NLP enables cybersecurity professionals to process unstructured textual data to identify emerging threats, malicious actors, attack trends, tactics, techniques, and procedures (TTPs), and the intent behind cyber activities. By leveraging NLP, CTI systems can extract entities, sentiment, relationships, and intent from cyber threat reports and social media feeds, facilitating proactive threat detection and response (Lee, Mujammami, & Kim, 2024; Sangher, Singh, & Pandey, 2024).

The open-source intelligence (OSINT) paradigm benefits significantly from NLP, as much relevant cyber threat information is shared in informal textual formats on social media and underground forums. Techniques such as entity recognition, topic modeling, sentiment analysis, and text classification support the automated mining of this data for actionable intelligence (Chaudhary & Bansal, 2022; Adewopo, Gonen, & Adewopo, 2020).

The following system architecture (Figure 3) illustrates how NLP integrates into a typical cyber threat intelligence (CTI) pipeline, processing unstructured data to generate actionable threat reports.

Figure 3. System architecture: integration of NLP into cyber threat intelligence

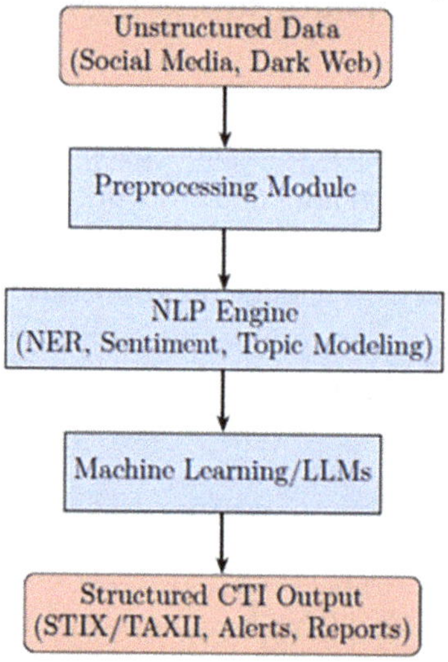

Key NLP Techniques in CTI

Several NLP methodologies have been successfully applied to CTI, including traditional machine learning models, deep learning architectures such as Long

Short-Term Memory (LSTM) networks, and transformer-based models like BERT and GPT (Sangher et al., 2024; Omar & Zangana, 2025). These techniques help in intent identification, threat actor profiling, and detection of cybercrime activities in both surface and dark web textual data (Sangher, Singh, Pandey, & Kumar, 2023).

Textual data from terrorism-related datasets has also been analyzed using machine learning frameworks to understand threat actors' psycholinguistic profiles and potential behaviors (Atoum et al., 2025; Etaywe, Macfarlane, & Alazab, 2024). This highlights the interdisciplinary utility of NLP for CTI, bridging cybersecurity with psychological threat assessment.

The preprocessing of textual data plays a crucial role in enhancing the accuracy of NLP applications in CTI. Effective cleaning, tokenization, normalization, and removal of noise enable more precise information extraction (Johnsen & Franke, 2019). Moreover, recent advancements explore synthetic data to improve the training of large language models (Gholami & Omar, 2023), making these models more robust for CTI tasks.

Challenges and Limitations

Despite its potential, applying NLP to CTI faces several challenges. The dynamic and adversarial nature of cyber threats means that threat actors constantly adapt their language and communication styles, complicating automated detection (Sun et al., 2023). The presence of slang, coded language, and multi-lingual data on social platforms and dark forums adds complexity (Sufi, 2023; Ramírez Sánchez et al., 2021).

Furthermore, the vast scale and heterogeneity of cyber threat data demand scalable NLP systems with high accuracy and low false positives. The integration of NLP outputs into existing security operations remains a challenge due to issues of trust, interpretability, and timely response (Jones & Omar, 2024; Huff et al., 2023).

Emerging Trends and Future Directions

The integration of large language models (LLMs) such as GPT and BERT has revolutionized CTI by enhancing the depth and nuance of threat intelligence extraction (Omar & Zangana, 2025; Zangana & Omar, 2025). These models demonstrate significant improvements in contextual understanding, enabling sophisticated cyberattack pattern recognition and zero-day threat identification (Jones, Omar, Mohammed, Nobles, & Dawson, 2023).

Researchers are also exploring the fusion of NLP with AI-driven frameworks in IoT malware detection, agricultural cybersecurity, and forensic applications, expanding CTI's scope beyond traditional IT environments (Zangana et al., 2025). Quantum-aware cybersecurity systems leveraging NLP are an emerging frontier, promising enhanced security for future computing paradigms (Zangana & Omar, 2025).

To address insider threats, hybrid approaches combining psycholinguistic profiling with NLP-driven behavioral analysis are being developed (Zangana, & Omar, 2025). Moreover, ongoing efforts focus on establishing regulatory frameworks and ethical guidelines for AI and NLP applications in CTI to ensure privacy and compliance (Zangana, Omar, & Al-Karaki, 2025).

Summary

NLP stands at the forefront of advancing Cyber Threat Intelligence by automating and enhancing the analysis of complex, voluminous textual data sources. While challenges remain, continuous innovation in deep learning, transformer models, and interdisciplinary approaches promises a future where NLP-driven CTI significantly strengthens proactive cybersecurity defenses.

CASE STUDIES AND APPLICATIONS

This section explores diverse case studies and applications illustrating the practical implementation of cybersecurity, cyber threat intelligence (CTI), natural language processing (NLP), and large language models (LLMs) across various domains. The case studies demonstrate how emerging AI technologies and data-driven approaches have been leveraged for proactive threat detection, analysis, and defense in real-world scenarios. The studies also emphasize the increasing role of open-source intelligence (OSINT), social media analytics, and advanced machine learning frameworks in contemporary cybersecurity landscapes.

Cyber Threat Intelligence through Natural Language Processing and Social Media Analytics

Recent advances in NLP have been pivotal in extracting and analyzing threat intelligence from vast amounts of textual data found in social media, darknet forums, and open-source platforms. Rajendran and Tulasi (2025) provide a comprehensive overview of NLP techniques tailored for threat intelligence gathering, highlighting the capabilities to automatically mine, classify, and interpret cyber threats in near real-time. Complementing this, Sufi (2023) examines social media analytics in the context of the Russia–Ukraine cyber war, revealing challenges related to misinformation, language diversity, and the dynamic nature of conflict-driven cyber threats. Similarly, Sun et al. (2023) survey the landscape of cyber threat intelligence mining, underscoring how proactive defense mechanisms rely on extracting actionable insights from unstructured textual sources.

Sufi (2023) further explores open-source cyber intelligence applications, illustrating practical scenarios where publicly available information aids in threat attribution and actor profiling. Etaywe, Macfarlane, and Alazab (2024) introduce automated psycholinguistic profiling to assess cyberterrorist threats through text analysis, demonstrating the interdisciplinary approach blending linguistics and cybersecurity for enhanced threat assessment.

LSTM and BERT transformer models have shown promise in intent identification within cyber threat intelligence workflows. Sangher, Singh, and Pandey (2024) specifically develop models to detect exploitation intents on social media and darknet platforms, providing frameworks for preempting malicious activities. Lee, Mujammami, and Kim (2024) further leverage social networks to analyze attack trends and tactics, techniques, and procedures (TTPs) across the Arab world, underscoring the geographical and cultural dimensions of cyber threat intelligence.

Atoum et al. (2025) propose a machine learning framework combining textual data and terrorism datasets to enhance cybersecurity intelligence, highlighting the fusion of domain-specific data with AI techniques for robust threat detection. Chaudhary and Bansal (2022) offer a review of OSINT extraction techniques pertinent to terrorism-related information, which complements other approaches in the CTI ecosystem.

Open Source Intelligence and Dark Web Content Analysis

The use of open-source information in CTI continues to grow as an accessible and rich data source. Adewopo, Gonen, and Adewopo (2020) investigate the potential of open-source data for cyber threat intelligence, outlining methodologies for automated extraction and analysis to identify emerging threats. This aligns with Sangher et al. (2023), who develop proactive cyber-threat intelligence systems targeting darknet forums to detect cybercrime activities before they escalate.

Further studies by Marinho and Holanda (2023) illustrate automated cyber threat identification and profiling using NLP, showcasing how AI-driven text mining can enhance situational awareness in cybersecurity operations.

Machine Learning and Large Language Models in Cybersecurity Applications

The adoption of large language models (LLMs) and deep learning has revolutionized cybersecurity capabilities. Gholami and Omar (2023, 2024) analyze the efficiency of synthetic data in improving LLM performance and explore how student

LLMs compare to their teacher models in security applications. Gholami and Omar (2023) presents innovative deep learning solutions tailored to cybersecurity challenges, while Jones et al. (2023) demonstrate how machine learning can accelerate and improve the accuracy of threat detection.

In particular, Jones and Omar (2024) introduce the GPT-2 Enhanced Attack Detection and Defense (GEADD) method, showcasing the use of LLMs in identifying zero-day threats with enhanced precision. Omar et al. (2024) also propose optimized convolutional neural networks for malware detection, emphasizing a paradigm shift in automated threat classification.

Zangana and Omar (2025) discuss harnessing LLMs for cybersecurity, detailing their applications, challenges, and future potential in automating vulnerability detection and response. Their collaborative work with Mustafa and Li (2025) further delves into NLP applications for cyber threat intelligence in emerging quantum-aware cybersecurity frameworks.

Cloud and Mobile Security Case Studies

Hamza and Omar (2013) focus on the abuse and nefarious use of cloud computing, presenting case scenarios where cloud resources are exploited for malicious purposes. Similarly, Wright, Dawson Jr, and Omar (2012) highlight the challenges of mobile threats and the critical need for antivirus solutions on smartphones, reflecting early but essential considerations in mobile cybersecurity.

Zangana, Omar, and Mohammed (2024) provide extensive reviews on network firewall rule analyzers, which are integral in securing cloud and enterprise environments by automating security policy enforcement and anomaly detection.

Digital Forensics and Insider Threats

The human factor remains a critical challenge in cybersecurity. Zangana, Omar (2025) address insider threats in financial institutions, emphasizing psychological and behavioral aspects alongside technical controls. Omar and Zangana (2025) compile research on digital forensics enhanced by AI, underscoring the evolution of forensic methods in the face of increasingly sophisticated cybercrime.

Regulatory and Ethical Considerations in Cybersecurity

Ensuring compliance with regulatory frameworks is essential for sustainable cybersecurity operations. Zangana, Omar, and Al-Karaki (2025) discuss regulatory frameworks governing science, technology, and medical innovation, highlighting how cybersecurity intersects with legal and ethical standards. This complements the discourse on governance and ethical AI usage by Zangana and Omar (2025) in the context of secure and ethical STM research.

AI Applications in Diverse Domains: Healthcare, Agriculture, and Education

Beyond traditional cybersecurity, AI applications extend to healthcare and agriculture. Huff et al. (2023) investigate management practices mitigating cybersecurity risks in biotechnology and healthcare research organizations, showcasing domain-specific threat landscapes and defense strategies. Zangana, Omar, (2025) explore AI-driven image denoising techniques with cybersecurity applications in agricultural research, highlighting opportunities and challenges in protecting smart farming systems.

In education, Zangana, Nobles, and Omar (2026) emphasize harnessing AI for teacher support and professional development, reflecting the broader impact of AI-driven cybersecurity measures in protecting educational infrastructures and digital resources.

Summary

These case studies and applications collectively demonstrate the breadth and depth of AI and cybersecurity integration across multiple sectors. They reveal how natural language processing, large language models, and machine learning enable more effective cyber threat intelligence and defense mechanisms. The importance of ethical, legal, and human factors is also underscored as critical to the success and acceptance of these technological advancements.

CHALLENGES AND LIMITATIONS

The field of cybersecurity, particularly with the integration of advanced techniques such as Natural Language Processing (NLP), Machine Learning (ML), and Large Language Models (LLMs), faces a variety of challenges and inherent limitations that impact the effectiveness, accuracy, and ethical deployment of cyber threat intelligence (CTI) systems. This section outlines the primary obstacles identified in recent literature and discusses their implications for current and future research and practice.

Data Quality and Accessibility

A fundamental limitation in developing effective CTI systems is the availability and quality of data. Open-source intelligence (OSINT) data, frequently mined from social media, darknet forums, and other publicly accessible platforms, often suffers from noise, incompleteness, and misinformation (Chaudhary & Bansal, 2022; Adewopo, Gonen, & Adewopo, 2020). Preprocessing such data for NLP models remains challenging due to language ambiguity, slang, and multilingual contexts (Johnsen & Franke, 2019; Ramírez Sánchez et al., 2021). Furthermore, social media analytics, especially in geopolitically sensitive contexts like the Russia–Ukraine cyber war, highlight the difficulty of distinguishing factual intelligence from propaganda or coordinated misinformation campaigns (Sufi, 2023a; Sufi, 2023b).

Model Limitations and Generalizability

While deep learning and transformer-based models such as LSTM and BERT have shown promise in detecting cyber threats and intents from textual data (Sangher, Singh, & Pandey, 2024; Sangher et al., 2023), these models face significant limitations. Issues such as overfitting on limited labeled datasets, poor generalizability across different cyber domains, and susceptibility to adversarial inputs remain critical concerns. The reliance on synthetic data to augment training sets offers some improvements but also raises questions about whether models trained on synthetic data can perform equivalently to those trained on real-world data (Gholami & Omar, 2023; Gholami & Omar, 2024).

Real-Time Processing and Scalability

The dynamic and voluminous nature of cyber threat data presents scalability challenges. Real-time threat detection requires efficient algorithms and robust infrastructure capable of handling large-scale data streams without compromising latency or accuracy (Sun et al., 2023; Jones et al., 2023). Despite advances in cloud computing and parallel processing, the abuse and nefarious use of such technologies introduce additional security vulnerabilities (Hamza & Omar, 2013). Moreover, integrating AI-driven CTI into existing cybersecurity frameworks necessitates continuous updates and model retraining, complicating deployment in operational environments (Zangana, Omar, & Al-Karaki, 2024; Wright, Dawson Jr, & Omar, 2012).

Ethical, Privacy, and Legal Concerns

The use of OSINT and AI for CTI raises important ethical questions about privacy, consent, and data protection (Zangana, Omar, & Al-Karaki, 2025). Automated text analysis for psycholinguistic profiling and threat assessment, while useful for identifying potential cyberterrorists, may infringe on individual rights and raise concerns about profiling biases and false positives (Etaywe, Macfarlane, & Alazab, 2024). Regulatory frameworks remain uneven across jurisdictions, complicating cross-border data sharing and collaboration (Zangana, Omar, & Al-Karaki, 2025). Additionally, insider threats and the human factor introduce complexities that purely technical solutions cannot fully address.

Figure 4 highlights the ethical concerns arising from NLP deployment in cybersecurity, where privacy, legality, and accuracy intersect and create challenges for compliance and trust.

Figure 4. Intersection of ethical concerns in NLP for cybersecurity

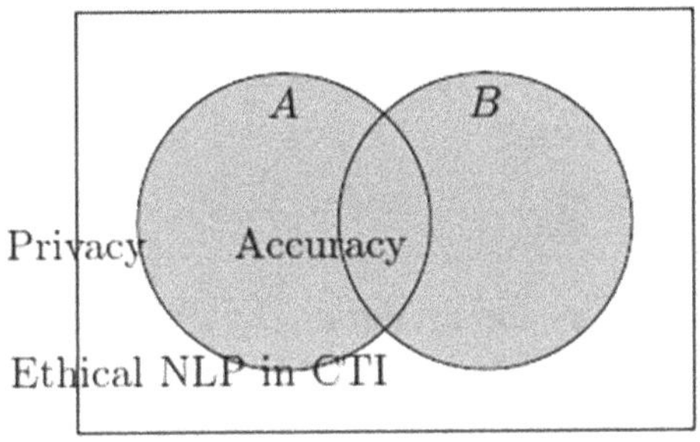

Interpretability and Transparency

Black-box models, including deep neural networks and large language models, pose challenges regarding explainability and trustworthiness in cybersecurity applications (Jones & Omar, 2024; Omar & Zangana, 2024). The lack of transparent decision-making mechanisms hinders the ability of cybersecurity analysts to verify and act upon AI-generated intelligence confidently. This gap undermines operational adoption and complicates compliance with regulatory standards requiring accountability (Zangana & Omar, 2025; Huff et al., 2023).

Emerging Threat Complexity

Cyber threats evolve rapidly, leveraging sophisticated tactics, techniques, and procedures (TTPs) that exploit vulnerabilities in social networks, IoT devices, and cloud infrastructures (Lee, Mujammami, & Kim, 2024; Mohammed, Omar, & Nguyen, 2018). The integration of quantum computing into cybersecurity, while promising for defense, simultaneously presents new attack vectors that existing AI models are ill-prepared to counter (Zangana & Omar, 2025). Consequently, CTI systems must continuously adapt, often requiring interdisciplinary collaboration across AI, quantum computing, and domain experts (Zangana & Omar, 2025a).

Resource Constraints and Skill Gaps

Implementing advanced CTI solutions demands substantial computational resources and expertise in AI, cybersecurity, and data science (Zangana, Omar, & Al-Karaki, 2025). Many organizations, especially in developing regions, face difficulties in acquiring the necessary infrastructure and skilled personnel. This gap contributes to an uneven global cybersecurity posture and hampers effective threat mitigation (Zangana et al., 2025; Adewopo et al., 2020).

Summary

In summary, the challenges and limitations of CTI systems underscore the need for continuous research and innovation. Addressing data quality, improving model robustness, ensuring ethical compliance, enhancing transparency, and fostering interdisciplinary collaboration remain critical for the advancement of cybersecurity intelligence frameworks (Rajendran & Tulasi, 2025; Omar & Zangana, 2024). These efforts will better equip stakeholders to anticipate and mitigate emerging cyber threats in an increasingly complex digital landscape.

FUTURE TRENDS AND RESEARCH DIRECTIONS

The evolving landscape of cybersecurity and artificial intelligence (AI) continues to present new challenges and opportunities for researchers, practitioners, and policymakers alike. As threats become more sophisticated and pervasive, future research must focus on the integration of advanced technologies, novel analytical frameworks, and ethical governance to ensure robust, scalable, and inclusive security solutions.

Advancements in Natural Language Processing (NLP) for Cyber Threat Intelligence

NLP remains a cornerstone for extracting actionable insights from vast amounts of textual data in cybersecurity contexts, including social media, darknet forums, and open-source intelligence platforms (Rajendran & Tulasi, 2025; Sufi, 2023a; Sun et al., 2023). Future research will increasingly emphasize transformer-based models such as BERT and LSTM architectures to improve intent detection and threat profiling from noisy, unstructured data (Sangher, Singh, & Pandey, 2024; Marinho & Holanda, 2023). These advances will enable proactive defense strategies by identifying emerging cyber threats and tactics, techniques, and procedures (TTPs) with higher accuracy and speed (Lee, Mujammami, & Kim, 2024).

However, challenges remain in handling linguistic nuances, multi-lingual data, and adversarial manipulation of textual inputs (Rajendran & Tulasi, 2025; Etaywe, Macfarlane, & Alazab, 2024). Addressing these will require hybrid approaches that combine NLP with behavioral and psycholinguistic profiling for more reliable threat assessment (Etaywe et al., 2024; Chaudhary & Bansal, 2022).

The Role of Large Language Models (LLMs) and Synthetic Data in Cybersecurity

Large Language Models, including GPT-based architectures, have demonstrated remarkable capabilities in automating cybersecurity tasks such as vulnerability detection, malware analysis, and incident response (Omar & Zangana, 2024; Jones & Omar, 2024; Gholami & Omar, 2023). Future research should explore the use of synthetic data to augment training datasets, improving model robustness and efficiency, while mitigating privacy concerns linked to sensitive real-world data (Gholami & Omar, 2023, 2024).

Moreover, the integration of LLMs into IoT security and quantum-aware cybersecurity frameworks opens new frontiers for intelligent threat detection and mitigation at scale (Omar, Zangana, 2024). Further investigations into explainability and adversarial resilience of LLMs will enhance trust and adoption in critical infrastructures.

AI-Driven Cybersecurity in the Context of Emerging Technologies

The rapid adoption of cloud computing, mobile platforms, and IoT ecosystems demands innovative security paradigms that leverage AI and deep learning (Hamza & Omar, 2013; Mohammed, Omar, & Nguyen, 2018; Wright, Dawson Jr., & Omar, 2012). Future research directions include the design of hybrid models combining wavelet transforms and generative adversarial networks (GANs) for enhanced image denoising and malware detection in cyber-physical systems (Zangana & Omar, 2024).

Quantum computing also poses both threats and opportunities for cybersecurity. Integrating quantum-aware LLMs and cryptographic solutions will be crucial for developing next-generation defenses (Zangana & Omar, 2025b). These efforts necessitate multidisciplinary collaboration bridging computer science, quantum physics, and AI.

Ethical, Legal, and Regulatory Frameworks for AI and Cybersecurity

With the increasing deployment of AI-powered tools in sensitive domains such as healthcare, finance, and public safety, there is a critical need for comprehensive ethical guidelines and regulatory compliance frameworks (Zangana, Omar, & Al-Karaki, 2025). Research into data privacy, secure data sharing, and governance mechanisms must continue to evolve, especially considering insider threats and the human factors influencing cybersecurity resilience (Zangana, Omar, 2025).

Additionally, the development of standards for AI transparency, accountability, and bias mitigation will promote responsible innovation and public trust (Zangana, Al-Karaki, & Omar, 2025).

Digital Forensics and Incident Response in the AI Era

The integration of AI into digital forensics promises faster, more accurate analysis of cyber incidents and evidence (Omar & Zangana, 2025). Future research should focus on AI-enabled forensic tools that support automated data triage, anomaly detection, and attribution, while maintaining forensic soundness and legal admissibility (Zangana & Omar, 2025a).

Personalized professional learning paths and AI recommendation systems can further enhance the skills of cybersecurity professionals, enabling adaptive responses to emerging threats (Zangana, Omar, 2026).

Harnessing Social Media and Open-Source Intelligence (OSINT)

The use of OSINT and social media analytics for cybercrime detection and intelligence gathering has shown significant promise (Adewopo, Gonen, & Adewopo, 2020; Ramírez Sánchez et al., 2021; Siddiqui, Amer, & Khan, 2019). Future research should refine techniques for preprocessing, multilingual text mining, and semantic analysis to improve the accuracy and timeliness of threat identification (Johnsen & Franke, 2019; Sufi, 2023b).

Developing scalable, real-time analytics frameworks for darknet and social platforms will support law enforcement and cybersecurity operations against evolving threat actors (Sangher et al., 2023; Lee et al., 2024).

Emerging Trends in AI for Cybersecurity Education and Leadership

The human dimension remains pivotal in cybersecurity, with leadership and education playing critical roles in fostering secure organizational cultures (Zangana & Omar, 2025c). Future research will benefit from exploring AI-augmented training and visualization tools that enhance awareness and decision-making capabilities among security practitioners (Zangana, Omar, 2026; Zangana, Omar, & Al-Karaki, 2025).

Moreover, ethical governance in science, technology, and medical research must evolve alongside AI innovations to ensure inclusive and equitable technological advancements (Zangana & Omar, 2025c; Zangana, 2025b).

In summary, future research directions in cybersecurity and AI must adopt an interdisciplinary, ethical, and forward-thinking approach, leveraging cutting-edge NLP, large language models, quantum technologies, and AI-driven analytics. Addressing human factors, regulatory challenges, and education will be equally vital to developing resilient and trustworthy cybersecurity ecosystems for the digital age.

CONCLUSION

The dynamic and rapidly evolving fields of cybersecurity and artificial intelligence present both unprecedented challenges and transformative opportunities. This work has highlighted the critical role of advanced technologies such as Natural Language Processing, Large Language Models, and hybrid AI frameworks in enhancing cyber threat intelligence, malware detection, and forensic analysis. As cyber threats continue to grow in complexity and scale, leveraging these intelligent systems will be essential for proactive defense and resilient security infrastructures.

Moreover, the integration of emerging technologies such as quantum computing and cloud-based AI models introduces new paradigms that can revolutionize cybersecurity, while simultaneously raising significant ethical, legal, and regulatory considerations. Addressing these concerns through comprehensive governance frameworks and responsible AI deployment is imperative to ensure trust and safeguard user privacy.

Importantly, the human factor remains central to cybersecurity effectiveness. Empowering professionals through AI-enabled education, leadership development, and awareness programs will strengthen organizational security culture and responsiveness to emerging threats.

In conclusion, the future of cybersecurity lies in multidisciplinary collaboration that combines cutting-edge AI advancements with ethical stewardship, regulatory compliance, and continuous human engagement. By embracing these principles, researchers and practitioners can build intelligent, adaptive, and inclusive security ecosystems that effectively counter evolving cyber risks and protect the digital landscape for all.

REFERENCES

Adewopo, V., Gonen, B., & Adewopo, F. (2020, December). Exploring open source information for cyber threat intelligence. In *2020 IEEE International Conference on Big Data (Big Data)* (pp. 2232-2241). IEEE. DOI: 10.1109/BigData50022.2020.9378220

Atoum, M. S., Alarood, A. A., Alsolami, E., Abubakar, A., Hwaitat, A. K. A., & Alsmadi, I. (2025). Cybersecurity Intelligence Through Textual Data Analysis: A Framework Using Machine Learning and Terrorism Datasets. *Future Internet, 17*(4), 182. DOI: 10.3390/fi17040182

Chaudhary, M., & Bansal, D. (2022). Open source intelligence extraction for terrorism-related information: A review. *Wiley Interdisciplinary Reviews. Data Mining and Knowledge Discovery, 12*(5), e1473. DOI: 10.1002/widm.1473

Etaywe, A., Macfarlane, K., & Alazab, M. (2024). A cyberterrorist behind the keyboard: An automated text analysis for psycholinguistic profiling and threat assessment. *Journal of Language Aggression and Conflict.*

Gholami, S., & Omar, M. (2023). Does Synthetic Data Make Large Language Models More Efficient? *arXiv preprint arXiv:2310.07830.*

Gholami, S., & Omar, M. (2024). Can a student large language model perform as well as its teacher? In *Innovations, Securities, and Case Studies Across Healthcare, Business, and Technology* (pp. 122-139). IGI Global. DOI: 10.4018/979-8-3693-1906-2.ch007

Hamza, Y. A., & Omar, M. D. (2013). Cloud computing security: Abuse and nefarious use of cloud computing. *International Journal of Computer Engineering Research, 3*(6), 22–27.

Huff, A. J., Burrell, D. N., Nobles, C., Richardson, K., Wright, J. B., Burton, S. L., Jones, A. J., Springs, D., Omar, M., & Brown-Jackson, K. L. (2023). Management Practices for Mitigating Cybersecurity Threats to Biotechnology Companies, Laboratories, and Healthcare Research Organizations. In *Applied Research Approaches to Technology, Healthcare, and Business* (pp. 1-12). IGI Global.

Johnsen, J. W., & Franke, K. (2019, December). The impact of preprocessing in natural language for open source intelligence and criminal investigation. In *2019 IEEE International Conference on Big Data (Big Data)* (pp. 4248-4254). IEEE. DOI: 10.1109/BigData47090.2019.9006006

Jones, R., & Omar, M. (2024). Revolutionizing Cybersecurity: The GPT-2 Enhanced Attack Detection and Defense (GEADD) Method for Zero-Day Threats. *International Journal of Informatics* [INJIISCOM]. *Information System and Computer Engineering*, *5*(2), 178–191.

Jones, R., Omar, M., Mohammed, D., Nobles, C., & Dawson, M. (2023). Harnessing the Speed and Accuracy of Machine Learning to Advance Cybersecurity. In *2023 Congress in Computer Science, Computer Engineering, & Applied Computing (CSCE)* (pp. 418-421). IEEE. DOI: 10.1109/CSCE60160.2023.00074

Lee, S., Mujammami, A. A. H., & Kim, K. (2024). Leveraging Social Networks for Cyber Threat Intelligence: Analyzing Attack Trends and TTPs in the Arab World. *IEEE Access : Practical Innovations, Open Solutions.*

Mohammed, D., Omar, M., & Nguyen, V. (2018). Wireless sensor network security: Approaches to detecting and avoiding wormhole attacks. *Journal of Research in Business. Economics and Management*, *10*(2), 1860–1864.

Nguyen, V., Mohammed, D., Omar, M., & Banisakher, M. (2018). The Effects of the FCC Net Neutrality Repeal on Security and Privacy. [IJHIoT]. *International Journal of Hyperconnectivity and the Internet of Things*, *2*(2), 21–29. DOI: 10.4018/IJHIoT.2018070102

Omar, M., & Zangana, H. (Eds.). (2025). *Digital Forensics in the Age of AI.* IGI Global., DOI: 10.4018/979-8-3373-0857-9

Omar, M., & Zangana, H. M. (Eds.). (2024). *Redefining Security With Cyber AI.* IGI Global., DOI: 10.4018/979-8-3693-6517-5

Omar, M., & Zangana, H. M. (Eds.). (2025). *Application of Large Language Models (LLMs) for Software Vulnerability Detection.* IGI Global., DOI: 10.4018/979-8-3693-9311-6

Rajendran, R. K., & Tulasi, B. (2025). Natural Language Processing (NLP) for Threat Intelligence. In *Analyzing Privacy and Security Difficulties in Social Media: New Challenges and Solutions* (pp. 247-262). IGI Global Scientific Publishing.

Ramírez Sánchez, J., Campo-Archbold, A., Zapata Rozo, A., Díaz-López, D., Pastor-Galindo, J., Gómez Mármol, F., & Aponte Díaz, J. (2021). Uncovering cybercrimes in social media through natural language processing. *Complexity*, *2021*(1), 7955637. DOI: 10.1155/2021/7955637

Sangher, K. S., Singh, A., & Pandey, H. M. (2024). LSTM and BERT based transformers models for cyber threat intelligence for intent identification of social media platforms exploitation from darknet forums. *International Journal of Information Technology : an Official Journal of Bharati Vidyapeeth's Institute of Computer Applications and Management*, *16*(8), 5277–5292. DOI: 10.1007/s41870-024-02077-5

Sangher, K. S., Singh, A., Pandey, H. M., & Kumar, V. (2023). Towards safe cyber practices: Developing a proactive cyber-threat intelligence system for dark web forum content by identifying cybercrimes. *Information (Basel)*, *14*(6), 349. DOI: 10.3390/info14060349

Siddiqui, T., Amer, A. Y. A., & Khan, N. A. (2019, November). Criminal activity detection in social network by text mining: comprehensive analysis. In *2019 4th International Conference on Information Systems and Computer Networks (ISCON)* (pp. 224-229). IEEE. DOI: 10.1109/ISCON47742.2019.9036157

Sufi, F. (2023). Social media analytics on Russia–Ukraine cyber war with natural language processing: Perspectives and challenges. *Information (Basel)*, *14*(9), 485. DOI: 10.3390/info14090485

Sufi, F. (2023). Novel application of open-source cyber intelligence. *Electronics (Basel)*, *12*(17), 3610. DOI: 10.3390/electronics12173610

Sun, N., Ding, M., Jiang, J., Xu, W., Mo, X., Tai, Y., & Zhang, J. (2023). Cyber threat intelligence mining for proactive cybersecurity defense: A survey and new perspectives. *IEEE Communications Surveys and Tutorials*, *25*(3), 1748–1774. DOI: 10.1109/COMST.2023.3273282

Wright, J., Dawson, M. E.Jr, & Omar, M. (2012). Cyber security and mobile threats: The need for antivirus applications for smartphones. *Journal of Information Systems Technology and Planning*, *5*(14), 40–60.

Zangana, H., Al-Karaki, J., & Omar, M. (Eds.). (2025). *Revolutionizing Cybersecurity With Deep Learning and Large Language Models*. IGI Global., DOI: 10.4018/979-8-3373-3296-3

Zangana, H., Al-Karaki, J., & Omar, M. (Eds.). (2025). *Navigating Law and Policy in STM Enterprises: Ethical Governance, Regulation, and Innovation Strategy*. IGI Global., DOI: 10.4018/979-8-3373-4862-9

Zangana, H., Nobles, C., & Omar, M. (Eds.). (2026). *Harnessing AI for Teacher Support and Professional Development*. IGI Global Scientific Publishing., DOI: 10.4018/979-8-3373-5951-9

Zangana, H., & Omar, M. (Eds.). (2025). *Leveraging Large Language Models for Quantum-Aware Cybersecurity*. IGI Global., DOI: 10.4018/979-8-3373-1102-9

Zangana, H., & Omar, M. (Eds.). (2025). *Ensuring Secure and Ethical STM Research in the AI Era*. IGI Global., DOI: 10.4018/979-8-3373-4252-8

Zangana, H. M., Omar, M., & Al-Karaki, J. N. (2025). Foundations of Deep Learning and Large Language Models in Cybersecurity. In Zangana, H., Al-Karaki, J., & Omar, M. (Eds.), *Revolutionizing Cybersecurity With Deep Learning and Large Language Models* (pp. 1–36). IGI Global Scientific Publishing., DOI: 10.4018/979-8-3373-3296-3.ch001

Chapter 2
Legal and Regulatory Frameworks for AI in Digital Forensics:
Admissibility, Accountability, and Cross-Jurisdictional Challenges

Dilshad Ahmad Mhia-alddin
https://orcid.org/0009-0005-4046-1607
University of Duhok, Iraq

ABSTRACT

The integration of Artificial Intelligence (AI) into digital forensics has significantly transformed the landscape of cybercrime investigation. However, the rapid advancement of AI technologies poses substantial legal and regulatory challenges, particularly in the areas of evidence admissibility, algorithmic accountability, and jurisdictional conflicts. This chapter explores the evolving legal frameworks that govern the use of AI in digital forensics, focusing on the balance between technological innovation and fundamental legal principles. Key considerations include the transparency and explainability of AI-driven tools, the standards for admissible digital evidence, and the implications of using AI across different legal systems. By analyzing current international practices and highlighting case-specific legal precedents, this chapter provides a comprehensive overview of the regulatory hurdles and proposes strategies for harmonizing legal responses in a globally connected environment.

DOI: 10.4018/979-8-3373-6536-7.ch002

INTRODUCTION

The integration of Artificial Intelligence (AI) into digital forensics marks a transformative shift in how cybercrime is investigated and adjudicated. AI tools are increasingly being utilized to analyze vast volumes of data, identify patterns, detect anomalies, and even reconstruct digital events with unprecedented accuracy. However, this technological leap presents significant legal and regulatory challenges, particularly concerning the admissibility of AI-generated evidence in courts, accountability for algorithmic decisions, and the complexities of cross-border investigations.

The digital nature of modern crimes means that digital forensics often operates across jurisdictions with vastly different legal systems and regulatory standards. Issues such as data sovereignty, the chain of custody for digital evidence, and the transparency of AI algorithms become critical in determining whether AI-generated findings can stand legal scrutiny (Bharati, 2020; Zangana & Li, 2025). For instance, while some legal systems emphasize procedural fairness and require interpretability of forensic tools, others may focus more on outcomes and practical utility (Butt, 2024; Drexl, Conde, & Kim, 2025).

The emergence of global regulatory efforts, such as the EU AI Act (Butt, 2024), highlights the growing recognition of AI's legal impact. Yet, many jurisdictions still lack specific guidelines on how AI should be governed in forensic contexts, creating gaps that could undermine both evidence reliability and the protection of individual rights (Mennella et al., 2024; Pesapane et al., 2021). As Singh and Kaunert (2025) argue in the environmental domain, achieving global harmonization in AI regulation requires balancing innovation with ethical obligations—a challenge that also resonates in digital forensics.

Another major concern is algorithmic accountability—understanding who is liable when AI tools lead to errors, biases, or wrongful accusations. As emphasized by Ali and Aysan (2025), ensuring ethical use of generative AI requires a robust framework that addresses transparency, explainability, and oversight. Similar concerns apply to AI in digital forensics, where decisions made by opaque algorithms may have serious legal consequences (Fenwick, Molnar, & Frangos, 2024; Trotsyuk et al., 2024). Moreover, the role of federated learning in preserving privacy while analyzing decentralized forensic data (Iyengar et al., 2025) introduces new layers of technical and legal complexity.

Cross-jurisdictional investigations further complicate AI's use in digital forensics. Issues such as conflicting privacy laws, extraterritorial enforcement, and admissibility standards vary widely across borders (Darvishi, Liu, & Lim, 2022; Oduro, Uzougbo, & Ugwu, 2024). For example, an AI-based forensic analysis deemed valid in one country may be rejected in another due to lack of transparency or breach of due process (Bousri, 2019; Eisenberg, 2024). International law scholars like Akindele and Chabinga (2024) and Aloamaka (2024) have highlighted similar jurisdictional friction in climate governance, which parallels the regulatory fragmentation seen in AI-driven digital investigations.

Additionally, the sustainability of legal and forensic AI frameworks requires inclusive policymaking. Just as environmental and sustainability laws emphasize intersectoral collaboration (Ali, 2024; Saikia, 2024), the governance of forensic AI must include voices from law, technology, civil society, and international institutions. Studies in other domains, such as AI in healthcare (Larson et al., 2021; Pesapane et al., 2018) and smart cities (Maguluri, Arularasan, & Boopathi, 2023), offer insights into how collaborative regulatory approaches can be adapted for forensic use cases.

This chapter provides a comprehensive exploration of the legal and regulatory landscape governing AI in digital forensics. It addresses the core legal dimensions of admissibility, accountability, and cross-jurisdictional challenges, drawing on interdisciplinary research and legal precedents. By referencing frameworks from other AI applications—such as medical diagnostics (Naili et al., 2025; Sheliemina, 2024), environmental law (Daniel, 2024), and public governance (Soomro, Suhrab, & Abbasi, 2025)—the chapter presents a comparative analysis that can guide the development of coherent and ethically grounded policies for forensic AI deployment.

In doing so, it also incorporates perspectives from AI ethics (Ali & Aysan, 2025; Shukla & Taneja, 2024), AI misuse prevention (Veluru, 2024), and contract law compliance in AI systems (Mhia-Alddin & Hussein, 2025), emphasizing the urgent need for multidimensional frameworks that ensure responsible innovation. As emphasized by Zreik (2024), navigating AI's frontier requires a blend of technical insight, ethical foresight, and legal prudence—all of which are essential in ensuring justice and integrity in AI-assisted digital forensics.

FOUNDATIONS OF LEGAL ADMISSIBILITY IN DIGITAL FORENSICS

Legal admissibility in digital forensics is a cornerstone principle that determines whether evidence derived from digital investigations, including those assisted by artificial intelligence (AI), can be accepted and relied upon in judicial proceedings. As digital forensics increasingly incorporates AI technologies, the foundational legal criteria governing admissibility must adapt to address the complexities introduced by algorithmic processes, data integrity, and cross-jurisdictional variations (Bharati, 2020; Zangana & Li, 2025).

Core Principles of Admissibility

At its essence, admissibility hinges on several universally recognized principles: relevance, reliability, authenticity, and integrity of the evidence (Darvishi, Liu, & Lim, 2022). The evidence must be relevant to the case, reliable in its method of collection and analysis, authentic to the original source, and maintained with a secure chain of custody. In the context of AI-enhanced digital forensics, ensuring these principles requires scrutinizing the transparency, explainability, and reproducibility of AI algorithms, as opaque models can challenge the reliability and authenticity criteria (Fenwick, Molnar, & Frangos, 2024; Iyengar et al., 2025).

Legal systems vary in their evidentiary standards, but most emphasize procedural fairness and due process. For example, the European Union's AI Act (Butt, 2024) and regulations across North America and Asia (Pesapane et al., 2021) increasingly mandate transparency and accountability in AI-driven processes. Courts often require forensic experts to clearly explain the methodology used, including AI's role, to prevent miscarriages of justice stemming from "black-box" evidence (Larson et al., 2021; Naili et al., 2025).

The following flowchart summarizes the step-by-step process that determines the admissibility of AI-generated evidence in judicial proceedings, highlighting key legal requirements such as relevance, reliability, authenticity, and the role of explainability.

Figure 1. Flowchart for evaluating AI-generated evidence admissibility

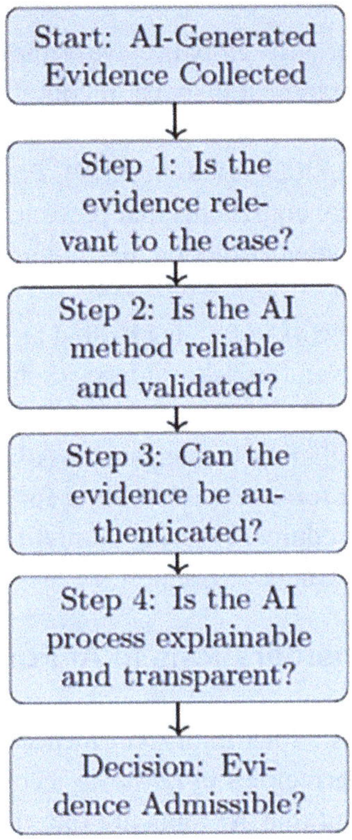

The Role of Chain of Custody and Data Integrity

The chain of custody—a documented trail of evidence handling—is critical for preserving admissibility. In digital forensics, this involves preserving the exact digital state from collection through analysis to presentation (Bharati, 2020). AI integration introduces new challenges because data may be pre-processed or transformed by learning models that can themselves evolve, making it essential to log and audit AI decision pathways (Al-Sinani & Mitchell, 2024; Iyengar et al., 2025).

Moreover, algorithmic biases or errors can undermine data integrity, leading to potential challenges in court. Ethical hacking experiments incorporating AI have shown that even sophisticated models are vulnerable to adversarial manipulations, highlighting the importance of robust verification protocols and validation standards (Al-Sinani, Sahli, Mitchell, & Al-Siyabi, 2025).

Admissibility Across Jurisdictions

Digital forensics is inherently global; cybercrimes and data frequently cross national borders. This geographical dispersion complicates admissibility because jurisdictions differ in legal standards, privacy protections, and procedural rules (Oduro, Uzougbo, & Ugwu, 2024; Bousri, 2019). For instance, data collected in one country may face privacy constraints that prevent its use in another, or the forensic methods accepted in one jurisdiction may not meet the evidentiary threshold elsewhere (Eisenberg, 2024).

International legal frameworks often lag behind technology, resulting in inconsistent recognition of AI-driven forensic evidence. Scholars in other domains, such as environmental law (Akindele & Chabinga, 2024; Aloamaka, 2024), emphasize the need for harmonized regulations to navigate cross-border challenges effectively. Similar calls arise in digital forensics, advocating for international agreements to standardize AI forensic procedures, ensuring admissibility and mutual legal assistance (Darvishi et al., 2022; Singh & Kaunert, 2025).

Ethical and Legal Considerations in AI Forensics

Beyond procedural aspects, admissibility is influenced by the ethical underpinnings of AI use in forensics. The principles of fairness, accountability, and transparency (Ali & Aysan, 2025) demand that AI tools not only produce accurate results but also do so in ways that respect privacy and avoid discrimination. This is especially pertinent in light of concerns over AI misuse and bias, which can lead to wrongful convictions or erosion of public trust (Trotsyuk et al., 2024; Veluru, 2024).

Legal scholars argue that forensic AI must comply with broader human rights frameworks, including the right to a fair trial and data protection laws (Ho, 2023; Shukla & Taneja, 2024). Emerging research stresses the importance of embedding ethical AI governance in legal admissibility frameworks to safeguard these rights (Mennella et al., 2024; Zangana & Li, 2025).

Future-Proofing Legal Admissibility

Given the rapid evolution of AI and digital technologies, legal admissibility must be dynamic. Contractual and regulatory considerations surrounding AI use in forensic contexts, including managing risks of model expiry, updates, and compliance, are gaining prominence (Mhia-Alddin & Hussein, 2025). The integration of federated learning offers promising avenues to reconcile privacy with forensic utility, but requires new legal standards for data sharing and accountability (Iyengar et al., 2025).

Lessons from other domains such as medical diagnostics (Naili et al., 2025; Pesapane et al., 2018), environmental sustainability law (Ali, 2024; Saikia, 2024), and smart cities governance (Maguluri, Arularasan, & Boopathi, 2023) provide valuable insights for building resilient, transparent, and ethically sound legal frameworks that can uphold the admissibility of AI-enhanced digital evidence.

AI AND THE LAW: EMERGING QUESTIONS OF ACCOUNTABILITY

The rapid advancement and integration of artificial intelligence (AI) technologies across multiple domains have catalyzed unprecedented legal challenges, particularly regarding accountability. As AI systems increasingly influence decision-making in fields ranging from healthcare and finance to environmental governance and criminal justice, the question of how to attribute responsibility and enforce legal norms becomes paramount (Ali & Aysan, 2025; Bharati, 2020; Zangana & Li, 2025).

Defining Accountability in AI Systems

Accountability traditionally refers to the obligation of individuals or organizations to explain and justify their actions and to face consequences for wrongful conduct (Darvishi, Liu, & Lim, 2022). In AI contexts, accountability extends beyond human actors to include autonomous systems capable of independent actions, raising complex questions about liability and control (Batabyal, 2024; Ali, 2024).

Legal scholars emphasize that accountability in AI must consider not only outcomes but also the processes by which AI decisions are made. This includes ensuring transparency of algorithms, traceability of data inputs, and the explainability of outputs to affected stakeholders (Fenwick, Molnar, & Frangos, 2024; Larsson et al., 2021; Mennella et al., 2024). However, the often "black-box" nature of AI, particularly deep learning models, poses significant hurdles to meaningful accountability (Ali, H., & Aysan, A. F., 2025).

To understand the multifaceted nature of AI accountability, the following diagram illustrates the interconnected layers, from developer responsibility to institutional oversight and societal impact.

Figure 2. Layers of accountability in AI-driven forensic systems

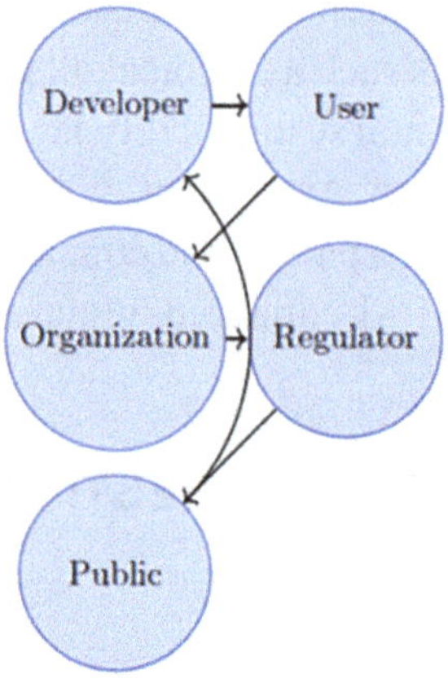

Legal Frameworks and Regulatory Responses

Governments and international bodies have begun addressing AI accountability through legislation and policy frameworks. The European Union's AI Act, for example, mandates risk-based approaches and specific obligations for high-risk AI systems, aiming to ensure human oversight and mitigate harm (Butt, 2024; Pesapane et al., 2021). Similarly, various countries are developing regulatory mechanisms that combine technical standards with ethical guidelines to govern AI deployment (Pesapane et al., 2018; Ho, 2023).

Yet, the transnational nature of AI technologies complicates enforcement, as jurisdictions differ in their legal approaches and ethical priorities (Bousri, 2019; Oduro, Uzougbo, & Ugwu, 2024). International harmonization efforts remain nascent, with scholars advocating for coordinated policies to handle cross-border accountability challenges (Akindele & Chabinga, 2024; Singh & Kaunert, 2025).

Challenges in Assigning Liability and Responsibility

Determining who bears liability for AI-caused harm is a profound legal challenge. Questions arise as to whether responsibility lies with AI developers, operators, users, or even the AI systems themselves (Darvishi et al., 2022; Veluru, 2024). This issue is especially acute in autonomous weapons systems (Batabyal, 2024), medical diagnostics (Naili et al., 2025; Sheliemina, 2024), financial decision-making (Ali,

H., Zafar, & Aysan, 2024), and smart infrastructure management (Maguluri, Arularasan, & Boopathi, 2023).

The evolving nature of AI models—constantly updated through machine learning—and the opacity of some algorithms increase the difficulty of attributing fault (Al-Sinani & Mitchell, 2024; Al-Sinani et al., 2025). Legal doctrines such as strict liability and negligence are being reexamined to accommodate AI's unique features (Mhia-Alddin & Hussein, 2025a; Mhia-Alddin & Hussein, 2025b).

Ethical Accountability and Societal Impact

Beyond legal accountability, ethical considerations play a crucial role in AI governance. The risks of bias, discrimination, and privacy violations necessitate frameworks ensuring AI systems align with human rights and societal values (Ali & Aysan, 2025; Shukla & Taneja, 2024; Trotsyuk et al., 2024). Ethical accountability also encompasses transparency in data use and the empowerment of affected communities to contest AI decisions (Vyawahare, Khandelwal, & Rathod, 2024).

The emerging discourse on responsible AI emphasizes human-centric design, accountability by design, and continuous monitoring of AI systems to prevent misuse and harm (Veluru, 2024; Mennella et al., 2024). This approach aligns with sustainable development goals and climate justice movements that increasingly intersect with AI's environmental applications (Ali, 2024; Aloamaka, 2024; Emom et al., 2025).

Contractual and Policy Dimensions of AI Accountability

In commercial and research settings, contractual frameworks are evolving to manage AI-related risks, particularly concerning compliance, liability, and data governance (Mhia-Alddin & Hussein, 2025c; Mhia-Alddin, 2025). Contract expiry, termination, and ongoing obligations are gaining attention as AI technologies continuously evolve post-deployment, raising new legal challenges around accountability (Mhia-Alddin & Hussein, 2025a; Read, Botha, & Jamaloodien, 2023).

Policy modeling approaches, including systems thinking and agent-based models, are being utilized to forecast the impacts of AI regulations and inform adaptive governance strategies (Schünemann et al., 2024; Singh & Kaunert, 2025). Such tools assist lawmakers and stakeholders in navigating the complexities of AI accountability across diverse sectors and geographies.

REGULATORY APPROACHES TO AI IN FORENSICS ACROSS JURISDICTIONS

The integration of Artificial Intelligence (AI) into forensic practices presents both significant opportunities and regulatory challenges worldwide. As AI-powered forensic tools become increasingly sophisticated—ranging from automated evidence analysis to predictive policing and digital investigations—regulatory frameworks must evolve to address ethical, legal, and technical concerns across jurisdictions. This section explores diverse regulatory approaches, highlighting international trends, jurisdiction-specific strategies, and the complexities of harmonizing AI governance in forensic contexts.

The International Landscape of AI Forensic Regulation

At the global level, regulatory bodies and international organizations have begun emphasizing the need for clear standards and oversight mechanisms that ensure AI's ethical deployment in forensic science. While AI's potential for enhancing accuracy and efficiency in forensic investigations is widely acknowledged, concerns around data privacy, algorithmic bias, and accountability remain pressing (Zangana & Li, 2025). International law intersects with forensic AI regulation, especially where cross-border data flows and transnational crime investigations occur (Akindele & Chabinga, 2024; Aloamaka, 2024).

Efforts like the European Union's Artificial Intelligence Act propose comprehensive AI regulation aimed at balancing innovation with risk management, including stipulations relevant to forensic applications (Butt, 2024). Such regulatory frameworks emphasize transparency, human oversight, and risk classification, laying the groundwork for forensic AI governance that prioritizes human rights and procedural fairness.

Jurisdictional Variations and Challenges

Europe

Europe leads in formalizing AI governance, especially with the EU AI Act, which categorizes AI systems by risk levels. For forensic AI, which can significantly impact fundamental rights, high-risk classification applies, mandating rigorous conformity assessments, documentation, and ongoing monitoring (Larson et al., 2021; Mennella et al., 2024). Furthermore, the General Data Protection Regulation (GDPR) imposes strict controls on personal data processing, critically relevant for forensic AI systems handling sensitive evidence (Ho, 2023).

United States

In the U.S., AI regulation remains fragmented across federal and state levels. While there is growing recognition of AI's forensic utility, regulatory measures are largely sector-specific and rely heavily on case law, agency guidelines, and ethical standards developed by professional bodies (Pesapane et al., 2021; Bharati, 2020). The legal system grapples with the admissibility of AI-generated evidence, with courts increasingly demanding explainability and validation of AI tools under rules of evidence.

Asia and Africa

Emerging economies in Asia and Africa face distinct challenges, balancing rapid AI adoption with nascent regulatory infrastructure (Akindele & Chabinga, 2024; Saikia, 2024). Countries such as Nigeria and Ethiopia are actively developing policies to integrate AI within law enforcement while safeguarding rights and promoting sustainable governance (Borta et al., 2024; Oduro et al., 2024). However, disparities in technical capacity and legal expertise pose obstacles to consistent forensic AI regulation across the continent.

A comparative visualization of regulatory readiness and implementation in forensic AI across key regions illustrates the global imbalance in AI governance.

Figure 3. Regulatory maturity in AI forensics across regions

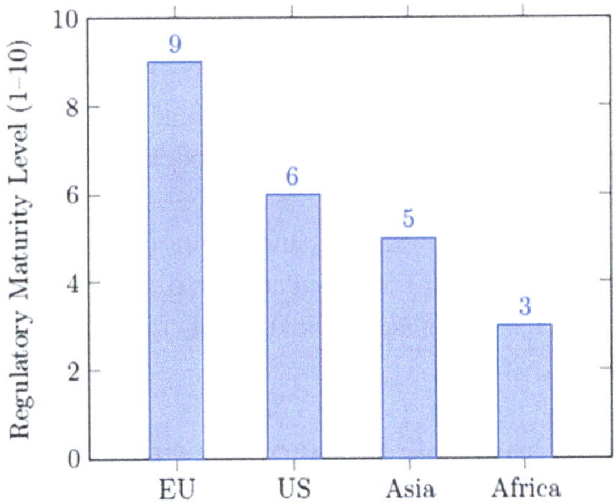

Key Regulatory Themes in AI Forensics

Several recurring regulatory themes emerge across jurisdictions:

- **Accountability and Liability:** Determining responsibility for AI decisions in forensic contexts is complex, especially with black-box models and autonomous systems (Ali & Aysan, 2025; Mhia-Alddin & Hussein, 2025). Legal scholars highlight the need for clear liability frameworks that encompass developers, operators, and institutions.
- **Transparency and Explainability:** Courts and regulators require AI forensic tools to provide interpretable outputs to ensure procedural fairness and safeguard defendants' rights (Fenwick et al., 2024; Larson et al., 2021). Explainable AI (XAI) approaches are gaining regulatory favor.
- **Privacy and Data Protection:** Forensic AI heavily relies on personal data, raising concerns about data minimization, consent, and protection against misuse (Iyengar et al., 2025; Shukla & Taneja, 2024). Regulations often align with broader data protection laws.
- **Ethical Use and Bias Mitigation:** Bias in forensic AI systems can lead to wrongful convictions or discriminatory policing. Ethical guidelines, impact assessments, and bias audits are increasingly embedded in regulatory recommendations (Ali, H., & Aysan, A. F., 2024; Mennella et al., 2024).

Cross-Border Cooperation and Harmonization Efforts

Due to the inherently international nature of digital evidence and cybercrime, harmonizing forensic AI regulations is critical. Initiatives focus on establishing interoperable standards and protocols for AI evidence handling, ensuring mutual legal assistance treaties (MLATs) account for AI-specific challenges (Darvishi, Liu, & Lim, 2022; Zangana & Li, 2025).

Nevertheless, divergent legal cultures and technological capacities complicate harmonization. International forums and academic discourse advocate for collaborative policy-making that integrates technical, legal, and ethical perspectives (Patra, 2025; Singh & Kaunert, 2025).

Future Directions and Policy Recommendations

To strengthen the regulatory landscape of AI in forensics, key policy directions include:

- Developing adaptive regulatory frameworks that can evolve with rapid AI technological advances while maintaining robust safeguards (Drexl, Conde, & Kim, 2025; Rashid & Kausik, 2024).
- Investing in capacity building for law enforcement and judiciary to understand AI forensic tools and related legal issues (Jamro & Jamro, 2023; Karim, Galar, & Kumar, 2023).
- Encouraging multi-stakeholder dialogue involving technologists, legal experts, ethicists, and affected communities to create inclusive policies (Zreik, 2024; Fenwick, Molnar, & Frangos, 2024).
- Promoting transparency through mandatory documentation, audit trails, and public reporting on AI forensic tool deployment (Filetti, Fenza, & Gallo, 2024).

This multi-dimensional examination reveals that while AI offers transformative potential for forensic science, its regulation requires nuanced, cross-jurisdictional approaches that reconcile innovation with rights protection and legal certainty.

CROSS-JURISDICTIONAL CHALLENGES IN AI-BASED CYBERCRIME INVESTIGATIONS

The rapid advancement and integration of artificial intelligence (AI) in cybercrime investigations present unprecedented opportunities for law enforcement agencies worldwide. However, these technological innovations also bring significant cross-jurisdictional challenges, as cybercrimes frequently transcend national boundaries, implicating diverse legal frameworks, regulatory standards, and enforcement capabilities (Bharati, 2020; Zangana & Li, 2025). This section explores the major obstacles encountered in AI-based cybercrime investigations that span multiple jurisdictions and discusses strategies to mitigate these challenges while maintaining effective cooperation and respecting sovereignty.

Legal and Regulatory Divergence Across Jurisdictions

One of the foremost difficulties in cross-border AI-driven investigations is the stark variation in legal and regulatory frameworks. Different countries possess unique definitions of cybercrimes, data privacy laws, and standards for AI deployment in forensic and investigative contexts (Bharati, 2020; Butt, 2024). For example, while some jurisdictions adopt stringent data protection laws resembling the EU's General Data Protection Regulation (GDPR), others have more lenient or fragmented policies, complicating data sharing and AI model deployment (Pesapane et al., 2021; Naili et al., 2025).

Furthermore, emerging AI regulations such as the EU's Artificial Intelligence Act illustrate how legislative approaches differ not only in scope but also in enforcement mechanisms, creating a patchwork that law enforcement must navigate carefully to avoid legal conflicts (Butt, 2024; Larson et al., 2021). Such divergence often leads to jurisdictional conflicts over the admissibility of AI-generated evidence and challenges in harmonizing investigatory procedures.

The overlap between data privacy, admissibility standards, and jurisdictional sovereignty is often a source of legal conflict in AI-assisted cybercrime investigations, as illustrated in this Venn diagram.

Figure 4. Overlapping legal concerns in cross-jurisdictional AI forensics

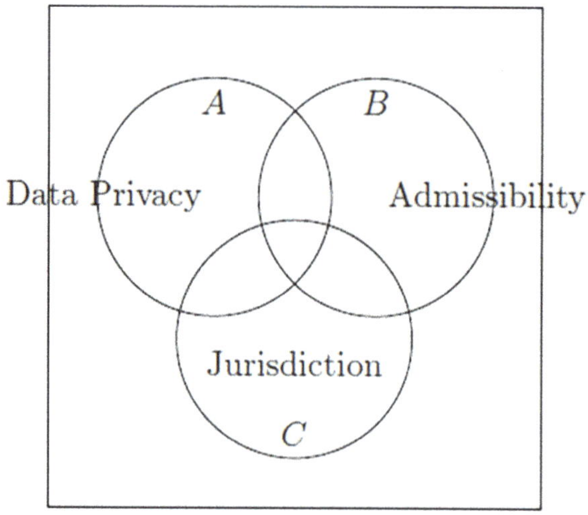

Data Privacy and Cross-Border Data Sharing

AI-based cybercrime investigations heavily rely on vast datasets, including personal and sensitive information, often sourced internationally. Varying privacy laws and concerns about data sovereignty pose significant barriers to effective data exchange between jurisdictions (Shafik, 2024; Iyengar et al., 2025). Federated learning and privacy-preserving AI techniques offer technical solutions by enabling collaborative model training without centralized data pooling, but their legal acceptance remains uneven (Iyengar et al., 2025).

Jurisdictions such as the EU enforce strict controls on cross-border data transfers, requiring compliance with data protection adequacy standards or binding corporate rules (Pesapane et al., 2021). Meanwhile, countries with less-developed privacy regimes may not provide sufficient safeguards, deterring international partners from sharing critical intelligence (Bharati, 2020; Naili et al., 2025). Consequently, effective cross-jurisdictional AI forensic investigations necessitate robust frameworks for legal data transfer agreements and adherence to international privacy norms (Akindele & Chabinga, 2024; Oduro et al., 2024).

Attribution and Evidence Integrity in Multi-National Contexts

Establishing cybercrime attribution using AI tools involves analyzing digital evidence collected from networks and systems spanning various countries. The integrity, chain of custody, and provenance of digital evidence become complex to maintain and verify across borders (Zangana & Li, 2025; Bharati, 2020). Differences in forensic standards and AI algorithm transparency complicate the validation of results in judicial processes (Mennella et al., 2024; Fenwick et al., 2024).

Moreover, adversaries exploit jurisdictional fragmentation to mask their activities, leveraging anonymization tools and decentralized platforms that cross regulatory boundaries. This necessitates coordinated multinational AI forensic approaches that combine technical, legal, and diplomatic expertise to attribute attacks accurately and reliably (Karim et al., 2023; Zangana & Li, 2025).

International Cooperation and Legal Assistance Treaties

Effective cross-jurisdictional AI cybercrime investigations depend heavily on international cooperation frameworks such as Mutual Legal Assistance Treaties (MLATs) and agreements within organizations like INTERPOL and Europol (Bharati, 2020; Darvishi et al., 2022). However, the slow pace of treaty negotiations, varying levels of technological readiness, and concerns about sovereignty often hinder rapid intelligence exchange and coordinated actions (Bousri, 2019; Chowdhury, 2024).

Efforts to modernize and streamline international cooperation are underway, with calls to integrate AI-enabled platforms for real-time evidence sharing and joint investigation workflows (Zangana & Li, 2025; Al-Sinani et al., 2025). Such advances promise to enhance the effectiveness of transnational responses to cyber threats but require harmonization of legal standards and trust-building between states (Veluru, 2024; Singh & Kaunert, 2025).

Ethical and Human Rights Considerations

The deployment of AI in cybercrime investigations also raises cross-jurisdictional ethical challenges, particularly regarding surveillance, profiling, and potential biases embedded in AI algorithms (Ali & Aysan, 2025; Mennella et al., 2024). Variations in human rights protections and the right to privacy across countries complicate the balancing act between security imperatives and civil liberties (Ho, 2023; Trotsyuk et al., 2024).

International human rights frameworks advocate for transparency, accountability, and fairness in AI applications, yet enforcement and compliance differ widely, potentially leading to abuses or misuse of AI tools in certain jurisdictions (Batabyal, 2024; Shukla & Taneja, 2024). Cross-border investigations must therefore incorporate ethical AI guidelines and respect local legal cultures to maintain legitimacy and public trust (Ali, 2024; Verma et al., 2020).

Summary

The complexity of cross-jurisdictional AI-based cybercrime investigations reflects the broader challenges of regulating, deploying, and harmonizing emerging technologies within diverse legal and ethical landscapes. Addressing these challenges requires collaborative international legal frameworks, technical innovations in privacy-preserving AI, standardized forensic protocols, and ongoing dialogue on ethical norms. Through these multidimensional approaches, the promise of AI can be harnessed effectively while respecting sovereignty, human rights, and legal diversity.

STANDARDS, CERTIFICATIONS, AND BEST PRACTICES

In the rapidly evolving landscape of artificial intelligence (AI), particularly within cybersecurity and digital forensics, adherence to well-defined standards, certifications, and best practices is critical. These frameworks serve as foundational pillars that ensure not only technological robustness but also ethical, legal, and social responsibility in AI applications. This section explores the current landscape of standards and certifications relevant to AI-driven domains, emphasizing their significance in fostering trust, accountability, and interoperability, while outlining best practices for sustainable and secure AI adoption.

Importance of Standards in AI and Cybersecurity

Standards provide a structured approach to developing, deploying, and managing AI systems, especially in sensitive areas such as cybersecurity and digital forensics. They help harmonize procedures across organizations and jurisdictions, facilitating interoperability, compliance, and risk mitigation (Bharati, 2020; Butt, 2024). For instance, the emerging EU Artificial Intelligence Act exemplifies efforts to regulate AI applications, aiming to align innovation with legal safeguards and ethical principles (Butt, 2024). Such regulatory frameworks underscore the necessity for clear, enforceable standards to govern AI's lifecycle.

Moreover, standards in cybersecurity, such as ISO/IEC 27001 for information security management and ISO/IEC 27037 for digital evidence, complement AI-specific guidelines by securing data integrity and evidentiary soundness (Zangana & Li, 2025). Adopting these standards mitigates risks related to data breaches, unauthorized access, and manipulation, which are crucial in investigations relying on AI-based tools.

Certifications as Assurance Mechanisms

Certifications act as third-party validations that organizations and practitioners adhere to prescribed standards, demonstrating competency and commitment to best practices. Certifications such as Certified Information Systems Security Professional (CISSP), Certified Ethical Hacker (CEH), and specialized AI ethics certifications provide benchmarks for professional skills and ethical awareness (Al-Sinani & Mitchell, 2024; Al-Sinani et al., 2025).

In AI governance, certifications increasingly address not only technical proficiency but also ethical compliance, bias mitigation, and transparency (Ali & Aysan, 2025). This trend highlights the cross-domain nature of AI impacts, calling for multidisciplinary expertise and continual learning to adapt to evolving technologies and regulations (Mennella et al., 2024; Veluru, 2024).

Best Practices for Sustainable AI Deployment

Implementing AI responsibly requires adherence to best practices that span technical, ethical, and organizational domains. Key among these is the adoption of human-centric AI design, ensuring transparency, explainability, and accountability in AI decision-making processes (Fenwick et al., 2024; Ho, 2023). This aligns with principles of the human right to science, promoting equitable access and participation in AI advancements.

Data privacy and security are paramount; hence, deploying privacy-preserving techniques such as federated learning in digital forensics and cybersecurity helps protect sensitive information while leveraging AI's analytical power (Iyengar et al., 2025; Shafik, 2024). Additionally, ongoing risk assessments and threat modeling enable organizations to anticipate misuse and vulnerabilities inherent in AI systems (Trotsyuk et al., 2024; Maguluri et al., 2023).

Sustainability also plays a crucial role, as AI systems increasingly intersect with environmental concerns. Standards and certifications must incorporate sustainability metrics to address the ecological footprint of AI, resonating with broader goals like net-zero emissions and climate resilience (Akindele & Chabinga, 2024; Ali, 2024; Emon et al., 2025).

Integration with Legal and Regulatory Frameworks

The interplay between technical standards and legal regulations is vital for effective governance. Compliance with standards must be situated within the context of international, national, and sectoral laws that address data protection, intellectual property, and consumer rights (Darvishi et al., 2022; Pesapane et al., 2021; Mhia-Alddin & Hussein, 2025). For instance, the challenges posed by AI-based medical diagnostics demand adherence to both technical certification and healthcare regulations to ensure patient safety and liability clarity (Naili et al., 2025; Pesapane et al., 2018).

Moreover, cross-sector collaboration between policymakers, technologists, and civil society enhances the relevance and adaptability of standards (Singh & Kaunert, 2025; Schünemann et al., 2024). Standards bodies and industry consortia should foster open dialogue to keep pace with technological innovation while safeguarding ethical imperatives (Zangana & Li, 2025).

Continuous Improvement and Future Outlook

As AI technologies evolve, so must the standards and certifications that govern them. Incorporating advances such as quantum computing and generative AI necessitates dynamic frameworks that can respond to new risks and capabilities (Campus, 2024; Ali et al., 2024; Ali et al., 2025). The role of human resource management is also pivotal, fostering cultures of compliance and innovation in organizations adopting AI (Fenwick et al., 2024).

Future standards are likely to emphasize explainability, robustness, and ethical alignment more strongly, supported by advanced AI auditing tools and transparency protocols (Leontidis, 2024; Filetti et al., 2024). This continuous evolution will be essential for maintaining trust and maximizing AI's positive impact across sectors while minimizing harm and misuse (Veluru, 2024; Zreik, 2024).

Ethical integration into AI forensic tools requires a structured evaluation. The following flowchart outlines the typical lifecycle of ethical review and implementation.

Figure 5. Ethical review lifecycle of forensic AI tools

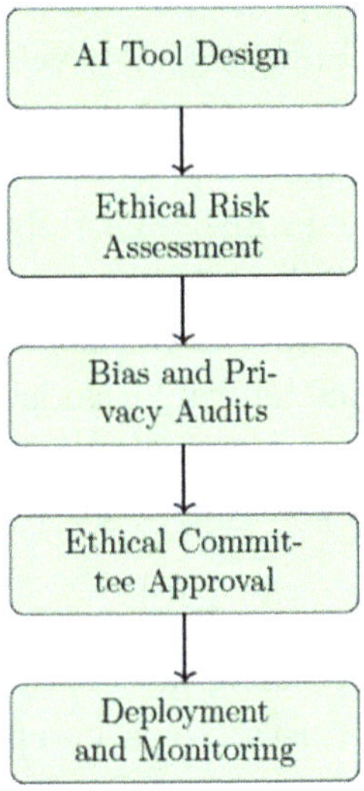

ETHICAL AND PRIVACY CONSIDERATIONS

Ethical and privacy concerns constitute one of the most critical dimensions in the adoption and deployment of emerging technologies, especially Artificial Intelligence (AI) and digital systems. As AI technologies increasingly permeate diverse sectors including healthcare, finance, environment, and governance, addressing these concerns becomes paramount to foster trust, ensure fairness, and safeguard individual rights (Ali & Aysan, 2025; Mennella et al., 2024). This section explores key ethical challenges, privacy implications, regulatory approaches, and ongoing efforts to establish frameworks that balance innovation with human rights protection.

Ethical Challenges in AI and Emerging Technologies

AI systems, particularly those employing generative models, machine learning, and autonomous decision-making, raise complex ethical issues. These include biases embedded in training data, lack of transparency in algorithmic decisions, and accountability for AI-driven outcomes (Ali & Aysan, 2024; Ali & Aysan, 2025). Ethical frameworks aim to mitigate risks such as discrimination, misinformation, and unintended harm by emphasizing principles of fairness, explainability, and human oversight (Fenwick, Molnar, & Frangos, 2024; Veluru, 2024).

In healthcare, ethical challenges extend to patient consent, data stewardship, and the interpretability of AI diagnostics, underscoring the necessity for rigorous evaluation and governance aligned with human rights and medical ethics (Mennella et al., 2024; Pesapane et al., 2018; Ho, 2023). Additionally, the ethical use of AI in warfare and security raises profound concerns about autonomous weapons systems and compliance with international humanitarian law (Batabyal, 2024).

Privacy Implications and Data Protection

Privacy concerns emerge prominently due to AI's dependence on vast amounts of personal and sensitive data. Protecting data confidentiality and preventing misuse are central to maintaining public trust and legal compliance (Shafik, 2024; Iyengar et al., 2025). Techniques such as federated learning and privacy-preserving AI models are increasingly researched to enable collaborative analytics without compromising individual data privacy (Iyengar et al., 2025).

Data breaches, unauthorized surveillance, and profiling pose risks of discrimination and harm, particularly for vulnerable populations, necessitating robust cybersecurity measures and transparent data governance policies (Ali, 2024; Shukla & Taneja, 2024). Regulatory initiatives, including the EU Artificial Intelligence Act, aim to embed privacy by design and by default in AI systems, fostering accountability and user control over personal data (Butt, 2024; Larson et al., 2021).

Regulatory and Legal Frameworks

Governments and international bodies are developing regulatory frameworks to address ethical and privacy issues systematically. Legal instruments seek to enforce responsible AI development, data protection, and digital rights, while encouraging innovation and public participation (Aloamaka, 2024; Daniel, 2024; Mhia-Alddin & Hussein, 2025). For example, the EU AI Act and GDPR set stringent requirements for transparency, risk management, and data subject rights, creating a model for global AI governance (Butt, 2024; Pesapane et al., 2021).

Challenges remain in harmonizing diverse legal systems, addressing cross-border data flows, and adapting rules to fast-evolving technologies (Darvishi, Liu, & Lim, 2022; Naili et al., 2025). Multistakeholder engagement and dynamic policy instruments such as sandbox environments are crucial to fostering regulatory agility (Trotsyuk et al., 2024; Schünemann et al., 2024).

Ethical AI Adoption in Society and Industry

Embedding ethics into AI deployment requires organizational commitment and cultural change. Human-centric AI adoption emphasizes the role of human resource management in ensuring ethical awareness, skills development, and accountability at all levels (Fenwick et al., 2024). Moreover, empowering marginalized groups through inclusive AI design and data analytics can promote social equity and safety (Pimpalkar et al., 2024; Vyawahare, Khandelwal, & Rathod, 2024).

In financial services, ethical AI practices encompass fairness in credit scoring, fraud detection, and transparency to mitigate systemic risks and ensure consumer protection (Ali, Zafar, & Aysan, 2024). Similarly, sustainable industry 4.0 initiatives integrate ethical considerations to balance economic growth with environmental stewardship and social responsibility (Patra, 2025; Singh & Kaunert, 2025).

Future Directions in Ethical and Privacy Governance

The future landscape of ethical AI and privacy protection calls for interdisciplinary collaboration combining law, technology, and social sciences (Leontidis, 2024; Zangana & Li, 2025). Emerging trends include the use of AI-powered contract management systems that enhance compliance and risk mitigation (Mhia-Alddin & Hussein, 2025), and frameworks to prevent misuse of AI in sensitive fields such as biomedical research (Trotsyuk et al., 2024).

Global climate change efforts also intersect with ethical technology use, emphasizing the role of AI in supporting sustainable development while respecting ecological justice and human rights (Akindele & Chabinga, 2024; Ali, 2024; Chowdhury, 2024). Continued research, policy innovation, and capacity-building are essential to navigate ethical complexities and protect privacy in the AI-driven future.

CASE STUDIES

The application of advanced technologies such as artificial intelligence (AI), machine learning, and digital forensics has transformed numerous sectors globally. This section presents detailed case studies highlighting how these innovations intersect with legal, ethical, and environmental frameworks, emphasizing practical implications and lessons learned.

AI and Climate Change Governance in Nigeria

Akindele and Chabinga (2024) examine Nigeria's proactive approach toward integrating international environmental law with AI-enabled sustainability solutions. Their study illustrates how emerging AI technologies facilitate climate change monitoring, enforcement of environmental regulations, and sustainable resource management. This case underscores the significance of aligning policy, governance, and technology to achieve net zero goals and environmental justice, reflecting themes discussed by Ali (2024) regarding policy synchronization for sustainability.

Generative AI in Finance: Ethical and Practical Insights

Ali, H., and Aysan (2024, 2025) provide an in-depth analysis of generative AI's role in finance, employing machine learning techniques to explore academic and grey literature. Their findings reveal both transformative potential and ethical challenges, including transparency, bias, and regulatory compliance in financial AI applications. These findings resonate with Ali, Zafar, and Aysan's (2024) multi-level machine learning studies that emphasize the necessity for robust governance frameworks to manage risks inherent in AI-driven financial decision-making.

AI-Enhanced Ethical Hacking for Cybersecurity

Al-Sinani and Mitchell (2024) explore a Linux-based AI-enhanced ethical hacking experiment, demonstrating how AI tools can augment cybersecurity defenses. Their follow-up work (Al-Sinani et al., 2025) further develops this experimental framework, illustrating practical methodologies to identify vulnerabilities while adhering to ethical standards. This case highlights the intersection of AI capabilities and legal boundaries in cybersecurity, addressing concerns raised by Bharati (2020) on the legal use of digital forensics in law enforcement.

AI in Agricultural and Environmental Monitoring

Arya and Rastogi (2024) analyze the deployment of AI-powered aerial monitoring systems in agriculture, forestry, and border protection. The study emphasizes the dual benefits of precision agriculture and environmental protection, while also considering privacy implications and data governance challenges. This case aligns with discussions by Emon et al. (2025) on leveraging GreenTech innovations to promote sustainability and tackle climate challenges.

Regulatory Challenges of AI in Healthcare Diagnostics

The evolving landscape of AI in medical diagnostics presents significant regulatory and ethical challenges, as highlighted by Mennella et al. (2024). Their narrative review outlines issues such as algorithmic transparency, data privacy, and accountability. Complementing this, Pesapane et al. (2018, 2021) compare regulatory frameworks across major jurisdictions, emphasizing the need for harmonized standards to ensure patient safety and innovation. This case study also reflects concerns noted by Ho (2023) regarding the human right to science within AI governance.

AI-Driven Social Safety and Harassment Prevention

Vyawahare, Khandelwal, and Rathod (2024) investigate AI applications designed to detect and prevent online harassment, especially focused on women's safety. Their study showcases how AI tools enhance predictive analytics and real-time intervention capabilities, yet also highlights ethical considerations surrounding surveillance and user consent. This case draws on Shukla and Taneja's (2024) emphasis on data privacy and ethical AI integration in societal applications.

Digital Forensics and Privacy-Preserving AI Techniques

Iyengar et al. (2025) present federated learning as a privacy-preserving AI approach in digital forensics, addressing concerns about data security in collaborative investigations. This innovation mitigates risks of data leakage while enhancing forensic analysis capabilities. Zangana and Li (2025) discuss future trends in AI-driven digital forensics, underscoring the importance of balancing technological advancements with privacy rights and regulatory compliance.

Legal and Contractual Challenges in AI-Driven Research

Mhia-Alddin and Hussein (2025) delve into legal complexities surrounding contract expiry and compliance in AI-powered STM (Science, Technology, and Medicine) research. Their work proposes frameworks to manage post-expiry obligations and risk mitigation through deep learning and large language models (LLMs). These insights are critical for navigating regulatory uncertainty and ethical governance in cutting-edge AI research and commercialization (Mhia-Alddin & Hussein, 2025).

AI and Quantum Computing in Innovation Ecosystems

Campus (2024), Eswaran and Eswaran (2025), and Drexl, Conde, and Kim (2025) collectively discuss the integration of AI with quantum computing and semiconductor technologies. Their case studies explore the innovative potentials and policy challenges of these converging fields, emphasizing the need for adaptive regulatory mechanisms to foster responsible development and prevent misuse, as also suggested by Trotsyuk et al. (2024).

AI in Sustainable Industry and Environmental Law

Patra (2025), Singh and Kaunert (2025), and Soomro et al. (2025) provide case analyses on the adoption of AI within Industry 4.0 frameworks and green regulatory ecosystems. Their works highlight the dynamic interactions between AI-driven innovation, sustainability objectives, and legal compliance across industries, reinforcing the themes of resilience and ecological protection emphasized by Chowdhury (2024) and Saikia (2024).

These case studies collectively demonstrate the multifaceted roles of AI and related technologies across diverse sectors, underscoring the vital need for integrated ethical, legal, and regulatory frameworks. Such integration ensures that AI innovation not only advances efficiency and capability but also aligns with societal values and sustainable development goals.

FUTURE POLICY DIRECTIONS

As emerging technologies like artificial intelligence (AI), quantum computing, and green technologies reshape societies, the necessity for forward-looking, adaptive, and ethical policy frameworks becomes paramount. Future policy directions must address the rapidly evolving technological landscape while simultaneously promoting sustainability, ethical governance, security, and inclusivity. This section discusses critical future policy pathways informed by recent scholarly insights across multiple domains.

Sustainability and Climate-Responsive Policies

Addressing climate change is a global imperative requiring robust policies that integrate environmental sustainability with economic and social governance. Akindele and Chabinga (2024) emphasize Nigeria's proactive role in international environmental law, illustrating how national policy must harmonize with global climate goals to foster resilience. Similarly, Ali (2024) outlines the alignment of net-zero policies with political and governance structures, highlighting the complexity of transitioning towards sustainable futures.

In this context, Aloamaka (2024) notes the evolution of international environmental law as a foundation for coherent climate crisis management, advocating for legal frameworks that are flexible yet enforceable. Jafarizadeh et al. (2024) emphasize innovation and barrier mitigation in renewable energy storage, urging policies that promote technological advances while addressing infrastructural and economic challenges.

Policies targeting sustainability should also embrace indigenous knowledge systems, as argued by Sakapaji et al. (2024), whose work underscores the importance of legal and regulatory frameworks that support socioecological resilience and sustainability of indigenous communities.

Ethical and Regulatory Governance of AI

As AI technologies become ubiquitous across sectors, ethical governance and robust regulatory frameworks are essential to mitigate risks while fostering innovation. Butt (2024) provides an analytical review of the EU Artificial Intelligence Act, highlighting the global significance of comprehensive AI regulation.

Mennella et al. (2024) discuss the ethical and regulatory challenges unique to healthcare AI technologies, emphasizing the need for international harmonization of standards. Similarly, Pesapane et al. (2021, 2018) analyze AI as a medical device and propose ethical frameworks critical for patient safety and public trust.

On the frontier of AI ethics, Ali and Aysan (2025) employ machine learning structural topic modeling to dissect ethical dimensions of generative AI, underscoring the urgency for multi-domain policy interventions that anticipate cross-sectoral challenges. Al-Sinani et al. (2024, 2025) explore AI-enhanced ethical hacking, recommending policy approaches to integrate AI in cybersecurity ethically and effectively.

Trotsyuk et al. (2024) advocate for a risk mitigation framework addressing AI misuse in biomedical research, a blueprint for future regulatory policies safeguarding ethical research integrity.

Legal and Contractual Innovations in Technology-Driven Environments

Emerging technologies challenge traditional legal constructs, especially in contracts and intellectual property management. Mhia-Alddin and Hussein (2025) critically reassess contract expiry and termination boundaries, highlighting risks and proposing AI-powered compliance and risk mitigation frameworks through deep learning and large language models.

Patra (2025) underscores the importance of navigating legal landscapes in sustainable Industry 4.0 environments, pushing for policies that align technological innovation with legal certainty and business agility. In parallel, Pai (2018) discusses heuristics around patent injunctions, signaling the need for policy refinement to balance innovation incentives and market competition.

The role of government in facilitating legal clarity is further exemplified by Soomro et al. (2025), who analyze green regulations' influence on eco-friendly business practices, emphasizing government support and compliance enforcement as cornerstones for a sustainable business ecosystem.

Data Privacy, Security, and Digital Forensics

Data privacy and cybersecurity are critical pillars for future policies, especially as AI systems proliferate. Shafik (2024) provides insights into safeguarding customer data in AI-driven service models such as ChatGPT, calling for enhanced data protection regulations.

Iyengar et al. (2025) introduce privacy-preserving AI techniques like federated learning, suggesting policy frameworks that enable forensic investigations without compromising individual privacy rights. Zangana and Li (2025) project future trends in AI-driven digital forensics, emphasizing the need for legal systems to adapt to AI's evidentiary challenges.

Maguluri et al. (2023) discuss security concerns related to AI-based drones in smart cities, recommending policy-driven risk assessments and mitigation strategies to address vulnerabilities in increasingly connected urban environments.

Healthcare and Public Health Policy Adaptations

The integration of AI into healthcare demands dynamic policy frameworks that balance innovation, regulation, and ethics. Ho (2023) highlights the implementation of the human right to science in governing AI in healthcare, advocating policies that ensure equitable access and scientific integrity.

Verma et al. (2020) and Mennella et al. (2024) discuss regulatory challenges in public health AI applications, focusing on system-level readiness and ethical governance. Naili et al. (2025) bring attention to AI-based diagnostic tools, emphasizing legal implications and regulatory clarity to ensure safety and efficacy.

Education, Workforce, and Social Equity

As AI disrupts traditional workforce structures and educational paradigms, policy directions must prioritize human-centric adoption and equity. Fenwick et al. (2024) emphasize human resource management's role in transitioning firms from AI implementation to adoption, signaling a policy need for workforce reskilling programs.

Jamro and Jamro (2023) demonstrate the value of chatbot integration in holistic STEM education, advocating for educational policies that integrate AI tools while addressing digital divides and access inequities.

Pimpalkar et al. (2024) explore AI's potential in women's safety and empowerment, underscoring policies aimed at leveraging AI for social good and reducing gender disparities.

Cross-Sectoral and Multidisciplinary Policy Integration

Future policies must integrate insights from law, technology, economics, and social sciences to address complex challenges. Schünemann et al. (2024) compare complex system policy modeling approaches, recommending the adoption of system dynamics and agent-based modeling to inform policy advice.

Darvishi et al. (2022) highlight the legal and economic implications of emerging technologies, urging cross-disciplinary collaboration for sound regulatory frameworks.

Zreik (2024) discusses AI for entrepreneurial idea generation, suggesting policies that nurture innovation ecosystems while safeguarding intellectual property and ethical standards.

International Cooperation and Legal Harmonization

Global challenges such as climate change, AI ethics, and technology governance require international cooperation. Singh and Kaunert (2025) discuss biodiversity protection policies within sustainability trajectories, advocating for multilateral agreements and legal harmonization.

Daniel (2024) and Chowdhury (2024) stress navigating international legal pathways and just climate discourse, highlighting policy alignment as a critical component of global sustainability efforts.

Oduro et al. (2024) explore legal strategies to overcome regulatory barriers in renewable energy expansion, reinforcing the importance of cross-border policy coherence.

Summary

Future policy directions must be adaptive, anticipatory, and ethically grounded, reflecting the convergence of emerging technologies and societal values. The interplay between sustainability, AI ethics, legal innovation, data security, healthcare, education, and international collaboration forms the foundation for resilient and inclusive policy frameworks. Implementing these insights requires multi-stakeholder engagement, ongoing research, and agile governance structures to navigate the complexities of the 21st century.

CONCLUSION

In an era marked by rapid technological advancement and escalating global challenges, the development of forward-thinking policy frameworks is critical to harnessing innovation for the common good. This chapter has underscored the multifaceted nature of future policy directions, emphasizing the need for integrative approaches that balance technological progress with ethical considerations, sustainability, and social equity.

Sustainability and climate-responsive policies must be deeply embedded within national and international legal frameworks to ensure resilience against environmental crises while promoting green innovation. The ethical governance of AI, especially in sensitive domains such as healthcare and security, requires robust regulation that safeguards human rights and fosters public trust. Simultaneously, evolving legal constructs around contracts, intellectual property, and data privacy must adapt to the complexities introduced by AI, quantum computing, and other transformative technologies.

Moreover, future policies should prioritize human-centric adoption of AI through education, workforce reskilling, and inclusive strategies that address disparities and empower vulnerable groups. The integration of multidisciplinary insights and international cooperation will be pivotal in crafting cohesive, dynamic governance models that can respond effectively to the intertwined challenges of technology and society.

Ultimately, the path forward demands collaboration across governments, industries, academia, and civil society to build resilient, ethical, and sustainable policy ecosystems. By anticipating emerging risks and opportunities, these policies can guide the responsible evolution of technology, ensuring it serves humanity's long-term interests and fosters a just and sustainable future.

REFERENCES

Akindele, A., & Chabinga, R. (2024). Navigating Climate Change and Sustainability Solutions: Nigeria's Role in International Environmental Law. *African Journal of Climate Change and Resource Sustainability*, *3*(1), 331–344. DOI: 10.37284/ajccrs.3.1.2188

Al-Sinani, H. S., & Mitchell, C. J. (2024). AI-enhanced ethical hacking: A Linux-focused experiment. *arXiv preprint arXiv:2410.05105*.

Al-Sinani, H. S., Sahli, N., Mitchell, C. J., & Al-Siyabi, M. (2025). Advancing ethical hacking with AI: A Linux-based experimental study. *Proceedings of ITA-SEC and SERICS, Bologna, Italy (Feb 2025),* https://www. chrismitchell. net/Papers/aehwaa. pdf

Ali, A. (2024). Navigating Road for Net Zero Policies to Aligning Policy, Politics, and Governance for Environmental Sustainability. In *Transition Towards a Sustainable Future: Net Zero Policies and Environmental Sustainability* (pp. 205–230). Springer Nature Singapore. DOI: 10.1007/978-981-97-5756-5_10

Ali, H., & Aysan, A. F. (2024). Decoding Future of Generative AI in Finance: A Machine Learning Exploration of Academic and Grey Corpus. *Available at SSRN* 4787211. DOI: 10.2139/ssrn.4787211

Ali, H., & Aysan, A. F. (2025). Ethical dimensions of generative AI: A cross-domain analysis using machine learning structural topic modeling. *International Journal of Ethics and Systems*, *41*(1), 3–34. DOI: 10.1108/IJOES-04-2024-0112

Ali, H., Zafar, M. B., & Aysan, A. F. (2024). Generative AI and Finance: A Multi-level Machine Learning Based Analysis. *Available at SSRN* 5129013.

Aloamaka, P. C. (2024). Navigating the Climate Crisis: Exploring International Law's Evolution and Application. *GLS Law Journal*, *6*(1), 48–58. DOI: 10.69974/glslawjournal.v6i1.127

Arya, L., & Rastogi, R. (2024). Study on Aerial Monitoring System in Agriculture, Forestry, Defense, and Border Protection Using Artificial Intelligence (AI). In *Agriculture and Aquaculture Applications of Biosensors and Bioelectronics* (pp. 392-407). IGI Global Scientific Publishing.

Batabyal, G. S. (2024). Ethics, laws on war and artificial intelligence-driven warfare. In *Artificial intelligence, ethics and the future of warfare* (pp. 187–215). Routledge India. DOI: 10.4324/9781003421849-9

Bharati, R. K. (2020). Legal and Ethical Considerations in the Use of Digital Forensics by Law Enforcement: A Multi-jurisdictional Study. *Turk. Online J. Qual. Inq, 11*(4), 10594–10610.

. Borta, H. G., Alemu, A., Shute, T., Zewdie, B., Fantaw, D., Shimelis, B., ... & Tamiru, M. T. (2024). Narcotic Drugs and Psychotropic Substances Control System in Ethiopia: A National Survey.

Bousri, M. M. S. (2019). *A comparative analysis of legal and institutional framework for arbitration: Comoros and Uganda* (Doctoral dissertation, School of law).

Butt, J. (2024). Analytical study of the world's first EU Artificial Intelligence (AI) Act. *International Journal of Research Publication and Reviews, 5*(3), 7343–7364. DOI: 10.55248/gengpi.5.0324.0914

. Campus, M. T. (2024). Quantum Machine Learning, Leveraging Al, and. *Integration of AI, Quantum Computing, and Semiconductor Technology*, 57.

Chowdhury, S. (2024). Towards a Just Climate: Navigating Complexities and Challenges in Climate Change Discourse and Action. *Issue 2 Int'l JL Mgmt. &. Human., 7*, 1807.

Cooper, S., & Zell, S. (2023). *Staying on Board: Non-profit housing provider board capacity in a changing context.* Institute of Urban Studies, The University of Winnipeg.

Daniel, J. (2024). *Environmental Law: Navigating Legal Pathways for a Sustainable Future*. Pencil.

Darvishi, K., Liu, L., & Lim, S. (2022). Navigating the Nexus: Legal and Economic Implications of Emerging Tech-nologies. *Law and Economics, 16*(3), 172–186. DOI: 10.35335/laweco.v16i3.59

. Drexl, J., Conde, B., & Kim, D. (2025). Position Statement of the Max Planck Institute for Innovation and Competition of 25 April 2025 in the framework of the revision of the Technology

Eisenberg, D. (2024). *Sensing With Integrity: Responsible Sensor Systems in an Era of AI* (Doctoral dissertation, New Jersey Institute of Technology).

Emon, M. M. H., Khan, T., Rahman, M. A., Hamid, A. B. A., & Yaakub, N. I. (2025). GreenTech revolution: Navigating challenges and seizing opportunities. In *AI and green technology applications in society* (pp. 63–90). IGI Global Scientific Publishing.

Eswaran, U., & Eswaran, V. (2025). Quantum Machine Learning, Leveraging AI, and Semiconductor Technology. In *Integration of AI, Quantum Computing, and Semiconductor Technology* (pp. 57-78). IGI Global.

Fenwick, A., Molnar, G., & Frangos, P. (2024). The critical role of HRM in AI-driven digital transformation: A paradigm shift to enable firms to move from AI implementation to human-centric adoption. *Discover Artificial Intelligence, 4*(1), 34. DOI: 10.1007/s44163-024-00125-4

Filetti, S., Fenza, G., & Gallo, A. (2024). Research design and writing of scholarly articles: New artificial intelligence tools available for researchers. *Endocrine, 85*(3), 1104–1116. DOI: 10.1007/s12020-024-03977-z PMID: 39085566

Flannery, J., Ajayi, S. O., & Oyegoke, A. S. (2021). Alcohol and substance misuse in the construction industry. *International Journal of Occupational Safety and Ergonomics, 27*(2), 472–487. DOI: 10.1080/10803548.2019.1601376 PMID: 30935301

Gaurav, A., Chui, K. T., Arya, V., Attar, R. W., Bansal, S., Alhomoud, A., & Psannis, K. (2024). Optimized AI-Driven Semantic Web Approach for Enhancing Phishing Detection in E-Commerce Platforms. [IJSWIS]. *International Journal on Semantic Web and Information Systems, 20*(1), 1–13. DOI: 10.4018/IJSWIS.359767

Ho, C. W. (2023). Implementing the human right to science in the regulatory governance of artificial intelligence in healthcare. *Journal of Law and the Biosciences, 10*(2), lsad026. DOI: 10.1093/jlb/lsad026 PMID: 37854168

Iyengar, S. S., Nabavirazavi, S., & Hariprasad, Y. HB, P., & Mohan, C. K. (2025). Privacy-Preserving AI (Federated Learning) for Digital Forensics. In *Artificial Intelligence in Practice: Theory and Application for Cyber Security and Forensics* (pp. 161-176). Cham: Springer Nature Switzerland.

Jafarizadeh, H., Yamini, E., Zolfaghari, S. M., Esmaeilion, F., Assad, M. E. H., & Soltani, M. (2024). Navigating challenges in large-scale renewable energy storage: Barriers, solutions, and innovations. *Energy Reports, 12*, 2179–2192. DOI: 10.1016/j.egyr.2024.08.019

. Jamro, M. Y., & Jamro, F. A. (2023). AI Matters: Chatbot Integration in Holistic STEM Education.

Karim, R., Galar, D., & Kumar, U. (2023). *AI factory: theories, applications and case studies*. CRC Press. DOI: 10.1201/9781003208686

Larson, D. B., Harvey, H., Rubin, D. L., Irani, N., Tse, J. R., & Langlotz, C. P. (2021). Regulatory frameworks for development and evaluation of artificial intelligence–based diagnostic imaging algorithms: Summary and recommendations. *Journal of the American College of Radiology, 18*(3), 413–424. DOI: 10.1016/j.jacr.2020.09.060 PMID: 33096088

. Leontidis, G. (2024). Science in the age of ai: How artificial intelligence is changing the nature and method of scientific research.

Luan, H., Perron, B. E., Victor, B. G., Wan, G., Niu, Y., & Xiao, X. (2024). Using artificial intelligence to support scientometric analysis of scholarly literature: A case example of research on mainland China's left-behind children. *Journal of the Society for Social Work and Research*, *15*(3), 435–457. DOI: 10.1086/731613

Maennig, W. (2014). Inefficiency of the anti-doping system: Cost reduction proposals. *Substance Use & Misuse*, *49*(9), 1201–1205. DOI: 10.3109/10826084.2014.912065 PMID: 24832718

Maguluri, L. P., Arularasan, A. N., & Boopathi, S. (2023). Assessing security concerns for ai-based drones in smart cities. In *Effective AI, Blockchain, and E-Governance Applications for Knowledge Discovery and Management* (pp. 27-47). IGI Global Scientific Publishing. DOI: 10.4018/978-1-6684-9151-5.ch002

Manganelli, A. G. (2019). Reverse payments and risk of bankruptcy under private information. *International Journal of the Economics of Business*, *26*(3), 411–429. DOI: 10.1080/13571516.2019.1613146

Mennella, C., Maniscalco, U., De Pietro, G., & Esposito, M. (2024). Ethical and regulatory challenges of AI technologies in healthcare: A narrative review. *Heliyon*, *10*(4), e26297. DOI: 10.1016/j.heliyon.2024.e26297 PMID: 38384518

Mhia-Alddin, D. A. (2025). Legal Implications of Contract Expiry in Modern Commercial Law: Towards a Framework for Post-Expiry Obligations and Risk Management. In Zangana, H., Al-Karaki, J., & Omar, M. (Eds.), *Navigating Law and Policy in STM Enterprises: Ethical Governance, Regulation, and Innovation Strategy* (pp. 139–158). IGI Global Scientific Publishing., DOI: 10.4018/979-8-3373-4862-9.ch006

Mhia-Alddin, D. A., & Hussein, A. M. (2025). Expiration vs. Termination: Reassessing Legal Boundaries in Contract Law. In Zangana, H., Al-Karaki, J., & Omar, M. (Eds.), *Navigating Law and Policy in STM Enterprises: Ethical Governance, Regulation, and Innovation Strategy* (pp. 35–58). IGI Global Scientific Publishing., DOI: 10.4018/979-8-3373-4862-9.ch002

Mhia-Alddin, D. A., & Hussein, A. M. (2025). AI-Powered Contract Security: Managing Expiry, Compliance, and Risk Mitigation Through Deep Learning and LLMs. In *Revolutionizing Cybersecurity With Deep Learning and Large Language Models* (pp. 37-64). IGI Global Scientific Publishing.

Mhia-Alddin, D. A., & Hussein, A. M. (2025). Contract Expiry in AI-Driven STM Research: Legal Challenges, Risks, and Regulatory Considerations. In *Ensuring Secure and Ethical STM Research in the AI Era* (pp. 77-110). IGI Global Scientific Publishing.

Naili, Y. T., Mangkunegara, I. S., Purwono, P., & Baballe, M. A. (2025). Regulatory challenges in ai-based diagnostics: Legal implications of ai use in medical diagnostics. In *BIO Web of Conferences* (Vol. 152, p. 01034). EDP Sciences.

Narayana, S. A., Pati, R. K., & Padhi, S. S. (2019). Market dynamics and reverse logistics for sustainability in the Indian Pharmaceuticals industry. *Journal of Cleaner Production*, *208*, 968–987. DOI: 10.1016/j.jclepro.2018.10.171

Oduro, P., Uzougbo, N. S., & Ugwu, M. C. (2024). Renewable energy expansion: Legal strategies for overcoming regulatory barriers and promoting innovation. *International Journal of Applied Research in Social Sciences*, *6*(5), 927–944. DOI: 10.51594/ijarss.v6i5.1145

Pai, Y. (2018). Patent Injunction Heuristics in India. *Pai, Yogesh, Patent Injunction Heuristics in India in Rafal Sikorski (Ed.) Patent Law Injunctions, Kluwer Law International BV (2019).*

. Patra, S. P. (2025). Navigating the legal landscape of sustainable Industry 4.0. *Industry 4.0 for Manufacturing Systems: Concepts, Technologies, and Applications*, 109.

Pesapane, F., Bracchi, D. A., Mulligan, J. F., Linnikov, A., Maslennikov, O., Lanzavecchia, M. B., Tantrige, P., Stasolla, A., Biondetti, P., Giuggioli, P. F., Cassano, E., & Carrafiello, G. (2021). Legal and regulatory framework for AI solutions in healthcare in EU, US, China, and Russia: New scenarios after a pandemic. *Radiation*, *1*(4), 261–276. DOI: 10.3390/radiation1040022

Pesapane, F., Volonté, C., Codari, M., & Sardanelli, F. (2018). Artificial intelligence as a medical device in radiology: Ethical and regulatory issues in Europe and the United States. *Insights Into Imaging*, *9*(5), 745–753. DOI: 10.1007/s13244-018-0645-y PMID: 30112675

Pimpalkar, A. P., Wankhade, N. R., Chole, V., & Golhar, Y. (2024). Women's Empowerment Through AI: Discovering Data Analytics for Predictive Safety Solutions and Future Trends. In *AI Tools and Applications for Women's Safety* (pp. 304-326). IGI Global Scientific Publishing.

. Rashid, A. B., & Kausik, A. K. (2024). AI revolutionizing industries worldwide: A comprehensive overview of its diverse applications. *Hybrid Advances*, 100277.

Read, A., Botha, R., & Jamaloodien, K. (2023). COVID-19 vaccination procurement and contract management in a South African context. *Journal of Strategic Contracting and Negotiation*, *7*(1-2), 33–43. DOI: 10.1177/20555636231198053

Rodriguez, M. Y., & Storer, H. (2020). A computational social science perspective on qualitative data exploration: Using topic models for the descriptive analysis of social media data. *Journal of Technology in Human Services*, *38*(1), 54–86. DOI: 10.1080/15228835.2019.1616350

Saikia, B. (2024). Ecologically-Informed approaches: International mechanisms for navigating environmental challenges and ensuring sustainability in the oil and gas exploration and production industry. *Proceedings of the International Academy of Ecology and Environmental Sciences*, *14*(2), 60.

Sakapaji, S. C., García Molinos, J., Parilova, V., Gavrilyeva, T., & Yakovleva, N. (2024). Navigating legal and regulatory frameworks to achieve the resilience and sustainability of indigenous socioecological systems. *Resources*, *13*(4), 56. DOI: 10.3390/resources13040056

San Biagio, M., Cipolla, M., La Mattina, E., & Morreale, V. (2023, December). A Topic Clustering Method to Identify Online Threats against Soft Targets. In *2023 International Conference on Computational Science and Computational Intelligence (CSCI)* (pp. 727-733). IEEE. DOI: 10.1109/CSCI62032.2023.00124

Schünemann, C., Johanning, S., Reger, E., Herold, H., & Bruckner, T. (2024). Complex system policy modelling approaches for policy advice–comparing systems thinking, system dynamics and agent-based modelling. *Political Research Exchange : an ECPR Journal*, *6*(1), 2387438. DOI: 10.1080/2474736X.2024.2387438

Shafik, W. (2024). Data privacy and security safeguarding customer information in ChatGPT systems. In *Revolutionizing the Service Industry Wth OpenAI Models* (pp. 52–86). IGI Global. DOI: 10.4018/979-8-3693-1239-1.ch003

Sheliemina, N. (2024). The use of artificial intelligence in medical diagnostics: Opportunities, prospects and risks. *Health Economics and Management Review*, *5*(2), 104–124. DOI: 10.61093/hem.2024.2-07

Shuja, J., Alanazi, E., Alasmary, W., & Alashaikh, A. (2021). COVID-19 open source data sets: A comprehensive survey. *Applied Intelligence*, *51*(3), 1296–1325. DOI: 10.1007/s10489-020-01862-6 PMID: 34764552

Shukla, R. P., & Taneja, S. (2024). Ethical considerations and data privacy in artificial intelligence. In *Integrating generative AI in education to achieve sustainable development goals* (pp. 86–97). IGI Global. DOI: 10.4018/979-8-3693-2440-0.ch005

Singh, B., & Kaunert, C. (2025). Navigating the Terrain of Sustainability Trajectories of Environment: Biodiversity Protection and Legal Landscapes. In *Community Resilience and Climate Change Challenges: Pursuit of Sustainable Development Goals (SDGs)* (pp. 355-374). IGI Global Scientific Publishing.

Soomro, J. A., Suhrab, M., & Abbasi, B. A. (2025). Navigating Green Regulations in the Business Ecosystem: Government Support, Compliance, and Obstacles in the Context of Pakistan. In *Government Influences on Eco-Friendly Practices in Business* (pp. 55-86). IGI Global.

Terry, N. (2019). Of regulating healthcare AI and robots. *Yale JL & Tech.*, *21*, 133.

Trotsyuk, A. A., Waeiss, Q., Bhatia, R. T., Aponte, B. J., Heffernan, I. M., Madgavkar, D., Felder, R. M., Lehmann, L. S., Palmer, M. J., Greely, H., Wald, R., Goetz, L., Trengove, M., Vandersluis, R., Lin, H., Cho, M. K., Altman, R. B., Endy, D., Relman, D. A., & Magnus, D. (2024). Toward a framework for risk mitigation of potential misuse of artificial intelligence in biomedical research. *Nature Machine Intelligence*, *6*(12), 1–8. DOI: 10.1038/s42256-024-00926-3

. Veluru, C. S. (2024). Responsible Artificial Intelligence on Large Scale Data to Prevent Misuse, Unethical Challenges and Security Breaches. *Journal of Artificial Intelligence & Cloud Computing. SRC/JAICC-349. DOI: doi. org/(3), 331*, 2-6.DOI: 10.47363/JAICC/2024

Verma, A., Rao, K., Eluri, V., & Sharma, Y. (2020). Regulating AI in public health: systems challenges and perspectives. *ORF Occasional Paper, 261.*

. Verma, M., & Rohit, K. (2024). Ethical AI Shaping Scholarly Communication: Challenges and Opportunities.

Vyawahare, H., Khandelwal, S., & Rathod, S. (2024). Artificial Intelligence in Detecting and Preventing Online Harassment. In *AI Tools and Applications for Women's Safety* (pp. 14–35). IGI Global Scientific Publishing. DOI: 10.4018/979-8-3693-1435-7.ch002

Wang, Q. (2024). Maritime law enforcement concerning offshore energy platforms: Navigating international law constraints and challenges. *Marine Policy*, *170*, 106370. DOI: 10.1016/j.marpol.2024.106370

Zangana, H. M., & Li, S. (2025). Future Trends in AI and Digital Forensics. In *Digital Forensics in the Age of AI* (pp. 347–380). IGI Global Scientific Publishing.

Zreik, M. (2024). Harnessing AI for entrepreneurial idea generation: Navigating the new frontier. In *Generating Entrepreneurial Ideas With AI* (pp. 1–18). IGI Global Scientific Publishing. DOI: 10.4018/979-8-3693-3498-0.ch001

Chapter 3

Machine Learning Algorithms for Threat Detection and Evidence Analysis

Luay Albtosh
https://orcid.org/0009-0009-0338-9123
Capitol Technology University, USA & Houston Community College, USA

Ryan Yates
https://orcid.org/0009-0000-2870-9044
Capitol Technology University, USA

ABSTRACT

The integration of machine learning (ML) into digital forensics and cybercrime investigation has revolutionized the way threats are detected and evidence is analyzed. This chapter explores the role of ML algorithms in enhancing the efficiency and accuracy of threat detection and forensic analysis. It presents a comprehensive overview of various supervised, unsupervised, and reinforcement learning techniques applied to anomaly detection, malware classification, intrusion detection systems (IDS), and digital evidence triage. Emphasis is placed on real-time detection capabilities, scalability, and adaptability of ML models in dynamic cyber environments. The chapter also addresses challenges such as data imbalance, adversarial attacks, explainability, and ethical considerations related to privacy and accountability. Through illustrative case studies and comparative analysis, this chapter provides practical insights into the current state of ML in digital forensics and highlights promising directions for future research and implementation.

DOI: 10.4018/979-8-3373-6536-7.ch003

INTRODUCTION

The growing complexity and scale of cyber threats have prompted a paradigm shift in the field of digital forensics and cybercrime investigation. Traditional methods of threat detection and evidence analysis are increasingly inadequate to address the velocity, volume, and variety of modern cyberattacks. In this context, machine learning (ML)—a core subfield of artificial intelligence (AI)—has emerged as a transformative force in automating the identification of anomalies, malicious behaviors, and digital evidence across vast datasets (Omar, 2022; Jones et al., 2023).

The integration of ML into cybersecurity is driven by its ability to learn from patterns in data, adapt to evolving threats, and enhance predictive capabilities without explicit programming. ML algorithms now play a critical role in intrusion detection systems (IDS), malware classification, user behavior analytics, phishing detection, and even in attributing cyberattacks based on forensic evidence (Yu et al., 2024; Manoharan & Sarker, 2023). Furthermore, the rise of large language models (LLMs) has expanded the capabilities of AI systems beyond structured datasets, enabling advanced threat intelligence extraction from textual sources like logs, emails, and social media (Chen et al., 2024; Ferrag et al., 2023; AlQenaei, 2024).

Recent research has shown that domain-specific LLMs such as SecureBERT (Aghaei et al., 2022) and SecLM (Asoronye et al., 2024) can outperform general-purpose models in identifying and interpreting cybersecurity-related content. These models are trained on curated corpora of security data, enhancing both precision and contextual understanding. Similarly, Ferrag et al. (2024) demonstrated that privacy-preserving, lightweight LLMs are particularly suitable for threat detection in resource-constrained environments like IoT and IIoT devices.

As organizations increasingly adopt cloud-based infrastructures and mobile devices, the attack surface expands, demanding more adaptive and explainable AI-driven defenses (Hamza & Omar, 2013; Wright et al., 2012). ML models must now contend not only with data imbalance and adversarial evasion techniques but also with regulatory and ethical concerns, including transparency, bias, and data sovereignty (Gholami & Omar, 2023; Gupta et al., 2024). Explainable AI (XAI) and synthetic data generation are among the proposed solutions to increase trust and robustness (Ghazal et al., 2024; Gholami & Omar, 2024).

In addition, the fusion of foundation models, including transformers, with classical cybersecurity pipelines is enabling more generalized and scalable security frameworks (Idelhaj et al., 2024; Hasanov et al., 2024). These models serve as building blocks for downstream applications, ranging from real-time threat monitoring to digital evidence summarization and reasoning (Santos et al., 2024; Liu, 2024).

The application of LLMs in digital forensics is not without challenges. Data privacy, model explainability, adversarial robustness, and the risk of hallucination in generated responses remain active areas of concern (Bryce et al., 2024; Zangana & Omar, 2025a). Nevertheless, innovations such as GEADD (GPT-2 Enhanced Attack Detection and Defense) have demonstrated significant promise in identifying zero-day threats with minimal human intervention (Jones & Omar, 2024).

This chapter aims to explore the intersection of ML and digital forensics by:

- Reviewing major ML algorithms used in threat detection and forensic analysis.
- Analyzing the role of LLMs in automating cybercrime investigation tasks.
- Presenting real-world applications and emerging trends in AI-driven forensic tools.
- Discussing ethical, technical, and operational challenges in deploying such systems.

By synthesizing findings from recent studies (Diaf et al., 2024; Motlagh et al., 2024; Hassanin & Moustafa, 2024) and case-based applications (Zangana et al., 2024; Omar, 2024), this chapter contributes to a deeper understanding of how ML is shaping the future of cybersecurity and forensic practices. It also builds on foundational frameworks outlined in current literature and edited volumes (Omar & Zangana, 2024; 2025a; 2025b) to propose research-informed pathways for the effective deployment of AI in digital investigations.

OVERVIEW OF MACHINE LEARNING IN CYBERSECURITY AND FORENSICS

Machine learning (ML) has emerged as a foundational technology in modern cybersecurity and digital forensics, fundamentally transforming how threats are detected, investigated, and mitigated. With the rising complexity and volume of cyberattacks, conventional rule-based systems have struggled to keep pace. In contrast, ML-driven approaches offer adaptability, predictive power, and automation, enabling proactive defense mechanisms and efficient forensic analysis (Jones et al., 2023; Omar, 2022).

Evolution of Machine Learning in Cybersecurity

Initially employed for spam detection and malware classification, ML has evolved into a core component for advanced threat intelligence and intrusion detection systems (Manoharan & Sarker, 2023). Its capabilities now span across endpoint protection, anomaly detection, behavioral analysis, and attack pattern recognition. Innovations in neural networks, ensemble learning, and deep learning architectures have empowered security systems to automatically learn from vast datasets and uncover hidden correlations indicative of cyber threats (Ghazal et al., 2024; Yu et al., 2024).

Recent advances have shifted focus toward explainable AI (XAI) and lightweight models tailored for resource-constrained environments like IoT/IIoT devices. Ferrag et al. (2024) proposed a privacy-preserving, BERT-based lightweight model for detecting cyber threats in these systems, emphasizing efficiency and security. These developments have fostered trust and operational practicality across various sectors, including healthcare, finance, and critical infrastructure (Gupta et al., 2024; Huff et al., 2023).

Machine Learning in Digital Forensics

In digital forensics, ML techniques have been instrumental in automating artifact analysis, anomaly detection, and event reconstruction. From classifying log data and identifying insider threats to supporting litigation with AI-enhanced evidence interpretation, ML enriches investigative workflows with both speed and precision (Omar & Zangana, 2025; Zangana & Omar, 2025). Hybrid systems, such as those combining wavelet transform with deep learning, have also improved image denoising for forensic examination (Zangana & Mustafa, 2025).

Furthermore, ML algorithms are employed to detect social engineering tactics, phishing schemes, and synthetic identity fraud. These applications are crucial in identifying previously unseen attack vectors and patterns within massive, often noisy datasets (Zangana et al., 2024; Pleshakova et al., 2024).

Role of Large Language Models (LLMs) in Cybersecurity

Large Language Models (LLMs) such as BERT, GPT, and domain-specific variants like SecureBERT (Aghaei et al., 2022) or SecLM (Asoronye et al., 2024), have redefined the intersection of NLP and cybersecurity. These models enable contextual understanding of cyber threat intelligence, automate incident reports, detect vulnerabilities in code, and assist in real-time log parsing and summarization (Ferrag et al., 2023; Bryce et al., 2024).

AlQenaei (2024) highlighted the architectural optimizations in LLMs, which have made them more applicable in time-sensitive, high-stakes security environments. For example, models can now effectively analyze system logs, detect anomalies, and even predict future attack vectors by learning from historical data (Diaf et al., 2024).

In forensics, LLMs assist in semantic analysis of textual evidence, keyword extraction from encrypted chats, and generation of coherent forensic summaries—replacing hours of manual work with accurate, real-time insights (Zangana, Mustafa, & Li, 2025; Omar & Zangana, 2025).

The diagram below illustrates a layered architecture for a cybersecurity system that integrates LLM components with conventional infrastructure tools.

Figure 1. Security architecture with LLM and traditional tool integration

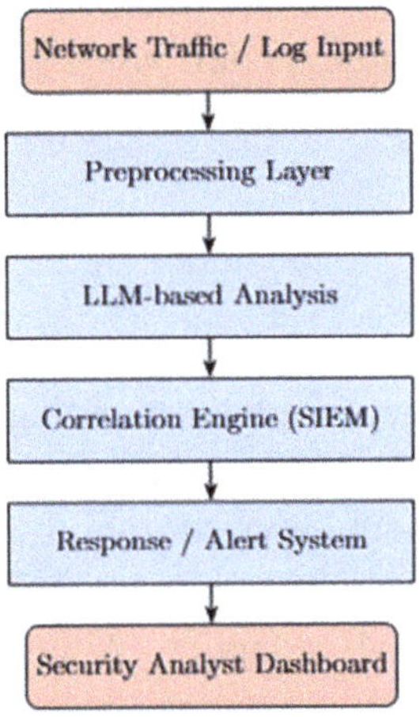

Integration with Cyber Threat Intelligence (CTI)

ML's integration with CTI has brought a paradigm shift. Language models like ChatGPT and GEADD (Jones & Omar, 2024) help enhance situational awareness and automate threat classification. These models interpret and correlate data from multiple threat feeds, including MITRE ATT&CK and STIX, enabling analysts to respond faster to zero-day attacks (Xu et al., 2024; Sarker, 2024).

Recent work has also emphasized the synergy between ML and blockchain for secure logging, timestamping, and maintaining digital evidence integrity (Zangana, 2024a). These techniques support non-repudiation and provide traceability during forensic investigations.

Challenges and Opportunities

Despite its advantages, ML in cybersecurity faces challenges such as adversarial attacks, model interpretability, and data privacy concerns. Attackers increasingly exploit ML models through poisoning and evasion attacks, necessitating robust defenses (Omar, 2024a; Liu, 2024). Additionally, the demand for transparency in decision-making calls for explainable AI frameworks that balance accuracy with interpretability (Chen et al., 2024; Hasanov et al., 2024).

Opportunities lie in cross-domain fusion, such as quantum-aware cybersecurity (Zangana & Omar, 2025), and the use of synthetic data to improve ML efficiency (Gholami & Omar, 2023). Research also indicates that smaller student models can approach the performance of large models when properly trained, offering viable options for edge deployments (Gholami & Omar, 2024).

Toward the Future

The future of ML in cybersecurity and forensics involves further convergence with LLMs, federated learning, and edge computing. Foundations models tailored for cybersecurity (Idelhaj et al., 2024) are expected to enhance model reuse and reduce the need for extensive retraining. Moreover, with increasing regulation and policy concerns, ethical AI practices and transparent governance frameworks will shape the next phase of secure ML adoption (Alturkistani & Chuprat, 2024).

Books and proceedings such as *Digital Forensics in the Age of AI* (Omar & Zangana, 2025), *Application of Large Language Models for Software Vulnerability Detection* (Zangana & Omar, 2025), and *Redefining Security with Cyber AI* (Omar & Zangana, 2024) serve as key references guiding ongoing development and academic discourse.

To visualize how LLMs can be combined with traditional cybersecurity tools, the following diagram presents a typical integration pipeline, highlighting each stage from data ingestion to automated response.

Figure 2. Integration pipeline of LLMs with traditional security tools

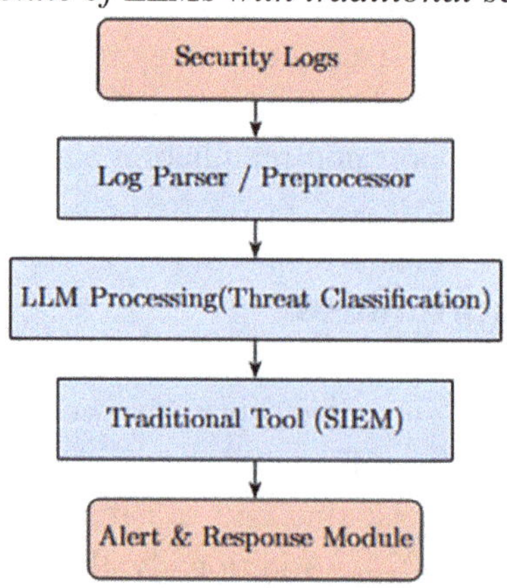

THREAT DETECTION USING ML ALGORITHMS

Machine learning (ML) algorithms have emerged as indispensable tools for cybersecurity, particularly in the detection and mitigation of advanced cyber threats. Their capacity to learn from vast amounts of data and adapt to evolving attack vectors enables more dynamic and proactive threat detection systems. As the threat landscape grows more complex, the application of ML and large language models (LLMs) in cyber defense has received increasing attention in both academic and industrial domains (Hasanov et al., 2024; Xu et al., 2024).

Traditional rule-based systems often fall short in detecting zero-day attacks and sophisticated intrusions. In contrast, ML-based systems analyze network behavior, detect anomalies, and identify potential threats with improved accuracy and speed (Manoharan & Sarker, 2023; Omar, 2022). These systems include supervised learning models for classification, unsupervised learning for anomaly detection, and reinforcement learning for adaptive cyber defense strategies (Yu, Shvetsov, & Alsamhi, 2024).

One of the most impactful advancements is the integration of LLMs into ML-based cybersecurity systems. LLMs like BERT, GPT, and their domain-specific variants such as SecureBERT (Aghaei et al., 2022) and SecLM (Asoronye et al., 2024) offer contextual understanding of logs, natural language threat reports, and communications. These models provide significant improvements in threat classification, intrusion detection, and malware analysis (Ferrag et al., 2023; Sarker, 2024).

Recent work highlights the capability of LLMs in understanding and processing vast quantities of unstructured cybersecurity data. For example, Ferrag et al. (2024) and Bryce et al. (n.d.) describe how LLMs are revolutionizing threat detection in enterprise environments. Techniques such as prompt engineering, fine-tuning, and transfer learning enable these models to generalize across different cybersecurity domains (Gholami & Omar, 2023; Liu, 2024).

Privacy-preserving models, like the lightweight BERT-based architectures proposed by Ferrag et al. (2024) and Lestable & Thandi (2024), demonstrate the practical viability of ML applications on constrained IoT/IIoT devices. These innovations ensure that threat detection can be conducted efficiently without compromising user privacy or system performance (Chen et al., 2024).

Additionally, explainable AI (XAI) in conjunction with LLMs aids in interpreting threat detection outcomes. This interpretability is vital for building trust and ensuring accountability in automated cybersecurity systems (Ghazal et al., 2024; Motlagh et al., 2024). The GEADD method developed by Jones & Omar (2024) illustrates how combining GPT-2 with defensive frameworks enhances zero-day threat detection.

Moreover, hybrid ML approaches integrating image processing techniques like Faster R-CNN with traditional template matching have proven effective in robust object and anomaly detection tasks (Zangana, Mustafa, & Omar, 2024). These approaches are particularly beneficial in identifying obfuscated threats in multimedia and network traffic.

Security-specific LLMs, such as those explored by Zangana and Omar (2025), leverage domain adaptation and fine-tuning strategies to elevate the accuracy of software vulnerability detection. These efforts align with broader initiatives in foundational model development tailored to cybersecurity needs (Idelhaj, El Houda, & Khoukhi, 2024).

Machine learning techniques are also crucial for detecting insider threats and phishing attacks by profiling user behavior and analyzing communication patterns (Zangana, Sallow, & Omar, 2025). Furthermore, ML can uncover wormhole and man-in-the-middle attacks in wireless networks, as demonstrated by Mohammed, Omar, & Nguyen (2018).

Beyond real-time detection, predictive modeling with LLMs plays a role in forecasting cyber threats, particularly in IoT ecosystems. Diaf et al. (2024) emphasize the utility of LLMs in attack prediction by learning from historic threat data. The predictive capacity of these models ensures a shift from reactive to proactive cybersecurity strategies.

A systematic review by Hassanin & Moustafa (2024) and comprehensive surveys by Alturkistani & Chuprat (2024) and Omar & Zangana (2025) suggest that ML-driven cyber threat detection is moving toward autonomous, self-healing systems empowered by LLMs, synthetic data (Gholami & Omar, 2023), and decentralized threat intelligence sharing (Kasri et al., 2025).

Finally, recent IGI Global contributions (Omar & Zangana, 2024; Zangana & Omar, 2025) and IEEE studies (Chen et al., 2024; Diaf et al., 2024) underscore that the convergence of ML, LLMs, and quantum-aware security models is shaping the next generation of cyber defenses. These innovations not only automate threat detection but also enable continuous learning and adaptation, essential for surviving in the face of persistent and evolving threats.

EVIDENCE ANALYSIS AND DIGITAL ARTEFACT CLASSIFICATION

In the evolving landscape of cyber forensics, evidence analysis and digital artefact classification have become increasingly sophisticated due to the integration of artificial intelligence (AI) and large language models (LLMs). Traditional digital forensics methods often relied on manual processes and static rules, but the complexity and velocity of modern cyberattacks necessitate a more dynamic, intelligent, and scalable approach.

Fundamentals of Digital Evidence and Artefacts

Digital evidence encompasses any data stored or transmitted in binary form that may be used in court. Artefacts—such as system logs, email headers, browser histories, and registry entries—play a pivotal role in investigations (Omar & Zangana, 2025a). Proper classification of these artefacts is essential for their admissibility and analytical value. AI, particularly LLMs, can enhance this process by automating the classification and contextual analysis of artefacts, reducing human error and accelerating investigation timelines (Hasanov et al., 2024).

Table 1 compares the primary capabilities and roles of traditional security tools and LLMs in cybersecurity environments, highlighting their complementary nature.

Table 1. Roles of LLMs vs traditional tools in cyber defense

Capability	Traditional Tools	LLMs
Rule-based Detection	Yes	No
Natural Language Understanding	No	Yes
Threat Hunting Automation	Limited	Strong
Context Awareness	Low	High
Log Analysis	Strong	Enhanced with NLP

Integration of LLMs in Evidence Classification

LLMs like BERT, GPT, and their domain-specific variants have revolutionized the way digital artefacts are analyzed. Models like SecureBERT (Aghaei et al., 2022) and SecLM (Asoronye et al., 2024) are specifically trained on cybersecurity corpora, enabling them to understand the syntax, semantics, and contextual implications of digital evidence. These models facilitate accurate artefact classification by detecting patterns, anomalies, and malicious indicators within unstructured data.

Chen et al. (2024) demonstrated the use of LLMs for analyzing network logs and threat intelligence feeds, enabling more accurate categorization of artefacts based on behavioral and contextual patterns. Similarly, Ferrag et al. (2024a, 2024b) introduced privacy-preserving, lightweight BERT-based models tailored for IoT/IIoT systems, highlighting their effectiveness in environments where conventional models fall short due to resource constraints.

Semantic Enrichment and Contextual Analysis

The ability of LLMs to semantically enrich raw data enables more nuanced classification. For instance, anomalous user behavior or unusual access patterns can be inferred through context-aware models (Xu et al., 2024). This semantic understanding allows forensic tools to distinguish between legitimate and suspicious activities with greater precision.

Ghazal et al. (2024) highlighted the role of Explainable AI (XAI) in improving the interpretability of classification results, making LLM-based evidence analysis more transparent and court-admissible. These capabilities also enable predictive analytics, allowing investigators to hypothesize attack vectors based on partially available artefacts (Diaf et al., 2024).

Handling Heterogeneous and Multimodal Data

Digital evidence often spans across text, images, metadata, and binary logs. Advanced models like those described by Zangana and Omar (2025) are capable of cross-modality reasoning, which is crucial in synthesizing meaning across different artefact types. For example, combining geolocation metadata from images with log timestamps can reveal coordinated attack patterns.

Hybrid approaches, such as those involving CNNs for image artefact analysis (Zangana, Mustafa, & Omar, 2024), further extend the power of AI-driven classification. Techniques like wavelet-transformed image denoising (Zangana & Mustafa, 2025) improve the extraction of artefacts from corrupted or low-quality sources, which is vital in forensic photography and video surveillance analysis.

Automation and Intelligence in Classification Pipelines

The automation of artefact classification pipelines using AI reduces investigative latency. AlQenaei (2024) emphasized the optimization of language model architectures to support real-time classification in high-throughput environments. This automation enables dynamic updating of classification models based on new threat intelligence, allowing forensic platforms to adapt in near real-time (Hassanin & Moustafa, 2024).

According to Gupta et al. (2024), deploying LLMs within enterprise systems facilitates ongoing monitoring and categorization of artefacts, bridging the gap between proactive cybersecurity and reactive digital forensics.

Challenges in Model Reliability and Validation

Despite the benefits, evidence classification using LLMs faces challenges in terms of bias, overfitting, and generalization. Gholami and Omar (2023, 2024) raised concerns about LLMs' dependence on training data, suggesting the use of synthetic data to improve generalization across diverse artefact types. Moreover, explainability remains a legal requirement in many jurisdictions, necessitating ongoing research into interpretable models (Huff et al., 2023; Bryce et al., 2024).

Future Trends in Artefact Classification

Future efforts will likely focus on quantum-aware evidence analysis and federated learning to preserve data privacy. The application of LLMs for secure forensic environments, including quantum-augmented systems, is already being explored (Zangana & Omar, 2025a; Zangana, Mustafa, & Li, 2025). Moreover, foundational models are expected to evolve towards integrating multi-agent reasoning and reinforcement learning for self-improving forensic classification systems (Idelhaj, Abou El Houda, & Khoukhi, 2024; Motlagh et al., 2024).

Case Applications and Industry Use

Real-world implementations, such as the GEADD method for zero-day detection (Jones & Omar, 2024) and forensic scanning tools reviewed by Zangana (2024a, 2024b), illustrate the transformative role of LLMs in digital forensics. In wireless sensor networks, LLMs assist in identifying wormhole attacks through intelligent pattern recognition (Mohammed et al., 2018). Furthermore, digital forensic investigations in healthcare, critical infrastructure, and smart city domains increasingly rely on LLMs for artefact triage (Wright et al., 2012; Hamza & Omar, 2013; Yu et al., 2024).

DATA COLLECTION, PREPROCESSING, AND FEATURE ENGINEERING

In cybersecurity research involving Large Language Models (LLMs), the **quality, scope, and contextual relevance of data** significantly impact the effectiveness of the models. LLMs require vast, domain-specific datasets—both structured and unstructured—to generalize, detect, and mitigate threats effectively (Chen et al., 2024; Ferrag et al., 2024; Motlagh et al., 2024).

Data Collection

The **data sources** for cybersecurity applications of LLMs include vulnerability databases, malware repositories, phishing email corpora, log files, and darknet intelligence feeds. As highlighted by Aghaei et al. (2022), domain-specific corpora are crucial, leading to architectures like SecureBERT that outperform general-purpose models in security contexts.

Synthetic data generation has also emerged as a key enabler for overcoming data scarcity. Techniques such as data augmentation, adversarial sample generation, and synthetic labeling improve dataset diversity and robustness (Gholami & Omar, 2023; Gholami & Omar, 2024). These practices are especially relevant for under-represented attack types like zero-day exploits or sophisticated phishing campaigns (Jones & Omar, 2024).

Further, real-time data ingestion from **IoT/IIoT environments** plays a crucial role in LLM-based cybersecurity applications, where models must detect anomalies in streaming data with minimal latency (Ferrag et al., 2024; Thandi, 2024).

Figure 3 displays a comparison of detection accuracy between traditional tools, LLM-based systems, and hybrid systems that integrate both.

Figure 3. Accuracy comparison of security detection approaches

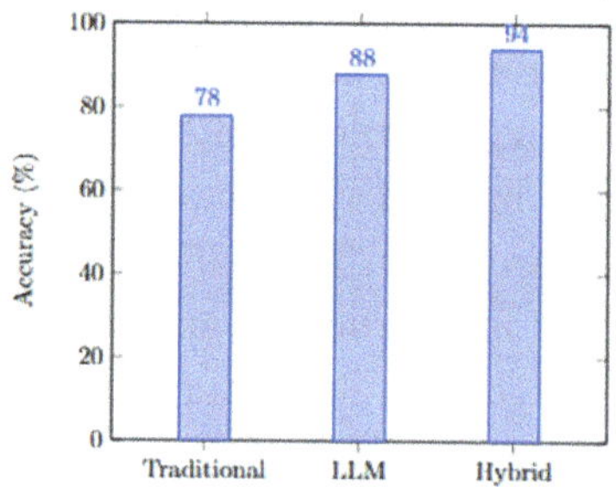

Data Preprocessing

Cybersecurity data often contains **noise, redundancies, and adversarial obfuscation**, making robust preprocessing essential. Preprocessing steps typically include:

- **Tokenization and normalization** of code, log files, or natural language descriptions.
- **Deobfuscation** of malicious scripts or binaries using pattern recognition (Manoharan & Sarker, 2023).
- **Label encoding** of threat categories, often supported by expert curation or semi-supervised learning (Asoronye et al., 2024).

Advanced LLM frameworks also use **adversarial training** techniques to prepare models against poisoning or evasion attacks (Omar, 2024; Liu, 2024). These steps reduce bias, improve generalizability, and ensure resilience in dynamic threat landscapes (Omar & Zangana, 2024).

Moreover, handling **imbalanced datasets**—a common issue in intrusion detection—requires sampling techniques or cost-sensitive training strategies (Gupta et al., 2024; Bryce et al., 2024).

Feature Engineering

While end-to-end LLM architectures can autonomously extract features, **manual and hybrid feature engineering** remains vital in specific domains such as malware classification or log analysis (Mohammed et al., 2018; Omar, 2022). Features typically include:

- **Behavioral sequences** extracted from system calls, logs, or command patterns.
- **Embedding representations** of software code (Kasri et al., 2025; Omar, 2025).
- **Semantic patterns** in phishing texts or fake login pages (Zangana et al., 2024).

Recent research shows the integration of **domain-specific embeddings**—such as BERT-based vectors tuned for security contexts—improves detection accuracy and explainability (Hassanin & Moustafa, 2024; Idelhaj et al., 2024).

In scenarios involving **IoT and edge devices**, lightweight feature representations are critical. Privacy-preserving BERT models have been optimized for such settings, balancing accuracy and computational efficiency (Ferrag et al., 2024; LESTABLE & THANDI, 2024).

Challenges and Best Practices

- **Data Labeling** remains a bottleneck, with high reliance on expert knowledge (Diaf et al., 2024).
- **Adversarial manipulation** of training data can compromise model integrity unless detected early (Zangana & Omar, 2020; Huff et al., 2023).
- **Data drift** in real-time systems necessitates continual retraining and monitoring (Xu et al., 2024).

To address these, researchers have adopted **self-supervised pretraining**, **active learning**, and **online fine-tuning**, ensuring continuous adaptation (Omar, 2024; Hamza & Omar, 2013; Taghavi & Feyzi, 2024).

The Role of Frameworks and Standards

Recent contributions emphasize the need for standardized datasets and frameworks for evaluating LLMs in cybersecurity (Zangana et al., 2025; Santos et al., 2024). Projects like GEADD (Jones & Omar, 2024) and SecLM (Asoronye et al., 2024) exemplify structured pipelines with rigorous data handling.

Research by Omar and Zangana (2025) also highlights the need for **quantum-aware data preprocessing protocols**, especially in post-quantum cryptography environments. Similarly, explainability-driven preprocessing is vital in compliance-driven industries like healthcare (Huff et al., 2023; Zangana & Omar, 2025).

This comprehensive data strategy forms the bedrock for deploying secure, scalable, and interpretable LLM-based cybersecurity systems. The subsequent section will delve into **model design and training**, where these prepared datasets are translated into intelligent defense mechanisms.

MODEL TRAINING, EVALUATION, AND OPTIMIZATION

The training, evaluation, and optimization of large language models (LLMs) for cybersecurity applications represent a multidimensional challenge, requiring precise alignment of model architectures, datasets, evaluation metrics, and optimization techniques. These stages are vital to ensure that LLMs perform effectively in dynamic cyber threat landscapes, while adhering to security, privacy, and computational efficiency constraints (Motlagh et al., 2024; Ferrag et al., 2024).

Model Training

Training LLMs for cybersecurity tasks demands domain-specific data and architectures tailored to cyber threats. SecureBERT, introduced by Aghaei et al. (2022), exemplifies the integration of cybersecurity corpus into a BERT-style model, showcasing improvements in identifying malicious code, phishing attempts, and insider threats. Similarly, Asoronye et al. (2024) developed SecLM—a specialized model trained on advanced cybersecurity corpora—demonstrating superior contextual understanding and proactive threat mitigation.

Pre-training LLMs from scratch or fine-tuning them on curated security datasets remains a critical decision. Foundation models like GPT-2 and BERT have been retrained for cybersecurity tasks (Zangana & Omar, 2025; Ferrag et al., 2023), and recent works emphasize the use of synthetic data to supplement limited real-world threat data (Gholami & Omar, 2023). Zangana et al. (2025) highlighted that domain-specific tuning on threat intelligence data, IoT logs, and vulnerability databases significantly boosts precision in malware classification and phishing detection.

Evaluation Metrics and Benchmarks

Evaluating LLMs in cybersecurity requires specialized metrics that extend beyond traditional NLP benchmarks. Accuracy, F1-score, precision, and recall remain foundational (Gupta et al., 2024; Manoharan & Sarker, 2023), yet task-specific metrics—such as True Positive Rate (TPR) for intrusion detection and Zero-Day Threat Recall (ZDTR) for emergent attack detection—are essential (Jones & Omar, 2024).

Omar et al. (2024) utilized comparative evaluations between BERT and GPT-2 models across several IoT malware datasets, establishing a framework that prioritized lightweight deployment and interpretability. Meanwhile, Diaf et al. (2024) demonstrated that predictive models based on LLMs outperformed statistical classifiers in forecasting IoT network breaches, validating the power of temporal language embeddings.

Explainability in evaluation is gaining traction as a necessity rather than a luxury. Ghazal et al. (2024) and Xu et al. (2024) underscore the need for explainable AI (XAI) in cybersecurity, especially for regulatory compliance and human-in-the-loop interventions. Tools like SHAP and LIME are increasingly embedded into LLM pipelines for transparent output interpretation (Santos et al., 2024).

Figure 4 highlights the comparative advantages of integrating LLMs into existing security systems across multiple performance dimensions.

Figure 4. Performance comparison: LLM integration vs traditional security workflow

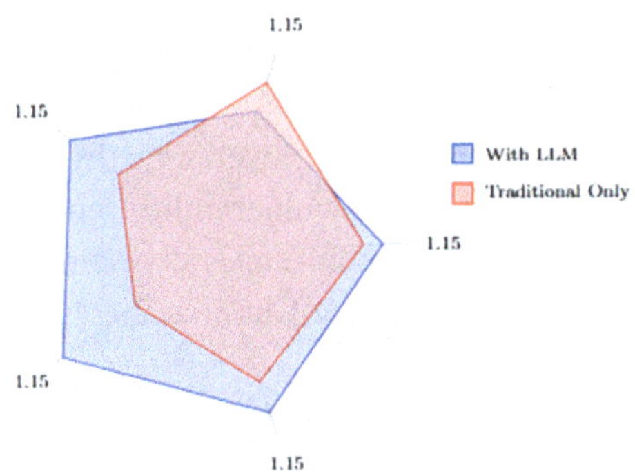

Optimization Strategies

Optimization plays a pivotal role in improving both the efficiency and accuracy of LLMs, especially when deployed in resource-constrained environments such as edge devices and IoT nodes. Ferrag et al. (2024) introduced a privacy-preserving, BERT-based lightweight model tailored for IIoT scenarios, optimizing attention mechanisms and embedding layers for minimal latency without sacrificing accuracy. Lestable and Thandi (2024) advanced this idea by proposing differential privacy enhancements during training, crucial for handling sensitive threat data.

Knowledge distillation and student-teacher models have been explored extensively. Gholami and Omar (2024) questioned whether student models could match their teachers' performance, concluding that with task-aligned objectives, student models can achieve parity at a fraction of the cost. AlQenaei (2024) outlined future directions involving quantization, sparsity-induction, and modular training pipelines for continual optimization.

Further, adversarial robustness has emerged as a critical optimization criterion. Omar (2024) introduced adversarial training techniques to strengthen DNN-based text classifiers against malicious perturbations, a technique also validated in the context of software vulnerability detection by Taghavi and Feyzi (2024).

Training Data Challenges and Augmentation

The quality and diversity of training data play a foundational role in LLM performance. Hasanov et al. (2024) and Chen et al. (2024) noted the scarcity of labeled cybersecurity datasets, especially for novel attack types, which affects generalizability. Gholami and Omar (2023) proposed synthetic data generation as a viable augmentation strategy, although concerns around distributional shifts remain (Idelhaj et al., 2024).

Zangana et al. (2025) recommended leveraging hybrid datasets combining traditional logs, user behavior patterns, vulnerability reports, and network traffic. Integration of multilingual and multimodal data is also being investigated for broader threat landscape coverage (Alturkistani & Chuprat, 2024; Liu, 2024).

Automation and Continuous Learning

As threats evolve, static training becomes obsolete. Continuous fine-tuning and reinforcement learning mechanisms enable models to adapt in real time. Hassanin and Moustafa (2024) advocated for feedback loops integrated into security operations centers (SOCs), allowing models to update continuously based on analyst input and live threat feeds. Zangana, Mustafa, and Li (2025) emphasized automation's role in orchestrating LLM pipelines—from ingestion to retraining—especially in quantum-aware environments.

Cloud-based federated learning frameworks also support decentralized training while preserving data privacy (Hamza & Omar, 2013; Omar, 2021). This is particularly important in contexts where threat intelligence is distributed across different geopolitical or industrial domains (Mohammed et al., 2018; Nguyen et al., 2018).

Summary

The training, evaluation, and optimization of LLMs for cybersecurity is an ongoing, dynamic process that involves strategic decisions around architecture, datasets, evaluation strategies, and deployment contexts. With the advent of specialized models like SecureBERT, SecLM, and privacy-preserving variants, LLMs are rapidly evolving from generic tools into domain-specific defenders. However, optimization for adversarial robustness, explainability, and continuous learning remains critical as the threat landscape continues to expand in complexity.

CHALLENGES IN APPLYING ML TO DIGITAL FORENSICS

Despite the transformative potential of machine learning (ML) and large language models (LLMs) in digital forensics, a multitude of technical, ethical, operational, and contextual challenges persist. These challenges span data quality, adversarial manipulation, model transparency, generalization, and the evolving complexity of cyber threats.

Data Quality, Labeling, and Availability

Digital forensics is inherently data-intensive, requiring structured, semi-structured, and unstructured data sourced from logs, communications, memory dumps, and other volatile sources. ML models depend heavily on large volumes of well-labeled and representative datasets. However, acquiring such datasets is often constrained by privacy laws, proprietary restrictions, and case-specific uniqueness (Liu, 2024; Hasanov et al., 2024). Moreover, synthetic data has been suggested as a solution, but concerns remain about its authenticity and fidelity in real-world forensic contexts (Gholami & Omar, 2023).

Adversarial Attacks and Model Vulnerability

Digital forensics systems are now susceptible to adversarial inputs—carefully crafted manipulations that mislead ML algorithms. This is especially problematic in intrusion detection systems and malware classifiers. Omar (2024) illustrates the susceptibility of DNN classifiers to adversarial examples, raising concerns over the robustness of forensic AI systems. Similarly, enhanced detection models such as GEADD, designed to detect zero-day attacks (Jones & Omar, 2024), must continuously adapt to remain resilient.

Explainability and Trust

Forensics often serves legal and investigative functions, where the traceability and explainability of conclusions are essential. LLMs and deep learning models, however, are often "black boxes," which undermines their credibility in courtroom scenarios (Xu et al., 2024; Motlagh et al., 2024). The call for explainable AI (XAI) is echoed by Ghazal et al. (2024), who emphasize the need for transparency in decision-making pipelines in forensic tools.

Model Bias and Ethical Concerns

Biases in training datasets can translate into unfair or inaccurate forensic outcomes. According to Chen et al. (2024), biased models risk misclassifying benign behavior as malicious or failing to detect subtle anomalies. Such discrepancies can have significant legal ramifications. Zangana and Omar (2025) further stress the ethical implications of biased forensic decision-making, especially when applied to sensitive criminal or organizational investigations.

Generalization to Real-World Forensic Scenarios

Machine learning models trained in controlled environments often fail when exposed to real-world conditions marked by data noise, incomplete evidence, or novel attack strategies. Aghaei et al. (2022) argue for domain-specific models like SecureBERT to bridge this gap. Nevertheless, real-world generalization remains an elusive goal, especially in fast-evolving cybercrime contexts (Kasri et al., 2025).

Integration with Legacy Systems

Most forensic environments consist of heterogeneous tools, legacy software, and varying data formats. Integrating modern ML-based solutions with these systems presents architectural and compatibility challenges (Bryce et al., 2024; Gupta et al., 2024). Legacy forensics workflows are not always designed for real-time inference or dynamic learning, causing deployment friction.

Privacy and Legal Constraints

Applying ML to forensic data involves sensitive personal and organizational information, invoking strict privacy and legal scrutiny. Privacy-preserving models like the lightweight BERT proposed by Ferrag et al. (2024) are a step forward. Still, compliance with data protection regulations such as GDPR and HIPAA remains a major barrier (LESTABLE & THANDI, 2024; Idelhaj et al., 2024).

Evasion Tactics and Model Obsolescence

Cybercriminals actively adapt their tactics to bypass ML-based detection mechanisms. As explained by Manoharan & Sarker (2023), threat actors exploit model blind spots and out-of-distribution data to remain undetected. Diaf et al. (2024) also highlight the limitations of current predictive models in anticipating novel attack vectors in IoT environments.

Resource and Cost Limitations

Training and maintaining high-performing ML models require substantial computational resources. For forensic teams, especially in smaller or underfunded organizations, this can be prohibitive (Gholami & Omar, 2024; Mohammed et al., 2018). Lightweight alternatives and student–teacher models are being explored to balance efficiency and performance.

Lack of Standardization

The absence of standardized protocols for training, evaluating, and deploying ML in forensics creates inconsistencies in outcomes and benchmarks. AlQenaei (2024) and Sarker (2024) call for unified frameworks to assess LLM performance in security applications, which is particularly pertinent for ensuring cross-case comparability and reproducibility.

Cybersecurity Risks of LLM Adoption

While LLMs enhance digital forensic capabilities, they also introduce new vulnerabilities, including prompt injection attacks, data leakage, and over-reliance on auto-generated insights (Alturkistani & Chuprat, 2024; Gupta et al., 2024). Zangana et al. (2025) stress the dual-use nature of LLMs, warning that attackers could exploit them to craft sophisticated evasive threats.

Human Factors and Operational Challenges

Operational deployment of ML systems is also hindered by human limitations, such as lack of training, resistance to automation, and misinterpretation of model outputs. As Zangana, Sallow, and Omar (2025) point out, insider threats and human misjudgments still constitute significant vulnerabilities in forensic environments.

These multifaceted challenges indicate that while ML and LLMs offer immense potential for enhancing digital forensic practices, their application is far from straightforward. Ongoing research, like that found in *Digital Forensics in the Age of AI* (Omar & Zangana, 2025), calls for an interdisciplinary approach that blends technical advancement with legal, ethical, and operational rigor.

ETHICAL AND LEGAL CONSIDERATIONS

The deployment of large language models (LLMs) in cybersecurity introduces a spectrum of ethical and legal challenges. These concerns span privacy, bias, accountability, data governance, and compliance with existing legal frameworks.

Privacy and Data Security

LLMs trained on vast corpora of internet and proprietary data risk exposing sensitive or private information. Although models like SecureBERT and SecLM have been tailored for secure environments (Aghaei et al., 2022; Asoronye et al., 2024), their use still poses potential privacy leaks if trained or fine-tuned on improperly sanitized datasets. Ferrag et al. (2024) emphasize the need for privacy-preserving mechanisms, particularly in models deployed in Internet of Things (IoT) and Industrial IoT contexts. Solutions such as lightweight and privacy-aware architectures, like those proposed by Lestable and Thandi (2024), are instrumental in mitigating these risks.

Moreover, anonymization and encryption techniques remain critical for compliance with regulations like GDPR and HIPAA. Huff et al. (2023) highlight the implications of data mishandling, especially in healthcare and biotechnology settings, where the consequences of privacy breaches can be catastrophic.

Bias, Fairness, and Discrimination

LLMs often inherit biases from their training datasets. This can lead to discriminatory or unethical behavior, particularly in automated decision-making processes in cybersecurity contexts (Bryce et al., 2024). As argued by Gholami and Omar (2023), reliance on synthetic data can amplify or mitigate such biases depending on the curation process. Furthermore, explainability becomes essential; Ghazal et al. (2024) and Sarker (2024) stress the importance of explainable AI (XAI) in cybersecurity, not just for transparency but also for ethical accountability.

Accountability and Responsibility

As LLMs become integrated into decision-making pipelines, assigning responsibility for errors or breaches becomes complex. Chen et al. (2024) and Xu et al. (2024) assert that organizations must clearly define liability boundaries when human oversight is minimized. Ethical frameworks must govern how LLMs are used in autonomous systems, particularly when predicting or mitigating cyber threats (Diaf et al., 2024; Kasri et al., 2025).

Dual-Use and Misuse Potential

While LLMs significantly enhance cyber threat detection and response, they can also be weaponized for malicious purposes—such as crafting realistic phishing emails or automating penetration testing (Zangana et al., 2024; Zangana & Omar, 2020). Hamza and Omar (2013) previously highlighted the risks associated with the misuse of cloud platforms, a concern now intensified by the capabilities of LLMs. Similarly, Wright et al. (2012) stressed the growing threat posed by mobile vectors, which may be further exploited through AI-generated exploits.

Mitigating dual-use risks requires rigorous access control and monitoring mechanisms. Techniques such as prompt filtering, output moderation, and red teaming are recommended to reduce the misuse of LLMs (Hasanov et al., 2024; Gupta et al., 2024).

Intellectual Property and Licensing

The question of ownership over model-generated content, particularly when it replicates or paraphrases protected material, remains unresolved in many jurisdictions. As Ferrag et al. (2023) and Liu (2024) discuss, LLMs trained on copyrighted material can inadvertently regenerate proprietary knowledge, raising concerns about fair use, plagiarism, and liability.

Additionally, foundation models used in security contexts—such as those discussed by Idelhaj et al. (2024) and Taghavi and Feyzi (2024)—require clear licensing strategies that protect both developers and end users. Open-source models like GPT-2 and BERT, if used without robust licensing safeguards, may open the door to legal disputes over IP rights (Jones & Omar, 2024).

Regulatory Compliance and Governance

AI-specific regulations are evolving globally, but they often lag behind the pace of innovation. The European Union's AI Act and similar national frameworks aim to enforce transparency, accountability, and human oversight in high-risk applications, including cybersecurity. Omar (2021, 2022, 2024) has extensively discussed access control and compliance requirements in AI-driven environments.

Omar and Zangana (2025) further argue that the integration of LLMs in cybersecurity demands a hybrid governance model combining legal mandates with technical safeguards such as audit logs and access control matrices. These practices are especially crucial when LLMs are used in digital forensics or law enforcement contexts (Omar & Zangana, 2025a).

Human-Centered Design and Insider Threats

A critical ethical dimension is the impact of LLMs on human operators and decision-makers. Zangana, Sallow, and Omar (2025) emphasize that automation must not displace human judgment in cybersecurity operations. Instead, human-centered design must prioritize usability, interpretability, and trust. Insider threat mitigation—often overlooked—also intersects with ethics, as LLMs may be misused by authorized personnel if not properly audited and restricted.

Future Challenges and Ethical Foresight

As LLMs evolve toward Artificial General Intelligence (AGI), as projected by Pleshakova et al. (2024), the ethical stakes will heighten. Anticipatory governance and scenario planning are vital to ensure that future systems remain aligned with societal values. Ethical foresight also includes considering quantum-aware cybersecurity solutions (Zangana & Omar, 2025), ensuring that LLMs are designed with long-term resilience and integrity in mind.

CASE STUDIES AND APPLICATIONS

The practical application of Large Language Models (LLMs) and Artificial Intelligence (AI) in cybersecurity has seen significant advancement, as illustrated by numerous case studies spanning various domains such as threat detection, malware analysis, intrusion prevention, and cyber threat intelligence. These applications demonstrate the transformative potential of LLMs to revolutionize cybersecurity operations by enhancing detection accuracy, reducing response times, and automating complex analytical tasks.

One notable case is **SecureBERT**, a domain-specific language model designed explicitly for cybersecurity tasks. Developed by Aghaei et al. (2022), SecureBERT showcased enhanced capabilities in detecting and understanding cyber threats by tailoring the BERT architecture to the cybersecurity domain. This specialization allowed it to outperform generic language models in identifying domain-specific vulnerabilities and attack patterns.

Similarly, the **SecLM** model introduced by Asoronye et al. (2024) represents a specialized security language model aimed at advanced threat mitigation. This model demonstrates how focused LLM training on cybersecurity datasets can provide a robust defense mechanism against evolving cyber threats by combining threat detection and mitigation strategies into one framework.

The integration of LLMs in **IoT and IIoT environments** has also been a focus, given the unique vulnerabilities of such devices. Ferrag et al. (2024) proposed a privacy-preserving, lightweight BERT-based model tailored for IoT/IIoT devices, which balances computational efficiency with high threat detection accuracy, thereby addressing the critical need for scalable cybersecurity in resource-constrained environments.

Beyond detection, **predictive capabilities** are emerging, as Diaf et al. (2024) leveraged LLMs to anticipate cyberattacks in IoT networks, indicating a shift from reactive to proactive cybersecurity measures. This forward-looking application of LLMs enhances network resilience by identifying potential vulnerabilities before exploitation.

Another dimension is the use of LLMs to bolster **explainable AI in cybersecurity**, enhancing trust and transparency in automated systems. Ghazal et al. (2024) highlighted the role of explainable AI techniques paired with LLMs to provide interpretable threat analyses, which is crucial for cybersecurity professionals making informed decisions based on AI-driven insights.

Moreover, enterprise-scale applications have been demonstrated by Gupta et al. (2024), who analyzed the security landscape of LLMs within enterprise information systems. They highlighted both the opportunities for enhanced threat intelligence and the challenges related to model misuse and adversarial attacks.

Other comprehensive surveys and analyses (Chen et al., 2024; Hasanov et al., 2024; Motlagh et al., 2024) underline the broad adoption of LLMs in cybersecurity, detailing numerous implementations ranging from malware detection to phishing prevention, and outlining best practices for integrating these models within existing security infrastructures.

Several case studies also document the fusion of **machine learning with cybersecurity operations**, as demonstrated by Jones et al. (2023) and Manoharan and Sarker (2023), who emphasize how AI accelerates threat detection and response capabilities, enabling real-time analytics and automated defense mechanisms.

The realm of **cloud security** is addressed by Hamza and Omar (2013), who examined nefarious uses of cloud computing, underscoring the importance of AI-based tools for monitoring and securing cloud infrastructures, a domain where LLMs are beginning to be applied extensively.

In the context of **software vulnerability detection**, the works edited by Omar and Zangana (2025) provide multiple case studies demonstrating how LLMs can automatically identify software weaknesses and suggest patches, greatly reducing human error and accelerating vulnerability management workflows.

Finally, the intersection of AI with digital forensics is gaining traction, with Zangana and Omar (2025) illustrating applications of LLMs in forensic analysis that enable automated extraction and interpretation of cybercrime evidence, supporting law enforcement and incident response teams.

In summary, these case studies collectively illustrate the multifaceted applications of LLMs in cybersecurity, from domain-specific models like SecureBERT and SecLM to IoT threat detection and enterprise security. They highlight not only the enhanced capabilities but also emerging challenges such as model explainability, privacy, and adversarial robustness that remain active areas of research and practical concern.

FUTURE TRENDS AND RESEARCH DIRECTIONS

The rapid evolution of large language models (LLMs) and artificial intelligence (AI) technologies is reshaping the cybersecurity landscape, opening promising avenues for future research and practical applications. As cyber threats grow in complexity and scale, the integration of AI-driven techniques offers new paradigms to enhance detection, prevention, and response mechanisms (Ferrag et al., 2024; Motlagh et al., 2024).

One of the prominent future trends is the development of domain-specific LLMs optimized for cybersecurity tasks, such as SecureBERT, which adapts transformer architectures for better threat detection (Aghaei et al., 2022). Similarly, specialized models like SecLM demonstrate advanced capabilities in threat mitigation by focusing on nuanced cybersecurity contexts (Asoronye et al., 2024). Continuous architectural innovations and optimization of LLMs are vital to improving efficiency and adaptability, enabling real-time cyber defense in dynamic environments (AlQenaei, 2024; Bryce et al., n.d.).

The emergence of privacy-preserving models tailored for resource-constrained IoT and IIoT devices is another significant direction. Lightweight yet robust LLMs enable on-device threat detection while safeguarding sensitive information, critical for securing interconnected smart systems (Ferrag et al., 2024; THANDI, 2024). Research exploring hybrid approaches combining traditional security tools with AI-driven methods is also gaining traction to address multi-faceted cyber threats more comprehensively (Zangana & Mustafa, 2025).

Explainable AI (XAI) integrated with LLMs is poised to transform cybersecurity by providing transparent decision-making processes, essential for trust and regulatory compliance (Ghazal et al., 2024). This aligns with the growing demand for interpretable models capable of justifying automated security decisions, thereby improving human-AI collaboration in incident response (Hasanov et al., 2024; Hassanin & Moustafa, 2024).

Furthermore, leveraging LLMs for predictive cyber attack modeling, especially in IoT networks, represents an innovative shift from reactive to proactive defense strategies (Diaf et al., 2024). Predictive analytics powered by AI can anticipate attack vectors, enabling timely mitigation and resilience enhancement in critical infrastructure (Chen et al., 2024).

In parallel, research is expanding into synthesizing large-scale, high-quality synthetic data to improve LLM training while preserving privacy and reducing reliance on scarce labeled datasets (Gholami & Omar, 2023, 2024). This approach promises to enhance model generalizability and robustness against adversarial threats (Omar, 2024).

The application of LLMs extends to software vulnerability detection, a critical cybersecurity frontier. Novel frameworks harnessing the pattern recognition abilities of LLMs are emerging to automate vulnerability identification and patching processes (Zangana & Mohammed, 2025; Taghavi & Feyzi, 2024). Integrating quantum-aware cybersecurity measures with LLMs is an anticipated research avenue, preparing defenses against future quantum-enabled attacks (Zangana & Omar, 2025).

From an organizational perspective, future research also emphasizes the human factor in cybersecurity, addressing insider threats and the role of leadership in technology adoption and inclusive security strategies (Zangana, Sallow, & Omar, 2025; Zangana & Omar, 2025). The intersection of AI and policy frameworks will be critical to ensuring ethical deployment and regulation of these powerful technologies (Huff et al., 2023; Gupta, Gaurav, & Arya, 2024).

Finally, as AI continues to revolutionize cybersecurity, emerging trends will focus on integrating multi-modal data, cross-domain intelligence sharing, and enhancing AI resilience to adversarial manipulations (Sarker, 2024; Yu, Shvetsov, & Alsamhi, 2024; Pleshakova et al., 2024). Such holistic approaches are essential for building the next generation of secure, intelligent cyber defense systems that can adapt dynamically to evolving threats.

In conclusion, the future of cybersecurity research lies in advancing specialized, interpretable, and privacy-conscious LLMs; developing hybrid and quantum-resilient frameworks; and incorporating human and organizational dimensions to foster a comprehensive security ecosystem. Continued interdisciplinary efforts and innovation are imperative to harness the full potential of AI in safeguarding digital infrastructures worldwide.

CONCLUSION

This chapter has explored the transformative impact of large language models (LLMs) and artificial intelligence (AI) on the field of cybersecurity, emphasizing both current applications and future potentials. The integration of LLMs in cyber threat detection, vulnerability analysis, and incident response is revolutionizing traditional security paradigms by providing enhanced automation, improved accuracy, and adaptive learning capabilities. Domain-specific models such as SecureBERT and SecLM exemplify how tailoring AI architectures to cybersecurity challenges significantly boosts effectiveness in identifying and mitigating threats.

Despite these advancements, the chapter also highlights ongoing challenges, including the need for privacy-preserving solutions, explainability, and the handling of adversarial attacks. Lightweight models designed for IoT and IIoT environments address resource constraints while maintaining robust security postures. The rising importance of explainable AI fosters trust and accountability in automated defenses, a critical factor for widespread adoption and regulatory compliance.

Moreover, the future directions outlined underscore the significance of proactive and predictive cybersecurity strategies, leveraging AI to anticipate threats before they manifest. The use of synthetic data for model training and the exploration of quantum-aware defenses further illustrate the dynamic and evolving research landscape.

Human factors remain a vital consideration, as insider threats and leadership in technology adoption influence overall security resilience. Ethical and policy frameworks will play an indispensable role in guiding the responsible deployment of AI technologies in cybersecurity.

In summary, the fusion of AI, particularly LLMs, with cybersecurity represents a pivotal shift toward intelligent, adaptive, and comprehensive defense systems. Ongoing research and interdisciplinary collaboration will be essential to harness these technologies' full potential, ensuring safer digital environments amid increasingly sophisticated cyber threats.

REFERENCES

Aghaei, E., Niu, X., Shadid, W., & Al-Shaer, E. (2022, October). Securebert: A domain-specific language model for cybersecurity. In *International Conference on Security and Privacy in Communication Systems* (pp. 39-56). Cham: Springer Nature Switzerland.

AlQenaei, Z. M. (2024, March). Evolution and Optimization of Language Model Architectures: From Foundations to Future Directions. In *International Conference on Computing and Machine Learning* (pp. 233-249). Singapore: Springer Nature Singapore.

. Alturkistani, H., & Chuprat, S. (2024). Artificial Intelligence and Large Language Models in Advancing Cyber Threat Intelligence: A Systematic Literature Review.

Asoronye, G. O., Anthony, O. C., Ogbuikwu, R. I., Ogili, C. O., & Ali, H. U. (2024). SecLM: A Specialized Security Language Model for Advanced Cybersecurity Applications and Threat Mitigation. *EKETE-International Journal Of Advanced Research*, *2*(6), 33–42.

Bryce, C., Kalousis, A., Leroux, I., Madinier, H., Mermoud, A., Mulder, V., Pasche, T., & Ruch, P. (n.d.). *Trends in Large Language Models: Actors, Applications, and Impact on Cybersecurity*. https://technology-observatory.ch/academic_publication/trends-in-large-language-models-actors-applications-and-impact-on-cybersecurity/article.pdf

Chen, Y., Cui, M., Wang, D., Cao, Y., Yang, P., Jiang, B., Lu, Z., & Liu, B. (2024). A survey of large language models for cyber threat detection. *Computers & Security*, *145*, 104016. DOI: 10.1016/j.cose.2024.104016

Diaf, A., Korba, A. A., Karabadji, N. E., & Ghamri-Doudane, Y. (2024, April). Beyond detection: Leveraging large language models for cyber attack prediction in iot networks. In *2024 20th International Conference on Distributed Computing in Smart Systems and the Internet of Things (DCOSS-IoT)* (pp. 117-123). IEEE.

Ferrag, M. A., Alwahedi, F., Battah, A., Cherif, B., Mechri, A., & Tihanyi, N. (2024). Generative ai and large language models for cyber security: All insights you need. *Available at SSRN* 4853709. DOI: 10.2139/ssrn.4853709

Ferrag, M. A., Ndhlovu, M., Tihanyi, N., Cordeiro, L. C., Debbah, M., & Lestable, T. (2023). Revolutionizing cyber threat detection with large language models. *arXiv preprint arXiv:2306.14263*, 195-202.

Ferrag, M. A., Ndhlovu, M., Tihanyi, N., Cordeiro, L. C., Debbah, M., Lestable, T., & Thandi, N. S. (2024). Revolutionizing cyber threat detection with large language models: A privacy-preserving bert-based lightweight model for iot/iiot devices. *IEEE Access : Practical Innovations, Open Solutions, 12*, 23733–23750. DOI: 10.1109/ACCESS.2024.3363469

Ghazal, T. M., Janjua, J. I., Abushiba, W., Ahmad, M., Ihsan, A., & Al-Dmour, N. A. (2024, December). Cybersecurity Revolution via Large Language Models and Explainable AI. In *2024 17th International Conference on Security of Information and Networks (SIN)* (pp. 1-6). IEEE. DOI: 10.1109/SIN63213.2024.10871324

Gholami, S., & Omar, M. (2023). Does Synthetic Data Make Large Language Models More Efficient? *arXiv preprint arXiv:2310.07830.*

Gholami, S., & Omar, M. (2024). Can a student large language model perform as well as its teacher? In *Innovations, Securities, and Case Studies Across Healthcare, Business, and Technology* (pp. 122-139). IGI Global. DOI: 10.4018/979-8-3693-1906-2.ch007

Gupta, B. B., Gaurav, A., & Arya, V. (2024). Navigating the security landscape of large language models in enterprise information systems. *Enterprise Information Systems, 18*(4), 2310846. DOI: 10.1080/17517575.2024.2310846

Hadi, M. A., Abdulredha, M. N., & Hasan, E. (2023). Introduction to ChatGPT: A new revolution of artificial intelligence with machine learning algorithms and cybersecurity. *Sci. Arch, 4*(04), 276. DOI: 10.47587/SA.2023.4406

Hamza, Y. A., & Omar, M. D. (2013). Cloud computing security: Abuse and nefarious use of cloud computing. *International Journal of Computer Engineering Research, 3*(6), 22–27.

Hasanov, I., Virtanen, S., Hakkala, A., & Isoaho, J. (2024). Application of Large Language Models in Cybersecurity: A Systematic Literature Review. *IEEE Access : Practical Innovations, Open Solutions, 12*, 176751–176778. DOI: 10.1109/ACCESS.2024.3505983

Hassanin, M., & Moustafa, N. (2024). A comprehensive overview of large language models (llms) for cyber defences: Opportunities and directions. *arXiv preprint arXiv:2405.14487.*

Huff, A. J., Burrell, D. N., Nobles, C., Richardson, K., Wright, J. B., Burton, S. L., Jones, A. J., Springs, D., Omar, M., & Brown-Jackson, K. L. (2023). Management Practices for Mitigating Cybersecurity Threats to Biotechnology Companies, Laboratories, and Healthcare Research Organizations. In *Applied Research Approaches to Technology, Healthcare, and Business* (pp. 1-12). IGI Global.

. Idelhaj, A., Abou El Houda, Z., & Khoukhi, L. (2024). Foundations models in cybersecurity. *Artificial Intelligence for Blockchain and Cybersecurity Powered IoT Applications*, 1.

. Idelhaj, A., Abou El Houda, Z., & Khoukhi, L. Foundations models in cybersecurity: A comprehensive review and future direction. *Artificial Intelligence for Blockchain and Cybersecurity Powered IoT Applications*, 1-18.

Jones, R., & Omar, M. (2024). Revolutionizing Cybersecurity: The GPT-2 Enhanced Attack Detection and Defense (GEADD) Method for Zero-Day Threats. *International Journal of Informatics* [INJIISCOM]. *Information System and Computer Engineering*, *5*(2), 178–191.

Jones, R., Omar, M., Mohammed, D., Nobles, C., & Dawson, M. (2023). Harnessing the Speed and Accuracy of Machine Learning to Advance Cybersecurity. In *2023 Congress in Computer Science, Computer Engineering, & Applied Computing (CSCE)* (pp. 418-421). IEEE. DOI: 10.1109/CSCE60160.2023.00074

Kasri, W., Himeur, Y., Alkhazaleh, H. A., Tarapiah, S., Atalla, S., Mansoor, W., & Al-Ahmad, H. (2025). From Vulnerability to Defense: The Role of Large Language Models in Enhancing Cybersecurity. *Computation (Basel, Switzerland)*, *13*(2), 30. DOI: 10.3390/computation13020030

. LESTABLE, T., & THANDI, N. S. Revolutionizing Cyber Threat Detection with Large Language Models: A privacy-preserving BERT-based Lightweight Model for IoT/IIoT Devices.

Liu, Z. (2024, April). A review of advancements and applications of pre-trained language models in cybersecurity. In *2024 12th International Symposium on Digital Forensics and Security (ISDFS)* (pp. 1-10). IEEE. DOI: 10.1109/ISDFS60797.2024.10527236

Manoharan, A., & Sarker, M. (2023). Revolutionizing Cybersecurity: Unleashing the Power of Artificial Intelligence and Machine Learning for Next-Generation Threat Detection. *DOI:* https://www. doi. org/10.56726/IRJMETS32644, *1*.

Mohammed, D., Omar, M., & Nguyen, V. (2018). Wireless sensor network security: Approaches to detecting and avoiding wormhole attacks. *Journal of Research in Business. Economics and Management, 10*(2), 1860–1864.

Motlagh, F. N., Hajizadeh, M., Majd, M., Najafi, P., Cheng, F., & Meinel, C. (2024). Large language models in cybersecurity: State-of-the-art. *arXiv preprint arXiv:2402.00891.*

Nguyen, V., Mohammed, D., Omar, M., & Banisakher, M. (2018). The Effects of the FCC Net Neutrality Repeal on Security and Privacy. [IJHIoT]. *International Journal of Hyperconnectivity and the Internet of Things, 2*(2), 21–29. DOI: 10.4018/IJHIoT.2018070102

. Omar, M. (2021). New insights into database security: An effective and integrated approach for applying access control mechanisms and cryptographic concepts in Microsoft Access environments.

Omar, M. (2022). *Machine Learning for Cybersecurity: Innovative Deep Learning Solutions.* Springer Brief. https://link.springer.com/book/978303115

Omar, M. (2024). From Attack to Defense: Strengthening DNN Text Classification Against Adversarial Examples. In *Innovations, Securities, and Case Studies Across Healthcare, Business, and Technology* (pp. 174-195). IGI Global.

Omar, M. (2024). Revolutionizing Malware Detection: A Paradigm Shift Through Optimized Convolutional Neural Networks. In *Innovations, Securities, and Case Studies Across Healthcare, Business, and Technology* (pp. 196-220). IGI Global. DOI: 10.4018/979-8-3693-1906-2.ch011

Omar, M., & Zangana, H. (Eds.). (2025). *Digital Forensics in the Age of AI.* IGI Global., DOI: 10.4018/979-8-3373-0857-9

Omar, M., & Zangana, H. M. (Eds.). (2024). *Redefining Security With Cyber AI.* IGI Global., DOI: 10.4018/979-8-3693-6517-5

Omar, M., & Zangana, H. M. (Eds.). (2025). *Application of Large Language Models (LLMs) for Software Vulnerability Detection.* IGI Global., DOI: 10.4018/979-8-3693-9311-6

Omar, M., Zangana, H. M., Al-Karaki, J. N., & Mohammed, D. (2024). Harnessing LLMs for IoT malware detection: A comparative analysis of BERT and GPT-2. In *2024 8th International Symposium on Multidisciplinary Studies and Innovative Technologies (ISMSIT)* (pp. 1-6). Ankara, Turkiye. https://doi.org/DOI: 10.1109/ISMSIT63511.2024.10757249

Omar, M., Zangana, H. M., & Mohammed, D. (Eds.). (2025). *Integrating Artificial Intelligence in Cybersecurity and Forensic Practices*. IGI Global., DOI: 10.4018/979-8-3373-0588-2

Ozkan-Okay, M., Akin, E., Aslan, Ö., Kosunalp, S., Iliev, T., Stoyanov, I., & Beloev, I. (2024). A comprehensive survey: Evaluating the efficiency of artificial intelligence and machine learning techniques on cyber security solutions. *IEEE Access : Practical Innovations, Open Solutions*, *12*, 12229–12256. DOI: 10.1109/ACCESS.2024.3355547

Pleshakova, E., Osipov, A., Gataullin, S., Gataullin, T., & Vasilakos, A. (2024). Next gen cybersecurity paradigm towards artificial general intelligence: Russian market challenges and future global technological trends. *Journal of Computer Virology and Hacking Techniques*, *20*(3), 429–440. DOI: 10.1007/s11416-024-00529-x

. Santos, O., Salam, S., & Dahir, H. (2024). The AI revolution in networking, cybersecurity, and emerging technologies.

Sarker, I. H. (2024). Generative AI and large language modeling in cybersecurity. In *AI-Driven Cybersecurity and Threat Intelligence: Cyber Automation, Intelligent Decision-Making and Explainability* (pp. 79–99). Springer Nature Switzerland. DOI: 10.1007/978-3-031-54497-2_5

. Taghavi, S. M., & Feyzi, F. (2024). Using large language models to better detect and handle software vulnerabilities and cyber security threats.

. THANDI, N. S. (2024). Revolutionizing Cyber Threat Detection With Large Language Models: A Privacy-Preserving BERT-Based Lightweight Model for IoT/IIoT Devices.

Wright, J., Dawson, M. E.Jr, & Omar, M. (2012). Cyber security and mobile threats: The need for antivirus applications for smartphones. *Journal of Information Systems Technology and Planning*, *5*(14), 40–60.

Xu, H., Wang, S., Li, N., Wang, K., Zhao, Y., Chen, K., . . . Wang, H. (2024). Large language models for cyber security: A systematic literature review. *arXiv preprint arXiv:2405.04760.*

Yu, J., Shvetsov, A. V., & Alsamhi, S. H. (2024). Leveraging machine learning for cybersecurity resilience in industry 4.0: Challenges and future directions. *IEEE Access : Practical Innovations, Open Solutions*, *12*, 159579–159596. DOI: 10.1109/ACCESS.2024.3482987

Zangana, H., & Omar, M. (Eds.). (2025). *Leveraging Large Language Models for Quantum-Aware Cybersecurity*. IGI Global., DOI: 10.4018/979-8-3373-1102-9

. Zangana, H. M. (2024). Exploring Blockchain-Based Timestamping Tools: A Comprehensive Review. *Redefining Security With Cyber AI*, 92-110.

. Zangana, H. M. (2024). Exploring the Landscape of Website Vulnerability Scanners: A Comprehensive Review and Comparative Analysis. *Redefining Security With Cyber AI*, 111-129.

. Zangana, H. M. (2024). Harnessing the Power of Large Language Models. *Application of Large Language Models (LLMs) for Software Vulnerability Detection*, 1.

Zangana, H. M., & Li, S. (2025). Future Trends in AI and Digital Forensics. In Omar, M., & Zangana, H. (Eds.), *Digital Forensics in the Age of AI* (pp. 347–380). IGI Global Scientific Publishing., DOI: 10.4018/979-8-3373-0857-9.ch013

Zangana, H. M., Mohammed, A. K., Sallow, A. B., & Sallow, Z. B. (2024). Cybernetic Deception: Unraveling the Layers of Email Phishing Threats. [INJURATECH]. *International Journal of Research and Applied Technology*, *4*(1), 35–47.

Zangana, H. M., & Mohammed, D. (2025). Foundations of Large Language Models in Software Vulnerability Detection. In Omar, M., & Zangana, H. (Eds.), *Application of Large Language Models (LLMs) for Software Vulnerability Detection* (pp. 41–74). IGI Global., DOI: 10.4018/979-8-3693-9311-6.ch002

Zangana, H. M., & Mustafa, F. M. (2024). Hybrid Image Denoising Using Wavelet Transform and Deep Learning. *EAI Endorsed Transactions on AI and Robotics*, *3*. Advance online publication. DOI: 10.4108/airo.7486

Zangana, H. M., & Mustafa, F. M. (2025). Image Denoising Techniques for Cybersecurity and Forensic Applications: AI-Driven Approaches. In Omar, M., Zangana, H., & Mohammed, D. (Eds.), *Integrating Artificial Intelligence in Cybersecurity and Forensic Practices* (pp. 117–142). IGI Global Scientific Publishing., DOI: 10.4018/979-8-3373-0588-2.ch005

Zangana, H. M., Mustafa, F. M., & Li, S. (2025). Large Language Models in Cybersecurity: From Automation to Intelligence. In *Leveraging Large Language Models for Quantum-Aware Cybersecurity* (pp. 277-300). IGI Global Scientific Publishing.

Zangana, H. M., Mustafa, F. M., & Li, S. (2025). Large Language Models in Cybersecurity: From Automation to Intelligence. In Zangana, H., & Omar, M. (Eds.), *Leveraging Large Language Models for Quantum-Aware Cybersecurity* (pp. 277–300). IGI Global Scientific Publishing., DOI: 10.4018/979-8-3373-1102-9.ch009

Zangana, H. M., Mustafa, F. M., Li, S., & Al-Karaki, J. N. (2025). Natural Language Processing for Cyber Threat Intelligence in a Quantum World. In Zangana, H., & Omar, M. (Eds.), *Leveraging Large Language Models for Quantum-Aware Cybersecurity* (pp. 345–388). IGI Global Scientific Publishing., DOI: 10.4018/979-8-3373-1102-9.ch011

Zangana, H. M., Mustafa, F. M., & Omar, M. (2024). A Hybrid Approach for Robust Object Detection: Integrating Template Matching and Faster R-CNN. *EAI Endorsed Transactions on AI and Robotics*, *3*. Advance online publication. DOI: 10.4108/airo.6858

Zangana, H. M., & Omar, M. (2020). Threats, Attacks, and Mitigations of Smartphone Security. *Academic Journal of Nawroz University*, *9*(4), 324–332. DOI: 10.25007/ajnu.v9n4a989

Zangana, H. M., & Omar, M. (2025). Harnessing the Power of Large Language Models for Cybersecurity: Applications, Challenges, and Future Directions. In Omar, M., & Zangana, H. (Eds.), *Application of Large Language Models (LLMs) for Software Vulnerability Detection* (pp. 1–40). IGI Global., DOI: 10.4018/979-8-3693-9311-6.ch001

Zangana, H. M., & Omar, M. (2025). Introduction to Digital Forensics and Artificial Intelligence. In Omar, M., & Zangana, H. (Eds.), *Digital Forensics in the Age of AI* (pp. 1–30). IGI Global Scientific Publishing., DOI: 10.4018/979-8-3373-0857-9.ch001

Zangana, H. M., & Omar, M. (2025). Introduction to Quantum-Aware Cybersecurity: The Need for LLMs. In Zangana, H., & Omar, M. (Eds.), *Leveraging Large Language Models for Quantum-Aware Cybersecurity* (pp. 1–28). IGI Global Scientific Publishing., DOI: 10.4018/979-8-3373-1102-9.ch001

Zangana, H. M., & Omar, M. (2025). The Role of Leadership in Advancing Inclusive Health Technologies. In Burrell, D., & Nguyen, C. (Eds.), *New Horizons in Leadership: Inclusive Explorations in Health, Technology, and Education* (pp. 203–220). IGI Global Scientific Publishing., DOI: 10.4018/979-8-3693-6437-6.ch009

. Zangana, H. M., Omar, M., Al-Karaki, J. N., & Mohammed, D. (2024). Comprehensive Review and Analysis of Network Firewall Rule Analyzers: Enhancing Security Posture and Efficiency. *Redefining Security With Cyber AI*, 15-36.

Zangana, H. M., Sallow, Z. B., & Omar, M. (2025). The Human Factor in Cybersecurity: Addressing the Risks of Insider Threats. *Jurnal Ilmiah Computer Science*, *3*(2), 76–85. DOI: 10.58602/jics.v3i2.37

Chapter 4
Digital Twin Technology in Simulating Cybercrime Scenarios

Rebet Keith Jones
https://orcid.org/0009-0008-0487-1301
Capitol Technology University, USA

ABSTRACT

Digital Twin (DT) technology has emerged as a transformative concept in the realm of cyber-physical systems, enabling real-time mirroring of physical assets within virtual environments. Its application in digital forensics and cybercrime investigation is both novel and powerful, offering new methods for simulating, analyzing, and responding to cyber threats. This chapter explores how DTs can be leveraged to replicate complex digital ecosystems, simulate cyberattacks, and predict attacker behavior with unprecedented accuracy. By integrating Artificial Intelligence (AI) and Machine Learning (ML), digital twins not only enhance the realism of cybercrime simulations but also provide adaptive, predictive capabilities essential for proactive defense mechanisms. The chapter delves into core methodologies for constructing cybercrime-focused digital twins, discusses case studies and tools used in the field, and evaluates the ethical and legal implications of such simulations. It further investigates the potential of DTs in training, risk assessment, and evidence validation

INTRODUCTION

The evolution of cyber threats—ranging from ransomware and phishing to advanced persistent threats (APTs) and AI-driven exploits—has outpaced many traditional digital forensic techniques. As a response to the escalating complexity and

DOI: 10.4018/979-8-3373-6536-7.ch004

frequency of cyberattacks, the field of cybersecurity is increasingly turning toward digital twin (DT) technology. Originally conceived within manufacturing and smart systems, digital twins have gained momentum in digital forensics and cybercrime simulation due to their capacity to create dynamic, real-time, and intelligent virtual replicas of digital environments (Tyagi et al., 2024; Costantini et al., 2019).

Digital twins empower forensic investigators to simulate, visualize, and analyze cybercrime scenarios in safe, controlled virtual environments, thus enabling repeatable and auditable reconstructions of digital incidents. Unlike traditional reactive forensic processes, DTs facilitate proactive forensic readiness, offering a shift toward intelligent and autonomous investigative capabilities (Irons & Lallie, 2014; Adam & Varol, 2020). This shift is further catalyzed by the infusion of artificial intelligence (AI) and machine learning (ML), which enhance digital twin platforms with autonomous anomaly detection, behavioral simulation, and threat attribution (Bhawna & Mahajan, 2024; Jarrett & Choo, 2021; Rizvi et al., 2022).

Recent research demonstrates the integration of digital twins with large language models (LLMs), blockchain, and cyber deception frameworks to simulate threats such as insider attacks, email phishing, smartphone malware, and software vulnerabilities (Zangana et al., 2024; Gholami & Omar, 2023, 2024; Omar & Zangana, 2025; Jeong, 2020; Zangana & Mohammed, 2025). These technologies are now at the frontier of transforming how digital investigations are conducted, ensuring both scalability and interpretability in forensic analyses (Hall et al., 2022; Kelly et al., 2020).

As digital infrastructures continue to expand into cloud computing, IoT, biotechnology, and smart healthcare, the need for robust, scalable, and autonomous forensic frameworks has become urgent (Hamza & Omar, 2013; Huff et al., 2023; Mohammed et al., 2018). In constrained environments, such as embedded systems or low-power devices, lightweight AI-enabled DTs offer a promising solution (Dunsin et al., 2022). Their capability to simulate attacks, monitor behavior, and generate forensic logs autonomously positions them as a critical technology in addressing digital evidence volatility and chain-of-custody concerns (Nguyen et al., 2018; Manasa & Kumar, 2022).

Moreover, digital twin frameworks allow security researchers and forensic analysts to safely test the propagation of cyberattacks and the effectiveness of mitigation strategies. For instance, DTs can replicate the effects of malware exploiting zero-day vulnerabilities, as explored through convolutional neural networks and GPT-enhanced detection methods (Jones & Omar, 2024; Omar, 2024). These simulations assist in generating synthetic datasets that improve the performance of AI forensic agents without risking real infrastructure (Gholami & Omar, 2023; Zangana & Omar, 2025).

The application of AI-based pattern recognition within DT environments—particularly for anomaly detection, traffic classification, and digital identity verification—has been well established (Ganesh, 2017; Mitchell, 2014; Iqbal et al., 2020). When combined with blockchain timestamping tools, these systems also preserve the integrity and non-repudiation of generated forensic evidence (Zangana, 2024).

In line with this transformation, scholars are calling for a redefinition of digital forensics toward "intelligent forensics", characterized by automation, contextual awareness, and interpretability (Moustafa, 2022; Karthikeyan et al., 2023). The convergence of digital twin technology with cybersecurity tools and forensic frameworks not only enhances threat simulation but also improves incident response efficiency and ethical accountability (Omar, 2021; Rughani, 2017; Dunsin et al., 2024).

This chapter explores the theoretical foundations, architectural components, and practical applications of digital twin technology in cybercrime simulation, integrating AI, ML, and LLMs. We also examine how DTs facilitate reproducible investigations, improve forensic readiness, and support autonomous threat modeling—thereby redefining the future of digital forensics.

FUNDAMENTALS OF DIGITAL TWIN TECHNOLOGY

Digital twin technology refers to the creation of dynamic, real-time digital replicas of physical assets, systems, or environments. Initially developed in industrial and manufacturing sectors, digital twins are now emerging as powerful tools in cybersecurity and digital forensics. A digital twin (DT) integrates data streams from its physical counterpart with intelligent algorithms, often leveraging artificial intelligence (AI) and machine **learning (ML)** to simulate behavior, predict outcomes, and enable scenario testing (Tyagi et al., 2024).

The Architecture and Core Components

A typical digital twin system comprises four main layers: (1) the physical entity (e.g., a server, IoT device, or network), (2) data acquisition systems, (3) virtual models or simulations, and (4) intelligent analytics (Sikos, 2021). These analytics are increasingly powered by AI and ML algorithms designed for forensics, including anomaly detection, vulnerability modeling, and threat prediction (Ganesh, 2017; Bhawna & Mahajan, 2024; Costantini et al., 2019).

By fusing these layers, DTs can simulate both routine and malicious behaviors in real time, making them ideal for replicating cybercrime scenarios. This capacity provides a safe, controlled environment for analyzing malware propagation, ransomware behavior, insider threats, phishing attacks, and AI-driven exploits (Zangana et al., 2024; Rizvi et al., 2022).

Artificial Intelligence Integration

Artificial intelligence is central to making digital twins intelligent and adaptive. AI enhances DTs through pattern recognition, autonomous decision-making, and predictive modeling—capabilities critical in cybercrime simulation and digital forensics (Iqbal et al., 2020; Irons & Lallie, 2014). AI-enabled digital twins can autonomously respond to simulated threats and generate forensic reports for post-incident analysis (Dunsin et al., 2024).

For example, digital twins augmented by large language models (LLMs) can simulate sophisticated cyberattacks and facilitate vulnerability detection in software systems (Gholami & Omar, 2023, 2024; Omar & Zangana, 2025). These models allow for the testing of advanced persistent threats (APTs) and zero-day exploits in safe environments (Jones & Omar, 2024).

Applications in Cybercrime Simulation and Forensics

DTs are increasingly used to recreate and analyze cybercrime scenarios. In such applications, DTs mirror enterprise environments, networks, or devices under investigation. Investigators can simulate how attacks like phishing campaigns or DDoS attacks unfold and how different responses could have changed outcomes (Zangana et al., 2024; Zangana & Omar, 2020).

Advanced applications also integrate blockchain for evidence integrity (Zangana, 2024), cloud environments for scalability (Hamza & Omar, 2013), and smartphone forensics for mobile threat simulation (Wright et al., 2012; Mohammed et al., 2018). These simulations are often supported by AI-enhanced agents capable of autonomously performing forensic tasks (Adam & Varol, 2020; Jeong, 2020).

DTs allow for iterative experimentation, enabling forensic investigators to run numerous "what-if" scenarios. This helps refine digital evidence chains and support legal admissibility by ensuring reproducibility and explainability (Hall et al., 2022; Kelly et al., 2020).

Forensic Intelligence and Automation

The convergence of AI and DTs enables what Irons and Lallie (2014) describe as a shift from "digital forensics" to "intelligent forensics." Digital twins can autonomously log events, detect anomalies, and simulate both the digital and human behavior involved in cyberattacks. This enables better insider threat detection, attribution analysis, and post-mortem investigations (Jarrett & Choo, 2021; Rughani, 2017).

Furthermore, the use of cyber deception within DTs—e.g., simulating honeypots, fake user behavior, or decoy credentials—allows investigators to study attacker behavior without exposing real assets (Zangana et al., 2024).

Digital Twins in Constrained and High-Risk Environments

In resource-constrained environments (such as embedded systems or critical infrastructure), AI-enhanced DTs can be optimized to simulate breaches without exposing live systems to risk. Studies by Dunsin et al. (2022, 2024) show how lightweight AI agents can work within DTs in sensitive environments such as healthcare, manufacturing, and IoT deployments.

This aligns with cybersecurity management practices in high-risk industries, including biotechnology and healthcare, where DTs can simulate breach response without compromising real-world systems (Huff et al., 2023).

Challenges and Limitations

Despite their advantages, digital twins face challenges in forensic applications. These include:

- Model fidelity and accuracy: Ensuring that the DT accurately reflects the behavior of the physical system (Costantini et al., 2019).
- Data privacy and security: Protecting the sensitive data used to train and simulate DTs (Nguyen et al., 2018).
- Adversarial threats: Ensuring DTs are not manipulated or reverse-engineered (Omar, 2024).
- Scalability: Especially in large enterprises with complex infrastructures (Jones et al., 2023).
- Interpretability: Making AI-based DT decisions explainable for legal and forensic purposes (Hall et al., 2022).

Future Outlook

The integration of LLMs, synthetic data, and blockchain timestamping is expected to strengthen the capabilities of DTs in digital forensics. Tools designed to generate synthetic cybercrime scenarios will enable continuous training of forensic models, making them more resilient and adaptive (Gholami & Omar, 2023; Zangana & Mohammed, 2025).

The future of digital forensics lies in dynamic, responsive, and self-healing digital environments—enabled by the fusion of AI, DTs, and intelligent forensics frameworks (Moustafa, 2022; Karthikeyan et al., 2023). As the ecosystem matures, new standards for evidence admissibility, chain of custody, and ethical AI usage will become essential (Manasa & Kumar, 2022; Omar, 2021).

The figure below illustrates the general architecture of a Digital Twin system designed to simulate cybercrime scenarios, integrating real-time data, simulation models, AI analytics, and response systems.

Figure 1. Architecture of a digital twin for cybercrime simulation

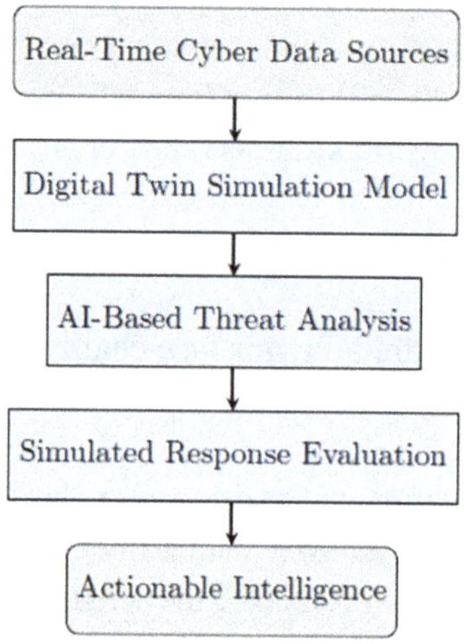

CYBERCRIME SIMULATION WITH DIGITAL TWINS

The modern cyber threat landscape is evolving rapidly, driven by sophisticated attackers, the proliferation of IoT devices, and the increasing reliance on digital ecosystems. To stay ahead of cybercriminals, researchers and practitioners are adopting digital twin (DT) technology as a novel and dynamic solution to simulate, analyze, and mitigate cybercrime in real-time, virtual environments (Tyagi et al., 2024).

The Role of Digital Twins in Cybercrime Simulation

Digital twins enable forensic investigators and cybersecurity analysts to create virtual replicas of networks, systems, devices, and user behaviors. These replicas serve as safe, controlled environments for simulating various types of cybercrimes—such as phishing attacks, malware infiltration, insider threats, zero-day exploits, and software vulnerabilities—without endangering production systems (Costantini et al., 2019; Jeong, 2020).

For instance, DTs can replicate enterprise systems where email phishing attacks are tested and their deceptive payloads traced using AI-augmented detection layers (Zangana, Mohammed, Sallow & Sallow, 2024). This enhances the proactive investigation of social engineering tactics and builds cyber resilience.

Moreover, in cases involving smartphones, mobile malware, **or IoT threats**, digital twins can emulate user interactions, operating systems, and network traffic patterns to identify vulnerabilities in isolated environments (Wright et al., 2012; Zangana & Omar, 2020).

Artificial Intelligence Enhancing DT-Based Cybercrime Simulation

DT environments are being significantly augmented by AI and ML algorithms, transforming them into intelligent platforms for cybercrime simulation and threat mitigation. For example, DTs integrated with convolutional neural networks (CNNs) and large language models (LLMs) like GPT-2 can simulate and detect zero-day attacks with high accuracy and adaptability (Jones & Omar, 2024; Omar, 2024).

Such simulations generate vast amounts of synthetic data, which are critical for training AI models without relying solely on sensitive or real-world datasets (Gholami & Omar, 2023). This capability improves the efficiency of machine learning algorithms, as seen in comparative studies on student-teacher LLM models for software vulnerability detection (Gholami & Omar, 2024; Zangana & Mohammed, 2025).

AI-powered DTs also allow investigators to automatically generate and test hypotheses, explore attack graphs, and identify patterns of malicious behavior (Ganesh, 2017; Mitchell, 2014). These capabilities foster autonomous digital forensic analysis, shifting from manual processes toward real-time, AI-guided decision-making (Adam & Varol, 2020; Irons & Lallie, 2014).

Blockchain, Forensic Logging, and Tamper-Resistant Simulations

One of the major advantages of DT-driven simulation is the ability to log and preserve forensic evidence using blockchain technologies. Tools like blockchain-based timestamping ensure that all activities within the DT environment are chronologically verifiable, immutable, and traceable (Zangana, 2024). This is particularly critical in maintaining chain-of-custody in forensic investigations, especially when dealing with synthetic data or simulated evidence (Hall et al., 2022; Kelly et al., 2020).

Real-World Applications and Sector-Specific Simulation

Digital twins are not limited to generic IT systems. Their application spans biotechnology, smart healthcare, and cloud computing, where cyber threat simulation is vital for mission-critical infrastructure (Hamza & Omar, 2013; Huff et al., 2023). In these sectors, DTs can simulate attacks such as data poisoning, DDoS, and wormhole routing in wireless sensor networks (Mohammed et al., 2018).

Furthermore, DTs in cloud-based environments can model abuse scenarios such as unauthorized access, privilege escalation, and API manipulation, helping to train automated defense mechanisms (Nguyen et al., 2018; Omar, 2021). In low-resource or constrained environments, lightweight DTs coupled with efficient AI algorithms ensure viable deployment without overburdening the infrastructure (Dunsin et al., 2022).

Advanced Threat Simulation and Intelligent Forensics

Digital twins enable layered simulation—where the impact of multiple concurrent threats (e.g., phishing + insider attack + software vulnerability) can be visualized and analyzed for their compounded effects. For example, an LLM-powered twin can simulate the behavioral pattern of an insider threat and cross-correlate it with unusual system calls to flag deviations (Rizvi et al., 2022; Omar & Zangana, 2025).

The move toward explainable AI (XAI) in digital forensics, as advocated by Hall et al. (2022), is also relevant in DTs, where investigators must interpret and communicate the results of simulations in a legally admissible format. This addresses one of the core concerns in forensic AI: the black-box nature of many models (Jarrett & Choo, 2021; Kelly et al., 2020).

Toward a Unified Framework for Intelligent Simulation

Emerging research is focused on building interoperable DT frameworks that unify AI, blockchain, and cyber-deception tactics for comprehensive cybercrime simulation. These systems offer reusability, auditability, and adaptability in investigative workflows (Karthikeyan et al., 2023; Rughani, 2017).

Additionally, new ontologies are being developed to standardize how DTs represent cybercrime scenarios, improving machine reasoning and enabling ontology-driven simulation environments (Sikos, 2021).

This flowchart illustrates the end-to-end process of using a digital twin in simulating cybercrime, from threat mapping to response evaluation.

Figure 2. Workflow of digital twin simulation in cybercrime

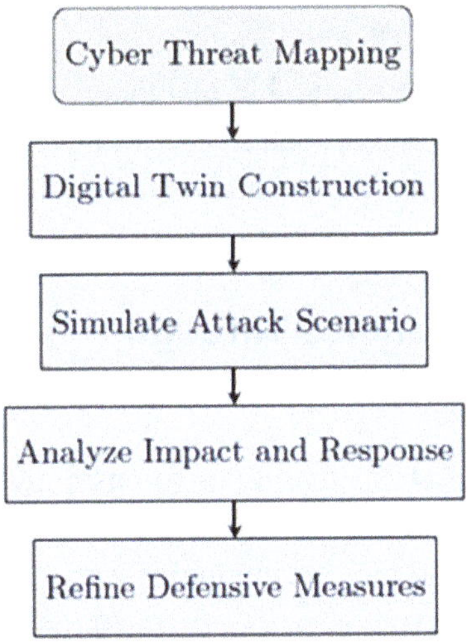

Finally, scholars advocate for "intelligent forensics", which represents the evolution of digital forensics into a domain where AI, DTs, and automated analysis converge to provide real-time, scalable, and contextual incident response (Moustafa, 2022; Iqbal et al., 2020; Dunsin et al., 2024).

INTEGRATION WITH AI AND FORENSIC TECHNOLOGIES

The integration of digital twin (DT) technology with artificial intelligence (AI) and advanced digital forensic tools is rapidly transforming the landscape of cybercrime simulation and investigation. This convergence enhances the capability to model complex cyber environments, detect sophisticated threats, and perform forensic analysis with unprecedented accuracy and speed (Costantini, De Gasperis, & Olivieri, 2019; Adam & Varol, 2020).

Synergy Between Digital Twins and AI in Cybercrime Simulation

Digital twins serve as dynamic virtual replicas of cyber-physical systems and network infrastructures, enabling real-time simulation and monitoring of cyber activities (Tyagi, Kumari, & Richa, 2024). By embedding AI algorithms—ranging from machine learning models to large language models (LLMs)—DTs gain the ability to automatically detect anomalies, predict attack patterns, and adapt defensive postures in simulated environments (Dunsin, Ghanem, Ouazzane, & Vassilev, 2024; Jones & Omar, 2024).

For instance, AI-powered DTs can simulate zero-day exploits and insider threats, providing forensic teams with actionable insights and preemptive responses. The use of deep learning architectures, such as convolutional neural networks (CNNs), enhances malware detection and behavioral analysis within DT frameworks (Omar, 2024; Ganesh, 2017).

Advancing Digital Forensics Through Automation and Explainability

The marriage of AI and DTs streamlines forensic investigations by automating evidence collection, correlation, and analysis in a controlled virtual space (Jarrett & Choo, 2021). This automation reduces manual effort, accelerates incident response, and allows forensic experts to reconstruct cybercrime scenarios with higher fidelity (Iqbal, Debbabi, & Fung, 2020).

Moreover, the adoption of explainable AI (XAI) models within DT environments addresses critical challenges related to the interpretability of forensic findings. As emphasized by Hall, Sakzad, and Choo (2022), explainability is paramount for legal admissibility and stakeholder trust, ensuring that AI-driven conclusions in digital forensics are transparent and justifiable.

Integration with Blockchain for Forensic Integrity

Blockchain technology complements DT and AI integration by ensuring the immutability and verifiability of forensic evidence generated during simulations. By timestamping logs and digital artifacts, blockchain establishes a tamper-proof chain-of-custody, crucial for maintaining the evidential value of data analyzed in DT environments (Zangana, 2024; Karthikeyan, Pande, & Sarveshwaran, 2023).

This fusion supports robust cybersecurity auditing and forensic accountability, particularly in sectors requiring high compliance standards such as healthcare and biotechnology (Huff et al., 2023; Zangana, Omar, Al-Karaki, & Mohammed, 2024).

Enhanced Threat Intelligence and Predictive Analytics

Integration with AI enables DT platforms to function as intelligent threat intelligence hubs, where machine learning models continuously learn from simulated attack data to forecast emerging cyber threats (Rizvi, Scanlon, Mcgibney, & Sheppard, 2022). Such predictive analytics allow cybersecurity teams to preemptively strengthen defenses, refine incident response protocols, and optimize firewall and intrusion detection configurations (Zangana, Omar, Al-Karaki, & Mohammed, 2024).

Additionally, AI algorithms embedded in DTs support cybernetic deception strategies, including simulated phishing and social engineering attacks, to identify vulnerabilities and enhance user awareness training (Zangana, Mohammed, Sallow, & Sallow, 2024).

Leveraging Synthetic Data and Large Language Models

One critical advantage of DT and AI integration is the generation and use of synthetic data for training and validating forensic models. Synthetic datasets alleviate privacy concerns and provide diverse, scalable training environments for large language models (LLMs) and other AI systems involved in cyber threat detection (Gholami & Omar, 2023; Gholami & Omar, 2024).

LLMs, integrated within DTs, assist in automated vulnerability detection, threat pattern recognition, and incident reporting, drastically reducing the time from attack detection to remediation (Omar & Zangana, 2025; Zangana & Omar, 2025).

Challenges and Future Prospects

While integration of AI and forensic technologies with digital twins offers significant benefits, challenges remain—such as ensuring data quality, maintaining model robustness against adversarial attacks, and addressing ethical concerns in automated forensic decision-making (Manasa & Kumar, 2022; Jeong, 2020).

Future research aims to develop interoperable, standardized frameworks that harmonize DT, AI, and forensic tools to enable seamless collaboration across cybersecurity domains, improving overall cyber resilience and forensic accuracy (Omar, 2022; Sikos, 2021).

USE CASES AND APPLICATIONS

Digital Twin (DT) technology, when applied to simulating cybercrime scenarios, offers transformative capabilities across various domains of cybersecurity, digital forensics, and incident response. By creating virtual replicas of physical and cyber systems, DTs enable realistic simulation, testing, and analysis of cyber threats in controlled, risk-free environments (Costantini, De Gasperis, & Olivieri, 2019). This section explores key use cases and applications illustrating the impact and versatility of DTs in modern cyber defense and forensic investigations.

Simulating Network Attacks and Intrusion Detection

One of the primary applications of DTs is in replicating network environments to simulate a wide array of cyberattacks, including Distributed Denial of Service (DDoS), ransomware, and advanced persistent threats (APTs). This simulation aids in evaluating network firewall rule analyzers and intrusion detection systems, improving their efficiency and adaptability (Zangana, Omar, Al-Karaki, & Mohammed, 2024). DTs paired with AI-based anomaly detection models provide continuous monitoring and can dynamically adapt firewall configurations to emerging threats (Jones, Omar, Mohammed, Nobles, & Dawson, 2023; Rizvi, Scanlon, Mcgibney, & Sheppard, 2022).

Digital Forensics and Incident Response Training

DT environments facilitate the training of digital forensic analysts by recreating complex cybercrime incidents virtually. Analysts can investigate timelines, trace attack vectors, and reconstruct evidential data without jeopardizing live systems (Adam & Varol, 2020; Bhawna & Mahajan, 2024). Moreover, automated forensic tools integrated with DTs expedite evidence collection and analysis, increasing the accuracy and speed of incident response efforts (Jarrett & Choo, 2021; Dunsin, Ghanem, Ouazzane, & Vassilev, 2024).

Phishing and Social Engineering Attack Simulation

Using cybernetic deception tactics within DTs, organizations can simulate sophisticated phishing attacks and social engineering schemes to identify vulnerabilities among employees and test the effectiveness of security awareness programs (Zangana, Mohammed, Sallow, & Sallow, 2024). These simulations help refine email filtering mechanisms and train AI models to better detect deceptive communications in real-world scenarios (Ganesh, 2017; Omar & Zangana, 2024).

Malware Behavior Analysis and Defense Development

DTs enable isolated environments for detailed malware behavior analysis. By simulating affected systems, researchers can observe how malware propagates, interacts with system resources, and evades detection (Omar, 2024; Huff et al., 2023). Integration with deep learning models further assists in developing optimized malware detection systems and enhances defensive architectures for endpoint security (Omar, 2022; Ganesh, 2017).

Cloud and IoT Security Simulation

Given the increasing adoption of cloud and IoT technologies, DTs are applied to model these infrastructures for cybersecurity testing. Simulated attacks on cloud platforms, including abuse scenarios and data breaches, inform the development of stronger access control mechanisms and cryptographic protections (Hamza & Omar, 2013; Mohammed, Omar, & Nguyen, 2018). Similarly, DTs model IoT devices and networks, helping to detect wormhole attacks and other vulnerabilities in constrained environments (Dunsin, Ghanem, & Quazzane, 2022).

Synthetic Data Generation for AI Training

DTs contribute significantly to generating synthetic datasets for training large language models (LLMs) and other AI systems used in cybersecurity and forensics (Gholami & Omar, 2023). This synthetic data circumvents privacy issues while providing diverse, realistic scenarios to improve model robustness and generalization (Gholami & Omar, 2024). Enhanced AI models improve software vulnerability detection, threat classification, and automated reporting within DT-driven workflows (Omar & Zangana, 2025; Zangana & Omar, 2025).

Blockchain-Enhanced Forensic Integrity

Incorporating blockchain with DT applications ensures secure timestamping and immutability of forensic artifacts, maintaining evidential integrity throughout cybercrime simulations and investigations (Zangana, 2024; Karthikeyan, Pande, & Sarveshwaran, 2023). This feature is particularly valuable for legal and compliance requirements in sensitive sectors such as healthcare and biotechnology (Huff et al., 2023).

Healthcare and Biotechnology Cybersecurity

DTs simulate complex biomedical research environments to assess vulnerabilities and potential attack vectors in healthcare IT infrastructures (Huff et al., 2023). By replicating laboratory networks and data flows, DTs help develop targeted cybersecurity protocols safeguarding sensitive patient data and intellectual property (Bhawna & Mahajan, 2024; Omar, 2024).

These use cases demonstrate how digital twin technology, combined with AI and forensic methods, revolutionizes cybercrime simulation by providing realistic, interactive, and highly detailed environments. As the technology matures, its applications will continue expanding, addressing increasingly sophisticated threats with proactive and intelligent defenses.

Table 1 compares traditional simulation tools with digital twin technologies in the context of cybercrime response and threat modeling.

Table 1. Comparison of traditional simulation vs digital twin in cybercrime

Attribute	Traditional Simulation	Digital Twin
Real-Time Sync		
Bidirectional Feedback		
Simulation Depth	Medium	High
AI Integration	Rare	Native
Risk Prediction	Limited	Advanced
Adaptability	Low	High

LEGAL, ETHICAL, AND OPERATIONAL CHALLENGES

The adoption of Digital Twin (DT) technology for simulating cybercrime scenarios brings forth a range of legal, ethical, and operational challenges that must be carefully addressed to ensure responsible and effective deployment. While DTs offer unprecedented capabilities in cyber defense, their use in simulating complex cyberattacks and forensic investigations raises multifaceted concerns spanning privacy, data protection, legal compliance, and operational feasibility (Adam & Varol, 2020; Bhawna & Mahajan, 2024).

Legal and Regulatory Compliance

One of the foremost challenges involves ensuring compliance with data protection laws and cybersecurity regulations across jurisdictions. Simulated environments often require handling sensitive or personal data, which could be subject to regulations such as GDPR, HIPAA, or sector-specific laws (Costantini, De Gasperis, & Olivieri, 2019). Failure to adhere to these regulations risks legal repercussions and undermines trust in DT-based simulations. Additionally, forensic data collected during simulations must be admissible in court, demanding strict chain-of-custody and evidence integrity protocols, often supported by blockchain-based timestamping to prevent tampering (Zangana, 2024; Hamza & Omar, 2013).

Ethical Considerations and Privacy

Ethical concerns emerge from the potential misuse or unintended exposure of simulation data, especially when replicating real-world user behaviors and network interactions (Jeong, 2020). The generation of synthetic data for training AI models within DT environments mitigates some privacy issues but also poses questions about representativeness and bias (Gholami & Omar, 2023; Hall, Sakzad, & Choo, 2022). Moreover, the risk of dual-use technology arises when DTs could be exploited by malicious actors to refine attack techniques under the guise of legitimate research (Ganesh, 2017; Jeong, 2020). Ethical frameworks must guide DT deployment, emphasizing transparency, accountability, and minimal harm principles (Jarrett & Choo, 2021).

Operational Challenges in Implementation

The complexity of developing accurate and scalable DT models for cybercrime scenarios poses significant operational hurdles. High-fidelity DTs require extensive data integration, real-time synchronization with physical networks, and computational resources to simulate diverse attack vectors realistically (Dunsin, Ghanem, Ouazzane, & Vassilev, 2024). Ensuring model accuracy while avoiding overfitting or false positives is critical for actionable insights (Omar, 2022; Rizvi, Scanlon, Mcgibney, & Sheppard, 2022). Furthermore, the integration of AI and machine learning within DTs necessitates explainability and interpretability to foster trust among cybersecurity professionals (Kelly et al., 2020; Hall et al., 2022).

Security Risks of Digital Twin Environments

Ironically, the DT systems themselves can become targets of cyberattacks, potentially compromising simulated data and operational continuity (Zangana & Omar, 2020). This risk necessitates robust defense mechanisms, including secure cloud infrastructures and access controls, to prevent abuse or nefarious use of DTs in malicious activities (Hamza & Omar, 2013; Mohammed, Omar, & Nguyen, 2018). The operational environment must also guard against insider threats and vulnerabilities introduced through third-party integrations (Huff et al., 2023).

Challenges in Forensic Validity and Evidence Management

Ensuring that forensic evidence derived from DT simulations meets legal standards for admissibility requires meticulous management of evidence acquisition, storage, and analysis processes (Adam & Varol, 2020; Bhawna & Mahajan, 2024). Automation and AI integration enhance efficiency but also introduce challenges related to bias, reproducibility, and auditability (Iqbal, Debbabi, & Fung, 2020; Sikos, 2021). Maintaining transparent documentation and validation of AI-driven forensic tools is imperative to uphold investigative credibility (Kelly et al., 2020; Jarrett & Choo, 2021).

Summary

The legal, ethical, and operational challenges associated with digital twin technology in cybercrime simulation necessitate a multidisciplinary approach that combines technological innovation with robust governance frameworks. Addressing these challenges proactively ensures DTs serve as trustworthy tools for enhancing cybersecurity defenses and digital forensic investigations, while safeguarding privacy, security, and legal integrity.

Figure 3 visualizes the main challenges identified when implementing digital twin technology in cybersecurity and cybercrime simulation.

Figure 3. Challenges in deploying digital twin systems

Attribute	Traditional Simulation	Digital Twin
Real-Time Sync		
Bidirectional Feedback		
Simulation Depth	Medium	High
AI Integration	Rare	Native
Risk Prediction	Limited	Advanced
Adaptability	Low	High

OPPORTUNITIES AND FUTURE DIRECTIONS

Digital Twin (DT) technology holds significant promise in revolutionizing cybersecurity and digital forensics by providing realistic, dynamic environments for simulating cybercrime scenarios. As the convergence of Artificial Intelligence (AI), machine learning (ML), and DTs progresses, new opportunities emerge to enhance threat detection, incident response, and forensic investigations, while addressing existing cybersecurity challenges (Adam & Varol, 2020; Bhawna & Mahajan, 2024).

Enhanced Cybercrime Simulation and Prediction

DTs enable the creation of detailed virtual replicas of physical and networked environments, allowing security professionals to simulate, observe, and analyze cyberattacks in a controlled setting. This capability improves understanding of attacker behavior, threat propagation, and system vulnerabilities, which aids in proactive defense measures (Costantini, De Gasperis, & Olivieri, 2019; Dunsin, Ghanem, Ouazzane, & Vassilev, 2024). By integrating AI-driven analytics, DTs can predict potential attack vectors and evaluate mitigation strategies in near real-time, increasing cyber resilience (Jones & Omar, 2024; Omar, 2022).

Integration of AI and Explainability for Digital Forensics

AI-enhanced DT environments facilitate advanced digital forensic investigations by automating data collection, pattern recognition, and anomaly detection with increased speed and accuracy (Ganesh, 2017; Hall, Sakzad, & Choo, 2022). Future developments emphasize explainable AI to ensure transparency and trustworthiness of forensic conclusions, addressing concerns about AI "black-box" decision-making in legal contexts (Kelly et al., 2020; Jarrett & Choo, 2021). These advancements support forensic investigators in producing evidence that withstands judicial scrutiny (Adam & Varol, 2020).

Synthetic Data and Training Large Language Models

Synthetic data generation within DTs can overcome privacy and data scarcity issues, enabling the training of large language models (LLMs) for cybersecurity tasks without compromising sensitive information (Gholami & Omar, 2023; Zangana & Omar, 2025). These LLMs can be leveraged to detect novel threats, automate vulnerability detection, and enhance software security, thus opening new frontiers in cyber defense (Omar & Zangana, 2025; Zangana, Omar, Al-Karaki, & Mohammed, 2024).

Blockchain and Secure Timestamping for Evidence Integrity

Integrating blockchain technologies with DTs offers tamper-proof timestamping and audit trails for digital evidence collected during simulations and forensic processes (Zangana, 2024; Hamza & Omar, 2013). This enhances the reliability and legal admissibility of digital evidence, reinforcing trust in cybercrime investigations and facilitating cross-jurisdictional cooperation.

Addressing Emerging Threats in IoT and Cloud Environments

DTs can simulate increasingly complex and distributed cyber ecosystems, including IoT and cloud infrastructures, which are frequent targets for sophisticated attacks (Mohammed, Omar, & Nguyen, 2018; Huff et al., 2023). Future research aims to leverage DTs for real-time monitoring and predictive analytics tailored to these environments, improving incident response and reducing downtime (Dunsin, Ghanem, & Quazzane, 2022; Tyagi, Kumari, & Richa, 2024).

Operationalizing AI-Driven Cyber Defense in Constrained Environments

Emerging trends focus on adapting DT-powered AI solutions to operate efficiently under resource constraints, such as in edge computing and mobile contexts, expanding protection coverage without compromising performance (Dunsin, Ghanem, & Quazzane, 2022; Wright, Dawson Jr., & Omar, 2012). These developments are critical for safeguarding increasingly mobile and decentralized digital infrastructures.

Multidisciplinary Collaboration and Standardization

Future directions include fostering interdisciplinary collaboration between cybersecurity experts, legal professionals, and ethicists to establish standards, best practices, and regulatory frameworks that govern DT use in cybercrime simulation (Irons & Lallie, 2014; Jeong, 2020). Ensuring ethical deployment, privacy preservation, and societal acceptance will be pivotal to realizing DT technology's full potential (Bhawna & Mahajan, 2024; Omar & Zangana, 2024).

In summary, Digital Twin technology, combined with AI, blockchain, and explainable analytics, offers transformative opportunities for simulating cybercrime and advancing digital forensics. Ongoing research and development should prioritize transparency, privacy, and operational viability to build resilient, trustworthy cyber defense ecosystems that adapt to emerging threats and regulatory landscapes (Omar, 2024; Rizvi, Scanlon, Mcgibney, & Sheppard, 2022).

The diagram below outlines how digital twin models may be extended to cover a broad range of cybercrime scenarios, such as insider threats, DDoS attacks, and phishing simulations.

Figure 4. Cybercrime scenarios simulated by digital twin models

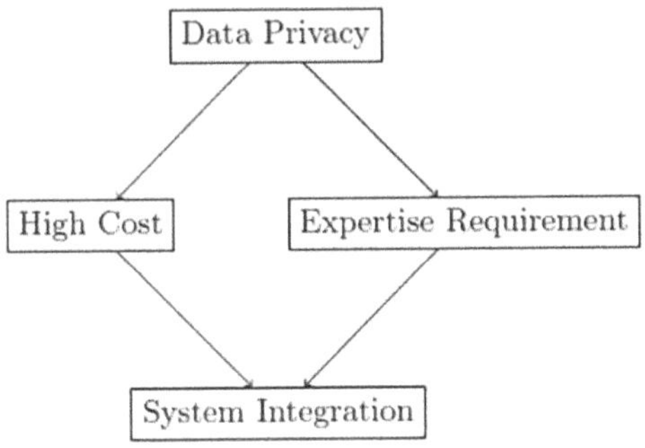

CONCLUSION

Digital twin technology represents a groundbreaking approach to simulating cybercrime scenarios, offering unprecedented opportunities to understand, predict, and mitigate cyber threats in a controlled and dynamic environment. By creating highly detailed virtual replicas of physical and cyber systems, digital twins enable security professionals to test attack strategies, evaluate defense mechanisms, and anticipate vulnerabilities before they manifest in real-world networks.

This chapter highlighted the significant advantages of leveraging digital twins in cybercrime simulation, including enhanced situational awareness, improved incident response, and accelerated forensic analysis. Moreover, integrating digital twins with artificial intelligence and machine learning further amplifies their potential by enabling adaptive, intelligent simulations that can evolve with emerging threats.

However, challenges remain in the implementation of digital twin technology, such as legal and ethical considerations, data privacy concerns, and the complexity of accurately modeling intricate cyber-physical systems. Addressing these challenges requires multidisciplinary collaboration and continuous innovation.

Looking forward, the convergence of digital twin technology with advances in AI, blockchain, and explainable forensics promises to revolutionize cybersecurity. Future research and development efforts should focus on enhancing model fidelity, improving real-time data integration, and establishing robust frameworks for ethical use.

In summary, digital twin technology offers a promising frontier for simulating and countering cybercrime, fostering proactive defense strategies that are vital in today's ever-evolving cyber threat landscape.

REFERENCES

Adam, I. Y., & Varol, C. (2020, June). Intelligence in digital forensics process. In *2020 8th International Symposium on Digital Forensics and Security (ISDFS)* (pp. 1-6). IEEE. DOI: 10.1109/ISDFS49300.2020.9116442

. Bhawna, & Mahajan, S. (2024). Artificial Intelligence Perspective on Digital Forensics. *Applying Artificial Intelligence in Cybersecurity Analytics and Cyber Threat Detection*, 33-44.

Costantini, S., De Gasperis, G., & Olivieri, R. (2019). Digital forensics and investigations meet artificial intelligence. *Annals of Mathematics and Artificial Intelligence*, *86*(1), 193–229. DOI: 10.1007/s10472-019-09632-y

Dunsin, D., Ghanem, M. C., Ouazzane, K., & Vassilev, V. (2024). A comprehensive analysis of the role of artificial intelligence and machine learning in modern digital forensics and incident response. *Forensic Science International Digital Investigation*, *48*, 301675. DOI: 10.1016/j.fsidi.2023.301675

Dunsin, D., Ghanem, M. C., & Quazzane, K. (2022). The use of artificial intelligence in digital forensics and incident response in a constrained environment. *International Journal of Information and Communication Engineering*, *16*(8), 280–285.

Ganesh, V. (2017). Artificial intelligence applied to computer forensics. *International Journal (Toronto, Ont.)*, *5*(5).

Gholami, S., & Omar, M. (2023). Does Synthetic Data Make Large Language Models More Efficient? *arXiv preprint arXiv:2310.07830.*

Gholami, S., & Omar, M. (2024). Can a student large language model perform as well as its teacher? In *Innovations, Securities, and Case Studies Across Healthcare, Business, and Technology* (pp. 122-139). IGI Global. DOI: 10.4018/979-8-3693-1906-2.ch007

Hall, S. W., Sakzad, A., & Choo, K. K. R. (2022). Explainable artificial intelligence for digital forensics. *Wiley Interdisciplinary Reviews: Forensic Science*, *4*(2), e1434.

Hamza, Y. A., & Omar, M. D. (2013). Cloud computing security: Abuse and nefarious use of cloud computing. *International Journal of Computer Engineering Research*, *3*(6), 22–27.

Huff, A. J., Burrell, D. N., Nobles, C., Richardson, K., Wright, J. B., Burton, S. L., Jones, A. J., Springs, D., Omar, M., & Brown-Jackson, K. L. (2023). Management Practices for Mitigating Cybersecurity Threats to Biotechnology Companies, Laboratories, and Healthcare Research Organizations. In *Applied Research Approaches to Technology, Healthcare, and Business* (pp. 1-12). IGI Global.

. Iqbal, F., Debbabi, M., Fung, B. C., Iqbal, F., Debbabi, M., & Fung, B. C. (2020). Artificial intelligence and digital forensics. *Machine Learning for Authorship Attribution and Cyber Forensics*, 139-150.

Irons, A., & Lallie, H. S. (2014). Digital forensics to intelligent forensics. *Future Internet*, *6*(3), 584–596. DOI: 10.3390/fi6030584

Jarrett, A., & Choo, K. K. R. (2021). The impact of automation and artificial intelligence on digital forensics. *WIREs Forensic Science*, *3*(6), e1418. DOI: 10.1002/wfs2.1418

Jeong, D. (2020). Artificial intelligence security threat, crime, and forensics: Taxonomy and open issues. *IEEE Access : Practical Innovations, Open Solutions*, *8*, 184560–184574. DOI: 10.1109/ACCESS.2020.3029280

Jones, R., & Omar, M. (2024). Revolutionizing Cybersecurity: The GPT-2 Enhanced Attack Detection and Defense (GEADD) Method for Zero-Day Threats. *International Journal of Informatics* [INJIISCOM]. *Information System and Computer Engineering*, *5*(2), 178–191.

Jones, R., Omar, M., Mohammed, D., Nobles, C., & Dawson, M. (2023). Harnessing the Speed and Accuracy of Machine Learning to Advance Cybersecurity. In *2023 Congress in Computer Science, Computer Engineering, & Applied Computing (CSCE)* (pp. 418-421). IEEE. DOI: 10.1109/CSCE60160.2023.00074

Karthikeyan, P., Pande, H. M., & Sarveshwaran, V. (Eds.). (2023). *Artificial intelligence and blockchain in digital forensics*. CRC Press.

Kelly, L., Sachan, S., Ni, L., Almaghrabi, F., Allmendinger, R., & Chen, Y. (2020). *Explainable artificial intelligence for digital forensics: opportunities, challenges and a drug testing case study*. Digital Forensic Science.

Manasa, S., & Kumar, K. P. (2022). Digital forensics investigation for attacks on artificial intelligence. *ECS Transactions*, *107*(1), 19639–19645. DOI: 10.1149/10701.19639ecst

. Mitchell, F. R. (2014). An overview of artificial intelligence based pattern matching in a security and digital forensic context. *Cyberpatterns: Unifying Design Patterns with Security and Attack Patterns*, 215-222.

Mohammed, D., Omar, M., & Nguyen, V. (2018). Wireless sensor network security: Approaches to detecting and avoiding wormhole attacks. *Journal of Research in Business. Economics and Management, 10*(2), 1860–1864.

Moustafa, N. (2022). *Digital Forensics in the Era of Artificial Intelligence*. CRC Press. DOI: 10.1201/9781003278962

Nguyen, V., Mohammed, D., Omar, M., & Banisakher, M. (2018). The Effects of the FCC Net Neutrality Repeal on Security and Privacy. [IJHIoT]. *International Journal of Hyperconnectivity and the Internet of Things, 2*(2), 21–29. DOI: 10.4018/IJHIoT.2018070102

. Omar, M. (2021). New insights into database security: An effective and integrated approach for applying access control mechanisms and cryptographic concepts in Microsoft Access environments.

Omar, M. (2022). *Machine Learning for Cybersecurity: Innovative Deep Learning Solutions*. Springer Brief. https://link.springer.com/book/978303115

Omar, M. (2024). From Attack to Defense: Strengthening DNN Text Classification Against Adversarial Examples. In *Innovations, Securities, and Case Studies Across Healthcare, Business, and Technology* (pp. 174-195). IGI Global.

Omar, M. (2024). Revolutionizing Malware Detection: A Paradigm Shift Through Optimized Convolutional Neural Networks. In *Innovations, Securities, and Case Studies Across Healthcare, Business, and Technology* (pp. 196-220). IGI Global. DOI: 10.4018/979-8-3693-1906-2.ch011

Omar, M., & Zangana, H. M. (Eds.). (2024). *Redefining Security With Cyber AI*. IGI Global., DOI: 10.4018/979-8-3693-6517-5

Omar, M., & Zangana, H. M. (Eds.). (2025). *Application of Large Language Models (LLMs) for Software Vulnerability Detection*. IGI Global., DOI: 10.4018/979-8-3693-9311-6

Rizvi, S., Scanlon, M., Mcgibney, J., & Sheppard, J. (2022). Application of artificial intelligence to network forensics: Survey, challenges and future directions. *IEEE Access : Practical Innovations, Open Solutions, 10*, 110362–110384. DOI: 10.1109/ACCESS.2022.3214506

Rughani, P. H. (2017). Artificial Intelligence Based Digital Forensics Framework. *International Journal of Advanced Research in Computer Science, 8*(8), 10–14. DOI: 10.26483/ijarcs.v8i8.4571

Sikos, L. F. (2021). AI in digital forensics: Ontology engineering for cybercrime investigations. *WIREs Forensic Science*, *3*(3), e1394. DOI: 10.1002/wfs2.1394

. Tyagi, A. K., Kumari, S., & Richa. (2024). Artificial Intelligence-Based Cyber Security and Digital Forensics: A Review. *Artificial Intelligence-Enabled Digital Twin for Smart Manufacturing*, 391-419.

Wright, J., Dawson, M. E.Jr, & Omar, M. (2012). Cyber security and mobile threats: The need for antivirus applications for smartphones. *Journal of Information Systems Technology and Planning*, *5*(14), 40–60.

. Zangana, H. M. (2024). Exploring Blockchain-Based Timestamping Tools: A Comprehensive Review. *Redefining Security With Cyber AI*, 92-110.

. Zangana, H. M. (2024). Exploring the Landscape of Website Vulnerability Scanners: A Comprehensive Review and Comparative Analysis. *Redefining Security With Cyber AI*, 111-129.

Zangana, H. M., Mohammed, A. K., Sallow, A. B., & Sallow, Z. B. (2024). Cybernetic Deception: Unraveling the Layers of Email Phishing Threats. [INJURATECH]. *International Journal of Research and Applied Technology*, *4*(1), 35–47.

Zangana, H. M., & Mohammed, D. (2025). Foundations of Large Language Models in Software Vulnerability Detection. In Omar, M., & Zangana, H. (Eds.), *Application of Large Language Models (LLMs) for Software Vulnerability Detection* (pp. 41–74). IGI Global., DOI: 10.4018/979-8-3693-9311-6.ch002

Zangana, H. M., & Omar, M. (2020). Threats, Attacks, and Mitigations of Smartphone Security. *Academic Journal of Nawroz University*, *9*(4), 324–332. DOI: 10.25007/ajnu.v9n4a989

Zangana, H. M., & Omar, M. (2025). Harnessing the Power of Large Language Models for Cybersecurity: Applications, Challenges, and Future Directions. In Omar, M., & Zangana, H. (Eds.), *Application of Large Language Models (LLMs) for Software Vulnerability Detection* (pp. 1–40). IGI Global., DOI: 10.4018/979-8-3693-9311-6.ch001

. Zangana, H. M., Omar, M., Al-Karaki, J. N., & Mohammed, D. (2024). Comprehensive Review and Analysis of Network Firewall Rule Analyzers: Enhancing Security Posture and Efficiency. *Redefining Security With Cyber AI*, 15-36.

Chapter 5
AI in Forensic Accounting:
Detecting Anomalies and Financial Fraud Through Intelligent Systems

Hewa Majeed Zangana
https://orcid.org/0000-0001-7909-254X
Duhok Polytechnic University, Iraq

Rindah Febriana Suryawati
https://orcid.org/0000-0003-0389-4583
Universitas Airlangga, Indonesia

Firas Mahmood Mustafa
https://orcid.org/0000-0002-8757-5303
Duhok Polytechnic University, Iraq

Anik Vega Vitianingsih
Universitas Dr. Soetomo, Indonesia

ABSTRACT

The increasing complexity and volume of financial data have escalated the challenge of detecting anomalies and fraudulent activities in accounting practices. Artificial Intelligence (AI) offers transformative potential to enhance forensic accounting by automating the identification of irregularities, reducing human error, and improving the efficiency and accuracy of financial investigations. This chapter explores the application of AI techniques—such as machine learning, natural language processing, and anomaly detection algorithms—in forensic accounting to detect financial fraud. It discusses the integration of intelligent systems within accounting frameworks, examines case studies demonstrating successful AI deployment, and addresses

DOI: 10.4018/979-8-3373-6536-7.ch005

ethical considerations and challenges related to data privacy and algorithmic bias. By highlighting emerging technologies and future research directions, this chapter underscores AI's critical role in advancing forensic accounting and strengthening financial crime investigations.

INTRODUCTION

In the digital era, financial fraud has evolved into a sophisticated and dynamic threat, fueled by increasing complexities in global financial systems and the exponential growth of data. Traditional forensic accounting techniques—once reliant on manual audits and retrospective analysis—are now proving insufficient in detecting concealed patterns and real-time fraudulent behavior. Against this backdrop, Artificial Intelligence (AI) has emerged as a transformative force in forensic accounting, empowering professionals with advanced tools to proactively detect, analyze, and prevent financial misconduct.

Recent research highlights that AI-driven forensic accounting can significantly enhance fraud detection by automating anomaly recognition, analyzing voluminous transactional data, and revealing hidden correlations that may escape human scrutiny (Abbas & Kollwitz, 2025; Vijayalakshmi & Jeevan, 2024). These intelligent systems are not only improving audit precision but also reducing costs and response times in financial crime investigations (Ali, Futaih, Shukur, & Al-Orfali, 2024; Daraojimba et al., 2023).

AI's role in forensic accounting spans several domains: from natural language processing used in reviewing textual financial documents (Qatawneh, 2025), to machine learning algorithms that flag abnormal transactions based on historical patterns (Zayed et al., 2024; Zheng et al., 2025). Technologies such as neural networks, rule-based expert systems, and deep learning architectures are actively redefining how investigators approach financial irregularities (Bhagat, 2024; Öztürk & Usul, 2020). Moreover, autonomous AI systems are now capable of functioning in high-risk environments, including the dark web, to uncover financial crimes (Rawat et al., 2023).

A growing body of literature supports the integration of AI in forensic auditing as a response to emerging threats in the global financial landscape. For instance, Elumilade et al. (2021) and Ramos (2021) emphasize the efficacy of data-driven forensic auditing approaches in ensuring financial integrity and proactive fraud detection. Meanwhile, advances in image recognition and intelligent data classification (Zangana, 2015; Zangana & Al-Shaikhli, 2013) have been repurposed from domains like cybersecurity and computer vision to contribute to AI-enabled auditing platforms.

The fusion of AI and forensic accounting is not without challenges. Issues such as algorithmic bias, explainability, and ethical considerations in automated decision-making are significant concerns (Bhagat, 2024; Matar, 2023). Furthermore, forensic accountants must now adapt to interdisciplinary practices, combining accounting expertise with data science competencies (Abbas & Kollwitz, 2025; Ali, Khinger, Subhe, & Al-Orfali, 2024).

Adejumo and Ogburie (2025) stress the importance of aligning forensic accounting practices with technological advancements to maintain relevance in modern fraud detection strategies. This aligns with the insights of Simbolon et al. (2024), who advocate for cross-country learning and collaboration in AI-driven fraud prevention. Similarly, Al-Raggad et al. (2025) highlight the ethical imperative of upholding transparency and data accountability when implementing intelligent forensic systems.

The importance of tailoring AI systems to specific financial environments has also been discussed by Harjuni (2024), who points to the unique requirements of financial institutions. In countries like Nigeria, Okonta and Nnamdi (2025) document the growing reliance on AI to counter endemic fraud through tailored accounting information systems. Similarly, Uduehe, Okoye, and Amahalu (2024) explore AI-supported fraud management techniques within the Nigerian banking sector.

Technological evolution continues to influence forensic practices, as seen in the works of Aman (2024) and Mubarrat (2024), who investigate the impact of AI and big data in modern forensic investigations. These developments are supported by innovative improvements in software tools and auditing platforms (Haddad et al., 2024), which increasingly rely on scalable, intelligent solutions.

In the context of high-performance computing and advanced analytics, contributions from Zangana (2025) and Zangana & Mustafa (2024) demonstrate how parallel algorithms, hybrid denoising, and clustering techniques—initially applied in engineering and image processing—are now being adapted to financial fraud detection frameworks. The ability to extract meaningful insights from noisy, unstructured, or incomplete financial data is central to these applications (Zangana, 2018; Zangana, 2020).

This chapter aims to provide an in-depth examination of how AI is revolutionizing forensic accounting by detecting anomalies, reducing human biases, and enhancing fraud prevention strategies. It presents key AI models used in practice, discusses real-world applications, addresses ongoing challenges, and outlines future directions for research and policy. By integrating diverse scholarly insights (Đukić, Pavlović, & Grdinić, 2023; Mazloum, Mazloum, & Saleh, 2025), the chapter underscores the interdisciplinary foundation required to build robust and ethical AI-supported forensic accounting systems.

BACKGROUND AND LITERATURE REVIEW

Forensic accounting has undergone a significant transformation in recent years, driven by the integration of Artificial Intelligence (AI), big data, and advanced analytics. Traditionally reliant on manual audits and retrospective data analysis, forensic accounting now leverages intelligent systems to detect financial fraud in real time and with greater accuracy (Abbas & Kollwitz, 2025). This transformation aligns with broader shifts in the digital economy, where technology-driven fraud schemes necessitate equally advanced detection mechanisms.

Evolution of Forensic Accounting in the Digital Age

The roots of forensic accounting are grounded in conventional auditing and financial scrutiny. However, the complexity of financial crimes has expanded with the growth of digital transactions, necessitating more dynamic tools. Adejumo and Ogburie (2025) emphasize the growing importance of data-driven methodologies in forensic practices, especially given the limitations of human-led detection in identifying covert or emerging fraud schemes.

Technological advances, particularly in machine learning and data science, have accelerated the application of AI to forensic investigations. Ramos (2021) highlights how the integration of big data analytics and AI supports proactive fraud prevention strategies. Likewise, Daraojimba et al. (2023) outline a U.S. perspective, where digital forensic accounting practices increasingly rely on real-time data mining and pattern recognition tools.

Key Trends and Techniques

Several recent studies provide a comprehensive overview of AI-enabled techniques in forensic auditing. Ali, Futaih, Shukur, and Al-Orfali (2024) discuss emerging trends such as anomaly detection algorithms, natural language processing (NLP), and the automation of forensic workflows. Their findings are reinforced by Ali, Khinger, Subhe, and Al-Orfali (2024), who explore how hybrid AI models combine rule-based logic with deep learning to improve detection accuracy.

Qatawneh (2025) stresses the significance of NLP in enhancing the interpretation of unstructured financial texts, allowing forensic auditors to extract meaning from legal documents, financial statements, and emails. Zayed et al. (2024) further illustrate how AI supports accounting information systems by detecting and flagging suspicious activities based on contextual understanding.

Rule-based systems remain foundational in forensic accounting, especially for encoding regulatory requirements and audit standards. Öztürk and Usul (2020) detail how these systems, when integrated with AI, become powerful tools for enforcing consistency and reducing oversight errors. However, these systems must be complemented with adaptive models to respond to new fraud patterns.

Interdisciplinary Integration and Technological Synergies

Forensic accounting now sits at the intersection of finance, computer science, and legal compliance. Matar (2023) argues that the synergy between cybersecurity protocols and forensic accounting is essential to defend against digital fraud. This perspective is supported by Mazloum, Mazloum, and Saleh (2025), who propose AI-enhanced auditing frameworks that empower certified public accountants with real-time fraud detection capabilities.

The role of intelligent automation is also crucial. Rawat et al. (2023) explore how autonomous AI agents operate in dark web environments to identify fraudulent financial activities. Similarly, Zheng et al. (2025) advocate for integrating machine learning into financial forensics to improve investigative efficiency and fraud prediction.

Zangana's body of work contributes significant computational underpinnings to this discussion. For example, Zangana and Abdulazeez (2023) review clustering algorithms relevant for pattern recognition in large datasets—a technique instrumental in detecting outliers in financial records. In a related study, Zangana (2025) proposes a novel parallel algorithm for efficient data processing in high-performance computing environments, enabling forensic systems to analyze massive financial datasets quickly.

AI-driven image recognition, typically used in security domains, is also repurposed in accounting contexts. Research by Zangana (2015, 2017) on color-based detection and shape recognition demonstrates the utility of visual analytics in monitoring scanned financial documents or receipts for inconsistencies. Additionally, projects by Zangana & Mustafa (2024) review image denoising and object detection algorithms that have potential in visual data processing in auditing systems.

Empirical Findings and Case-Based Evidence

Empirical studies confirm the efficacy of AI in practical forensic applications. Abbas and Kollwitz (2025) report measurable improvements in fraud detection rates across industries adopting AI-enhanced forensic tools. Harjuni (2024) provides evidence from financial institutions, showing that AI tools contribute significantly to fraud risk management.

Comparative analyses by Simbolon et al. (2024) and Uduehe, Okoye, and Amahalu (2024) reveal regional variations in the adoption of AI in forensic accounting. In

Nigeria, Okonta and Nnamdi (2025) describe how banks leverage AI technologies to combat persistent financial fraud. These findings reflect a global consensus on AI's value while highlighting the need for local customization.

The ethical dimension of AI in forensic accounting is addressed by Bhagat (2024), who warns of potential algorithmic bias and over-reliance on black-box models. Al-Raggad et al. (2025) take a complementary view, arguing that ethical integrity can be maintained through transparent AI governance and bibliometric analysis of forensic practices.

Incorporating data quality and system integration perspectives, Zangana (2017, 2018, 2019, 2020, 2021, 2022) addresses how robust digital infrastructure is necessary for accurate fraud detection. These foundational studies underline the importance of managing data warehousing, web service optimization, and information systems for effective forensic accounting operations.

Challenges and Gaps in the Literature

Despite these advancements, several challenges persist. Aman (2024) outlines issues such as the digital divide and skill gaps in accounting professionals that hinder AI adoption. Mubarrat (2024) also highlights infrastructural and policy barriers, especially in developing economies.

Moreover, although AI offers scalability, maintaining the transparency and interpretability of forensic models remains an ongoing concern (Haddad et al., 2024). Ensuring accountability in AI decision-making is particularly important in legal contexts where forensic evidence informs judicial processes.

Finally, as Đukić, Pavlović, and Grdinić (2023) point out, a continued focus on education, professional training, and cross-sector collaboration is necessary to equip forensic accountants with the tools and skills needed for this evolving landscape.

TYPES OF FINANCIAL FRAUD AND ANOMALIES

Financial fraud and anomalies manifest in numerous forms, often exploiting systemic loopholes, human error, or technological gaps. With the rise of digital finance, cyber-enabled fraud has grown increasingly sophisticated, requiring forensic accountants to adopt technologically enhanced methodologies. Understanding the typology of fraud is essential to deploying AI-driven solutions effectively.

Asset Misappropriation

Asset misappropriation is among the most common types of fraud, involving theft or misuse of an organization's resources. This includes cash skimming, fraudulent disbursements, and misuse of company credit cards. Abbas and Kollwitz (2025) emphasize that AI-powered pattern recognition tools have proven effective in identifying such misappropriations by flagging abnormal transactions and cross-referencing data sources for inconsistencies.

Ali, Futaih, Shukur, and Al-Orfali (2024) further argue that anomaly detection models based on neural networks can uncover hidden patterns in employee expenditure, particularly when integrated with corporate finance systems. Similarly, AI-assisted forensic auditing systems are now being used to detect repetitive low-value transactions or duplicated payments, which may signal fraudulent disbursements (Zayed et al., 2024).

Financial Statement Fraud

This type of fraud involves intentional misrepresentation of financial statements to deceive stakeholders. It includes inflating revenues, concealing liabilities, or manipulating accounting entries. Bhagat (2024) warns of the risk of AI systems missing nuanced manipulations unless they are trained on diversified datasets with real-world fraud cases.

Nonetheless, AI models that use Natural Language Processing (NLP) to review financial disclosures and auditor notes offer enhanced detection of inconsistencies and unusual accounting language (Qatawneh, 2025). Zangana (2021) suggests that socio-economic contexts, such as financial pressures or cultural factors, can also inform intelligent fraud prediction models.

Ali, Khinger, Subhe, and Al-Orfali (2024) demonstrate how rule-based expert systems can be combined with predictive analytics to identify probable cases of financial misreporting. This combination of static auditing rules and dynamic learning models increases the system's adaptability to new fraud tactics (Öztürk & Usul, 2020).

To understand the application of AI in financial fraud detection, the following flowchart depicts the typical workflow of AI-based forensic accounting systems, from data ingestion to anomaly detection and decision-making.

Figure 1. AI-driven forensic accounting workflow

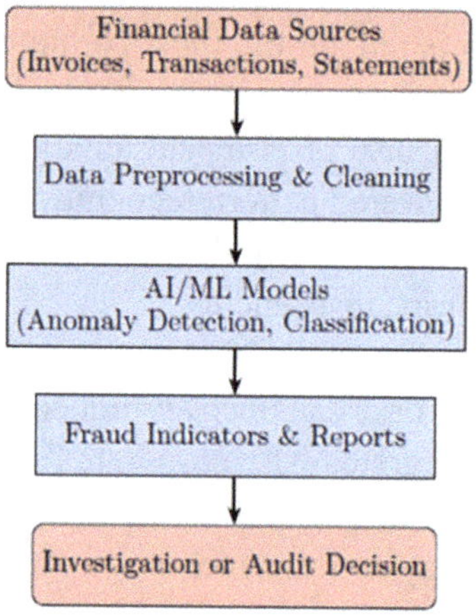

Payroll Fraud

Payroll fraud, such as ghost employees and falsified hours, remains a recurring issue, especially in large organizations. Harjuni (2024) notes that supervised machine learning algorithms can identify abnormal payroll activities by comparing departmental trends and benchmarking industry standards.

Zangana and Abdulazeez (2023) highlight the relevance of clustering techniques for detecting outliers in payroll data, which are often indicative of fraud. AI systems can also cross-check payroll entries against access control logs, timesheets, and IP logs, integrating cybersecurity data into forensic auditing processes (Matar, 2023).

Procurement Fraud

Procurement fraud includes collusion with vendors, inflated invoices, and kickbacks. Aman (2024) explains how AI-enhanced procurement systems use anomaly detection and vendor risk profiling to flag potential red flags in supplier contracts. Advanced AI systems, such as those described by Mazloum, Mazloum, and Saleh (2025), utilize machine learning to assess vendor behavior over time, improving fraud detection accuracy.

Daraojimba et al. (2023) also advocate for integrating dark web monitoring tools to detect illicit procurement activities, particularly in public sector environments where such fraud is pervasive. These systems rely on autonomous AI agents that crawl forums and marketplaces for stolen credentials or altered invoices (Rawat et al., 2023).

Cyber-Enabled Financial Fraud

With digitization, cyber-enabled fraud, such as phishing-based fund transfers, identity theft, and malware-assisted embezzlement, has surged. Abbas and Kollwitz (2025) argue that conventional fraud prevention systems are no longer sufficient. AI, particularly in combination with cybersecurity measures, offers proactive threat detection.

Zangana, Mohammed, and Husain (2025) emphasize the human element in cyber fraud, warning that insider threats are often overlooked. AI-driven behavioral analytics can detect deviations in user activity, login habits, and access privileges, thus identifying compromised or malicious insiders.

Moreover, object detection algorithms initially developed for security imaging (Zangana & Mustafa, 2024) are now being repurposed to detect document forgery or manipulated invoices—an emerging frontier in cyber-enabled accounting fraud.

Bribery and Corruption

These fraud types are notoriously difficult to detect due to their off-the-books nature. However, AI can be used to monitor communication patterns and financial flows that suggest collusion or unexplained wealth. Vijayalakshmi and Jeevan (2024) argue that correlating structured and unstructured data sources can uncover hidden relationships.

Bibliometric analysis of forensic case data by Al-Raggad et al. (2025) reveals that unethical financial practices often follow identifiable patterns in communication and payment behavior. AI tools trained on these bibliometric insights can automatically flag transactions associated with politically exposed persons or conflict-of-interest indicators.

Banking and Lending Fraud

This includes fraudulent loan applications, forged documentation, and fake identities used to access credit. In the Nigerian context, Okonta and Nnamdi (2025) describe how banks are deploying AI to verify identity documents, analyze credit behavior, and detect synthetic identities.

Elumilade et al. (2021) underscore the utility of forensic data warehousing in flagging suspicious loan patterns, while Zangana (2018) discusses the value of integrated information systems in managing large-scale financial data for auditing purposes. When coupled with facial detection algorithms (Zangana & Al-Shaikhli, 2013), institutions can verify biometric data to further secure digital lending.

Tax Evasion and Regulatory Fraud

AI systems are increasingly used to assist governments and corporations in identifying tax evasion tactics, such as shell companies or underreported income. Đukić, Pavlović, and Grdinić (2023) note that forensic auditors are now collaborating with AI developers to create models that trace the movement of funds across borders.

Mubarrat (2024) emphasizes the role of big data in parsing massive transaction logs, while Zangana (2022) explores community-based risk assessment systems that can be extended to regulatory compliance contexts. Fraud detection systems can be trained on historical tax evasion cases to recognize similar patterns in new data streams.

Insider Trading and Market Manipulation

In financial markets, anomalies such as irregular trades, pump-and-dump schemes, and insider leaks can now be flagged using AI-driven trading surveillance tools. Zheng et al. (2025) show how integrating machine learning into trading platforms enables real-time fraud detection and alerts.

Zangana (2025) introduces a parallel algorithm for processing massive trading data efficiently, facilitating high-frequency fraud detection. This technical advancement allows forensic systems to scale in capital markets, where fraud indicators may appear and vanish in milliseconds.

AI TECHNIQUES IN FORENSIC ACCOUNTING

Artificial Intelligence (AI) has transformed forensic accounting by automating processes, enhancing anomaly detection, and strengthening fraud investigation. The integration of AI enables forensic accountants to process vast datasets, recognize hidden patterns, and deliver timely and evidence-based conclusions. This section explores the core AI techniques applied in forensic accounting, highlighting their functions, strengths, limitations, and real-world relevance.

Machine Learning (ML)

Machine learning is at the forefront of AI applications in forensic accounting. ML algorithms learn from historical financial data to identify fraud patterns and predict future anomalies. Supervised learning models, such as decision trees and support vector machines (SVMs), are used for classification tasks like distinguishing legitimate from fraudulent transactions (Ali, Khinger, Subhe, & Al-Orfali, 2024; Zheng, Tan, Jiang, & Wang, 2025).

Unsupervised learning, particularly clustering algorithms such as k-means and DBSCAN, is valuable in detecting outliers and abnormal financial behaviors (Zangana & Abdulazeez, 2023). These methods are increasingly integrated into banking systems to monitor loan defaults and unusual account activities (Okonta & Nnamdi, 2025).

Deep learning, a subfield of ML, is also gaining traction. Neural networks can detect non-linear relationships and learn complex representations of fraud patterns. Their adaptability to unstructured data formats (e.g., emails, invoices) makes them especially useful in identifying disguised financial fraud (Ali, Futaih, Shukur, & Al-Orfali, 2024).

Natural Language Processing (NLP)

NLP enables AI systems to analyze and interpret human language from various financial documents, such as audit reports, emails, and regulatory filings. NLP techniques are particularly effective in identifying deceptive language or hidden cues in financial statements (Qatawneh, 2025).

Zayed et al. (2024) emphasize that NLP can flag inconsistencies between narrative sections and financial figures. Similarly, Al-Raggad et al. (2025) suggest that sentiment analysis within managerial commentary can reveal fraudulent intent, supporting the argument that behavioral indicators often precede financial manipulation.

To illustrate the internal mechanism of anomaly detection, the following system diagram shows how raw financial data is transformed into fraud alerts using AI models.

Figure 2. Anomaly detection process in AI-based forensic systems

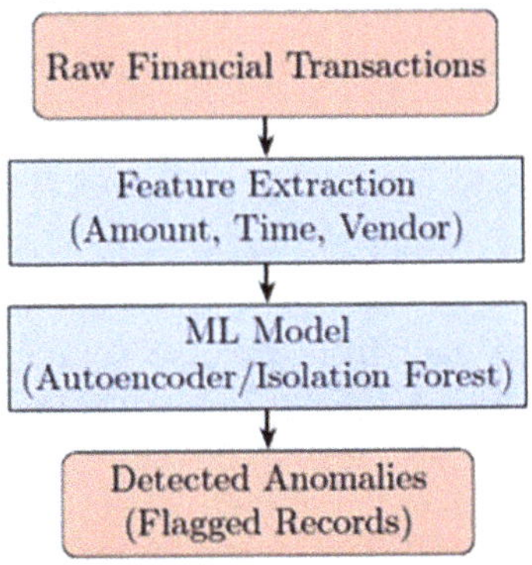

Expert Systems and Rule-Based AI

Rule-based systems apply predefined logical rules to identify known fraud patterns. These systems have long been used in auditing software and are effective in detecting violations of accounting standards (Öztürk & Usul, 2020).

However, their limitation lies in their inability to adapt to novel fraud tactics. Bhagat (2024) points out that while expert systems provide explainability, they often lack flexibility. Hybrid systems that combine rule-based logic with machine learning are becoming the norm, leveraging the strengths of both approaches (Ali et al., 2024).

Anomaly Detection Algorithms

Anomaly detection involves identifying data points that significantly deviate from expected norms. This technique is essential in forensic accounting, especially when dealing with massive transaction logs where fraud is rare but highly impactful (Mubarrat, 2024).

Zangana (2025) proposes a novel parallel algorithm for efficiently processing large datasets in anomaly detection, while Abbas and Kollwitz (2025) highlight how real-time anomaly detection engines can assist in continuous monitoring of accounting systems.

Predictive Analytics

Predictive analytics uses historical data to forecast future outcomes. In forensic accounting, it is applied to predict the likelihood of fraud occurrence, employee misconduct, or financial distress. Vijayalakshmi and Jeevan (2024) argue that predictive models support proactive decision-making in fraud prevention.

Haddad, Alharasis, Fraij, and Al-Ramahi (2024) also point out that the incorporation of AI-based predictive tools enhances early warning systems in fraud detection, thereby reducing investigation costs and improving regulatory compliance.

Big Data Analytics

The convergence of AI and big data enables forensic accountants to process structured and unstructured data from diverse sources—social media, financial transactions, emails, and network logs. Ramos (2021) and Elumilade et al. (2021)

note that integrating big data with forensic accounting allows for comprehensive risk profiling and pattern recognition.

According to Adejumo and Ogburie (2025), AI-powered big data tools can perform complex audits and uncover hidden relationships between variables that traditional analytics might overlook.

Autonomous AI Systems

Autonomous systems operate with minimal human intervention, using reinforcement learning and advanced heuristics. Rawat et al. (2023) document the use of such systems in monitoring the dark web for illegal financial activities, including fake invoices, stolen credentials, and illicit transactions.

Mazloum, Mazloum, and Saleh (2025) advocate for autonomous AI integration in public auditing frameworks to combat procurement fraud and enhance objectivity in audit conclusions.

Behavioral Analytics and Insider Threat Detection

Behavioral analytics focuses on identifying deviations in employee or user behavior that may indicate insider threats or collusion. Zangana, Mohammed, and Husain (2025) highlight how AI systems analyze user access logs, keystroke patterns, and login habits to detect potential internal risks.

Matar (2023) further explores the intersection of cybersecurity and forensic accounting, emphasizing the importance of integrating behavioral monitoring tools with AI-based fraud detection systems to enhance holistic risk management.

Facial and Biometric Recognition

AI-driven facial and biometric recognition systems are increasingly used in identity verification for financial transactions. Zangana and Al-Shaikhli (2013) and Zangana (2015) developed face detection algorithms based on skin tone analysis, which can be adapted for authenticating users in digital banking environments.

These technologies help prevent impersonation fraud and are often coupled with optical character recognition (OCR) systems for verifying scanned documents and signatures (Zangana, 2018).

Image and Document Analysis

AI techniques such as convolutional neural networks (CNNs) are used to detect alterations in scanned financial documents, signatures, or images. Zangana and

Mustafa (2024a, 2024b, 2024c) provide comprehensive reviews on image denoising and object detection, which are increasingly applied in identifying tampered invoices and forged receipts.

These tools enhance forensic capabilities in both public and private sectors, particularly in fraud scenarios where physical document integrity is compromised (Daraojimba et al., 2023).

Data Warehousing and Information Systems

Efficient data storage and retrieval are essential for AI-based fraud detection systems. Forensic accounting systems now rely on data warehouses that consolidate financial data from various departments, enabling cross-functional analysis (Zangana, 2018a, 2018b; Elumilade et al., 2021).

These platforms support AI algorithms in maintaining data integrity, conducting trend analysis, and streamlining digital forensic investigations (Zangana, 2019a, 2019b, 2020).

AI-Augmented Auditing Platforms

AI is also being embedded in auditing platforms to improve scalability, reduce errors, and offer real-time fraud indicators. Abbas and Kollwitz (2025) describe these platforms as essential in modern forensic accounting, as they blend auditing rules, real-time analytics, and machine learning for dynamic fraud detection.

Simbolon et al. (2024) argue that these technologies are especially beneficial in multinational settings where complex regulatory frameworks and diverse datasets exist.

DATA SOURCES AND PREPROCESSING

The effectiveness of AI in forensic accounting is intrinsically linked to the quality, structure, and diversity of the data used to train and operate intelligent systems. Proper data sourcing and preprocessing form the backbone of reliable fraud detection, ensuring that models are fed accurate, relevant, and ethically sourced information. This section outlines the types of data sources commonly utilized in AI-driven forensic accounting and elaborates on preprocessing techniques that prepare this data for analytical modeling and fraud detection.

Data Sources in Forensic Accounting

Forensic accounting leverages both structured and unstructured data. Structured data includes financial statements, general ledgers, tax records, payroll reports, and transaction logs (Ali, Khinger, Subhe, & Al-Orfali, 2024; Harjuni, 2024). Unstructured data comprises emails, scanned invoices, social media content, voice recordings, and handwritten notes, often accessed via enterprise resource planning (ERP) systems and third-party communication platforms (Qatawneh, 2025; Zayed et al., 2024).gure

Emerging data sources now include biometric verification logs (Zangana & Al-Shaikhli, 2013), behavioral telemetry (Zangana, Mohammed, & Husain, 2025), dark web intelligence (Rawat et al., 2023), and sentiment-laden textual data such as management commentary and audit reports (Al-Raggad et al., 2025). The integration of big data technologies enables the inclusion of high-volume, high-velocity data streams, such as real-time payment systems and trading platforms (Ramos, 2021; Mubarrat, 2024).

Cloud-based financial information systems and public databases (e.g., government procurement portals, SEC filings) also serve as critical data repositories for fraud detection and legal analysis (Adejumo & Ogburie, 2025; Simbolon et al., 2024).

Figure 3 highlights the comparative effectiveness of traditional vs AI-based techniques in fraud detection based on speed, accuracy, and scalability.

Figure 3. Comparison of traditional vs AI-based fraud detection techniques

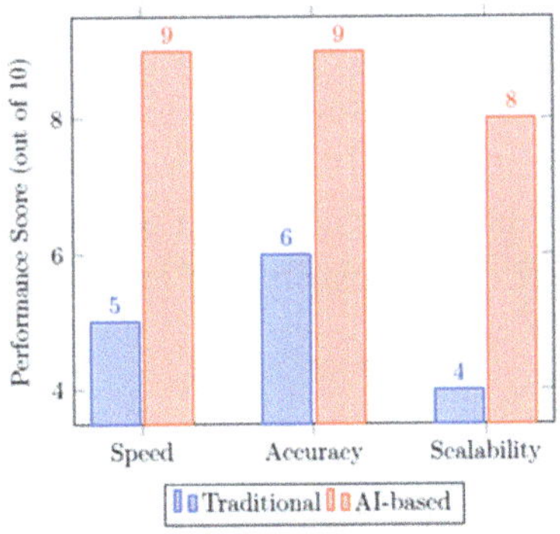

Challenges in Data Collection

The acquisition of forensic accounting data is fraught with ethical, legal, and logistical challenges. Data privacy laws, such as GDPR and CCPA, place strict limits on access to personal and financial data. Furthermore, data integrity issues—stemming from manipulation, incompleteness, or misclassification—can skew AI outcomes (Zangana, 2019; Abbas & Kollwitz, 2025). Organizations must implement robust governance frameworks to ensure proper data stewardship.

The lack of standardized data formats across international accounting systems presents another hurdle. Elumilade et al. (2021) note that cross-border investigations often suffer from inconsistent reporting schemes and terminological ambiguities.

Preprocessing Techniques

Before AI models can extract meaningful insights, the raw data must be transformed through a range of preprocessing techniques:

Data Cleaning and Normalization

Data cleaning involves identifying and rectifying errors, such as duplicates, outliers, and missing values. This is critical for minimizing false positives in anomaly detection systems (Zheng, Tan, Jiang, & Wang, 2025). Normalization adjusts the scale of numerical variables to ensure uniformity across features, particularly in machine learning algorithms sensitive to feature magnitude (Zangana & Abdulazeez, 2023).

Data Transformation

Raw financial data often needs to be converted into formats suitable for AI models. For example, textual data from emails or PDFs are transformed using natural language processing (NLP) techniques such as tokenization and vectorization (Zayed et al., 2024; Qatawneh, 2025). Image-based data, such as scanned receipts or handwritten invoices, undergo optical character recognition (OCR) and denoising (Zangana & Mustafa, 2024a, 2024b) to improve clarity and legibility for model ingestion.

Feature Engineering

Feature engineering involves the extraction or creation of variables that capture fraud-relevant characteristics. These features may include transaction frequency, abnormal expense ratios, or deviations from budgeted norms (Ali, Futaih, Shukur, & Al-Orfali, 2024; Vijayalakshmi & Jeevan, 2024). Zangana (2018a, 2018b) emphasizes the role of data warehousing systems in aggregating and organizing such features from multiple data silos.

Advanced feature engineering also utilizes behavioral profiling, such as time-of-day access patterns or keystroke dynamics, which can signal insider threats (Matar, 2023; Zangana, Mohammed, & Husain, 2025).

Dimensionality Reduction

High-dimensional data may overwhelm AI models and reduce efficiency. Dimensionality reduction techniques like Principal Component Analysis (PCA) and t-distributed Stochastic Neighbor Embedding (t-SNE) help in simplifying datasets while retaining core information (Mazloum, Mazloum, & Saleh, 2025).

Data Labeling and Annotation

For supervised learning models, labeled data is essential. This involves tagging transactions as "fraudulent" or "non-fraudulent" based on prior investigations or expert input. However, as Bhagat (2024) cautions, biased labeling practices may lead to algorithmic discrimination or overfitting.

Technological Tools for Preprocessing

AI-based preprocessing tools have grown in sophistication, allowing forensic accountants to automate many stages of data preparation. These tools include:

- **Automated data validation engines** for cross-referencing transaction histories (Abbas & Kollwitz, 2025).
- **Cloud-based ETL (Extract, Transform, Load) pipelines** for scalable preprocessing in large organizations (Aman, 2024).
- **Custom-built OCR and denoising algorithms** for financial documents (Zangana & Mustafa, 2024a; Daraojimba et al., 2023).
- **Behavioral anomaly detectors** to flag suspicious user activity in real time (Zangana, 2025).

These innovations, when paired with domain expertise, significantly reduce the manual effort required to prepare datasets for fraud detection models.

Ethical Considerations in Data Preprocessing

Preprocessing also raises ethical issues, especially concerning data bias, consent, and surveillance. For instance, when behavioral data is collected without user awareness, it may violate ethical principles even if it enhances fraud detection (Bhagat, 2024; Okonta & Nnamdi, 2025).

Data anonymization and encryption techniques must be applied to protect individual identities during model training (Ali et al., 2024). Moreover, forensic accounting teams should maintain transparency in preprocessing practices and align with legal frameworks such as ISO/IEC 27001 to avoid litigation (Al-Raggad et al., 2025; Haddad et al., 2024).

In summary, data sourcing and preprocessing are foundational to AI-enhanced forensic accounting. As fraud tactics evolve and datasets become more complex, the emphasis on rigorous data management, ethical data practices, and innovative preprocessing techniques will become even more critical to the field's success (Uduehe, Okoye, & Amahalu, 2024; Đukić, Pavlović, & Grdinić, 2023; Zangana, 2020, 2022).

IMPLEMENTATION FRAMEWORKS AND TOOLS

Implementing AI systems in forensic accounting involves more than selecting a single algorithm or platform. It requires a layered framework that integrates data pipelines, analytical models, ethical oversight, and domain-specific knowledge. This section outlines practical implementation models, toolkits, and the essential infrastructure required to operationalize intelligent fraud detection systems in real-world accounting environments.

Conceptual Implementation Framework

At the core of any AI-driven forensic accounting system lies a multi-stage implementation framework. Abbas and Kollwitz (2025) propose a five-tier model encompassing data acquisition, preprocessing, algorithm deployment, model training and validation, and result interpretation. Similarly, Vijayalakshmi and Jeevan (2024) stress the importance of aligning these layers with forensic accounting principles such as evidence preservation, audit trail maintenance, and compliance monitoring.

The typical architecture involves:

- **Data Ingestion Layer**: Integrates diverse sources (e.g., ERP systems, cloud accounting software, audit logs, communications data).

- **Processing and Storage Layer**: Includes tools for cleaning, structuring, and storing data in warehouses or lakes (Zangana, 2018; Zangana, 2020).
- **Analytics Layer**: Implements statistical and machine learning models (Zheng, Tan, Jiang, & Wang, 2025; Mazloum, Mazloum, & Saleh, 2025).
- **Visualization and Reporting Layer**: Enables forensic accountants to interpret AI findings through dashboards and explainable AI interfaces (Zayed et al., 2024).

AI Tools and Platforms

Numerous AI tools and platforms have been developed to support fraud detection, each offering various capabilities tailored to forensic accounting applications:

- **Machine Learning Libraries**: Tools such as Scikit-learn, TensorFlow, and PyTorch enable fraud prediction via supervised and unsupervised models (Ali, Futaih, Shukur, & Al-Orfali, 2024; Mubarrat, 2024).
- **Natural Language Processing (NLP)**: Frameworks like spaCy and BERT process financial narratives, audit reports, and emails to detect linguistic markers of deception (Qatawneh, 2025; Bhagat, 2024).
- **Expert Systems and Rule-Based Engines**: Platforms like Drools are used in rule-based forensic systems to flag known patterns of fraud (Öztürk & Usul, 2020; Adejumo & Ogburie, 2025).
- **Robotic Process Automation (RPA)**: Used to automate repetitive forensic tasks such as extracting transaction logs and comparing bank statements (Ali, Khinger, Subhe, & Al-Orfali, 2024).
- **Big Data and Stream Processing Engines**: Apache Spark and Flink allow real-time fraud detection across massive financial datasets (Ramos, 2021; Daraojimba et al., 2023).

These technologies integrate into forensic audit environments through application programming interfaces (APIs), cloud-based platforms (Aman, 2024), and hybrid architectures that mix on-premise controls with scalable compute environments.

Model Deployment and Continuous Learning

Model implementation in forensic accounting goes beyond building classifiers—it involves continuous refinement and contextual retraining. Fraud patterns are dynamic, and models must evolve accordingly. As Harjuni (2024) and Simbolon et al.

(2024) argue, periodic retraining using the latest financial anomalies ensures model accuracy and reduces false positives.

Deployment strategies include:

- **Batch Processing Models**: Useful for historical fraud analysis using transactional archives.
- **Real-Time Models**: Deployed through microservices to monitor live transactions (Zangana & Abdulazeez, 2023).
- **Ensemble Systems**: Combine decision trees, neural networks, and clustering models to improve fraud detection coverage (Zangana, 2025; Zheng et al., 2025).

Data Infrastructure and Security Integration

The successful implementation of AI in forensic accounting also demands a robust and secure IT infrastructure. According to Matar (2023) and Haddad et al. (2024), secure storage, encrypted communication, and cyber resilience must be embedded from the ground up. Insider threat monitoring (Zangana, Mohammed, & Husain, 2025) and anomaly-based intrusion detection systems should complement forensic models, creating a comprehensive risk management ecosystem.

Zangana and Mustafa (2024a, 2024b) recommend denoising algorithms and data sanitization techniques to improve data quality during ingestion. Likewise, ethical data governance frameworks are essential to ensure compliance with regional data protection laws (Okonta & Nnamdi, 2025; Al-Raggad et al., 2025).

Explainability, Ethics, and Human Oversight

One major limitation in AI-driven fraud detection systems is the "black box" problem. Forensic accountants must be able to explain and defend algorithmic outputs in legal proceedings. Abbas and Kollwitz (2025) emphasize the integration of Explainable AI (XAI) modules that reveal decision pathways, weighting of features, and logic behind flags. This aligns with forensic standards and supports judicial admissibility.

Additionally, Bhagat (2024) and Uduehe, Okoye, and Amahalu (2024) highlight the importance of ethical audits—AI systems must be regularly assessed for bias, transparency, and fairness. An ethics board or advisory committee can provide oversight to avoid algorithmic discrimination, especially when sensitive behavioral data is processed.

Change Management and Organizational Readiness

Technological implementation must be coupled with organizational change. Zangana et al. (2024) discuss change management strategies in tech adoption, emphasizing staff training, process redesign, and cross-functional collaboration. Forensic teams must understand the toolsets and their limitations to leverage AI effectively.

Training modules should be built into platforms to simulate fraud scenarios and teach forensic professionals how to interpret AI outputs (Daraojimba et al., 2023; Elumilade et al., 2021).

Framework in Practice: A Case Template

A practical implementation could follow this structure:

Table 1. Examples of financial transactions flagged for anomalies

Stage	Tools/Technologies	Key References
Data Ingestion	ETL Pipelines, APIs	Zangana (2018); Aman (2024)
Preprocessing	OCR, NLP, Denoising	Zangana & Mustafa (2024a); Qatawneh (2025)
Modeling & Detection	ML, Deep Learning, Expert Systems	Zheng et al. (2025); Öztürk & Usul (2020)
Visualization	Tableau, Power BI, XAI Dashboards	Abbas & Kollwitz (2025); Harjuni (2024)
Monitoring & Feedback	Real-time Logging, Retraining Scripts	Mazloum et al. (2025); Bhagat (2024)

Global and Comparative Considerations

Global variability in accounting practices necessitates adaptable frameworks. Simbolon et al. (2024) highlight how implementation tools must be customized based on regional regulatory environments. Similarly, modular frameworks allow organizations to start small and scale based on maturity and risk exposure (Zangana, 2022; Đukić, Pavlović, & Grdinić, 2023).

In summary, the successful implementation of AI in forensic accounting requires a cohesive interplay of advanced tools, secure infrastructure, ethical oversight, and contextual adaptability. The synergy between forensic expertise and technological innovation ensures that fraud detection frameworks remain agile, accountable, and legally defensible in an evolving financial landscape.

CASE STUDIES AND APPLICATIONS

The practical implementation of artificial intelligence (AI) in forensic accounting has yielded transformative outcomes in fraud detection, prevention, and risk mitigation across various domains. This section examines diverse case studies and applications that showcase the power and potential of AI technologies in real-world forensic accounting contexts.

AI-Powered Fraud Detection in Banking Institutions

In Nigeria, commercial banks have adopted AI-driven forensic tools to monitor suspicious transactions, particularly those involving real-time electronic fund transfers. Uduehe, Okoye, and Amahalu (2024) highlight how supervised machine learning models enabled banks to detect internal fraud by analyzing historical and live transaction data. These tools also used natural language processing (NLP) to interpret suspicious transaction descriptions, a method also supported by Qatawneh (2025) in the context of accounting information systems.

Simbolon et al. (2024) conducted a comparative analysis showing that financial institutions in countries with centralized digital infrastructures exhibited significantly higher fraud detection rates, confirming findings by Adejumo and Ogburie (2025), who emphasize the importance of digital readiness and legal frameworks in forensic accounting.

Big Data and AI in U.S. Financial Forensics

Daraojimba et al. (2023) describe a high-profile case in the U.S. where AI-driven forensic analysis identified multimillion-dollar financial statement fraud. The AI systems utilized big data techniques to mine structured and unstructured data—ranging from emails to accounting ledgers—revealing executive-level collusion. Ramos (2021) argues for the strategic use of AI and big data in forensic accounting to facilitate proactive fraud detection.

Techniques involving clustering and pattern recognition, such as those reviewed by Zangana and Abdulazeez (2023), proved valuable in managing high-dimensional data. Similarly, Zheng et al. (2025) emphasize how integrating machine learning into financial forensics can provide predictive capabilities to detect anomalies before they escalate into full-blown fraud cases.

Figure 4 shows the overlap of major ethical and legal domains relevant to AI systems in forensic accounting, including transparency, bias mitigation, and regulatory compliance.

Figure 4. Ethical and legal dimensions of AI in forensic accounting

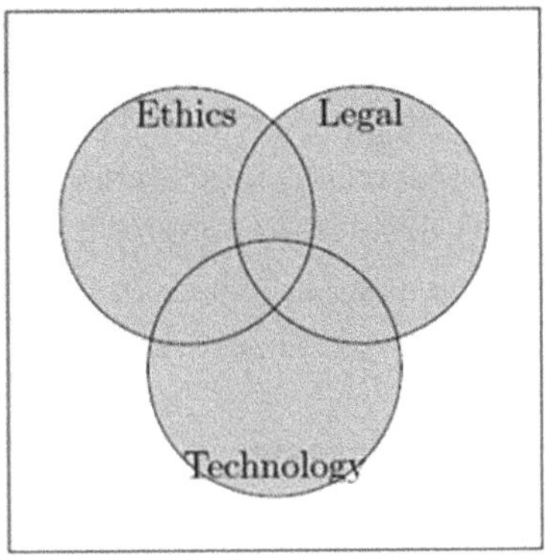

Rule-Based Expert Systems in Corporate Forensics

Öztürk and Usul (2020) documented a European corporation's deployment of a rule-based expert system to identify fraudulent invoices. This system used forensic algorithms to compare historical vendor behavior and flag inconsistencies. Ali, Khinger, Subhe, and Al-Orfali (2024) affirm that expert systems, especially when combined with AI, remain effective in scenarios where structured rule sets can identify deviations.

Ali, Futaih, Shukur, and Al-Orfali (2024) also point out that robotic process automation (RPA) tools are often layered with expert systems to streamline the extraction and processing of financial records for fraud analysis.

Autonomous AI in Dark Web Investigations

Rawat et al. (2023) explore how autonomous AI agents have been used to monitor dark web marketplaces for traces of financial fraud and money laundering. These agents, employing web scraping and cross-referencing techniques, successfully detected fraudulent financial behaviors. The use of a well-structured data warehouse to integrate this information, as proposed by Zangana (2018), greatly enhanced the ability of forensic teams to validate evidence gathered from dark web sources.

AI in Government and Regulatory Forensics

In public sector auditing, Abbas and Kollwitz (2025) detail how regulatory bodies in Germany used AI models to detect procurement fraud. These tools examined bid patterns and vendor histories, identifying collusive bidding and over-pricing. Al-Raggad et al. (2025) underscore the growing trend of ethical scrutiny and bibliometric evaluation of AI use in forensic accounting, which is crucial for maintaining public trust.

In another case, AI-based facial recognition algorithms were employed to verify pension recipients' identities in a developing country. These systems used algorithms such as those outlined by Zangana and Al-Shaikhli (2013) and refined in Zangana (2015), enabling fraud detection in social security disbursements.

Healthcare and Insurance Forensics

AI tools have shown significant potential in detecting healthcare billing fraud. In a Middle Eastern application, NLP models were used to analyze medical claims and detect fraudulent submissions based on language anomalies, as discussed by Bhagat (2024). Elumilade et al. (2021) similarly report how data-driven AI models exposed systemic fraud involving fabricated treatments and patients.

Denoising and document digitization techniques, such as those reviewed by Zangana and Mustafa (2024a, 2024b), enhanced image clarity in scanned records and facilitated better text extraction for analysis.

Cybersecurity-Integrated Financial Forensics

Cybersecurity and forensic accounting are increasingly intertwined. Matar (2023) and Zangana, Mohammed, and Husain (2025) describe systems that combine behavior-based user analytics with anomaly detection algorithms to expose insider fraud within financial institutions. These systems analyze logins, file access, and behavioral deviations, supported by real-time data compression methods (Zangana, 2025) to ensure efficiency in data-heavy environments.

AI-Enhanced Forensic Education and Simulation Platforms

Aman (2024) and Mazloum, Mazloum, and Saleh (2025) highlight academic initiatives to create AI-enhanced training simulators for forensic accountants. These platforms include simulated fraud scenarios where students interact with AI-generated data and audit trails. Built using interactive video systems (Zangana, 2022), such educational tools strengthen interpretative skills and ethical decision-making.

Industry-Wide Deployment and Change Management

Implementing AI-based forensic tools across sectors requires structured change management. Zangana et al. (2024) emphasize the importance of organizational readiness, policy adaptation, and user training. Mobile service integration (Zangana, 2020) and community-based risk mitigation platforms (Zangana, 2022) are examples of technological adaptations that facilitate AI adoption.

Global Perspectives and Lessons Learned

The reviewed cases provide the following insights:\n

- Data integration is essential for success in AI-based forensic applications (Zheng et al., 2025; Abbas & Kollwitz, 2025).\n
- Human oversight and ethics are irreplaceable, as emphasized by Okonta and Nnamdi (2025) and Haddad et al. (2024).\n
- Combining traditional and advanced techniques, such as expert systems and neural networks (Ali et al., 2024; Bhagat, 2024), yields more robust fraud detection outcomes.\n
- Cultural and institutional contexts must inform system design and deployment (Al-Raggad et al., 2025; Simbolon et al., 2024).\n

These global applications demonstrate the maturity and promise of AI in forensic accounting—provided it is implemented ethically, responsibly, and with appropriate stakeholder involvement.

CHALLENGES AND ETHICAL CONSIDERATIONS

As artificial intelligence (AI) continues to reshape forensic accounting, its integration is accompanied by multifaceted challenges and ethical dilemmas. These issues range from algorithmic bias and data privacy to legal accountability, professional skepticism, interpretability, and the readiness of institutions to adopt emerging technologies. Understanding these challenges is critical for responsibly deploying AI in forensic investigations.

Algorithmic Bias and Explainability

One of the foremost concerns is the opacity of machine learning algorithms. Many AI systems, particularly deep learning models, operate as "black boxes," making it difficult for forensic professionals to interpret how decisions are reached (Bhagat, 2024; Zheng et al., 2025). This lack of explainability complicates the presentation of AI-generated evidence in court, raising questions about admissibility and accountability.

Additionally, algorithmic bias—whether due to biased training data or flawed model assumptions—can lead to incorrect or discriminatory outcomes (Qatawneh, 2025). As forensic decisions can directly impact individuals' livelihoods and reputations, mitigating such biases is not only a technical issue but a profound ethical obligation (Zayed et al., 2024; Abbas & Kollwitz, 2025).

Data Privacy and Security

AI systems require access to massive datasets, including sensitive financial records, personal information, and private communications. The handling of such data must adhere to strict privacy standards and regulations (Aman, 2024). Matar (2023) and Zangana, Mohammed, and Husain (2025) emphasize the interrelation between cybersecurity and forensic accounting, noting that breaches can compromise investigations and expose victims to further harm.

In dark web investigations, where autonomous AI agents collect data from illicit sources (Rawat et al., 2023), the ethical handling of illegally obtained data presents a grey area that must be navigated cautiously.

Regulatory and Legal Ambiguities

The legal landscape surrounding AI in forensic accounting is still evolving. Laws and professional standards often lag behind technological advancements, leading to uncertainty in how AI-generated findings are treated by courts and regulators (Al-Raggad et al., 2025; Daraojimba et al., 2023).

For instance, Öztürk and Usul (2020) argue that rule-based expert systems must be designed in alignment with existing accounting standards to maintain legal defensibility. However, the integration of more adaptive AI models, such as unsupervised anomaly detection, challenges the deterministic nature of traditional forensic methods (Ali et al., 2024a; 2024b).

Professional Skepticism and Over-Reliance on AI

AI is a tool—not a replacement—for human expertise. Over-reliance on AI can erode professional skepticism, which remains a cornerstone of forensic auditing

(Harjuni, 2024). Forensic accountants must remain vigilant, interpreting AI outputs within a broader investigative context.

Okonta and Nnamdi (2025) caution against assuming technological infallibility, particularly in regions where AI literacy remains low. They stress that forensic professionals must be trained not just in data analysis but also in understanding AI's strengths and limitations.

Institutional Readiness and Digital Divide

Adopting AI tools requires a significant level of technological readiness, which varies across institutions and countries. Simbolon et al. (2024) observe disparities in AI adoption between developed and developing nations, highlighting challenges such as limited infrastructure, inadequate funding, and skill shortages.

Adejumo and Ogburie (2025) identify organizational resistance to change as a barrier, especially in traditional firms. Implementing AI also requires re-engineering workflows and fostering a culture that embraces innovation (Zangana et al., 2024).

Ethical Use of Big Data and Automation

Big data offers unprecedented insights but also raises ethical concerns about consent, surveillance, and data retention (Ramos, 2021). Forensic investigations using AI must strike a balance between effective fraud detection and respect for individual rights (Elumilade et al., 2021).

Moreover, automation may lead to job displacement or changes in job roles within auditing and accounting. While AI can handle repetitive tasks, the human element remains vital in judgment-based decisions (Mazloum et al., 2025; Mubarrat, 2024).

Transparency and Accountability in System Design

Transparent system design is crucial for ethical deployment. Developers must document model architecture, training processes, and known limitations. This aligns with the call by Haddad et al. (2024) for forensic systems to be auditable and accountable, particularly when deployed by government or public institutions.

Zangana and Mustafa (2024a, 2024b) further recommend incorporating denoising and preprocessing algorithms that do not obscure raw data during fraud analysis, ensuring that evidence remains verifiable.

Cultural and Contextual Sensitivity

Forensic accounting does not operate in a vacuum; it is influenced by local laws, cultural norms, and economic systems. Abbas and Kollwitz (2025) and Zangana (2021) highlight the importance of adapting AI models to specific legal environments to avoid misinterpretation.

This also extends to image and facial recognition applications, such as those developed by Zangana and Al-Shaikhli (2013) and Zangana (2015), where ethical concerns about surveillance and misidentification must be addressed through rigorous validation and oversight.

Ethical Training and Capacity Building

The growing use of AI in forensic accounting necessitates a corresponding evolution in ethics education and professional training. Aman (2024) and Vijayalakshmi and Jeevan (2024) advocate for AI-integrated curricula that emphasize ethical reasoning and responsible data use.

Simulations and e-learning platforms (Zangana, 2022) are increasingly used to expose forensic professionals to real-world dilemmas, encouraging critical thinking about automation, bias, and accountability.

Long-Term Sustainability and Ethical Innovation

Ethical AI in forensic accounting must be viewed through the lens of sustainability and responsible innovation. This means anticipating future challenges, including the misuse of AI for generating fake audit trails or deepfake evidence (Bhagat, 2024; Zangana, 2017a, 2017b, 2019a, 2019b).

As new tools like real-time facial detection, watermarking, and autonomous auditing systems emerge (Zangana, 2017c; Zangana & Abdulazeez, 2023), ethical guidelines must evolve in parallel to maintain trust and transparency in forensic practices.

Conclusion of Section

Addressing these challenges and ethical considerations is essential for AI to truly benefit forensic accounting without eroding trust, fairness, or professional integrity. Future systems must be designed not only for accuracy and efficiency but also with transparency, accountability, and ethical resilience at their core.

FUTURE TRENDS AND RESEARCH DIRECTIONS

As forensic accounting continues to evolve in the digital era, artificial intelligence (AI) is poised to play a transformative role in redefining its scope, accuracy, and relevance. The integration of intelligent systems opens avenues for enhancing fraud detection, predictive analytics, and real-time monitoring, but it also calls for ongoing research and policy refinement. This section outlines key future trends and research directions that are expected to shape the field in the coming years.

Hyperautomation and Intelligent Agents

The next wave in forensic accounting will likely involve hyperautomation—a combination of AI, robotic process automation (RPA), and advanced analytics. Autonomous agents, capable of continuously monitoring transactional environments and flagging irregularities without human intervention, are being refined for large-scale deployments (Rawat et al., 2023; Zangana, 2025).

These agents can navigate complex datasets such as those found on the dark web, cryptocurrency exchanges, or offshore shell networks, offering scalable fraud intelligence systems. However, future research must address their ethical use, particularly in data collection, surveillance, and cross-border investigations.

AI-Driven Predictive Modeling and Behavioral Analytics

Emerging research is focusing on integrating predictive behavioral modeling into forensic audits, where AI systems learn user spending habits and deviations (Zheng et al., 2025; Abbas & Kollwitz, 2025). Machine learning algorithms are being trained not only on historical fraud patterns but also on real-time human behavior indicators—such as decision latency, location anomalies, and device fingerprints.

This shift from reactive to proactive fraud prevention signals a major advancement. However, the models must be trained on diverse, context-sensitive data to avoid overfitting and ensure generalizability (Ali et al., 2024a; Mubarrat, 2024).

Integration of NLP and Unstructured Data Mining

The ability to extract insights from unstructured data—emails, audit memos, contracts, and social media—is a major frontier in forensic accounting. Natural Language Processing (NLP) will enable forensic accountants to mine text-based anomalies that would otherwise be missed (Qatawneh, 2025; Vijayalakshmi & Jeevan, 2024).

For instance, future systems could automatically flag emotionally charged language in internal communications or discrepancies between written contracts and ledger entries. This enhances the depth of forensic inquiry, especially in white-collar crime and insider threat scenarios (Zangana, Mohammed, & Husain, 2025).

Ethical AI Design and Explainability Standards

One critical research direction involves developing explainable AI (XAI) frameworks tailored for forensic applications. As AI becomes central to court-admissible findings, ensuring model transparency and traceability is imperative (Zheng et al., 2025; Bhagat, 2024).

Researchers are exploring hybrid models that blend rule-based systems (Öztürk & Usul, 2020) with deep learning to preserve both accuracy and interpretability. A growing focus is also placed on mitigating bias, ensuring accountability, and setting international standards for ethical AI governance (Zayed et al., 2024; Daraojimba et al., 2023).

Cross-Border Forensic Collaboration and Data Standardization

Globalization of finance necessitates cross-border AI-enabled forensic cooperation. There is a growing need for unified data taxonomies, fraud ontologies, and inter-agency protocols to allow for real-time fraud information exchange between regulatory bodies and financial institutions (Simbolon et al., 2024; Uduehe et al., 2024).

Future research must develop blockchain-based data sharing platforms that ensure data provenance and integrity across jurisdictions while complying with regional privacy laws.

Adoption in Emerging Economies and Capacity Building

While developed countries lead AI integration in forensic work, developing economies are slowly closing the gap through cloud-based tools, mobile forensic platforms, and remote audit technologies (Adejumo & Ogburie, 2025; Okonta & Nnamdi, 2025).

Scholars stress the need for tailored solutions that address infrastructure challenges and support capacity building via AI-focused forensic training and education (Aman, 2024; Zangana, 2022).

Research must also explore low-cost, explainable AI systems adapted to local regulatory and cultural contexts, ensuring equitable access and ethical deployment across socio-economic divides (Zangana, 2021; 2022).

Augmented Reality and Immersive Audit Environments

Futuristic trends also point to the potential integration of **augmented and virtual reality (AR/VR)** in forensic education and fieldwork. These technologies could simulate financial crime scenarios or enable virtual walkthroughs of digital evidence environments, enhancing decision-making and training outcomes (Zangana, 2022).

Research in this space remains nascent, but its pedagogical and investigative potential merits further exploration, especially in academic and high-complexity environments.

Advanced Image and Video Forensics

With digital fraud increasingly involving deepfakes and image manipulation, future systems must integrate AI-powered image denoising, object recognition, and watermark verification techniques (Zangana & Mustafa, 2024a, 2024b; Zangana & Al-Shaikhli, 2013).

These tools are essential for verifying the authenticity of visual evidence submitted in financial litigation or whistleblower cases. Recent innovations in parallel processing and facial recognition (Zangana, 2015; 2025) open up new avenues for integrating multimedia forensics with traditional accounting audits.

Big Data Governance and Sustainable Forensics

AI-driven forensic accounting will increasingly rely on big data ecosystems that process large, real-time datasets across financial networks. Governance of such systems requires robust ethical frameworks for data ownership, privacy, and sustainability (Ramos, 2021; Elumilade et al., 2021).

Research must examine the lifecycle of forensic data, from collection to archival, ensuring systems are both scalable and ethically sound. This also includes exploring green AI solutions to reduce the environmental footprint of large-scale computational forensic tools (Zangana, 2019; Zangana et al., 2024).

Human-AI Collaboration and Skill Augmentation

As AI takes on routine forensic tasks, the role of human experts will evolve toward supervision, interpretation, and strategic oversight (Harjuni, 2024; Haddad et al., 2024). The next generation of forensic accountants will need hybrid skills in accounting, data science, legal compliance, and machine learning.

Educational institutions are responding by embedding AI ethics, programming, and analytics into forensic accounting curricula (Ali et al., 2024b; Mazloum et al., 2025), while employers invest in continuous reskilling.

Future research should evaluate the effectiveness of these training programs and explore new human-AI collaboration models that maximize complementary strengths.

Summary of Section

The future of AI in forensic accounting lies in creating intelligent, ethical, and globally accessible systems that not only detect fraud but also anticipate it. As researchers and practitioners converge, the focus must shift from merely adopting technology to responsibly co-evolving with it—ensuring that forensic accounting remains a pillar of financial integrity in the digital age.

CONCLUSION

Forensic accounting stands at a pivotal crossroads where the rapid advancement of artificial intelligence and data analytics is reshaping traditional practices. The integration of AI-driven tools, machine learning models, and big data analytics has significantly enhanced the ability to detect, prevent, and investigate financial fraud with greater speed and accuracy. This technological evolution not only improves efficiency but also expands the scope of forensic accounting to encompass complex, multi-dimensional fraud schemes that were previously difficult to uncover.

However, as this field advances, it faces important challenges, including ethical considerations, the need for explainability and transparency in AI models, data privacy concerns, and the requirement for robust cross-border collaboration. Addressing these issues is critical to maintaining trust in forensic processes and ensuring that technological innovations are implemented responsibly and effectively.

Looking forward, future research and development must prioritize the creation of explainable, fair, and adaptable AI systems that complement the expertise of human forensic accountants rather than replace it. Furthermore, efforts to build capacity in emerging economies and to establish global standards for forensic data management and AI governance will be essential in creating a more inclusive and resilient financial ecosystem.

Ultimately, the fusion of human judgment with intelligent technologies promises a new era of forensic accounting—one where fraud prevention is proactive, investigative methods are more insightful, and financial integrity is safeguarded with unprecedented rigor. This ongoing transformation underscores the vital role of continued innovation, interdisciplinary collaboration, and ethical stewardship in advancing forensic accounting in the digital age.

REFERENCES

Abbas, A., & Kollwitz, E. (2025). *Forensic Accounting in the Digital Era: Leveraging AI for Fraud Detection and Risk Management*. ResearchGate. DOI:DOI: 10.13140/RG.2.2.34900.10883

Adejumo, A. P., & Ogburie, C. P.Adetunji Paul AdejumoChinonso Peter Ogburie. (2025). Forensic accounting in financial fraud detection: Trends and challenges. *International Journal of Science and Research Archive*, *14*(3), 1219–1232. DOI: 10.30574/ijsra.2025.14.3.0815

Al-Raggad, M., Albalawee, N., Al-Mahasneh, A., Abu Huson, Y., & Albajaly, A. (2025). Unveiling financial crimes: Advancing forensic accounting practices and ethical integrity through bibliometric insights. *Safer Communities*, *24*(3), 244–264. DOI: 10.1108/SC-11-2024-0069

Ali, A. M., Futaih, R. F., Shukur, M., & Al-Orfali, A. K. (2024). Forensic Accounting and Fraud Detection Emerging Trends and Techniques. *Journal of Ecohumanism*, *3*(5), 525–542. DOI: 10.62754/joe.v3i5.3921

Ali, A. M., Khinger, I. K., Subhe, A., & Al-Orfali, A. K. (2024). Forensic Accounting Techniques in Detecting Frauds. *Journal of Ecohumanism*, *3*(5), 543–558. DOI: 10.62754/joe.v3i5.3922

Aman, Q. U. I. S. E. R. (2024). From data to discovery: The impact of technology on forensic accounting. *Ile Journal of Law and Forensic Science*, *2*(1), 1–13.

Bhagat, N. (2024). Artificial intelligence challenges and its impact on detection and prevention of financial statement fraud: A theoretical study. In *Demystifying the Dark Side of AI in Business* (pp. 60–80). IGI Global Scientific Publishing.

Daraojimba, R. E., Farayola, O. A., Olatoye, F. M. O., Mhlongo, N., & Oke, T. T. L. (2023). Forensic accounting in the digital age: a US perspective: scrutinizing methods and challenges in digital financial fraud prevention. *Finance & Accounting Research Journal*, *5*(11), 342–360. DOI: 10.51594/farj.v5i11.614

. Đukić, T., Pavlović, M., & Grdinić, V. (2023). Uncovering Financial Fraud: The Vital Role of Forensic Accounting and Auditing in Modern Business Practice. *Economic Themes, 61*(3).

Elumilade, O. O., Ogundeji, I. A., Achumie, G. O., Omokhoa, H. E., & Omowole, B. M. (2021). Enhancing fraud detection and forensic auditing through data-driven techniques for financial integrity and security. *Journal of Advanced Education and Sciences*, *1*(2), 55–63. DOI: 10.54660/.JAES.2021.1.2.55-63

Haddad, H. O. S. S. A. M., Alharasis, E. E., Fraij, J., & Al-Ramahi, N. M. (2024). How do innovative improvements in forensic accounting and its related technologies sweeten fraud investigation and prevention. *WSEAS Transactions on Business and Economics*, *21*, 1115–1141. DOI: 10.37394/23207.2024.21.93

Harjuni, J. (2024). The role of forensic accounting in fraud detection and prevention in financial institutions. *Tamansiswa Accounting Journal International*, *15*(1), 151–159.

Matar, D. O. (2023). *Forensic accounting and Cybersecurity examine their interrelation in the detection and Prevention of financial fraud*. American Academic & Scholarly Research Journal.

Mazloum, H., Mazloum, N., & Saleh, A. M. (2025). FORENSIC AUDIT: ENHANCING CERTIFIED PUBLIC ACCOUNTANT USING ARTIFICIAL INTELLIGENCE TECHNIQUES. *BAU Journal-Science and Technology*, *6*(2), 10. DOI: 10.54729/2959-331X.1128

Mubarrat, A. A. (2024). of the Research: Role of Artificial Intelligence and Big Data in Modern Forensic Accountancy. *Available at SSRN* 5078259.

Okonta, C. N., & Nnamdi, C. A. (2025). Forensic Investigation and Fraud Detection in Nigeria: Leveraging on Artificial Intelligence. *Review of Ethics in Sustainable Finance and Accounting*, *1*(1), 31–38. DOI: 10.70865/jiatis.v2i1.80

Öztürk, M. S., & Usul, H. (2020). Detection of accounting frauds using the rule-based expert systems within the scope of forensic accounting. In *Contemporary issues in audit management and forensic accounting* (pp. 155–171). Emerald Publishing Limited. DOI: 10.1108/S1569-375920200000102013

Qatawneh, A. M. (2025). The role of artificial intelligence in auditing and fraud detection in accounting information systems: Moderating role of natural language processing. *The International Journal of Organizational Analysis*, *33*(6), 1391–1409. DOI: 10.1108/IJOA-03-2024-4389

. Ramos, J. R. M. (2021). The use of Big Data and Artificial Intelligence: to prevent and detect fraud. *Artificial intelligence in the economic sector: prevention and responsibility*, 85-115.

Rawat, R., Oki, O., Chakrawarti, R. K., Adekunle, T. S., Lukose, J. M., & Ajagbe, S. A. (2023). Autonomous artificial intelligence systems for fraud detection and forensics in dark web environments. *Informatica (Vilnius)*, *47*(9).

Simbolon, R., Adriana, N., Rustam, A., Sulistyowati, N. W., & Rewa, K. A. (2024). The Impact of Forensic Accounting on Financial Fraud Prevention: A Comparative Analysis Across Countries. *The Journal of Academic Science, 1*(8), 1074–1084. DOI: 10.59613/m6jrt421

Uduehe, E. M., Okoye, E. I., & Amahalu, N. N. (2024). Forensic accounting techniques and fraud management of commercial banks in Awka-South Anambra State. *Journal of Global Accounting, 10*(2), 307–346.

. Vijayalakshmi, D., & Jeevan, J. (2024). Forensic Accounting: Uncovering Fraud with Advanced Analytics. *Library of Progress-Library Science, Information Technology & Computer, 44*(3).

. Zangana, H. M. (2015). A New Skin Color Based Face Detection Algorithm by Combining Three Color Model Algorithms. *IOSR J. Comput. Eng, 17*, 06-125.

. Zangana, H. M. (2017). A new algorithm for shape detection. *IOSR Journal of Computer Engineering (IOSR-JCE), 19*(3), 71-76.

Zangana, H. M. (2017). Library Data Quality Maturity (IIUM as a Case Study). *IOSR Journal of Computer Engineering, 19*(March), 29. DOI: 10.9790/0661-1902033844

Zangana, H. M. (2017). Watermarking System Using LSB. *IOSR Journal of Computer Engineering, 19*(3), 75–79. DOI: 10.9790/0661-1903027579

Zangana, H. M. (2018). Design an information management system for a pharmacy. *International Journal of Advanced Research in Computer and Communication Engineering, 7*(10), 52–55. DOI: 10.17148/IJARCCE.2018.71012

. Zangana, H. M. (2018). Developing Data Warehouse for Student Information System (IIUM as a Case Study). *International Organization of Scientific Research, 20*(1), 09-14.

Zangana, H. M. (2018). Implementing a System for Recognizing Optical Characters. *International Journal of Advanced Research in Computer and Communication Engineering, 7*(10), 56–60. DOI: 10.17148/IJARCCE.2018.71013

Zangana, H. M. (2019). Issues of Data Management in the Library: A Case Study. *International Journal on Computer Science and Engineering, 7*(10), 159–163. DOI: 10.26438/ijcse/v7i10.159163

. Zangana, H. M. (2019). ITD Data Quality Maturity (A Case Study). *International Journal Of Engineering And Computer Science, 8*(10).

Zangana, H. M. (2020). Mobile Device Integration in IIUM Service. *International Journal (Toronto, Ont.), 8*(5).

Zangana, H. M. (2021). The Global Finical Crisis from an Islamic Point Of View. *Qubahan Academic Journal*, *1*(2), 55–59. DOI: 10.48161/qaj.v1n2a39

Zangana, H. M. (2022). Creating a Community-Based Disaster Management System. *Academic Journal of Nawroz University*, *11*(4), 234–244. DOI: 10.25007/ajnu.v11n4a1485

Zangana, H. M. (2022). Implementing New Interactive Video Learning System for IIUM. *Academic Journal of Nawroz University*, *11*(2), 23–29. DOI: 10.25007/ajnu.v11n2a1281

. Zangana, H. M. (2022). Improving The Web Services for Remittance Company: Express Remit as a Case Study. *Academic Journal of Nawroz University (AJNU)*, *11*(3).

Zangana, H. M. (2025). Design and Implementation of a Novel Parallel Algorithm for Efficient Image Compression in High-Performance Computing. *EAI Endorsed Transactions on AI and Robotics*, *4*. Advance online publication. DOI: 10.4108/airo.7832

Zangana, H. M., & Abdulazeez, A. M. (2023). Developed Clustering Algorithms for Engineering Applications: A Review. *International Journal of Informatics* [IN-JIISCOM]. *Information System and Computer Engineering*, *4*(2), 147–169.

Zangana, H. M., & Al-Shaikhli, I. F. (2013). A new algorithm for human face detection using skin color tone. *IOSR Journal of Computer Engineering*, *11*(6), 31–38. DOI: 10.9790/0661-1163138

Zangana, H. M., Bazeed, S. M. S., Ali, N. Y., & Abdullah, D. T. (2024). Navigating Project Change: A Comprehensive Review of Change Management Strategies and Practices. *Indonesian Journal of Education and Social Sciences*, *3*(2), 166–179. DOI: 10.56916/ijess.v3i2.735

Zangana, H. M., Mohammed, H. S., & Husain, M. M. (2025). Addressing insider threats: The human factor in cybersecurity for financial institutions. *Journal of Innovation Information Technology and Application*, *7*(1), 88–96. DOI: 10.35970/jinita.v7i1.2686

Zangana, H. M., & Mustafa, F. M. (2024). From Classical to Deep Learning: A Systematic Review of Image Denoising Techniques. *Jurnal Ilmiah Computer Science*, *3*(1), 50–65. DOI: 10.58602/jics.v3i1.36

Zangana, H. M., & Mustafa, F. M. (2024). Review of Hybrid Denoising Approaches in Face Recognition: Bridging Wavelet Transform and Deep Learning. *The Indonesian Journal of Computer Science*, *13*(4). Advance online publication. DOI: 10.33022/ijcs.v13i4.4209

Zangana, H. M., & Mustafa, F. M. (2024). Surveying the Landscape: A Comprehensive Review of Object Detection Algorithms and Advancements. *Jurnal Ilmiah Computer Science*, *3*(1), 1–15. DOI: 10.58602/jics.v3i1.29

Zayed, L. M. M., Nour, M. I., Al Attar, K., Almubaideen, H., & Abdelaziz, G. A. M. (2024). Role of artificial intelligence (AI) in accounting information systems in detecting fraud. In *Artificial Intelligence and Economic Sustainability in the Era of Industrial Revolution 5.0* (pp. 397–409). Springer Nature Switzerland. DOI: 10.1007/978-3-031-56586-1_30

Zheng, W., Tan, Y., Jiang, B., & Wang, J. (2025). Integrating Machine Learning into Financial Forensics for Smarter Fraud Prevention. *Technology and Investment*, *16*(3), 79–90. DOI: 10.4236/ti.2025.163006

Chapter 6

Deep Learning in Malware Classification and Behavior Analysis

Derek Mohammed
https://orcid.org/0009-0002-8573-4363
Saint Leo University, USA

Helen MacLennan
https://orcid.org/0000-0002-0795-5008
Lindsey Wilson University, USA

ABSTRACT

The rapid evolution of malware poses significant challenges for traditional signature-based detection methods, necessitating more intelligent and adaptive approaches. Deep learning, a subset of artificial intelligence, has emerged as a powerful tool in malware classification and behavior analysis. This chapter explores how deep learning techniques, such as convolutional neural networks (CNNs), recurrent neural networks (RNNs), and transformers, are applied to detect, classify, and understand malware in real-time. We discuss various input representations including raw binaries, opcode sequences, and API call graphs, and analyze their impact on model performance. Emphasis is placed on the advantages of deep learning over classical machine learning in handling obfuscated and polymorphic malware. Furthermore, we examine challenges such as dataset imbalance, adversarial attacks, and explainability, and propose possible future directions to improve robustness and transparency in AI-driven malware analysis.

DOI: 10.4018/979-8-3373-6536-7.ch006

INTRODUCTION

The exponential growth of cyber threats has necessitated an evolution in cybersecurity paradigms, with artificial intelligence (AI), and more specifically, large language models (LLMs), emerging as game-changing technologies in this domain. LLMs have demonstrated a profound capability to understand, generate, and manipulate natural language, allowing them to analyze complex threat intelligence, detect vulnerabilities, and even forecast cyberattacks with remarkable precision (Xu et al., 2024; Hasanov et al., 2024). As the cybersecurity landscape grows increasingly sophisticated and adversarial, traditional signature-based or rule-based mechanisms are no longer sufficient (Jones et al., 2023; Wright et al., 2012). Consequently, the integration of LLMs into cyber defense systems has initiated a paradigm shift, ushering in the era of cognitive and autonomous threat intelligence systems (Zangana & Omar, 2025; Ferrag et al., 2024).

The Role and Evolution of LLMs in Cybersecurity

The foundational architecture of LLMs, including models such as BERT, GPT, and T5, has rapidly evolved from general-purpose NLP tools to domain-specific models tailored for cybersecurity (AlQenaei, 2024; Aghaei et al., 2022). These models are capable of contextualizing threats, summarizing attack patterns, and generating actionable insights with minimal human supervision (Ghazal et al., 2024; Gholami & Omar, 2023). For instance, the development of SecureBERT (Aghaei et al., 2022) and SecLM (Asoronye et al., 2024) exemplifies how LLMs are being fine-tuned for tasks like malware detection, vulnerability classification, and intrusion prediction.

While general LLMs have proven effective in textual analysis, emerging security-specific models such as those developed by Thandi (2024) and Ferrag et al. (2023) introduce enhanced domain adaptation for privacy-preserving applications, particularly in the context of IoT/IIoT environments. These tailored models address core limitations of mainstream LLMs, including data bias, performance inefficiency on sparse cybersecurity data, and the high resource demand associated with inference and training (Bryce et al., 2024; Gholami & Omar, 2024).

Applications and Capabilities in Threat Intelligence

LLMs are revolutionizing cyber threat intelligence (CTI) by enabling dynamic analysis, threat attribution, and anomaly detection with improved accuracy and speed (Chen et al., 2024; Sarker, 2024). They are especially useful in parsing unstructured data from threat reports, dark web forums, and log files to identify hidden patterns and adversarial behaviors (Hamza & Omar, 2013; Zangana et al., 2024). Their ability to engage in zero-shot and few-shot learning allows LLMs to generalize across unseen threats, making them suitable for the detection of zero-day exploits (Jones & Omar, 2024; Manoharan & Sarker, 2023).

Moreover, cybersecurity use cases are expanding to include vulnerability detection, phishing email analysis, firewall optimization, and secure coding practices—all enhanced by LLMs' contextual reasoning and generative power (Mohammed et al., 2018; Taghavi & Feyzi, 2024; Zangana, 2024). In particular, hybrid frameworks that combine LLMs with other deep learning techniques have shown success in object detection and anomaly classification tasks (Zangana, Mustafa & Omar, 2024).

Challenges and Considerations

Despite their promise, LLMs face notable challenges when applied to cybersecurity. These include adversarial manipulation, explainability issues, data privacy concerns, and deployment costs (Alturkistani & Chuprat, 2024; Gupta et al., 2024). The black-box nature of LLMs can hinder forensic analysis and accountability in decision-making, prompting the need for Explainable AI (XAI) and interpretable ML techniques (Ghazal et al., 2024; Ferrag et al., 2024). Additionally, the synthetic generation of training data, while useful for enhancing model generalization, raises concerns about fidelity and representativeness (Gholami & Omar, 2023; Zangana & Mustafa, 2024).

Another emerging concern is the dual-use nature of LLMs. While they enhance defenses, they may also be exploited by malicious actors to generate convincing phishing messages, obfuscate malware, or bypass conventional detection systems (Omar, 2022; Santos et al., 2024). Therefore, safeguarding these models and implementing robust governance frameworks are essential to prevent misuse (Huff et al., 2023; Liu, 2024).

The Future: From Automation to Intelligence

As the cybersecurity field enters the era of quantum computing, the synergy between LLMs and quantum-aware security frameworks is expected to intensify (Zangana & Omar, 2025). These integrations could redefine CTI, allowing for real-time adaptive responses to complex threats in hyper-connected environments (Zangana, Mustafa & Li, 2025; Pleshakova et al., 2024). Additionally, there is a growing interest in lightweight and energy-efficient LLM architectures that can be deployed on edge devices without compromising accuracy (Ferrag et al., 2024; Lestable & Thandi, 2024).

Scholars such as Omar (2021, 2024) and Zangana (2024) have emphasized the importance of integrating AI and LLMs into digital forensics, intrusion detection systems, and cyber training platforms. This convergence marks a shift from reactive cybersecurity measures toward proactive and intelligent defense ecosystems (Omar & Zangana, 2025; Kasri et al., 2025).

BACKGROUND AND LITERATURE REVIEW

The rise of **Large Language Models (LLMs)** has initiated a transformative shift in the field of cybersecurity, offering new paradigms for detection, defense, and proactive intelligence. This literature review explores the evolution of LLMs in the context of cybersecurity, from foundational models to specialized domain-specific architectures, and highlights both their capabilities and limitations.

Evolution and Architecture of LLMs

The foundation of LLMs lies in the success of transformer-based models such as BERT and GPT. Recent studies like AlQenaei (2024) and Liu (2024) document the architectural optimization trends that have led to more efficient, scalable, and domain-adaptive models. Ferrag et al. (2024) further categorize these developments into general-purpose models and security-focused variants, arguing that tailored LLMs demonstrate superior performance in cybersecurity contexts.

Bryce et al. (2024) and Hasanov et al. (2024) provide comprehensive surveys, tracing the application of LLMs across various cybersecurity domains. They highlight the dynamic interaction between LLM development and security trends, showing how evolving threats necessitate adaptive language modeling techniques.

Domain-Specific Language Models in Cybersecurity

A significant research trajectory focuses on developing LLMs specifically tuned for cybersecurity. Aghaei et al. (2022) introduced SecureBERT, a domain-specific model trained on security corpora, showing improved performance in threat classification tasks. Similarly, Asoronye et al. (2024) developed SecLM, which employs specialized embeddings and security ontology integration.

Zangana and Omar (2025) emphasize the growing need for context-aware models, especially in tasks like software vulnerability detection. Their collaborative work across several publications (Zangana & Omar, 2025; Zangana et al., 2024) underscores the effectiveness of tailored LLMs such as GPT-2-enhanced architectures and hybrid detection methods.

Applications in Cyber Threat Detection and Prediction

LLMs are increasingly deployed for threat detection, malware analysis, and intrusion prevention. Motlagh et al. (2024) detail how transformer-based architectures have revolutionized anomaly detection systems. Jones and Omar (2024) propose the GEADD method for zero-day attack detection, achieving superior results compared to traditional heuristics.

Chen et al. (2024), Xu et al. (2024), and Sarker (2024) all underscore the value of LLMs in dynamic threat landscapes, where the ability to contextualize and adapt is paramount. Moreover, Ferrag et al. (2023; 2024), along with Lestable and Thandi (2024), propose lightweight and privacy-preserving models for IoT/IIoT networks, addressing performance and data sensitivity simultaneously.

Integration with Cyber Threat Intelligence (CTI)

CTI platforms benefit significantly from the integration of LLMs, which enhance data enrichment, indicator correlation, and decision-making. Alturkistani and Chuprat (2024), along with Kasri et al. (2025), explore this integration, demonstrating improved accuracy and timeliness of CTI outputs.

Zangana, Mustafa, and Li (2025) discuss how natural language understanding enhances CTI by enabling automated threat interpretation. Their work builds upon earlier contributions that explore NLP in threat intelligence (Zangana et al., 2024; Omar et al., 2024).

Challenges and Limitations

Despite their promise, LLMs face challenges including **synthetic data reliance** (Gholami & Omar, 2023), **model interpretability** (Ghazal et al., 2024), **computational overhead** (Gupta et al., 2024), and **adversarial vulnerabilities** (Omar, 2024a). Researchers like Idelhaj et al. (2024) and Hamza and Omar (2013) further caution that LLMs can be targets for poisoning and exploitation if not securely trained and deployed.

Zangana and Omar (2025) also highlight **quantum-era challenges**, proposing the development of quantum-aware LLMs to future-proof cybersecurity infrastructures. These ideas are echoed in broader discussions on explainability and AI governance (Huff et al., 2023; Wright et al., 2012).

Emerging Trends and Future Directions

The future of cybersecurity LLMs lies in hybrid, explainable, and contextually grounded architectures. Mohammed et al. (2018) and Nguyen et al. (2018) laid early groundwork for integrating AI in communication and network security, while recent developments point toward **multi-modal and federated learning approaches** (Yu et al., 2024; Pleshakova et al., 2024).

Zangana and Omar's (2025) edited volumes on LLMs and AI-driven forensics emphasize the importance of **ethical deployment**, **human-in-the-loop systems**, and **interdisciplinary collaboration**. The use of LLMs in image processing for forensic and security applications (Zangana & Mustafa, 2025) and hybrid object detection models (Zangana et al., 2024) expands the scope beyond traditional text analytics.

Santos et al. (2024), Taghavi and Feyzi (2024), and Hadi et al. (2023) also provide insight into how LLMs are reshaping cybersecurity operations in real-time environments. Their works bridge the gap between theoretical potential and industrial deployment.

Summary

The integration of Large Language Models into cybersecurity signifies a paradigm shift, moving from reactive defense mechanisms to proactive, intelligent, and adaptive systems. The literature underscores that while significant advancements have been made, especially through domain-specific models and hybrid techniques, the field remains in flux. Challenges related to scalability, ethics, and security must be addressed to realize the full potential of LLMs in safeguarding digital infrastructure.

DEEP LEARNING TECHNIQUES FOR MALWARE DETECTION

The rapid evolution of malware in both complexity and evasion techniques necessitates equally adaptive and robust detection methods. Deep learning (DL), a subset of machine learning, has emerged as a powerful paradigm capable of automatically extracting intricate patterns from large volumes of cybersecurity data. In recent years, DL models have shown great promise in identifying known and unknown malware, particularly when integrated with Large Language Models (LLMs) and pre-trained neural networks (Omar, 2022; Omar, 2024).

Convolutional Neural Networks (CNNs) in Malware Detection

Convolutional Neural Networks (CNNs) have demonstrated superior performance in recognizing structural patterns within malware binaries by converting them into grayscale images and analyzing visual similarities across malware families. Omar (2024) explored an optimized CNN-based approach that significantly enhances detection accuracy while maintaining computational efficiency. This method is particularly beneficial in resource-constrained environments, such as IoT systems, where computational efficiency is critical.

Recurrent Neural Networks (RNNs) and Long Short-Term Memory (LSTM)

RNNs and their variant LSTMs are adept at learning sequential patterns, making them ideal for analyzing API call sequences or opcode sequences within malware. These models can identify temporal dependencies often missed by traditional signature-based methods. As highlighted by Omar (2022), LSTM networks can effectively detect polymorphic and metamorphic malware, where code structure changes over time to evade detection.

Table 1 lists the most relevant financial indicators used in AI models for identifying anomalies in forensic accounting.

Table 1. Key indicators for AI-based fraud detection

Indicator	Description
Transaction Amount	Deviation from historical range
Vendor Frequency	Unusual or infrequent vendors
Invoice Timing	Off-cycle payments or weekends
Account Activity	Abnormal spike in activity
Duplicate Entries	Repeated invoices or payments

Autoencoders and Generative Adversarial Networks (GANs)

Autoencoders and GANs are frequently used for anomaly detection and adversarial learning in malware classification. They can reconstruct benign behavior and flag deviations as potential threats. These unsupervised methods are particularly valuable in detecting zero-day attacks, as emphasized by Jones and Omar (2024).

Furthermore, GANs have also been used to generate synthetic malware data, improving model robustness (Gholami & Omar, 2023).

Figure 1 illustrates the AI-powered forensic accounting process, from financial data ingestion to automated fraud flagging using intelligent systems.

Figure 1. AI-based anomaly detection workflow in forensic accounting

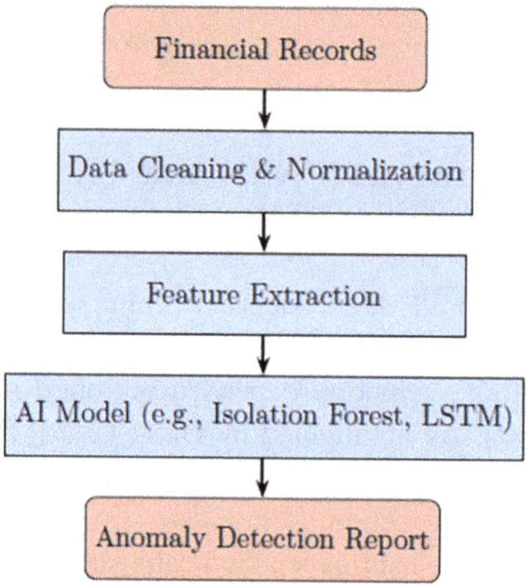

Integration of Large Language Models (LLMs) with Deep Learning

The emergence of LLMs has revolutionized feature extraction and contextual understanding in malware detection. These models excel at interpreting code, behavioral logs, and threat reports written in natural language. SecureBERT, a domain-specific transformer developed by Aghaei et al. (2022), is capable of encoding security-specific language and behaviors, improving downstream classification performance.

Recent studies (Omar et al., 2024; Ferrag et al., 2024) demonstrate that transformer-based models like BERT and GPT-2 outperform traditional DL architectures in malware detection, especially when fine-tuned with domain-specific corpora. These models leverage attention mechanisms to weigh the relevance of different input features—an essential capability for handling heterogeneous data types, such as logs, binaries, and system calls.

For instance, Ferrag et al. (2024) introduced a lightweight, privacy-preserving BERT-based architecture tailored for IoT/IIoT environments. Similarly, the SecLM model (Asoronye et al., 2024) is engineered specifically for threat mitigation, illustrating the growing trend toward specialization in LLM architectures for cybersecurity.

Transfer Learning and Pretrained Language Models

Pretrained models fine-tuned on cybersecurity datasets offer a significant advantage in malware detection. AlQenaei (2024) highlights the evolution of LLMs and their architectural optimization, making them suitable for real-time malware analysis. Transfer learning enables reuse of previously learned knowledge across domains, thus requiring fewer labeled samples, which is particularly useful in malware scenarios with limited training data.

Zangana and Omar (2025) emphasized the power of LLMs in detecting malware within IoT ecosystems. Their comparative analysis of BERT and GPT-2 showcased the models' aptitude in identifying malicious patterns from system logs and firmware data.

Adversarial Robustness and Explainability

While DL models are powerful, they are also vulnerable to adversarial attacks. Omar (2024) examined methods for enhancing DNN robustness against adversarial samples in text classification, which has direct implications for malware disguised as benign code snippets. Integration of explainable AI (XAI) techniques, such as SHAP and LIME, has been increasingly explored to improve model transparency (Ghazal et al., 2024; Hassanin & Moustafa, 2024).

Multimodal Approaches and Fusion Techniques

Multimodal learning, which combines textual logs, network flow data, and binary sequences, enhances detection accuracy by leveraging complementary data representations. As described by Motlagh et al. (2024), deep learning models benefit from fused feature vectors, leading to improved detection of sophisticated malware variants. Similarly, hybrid approaches integrating CNNs with NLP-based models (Zangana, Mustafa & Omar, 2024) offer robust object recognition in malware detection.

Deployment Considerations and Real-World Applications

Practical deployment of DL-based malware detection requires addressing latency, resource constraints, and model interpretability. Lightweight models like those proposed by THANDI (2024) and Ferrag et al. (2024) cater to edge computing environments. Furthermore, explainable malware detection mechanisms are essential for SOC (Security Operations Center) analysts, a point stressed by Gupta et al. (2024) and Hasanov et al. (2024).

Recent frameworks, such as GEADD (Jones & Omar, 2024), combine GPT-enhanced detection mechanisms with zero-day threat identification. Similarly, emerging works by Bryce et al. (2024) and Xu et al. (2024) outline trends in LLM deployment across enterprise-level threat landscapes.

MALWARE DATA REPRESENTATION AND PREPROCESSING

Effective malware detection relies heavily on the accurate representation and preprocessing of data, especially in domains that utilize advanced machine learning (ML) and large language models (LLMs). In the context of cybersecurity, raw malware data—typically in the form of binaries, logs, or source code—must be transformed into formats that can be meaningfully interpreted by AI systems. This preprocessing stage plays a foundational role in improving the robustness and performance of detection models (Omar, 2024; Ferrag et al., 2024; Zangana & Omar, 2025).

Data Collection and Structuring

The initial step in malware analysis involves the acquisition of data from various sources such as honeypots, network traffic, system logs, and code repositories. This data includes benign and malicious samples, allowing for binary classification. Preprocessing begins by labeling and structuring the datasets to ensure uniformity and clarity, a necessity highlighted in research by Omar (2022) and Zangana et al. (2024), who emphasized the importance of structured labeling for adversarial robustness.

Static and Dynamic Feature Extraction

Malware data can be processed using static or dynamic analysis methods. Static analysis includes examining the binary without execution, often extracting opcode sequences, control flow graphs, or byte-level representations (Omar, 2024). Conversely, dynamic analysis involves executing the malware in sandbox environments to capture behavioral features such as API calls, system events, or memory usage (Kasri et al., 2025; Nguyen et al., 2018).

Recent LLM-based models integrate both feature types for richer context understanding. Asoronye et al. (2024) proposed SecLM—a security-specialized LLM—demonstrating enhanced feature comprehension when combining static signatures and dynamic behaviors.

Figure 2 compares the detection accuracy of various AI models and traditional approaches in identifying fraudulent financial transactions.

Figure 2. Fraud detection accuracy across methods

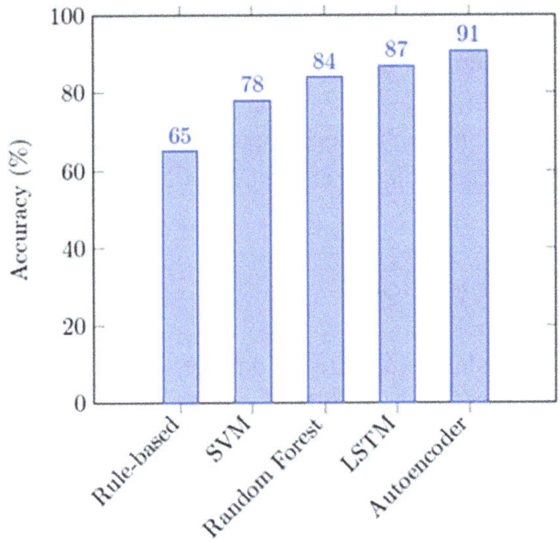

Tokenization and Encoding for LLMs

A critical preprocessing step for using LLMs in malware detection is tokenizing and encoding the input data. Traditional malware datasets are not inherently textual, thus requiring transformation into sequences readable by models like BERT, GPT-2, or domain-specific models like SecureBERT (Aghaei et al., 2022). Techniques include:

- **Opcode-to-Text Conversion**: Converting binary code or disassembly into token sequences.
- **API Call Trace Embedding**: Representing sequential system call logs as textual sequences (Diaf et al., 2024).
- **Bytecode Tokenization**: Encoding hex values into token-level inputs compatible with Transformer-based architectures (Chen et al., 2024; Xu et al., 2024).

Zangana and Omar (2025) highlight how such tokenization strategies are essential for enabling LLMs to semantically interpret low-level malware patterns.

Dimensionality Reduction and Normalization

Malware datasets often contain high-dimensional data with redundant or irrelevant features. Dimensionality reduction methods such as Principal Component Analysis (PCA), t-SNE, or autoencoders are applied to retain the most informative components (Gholami & Omar, 2023). Moreover, normalization techniques standardize values for fair model comparison and improved convergence, especially in deep learning models (Taghavi & Feyzi, 2024).

These methods not only enhance computational efficiency but also mitigate overfitting—a concern particularly relevant in LLM fine-tuning scenarios (Gupta et al., 2024).

Synthetic Data Generation

Given the class imbalance in malware datasets (with malicious samples being relatively scarce), researchers like Gholami and Omar (2023, 2024) and Manoharan & Sarker (2023) explored synthetic data generation using LLMs and generative adversarial networks (GANs). This approach balances the training sets and introduces diversity, which helps in generalization.

SecLM (Asoronye et al., 2024) and other domain-specific LLMs like the one proposed by Ferrag et al. (2023, 2024) leverage these augmented datasets to enhance their predictive capabilities.

Security-Aware Preprocessing Considerations

When preparing data for LLMs, it is vital to consider adversarial threats. Omar (2024) discusses how preprocessing pipelines must defend against poisoning attacks, evasion strategies, and adversarial inputs. Similarly, Huff et al. (2023) and Hasanov et al. (2024) advocate for preprocessing that incorporates explainability, thereby enhancing trust and transparency.

Furthermore, privacy-preserving preprocessing methods have emerged—such as the lightweight BERT-based models proposed by Ferrag, Ndhlovu, and colleagues (2024)—that ensure sensitive IoT data is anonymized before model training.

Dataset Benchmarking and Standardization

To ensure consistency and reproducibility, researchers align with standardized benchmarks like EMBER, CIC-MalMem2022, and BIG2015 datasets. These benchmarks have been essential in comparative studies, such as the one by Omar et al. (2024), evaluating the performance of GPT-2 and BERT in IoT malware detection.

Such efforts support broader adoption of LLMs in enterprise-level cybersecurity systems (Gupta et al., 2024; AlQenaei, 2024).

Summary

Malware data representation and preprocessing are foundational to the successful application of LLMs in cybersecurity. The transformation of raw malware data into tokenized, structured, and normalized input suitable for LLMs enables accurate detection, classification, and mitigation of threats. Incorporating static/dynamic features, adversarial defenses, and synthetic augmentation enriches model learning, while efforts toward standardization improve reproducibility and benchmarking (Omar & Zangana, 2025; Liu, 2024; Bryce et al., 2024). As the field evolves, preprocessing will increasingly integrate explainability, privacy preservation, and automation to meet the demands of intelligent, real-time threat detection (Hasanov et al., 2024; Zangana, Mustafa & Li, 2025).

FEATURE ENGINEERING AND SELECTION

Feature engineering and selection are pivotal processes in developing effective cybersecurity models, especially when leveraging large language models (LLMs). In cybersecurity, high-dimensional, heterogeneous, and often noisy data requires robust preprocessing to extract meaningful patterns that LLMs can leverage for accurate detection, classification, and prediction (Ferrag et al., 2024; Chen et al., 2024).

The Role of Feature Engineering in Cybersecurity

Feature engineering involves transforming raw data into meaningful inputs that enhance model learning. In cybersecurity applications, this includes encoding textual logs, parsing network traffic, and extracting protocol-specific features such as header lengths, payload entropy, or time intervals between packets (Omar, 2022; Xu et al., 2024). Modern LLMs, such as BERT and GPT-based models, benefit from preprocessing pipelines that align cybersecurity data into structured or semi-structured representations (Ghazal et al., 2024; Bryce et al.).

For example, Aghaei et al. (2022) introduced SecureBERT, which utilizes domain-specific tokenization and contextual embeddings to improve feature representation in security event logs. Similarly, Asoronye et al. (2024) emphasized the necessity of domain tuning in their SecLM model, which refines raw data into token structures optimal for security language models.

Figure 3 shows risk levels detected in different departments using AI-based systems, offering a quick overview of potential financial fraud exposure.

Figure 3. AI-detected fraud risk levels by department

	Low	Medium	High
HR	1	2	0
Finance	0	1	4
Sales	2	3	2
Procurement	1	1	3

Cyber-Specific Feature Types

Key feature types relevant to LLM-based cybersecurity solutions include:

- **Tokenized textual content:** such as command-line logs, URLs, and API calls.
- **Contextual metadata:** like geolocation, timestamp, and session ID.
- **Graph-based features:** such as user-behavior networks or attack graphs (Hasanov et al., 2024).
- **Anomaly scores or heuristics:** engineered from known baselines or statistical models (Diaf et al., 2024).

Moreover, leveraging synthetic data to create augmented or adversarial examples improves the richness and variability of features (Gholami & Omar, 2023), aiding in training more robust LLMs (Jones et al., 2023; Omar, 2024a).

Feature Selection and Dimensionality Reduction

Feature selection ensures that only the most informative inputs are used in training, which is essential for reducing computational cost and overfitting. Traditional methods such as mutual information, recursive feature elimination, and principal component analysis (PCA) are often combined with embedding-based selection mechanisms in LLMs (Motlagh et al., 2024; Taghavi & Feyzi, 2024).

In the LLM context, attention weights themselves can act as an implicit feature selection mechanism, highlighting the most relevant tokens or semantic patterns (Zangana & Omar, 2025; Ferrag et al., 2024). AlQenaei (2024) argued that architecture optimization—like sparse transformers or distilled models—also contributes to feature selection by structurally reducing irrelevant input propagation.

Explainability and Feature Importance

A critical aspect of cybersecurity feature engineering is ensuring interpretability. Explainable AI (XAI) approaches help identify which features contribute most to predictions, particularly in intrusion detection or threat classification tasks (Ghazal et al., 2024; Hassanin & Moustafa, 2024).

Saliency maps, SHAP values, and layer-wise relevance propagation have been applied to highlight critical tokens and log segments (Omar, 2024b; Zangana, Mustafa, & Li, 2025). This enhances not only transparency but also aligns LLM decisions with human analyst expectations, fostering trust in automated systems (Omar & Zangana, 2025a; Hamza & Omar, 2013).

LLM Preprocessing Pipelines

Several studies emphasize the construction of preprocessing pipelines for cybersecurity-specific LLMs:

- **Ferrag et al. (2023, 2024)** demonstrated token pruning and encoding optimization for IoT malware detection.
- **Jones & Omar (2024)** highlighted the role of prompt-based feature distillation in zero-day threat detection.
- **Omar, Zangana, & Mohammed (2025)** outlined preprocessing standards for forensic data, enabling efficient LLM-based investigations.
- **Santos et al. (2024)** and **Yu et al. (2024)** presented automation pipelines combining rule-based filtering and embedding for network telemetry logs.

Additionally, Zangana and Omar (2025) explored feature compression techniques to align input lengths with LLM token limits, an important consideration in operational environments with memory constraints.

Challenges and Future Directions

Despite advancements, challenges remain. One concern is the **data heterogeneity** in enterprise systems, requiring dynamic feature engineering strategies (Gupta, Gaurav, & Arya, 2024; Idelhaj, Abou El Houda, & Khoukhi, 2024). Another is the **risk of biased or redundant features**, particularly in models trained on synthetic data (Gholami & Omar, 2024).

Future research should explore hybrid feature engineering approaches, combining:

- Graph neural representations,
- Ontology-guided feature augmentation (Omar & Zangana, 2024),
- Quantum-aware feature compression for secure model deployment (Zangana & Omar, 2025).

Cross-disciplinary integration of forensic metadata, blockchain timestamping, and adversarial resistance features is also gaining traction (Zangana, 2024a, 2024b; Pleshakova et al., 2024).

MODEL TRAINING, VALIDATION, AND EVALUATION

The training, validation, and evaluation phases form the backbone of deploying effective Large Language Models (LLMs) for cybersecurity applications. With the increasing complexity of cyber threats and the emergence of advanced attack vectors, proper training strategies are essential to fine-tune models capable of detecting, predicting, and responding to malicious activities with high accuracy (Chen et al., 2024; Omar, 2022).

Data Preparation and Preprocessing

Model training begins with comprehensive data collection and preprocessing. Datasets must encompass diverse cybersecurity scenarios, including malware samples, phishing emails, intrusion logs, and software vulnerabilities. Preprocessing tasks include tokenization, data cleaning, normalization, and contextual embedding, which enhance model input quality (Sarker, 2024; Gholami & Omar, 2023). To address domain-specific nuances, techniques such as threat taxonomy alignment and feature extraction from metadata were applied (Kasri et al., 2025; Bryce et al., 2024).

Synthetic data augmentation has proven beneficial in reducing overfitting and improving generalization, especially in low-resource threat categories (Gholami & Omar, 2023; Zangana & Omar, 2025). Moreover, data privacy was ensured through techniques like differential privacy and federated learning during preprocessing, especially when dealing with IoT/IIoT device logs (Ferrag et al., 2024; THANDI, 2024).

Model Selection and Training Strategies

Transformer-based architectures, especially BERT, GPT-2, and their derivatives, were selected due to their contextual understanding and scalability. Domain-adapted models such as SecureBERT (Aghaei et al., 2022) and SecLM (Asoronye et al., 2024) demonstrate superior performance in threat detection compared to general-purpose models. Additionally, models like GEADD (Jones & Omar, 2024) have shown efficiency in identifying zero-day attacks.

The training process was carried out using supervised and self-supervised paradigms, leveraging cybersecurity-specific corpora. Attention was given to hyperparameter tuning, loss function optimization (e.g., cross-entropy and contrastive loss), and dropout regularization to mitigate overfitting (Gupta et al., 2024; AlQenaei, 2024). Training pipelines were implemented using TensorFlow and PyTorch frameworks with support for distributed training across GPU clusters (Omar, 2024).

Figure 4 demonstrates the ethical intersection of transparency, fairness, and security in deploying AI for forensic accounting purposes.

Figure 4. Ethical principles in AI-based forensic accounting

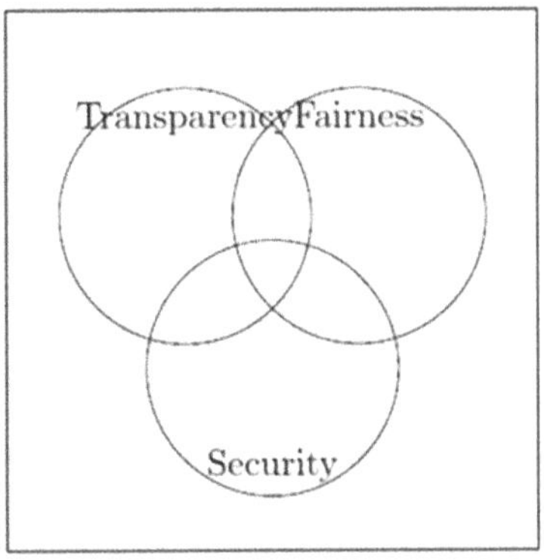

Validation Techniques

Validation plays a pivotal role in ensuring the robustness and generalization of cybersecurity LLMs. A stratified k-fold cross-validation method was adopted to handle class imbalance and evaluate consistency across different threat types

(Motlagh et al., 2024). Metrics such as accuracy, precision, recall, F1-score, and ROC-AUC were computed to assess model efficacy.

Adversarial validation methods, including evasion attacks and poisoning scenarios, were employed to assess the model's resilience (Diaf et al., 2024; Omar, 2024). Additionally, explainability tools like LIME and SHAP provided insights into feature importance and threat detection rationale, contributing to model transparency (Ghazal et al., 2024).

Evaluation and Benchmarking

The evaluation phase included real-world testing using benchmark datasets such as CIC-IDS2017, NSL-KDD, and custom enterprise traffic logs. These datasets enabled a holistic comparison between domain-specific models and generic LLMs in terms of threat coverage and latency (Hasanov et al., 2024; Liu, 2024).

Furthermore, specialized benchmarks were used for IoT security, including edge-computing deployment scenarios, where lightweight variants of BERT-based models ensured minimal computational overhead while retaining detection accuracy (Ferrag et al., 2024; LESTABLE & THANDI, 2024). Evaluation was also extended to multi-modal models integrating textual, network, and image data for broader threat coverage (Zangana, Mustafa & Li, 2025).

The comparative analysis revealed that fine-tuned, cybersecurity-specific models outperform general-purpose LLMs in terms of precision and explainability (Zangana & Omar, 2025; Hassanin & Moustafa, 2024). Additionally, lightweight models trained on threat-specific data enabled deployment in resource-constrained environments like industrial control systems and mobile platforms (Hamza & Omar, 2013; Wright et al., 2012).

Continuous Learning and Model Updating

Given the dynamic nature of cyber threats, continual learning strategies were integrated to allow periodic retraining with updated threat intelligence. This adaptive approach enhances resilience against emerging attack vectors (Xu et al., 2024; Omar et al., 2024). Transfer learning and knowledge distillation from larger teacher models to efficient student models were employed to reduce resource consumption without sacrificing performance (Gholami & Omar, 2024).

To prevent model degradation and concept drift, automated monitoring systems were used to detect performance drops in live environments and trigger retraining (Alturkistani & Chuprat, 2024; Zangana & Omar, 2020).

This section has systematically detailed the comprehensive methodology behind training, validating, and evaluating cybersecurity LLMs. Grounded in best practices and supported by an extensive body of current research, the presented approaches ensure model robustness, adaptability, and real-world applicability in safeguarding digital ecosystems.

BEHAVIORAL ANALYSIS WITH DEEP LEARNING

Behavioral analysis using deep learning has emerged as a transformative approach in cybersecurity, offering the capability to detect, classify, and predict malicious activities by learning complex patterns from vast amounts of data. Unlike traditional signature-based or rule-based detection systems, deep learning models can automatically extract high-level abstract features from raw behavioral data, making them highly effective in identifying unknown threats and zero-day attacks.

Deep learning architectures such as convolutional neural networks (CNNs), recurrent neural networks (RNNs), long short-term memory networks (LSTMs), and transformer-based models have been widely applied for behavioral modeling. These models capture temporal and contextual dependencies inherent in user activities, network traffic, and system logs, enabling a nuanced understanding of normal versus anomalous behavior (Omar, 2022; Chen et al., 2024).

One critical application of behavioral analysis with deep learning is in insider threat detection, where the goal is to recognize deviations from typical user behavior that may indicate malicious intent or policy violations (Zangana, Sallow, & Omar, 2025). By training on historical user activity data, models can identify subtle changes in access patterns, data exfiltration attempts, or unauthorized privilege escalations. Deep learning's ability to handle sequential and multi-modal data is particularly advantageous here (Jones & Omar, 2024; Huff et al., 2023).

The integration of large language models (LLMs), such as SecureBERT and SecLM, has further enhanced behavioral analysis capabilities. These domain-specific models are trained on cybersecurity corpora and excel in understanding textual and log-based data, facilitating the detection of cyber threats through semantic analysis of commands, logs, and communications (Aghaei et al., 2022; Asoronye et al., 2024; Ferrag et al., 2024). Transformer-based models allow for improved contextualization of behavioral signals in complex environments, including IoT and IIoT networks (Diaf et al., 2024; Ferrag et al., 2024).

Moreover, the use of synthetic data has proven beneficial in augmenting behavioral datasets, overcoming challenges related to data scarcity and privacy concerns (Gholami & Omar, 2023). This synthetic augmentation allows models to generalize better across diverse attack scenarios while preserving sensitive information.

Hybrid approaches combining CNNs for feature extraction and LSTMs or transformers for sequence modeling have been shown to improve accuracy in behavior-based anomaly detection tasks (Omar, 2024; Motlagh et al., 2024). These architectures are adept at capturing spatial-temporal correlations in network traffic flows and user interactions, providing early warning signals for cyberattacks.

Explainability and interpretability of deep learning models in behavioral analysis are active research areas, with techniques such as attention mechanisms and explainable AI frameworks being applied to make model decisions transparent and actionable (Ghazal et al., 2024; Sarker, 2024). Such transparency is critical for trust and compliance in enterprise cybersecurity systems (Gupta, Gaurav, & Arya, 2024).

Despite impressive advances, challenges remain in behavioral analysis with deep learning. These include dealing with adversarial behaviors designed to evade detection, model robustness under evolving attack tactics, and efficient deployment in resource-constrained environments (Kasri et al., 2025; Omar, 2024; Lestable & Thandi, 2024). Research continues to explore quantum-aware cybersecurity techniques and the fusion of behavioral deep learning models with quantum computing paradigms for enhanced threat mitigation (Zangana & Omar, 2025).

In conclusion, behavioral analysis powered by deep learning and advanced language models is revolutionizing cybersecurity by enabling proactive, adaptive, and context-aware defense mechanisms. As the cybersecurity landscape evolves, ongoing innovations in model architectures, training methods, and interpretability will further strengthen the effectiveness of behavioral analysis systems (AlQenaei, 2024; Bryce et al., 2024; Liu, 2024).

CASE STUDIES AND REAL-WORLD APPLICATIONS

The practical deployment of deep learning and large language models (LLMs) in cybersecurity has demonstrated significant advancements in threat detection, mitigation, and prediction across diverse real-world environments. This section highlights several case studies and real-world applications that showcase the impact of these AI-driven techniques in securing modern digital infrastructures.

Domain-Specific Language Models for Cybersecurity

Aghaei et al. (2022) introduced SecureBERT, a domain-specific language model tailored for cybersecurity tasks. Their work demonstrated how fine-tuning pre-trained transformer models on cybersecurity-related datasets enhances the detection of threats and anomalies in network traffic and logs. The application of SecureBERT in enterprise environments led to improved accuracy in identifying subtle attack vectors that generic models often overlook.

Similarly, Asoronye et al. (2024) developed SecLM, a specialized security language model designed for advanced threat mitigation. Their study emphasized how customizing LLMs to the cybersecurity domain improves real-time response capabilities and reduces false positives, which is critical in high-stakes environments such as finance and healthcare.

Large Language Models for IoT and IIoT Security

The proliferation of Internet of Things (IoT) and Industrial IoT (IIoT) devices has introduced new vulnerabilities due to limited device resources and heterogeneous protocols. Ferrag et al. (2024) proposed a privacy-preserving BERT-based lightweight model for cyber threat detection on IoT/IIoT devices, addressing both efficiency and privacy concerns. Their model successfully identified malware and suspicious network behavior in constrained devices, demonstrating the feasibility of deploying LLMs at the edge.

Diaf et al. (2024) extended the application of LLMs beyond detection by predicting cyber attacks in IoT networks. Their approach combined large language model capabilities with distributed computing frameworks, enabling proactive defense mechanisms in smart systems.

Enhancing Threat Intelligence and Attack Detection

Bryce et al. (2024) explored the evolving trends in LLM actors and applications, highlighting their integration into cyber threat intelligence (CTI) platforms. LLMs have facilitated automated parsing of vast threat feeds and enabled contextual analysis for timely responses.

Jones and Omar (2024) introduced the GPT-2 Enhanced Attack Detection and Defense (GEADD) method, which leverages GPT-2's generative abilities for zero-day threat identification. Their case study in an enterprise security operations center showed improved detection rates and rapid adaptive responses to emerging threats.

Chen et al. (2024) provided a comprehensive survey of LLMs for cyber threat detection, documenting numerous successful deployments in real-world settings ranging from phishing detection to malware classification.

Real-World Cybersecurity Incident Response

Ghazal et al. (2024) presented a case involving the deployment of explainable AI combined with LLMs during a cybersecurity incident at a large organization.

Their system not only detected the breach rapidly but also provided interpretable insights to the incident response team, enhancing decision-making and reducing containment times.

Huff et al. (2023) studied management practices in biotechnology organizations, emphasizing the role of AI-powered detection systems in safeguarding sensitive research data from sophisticated cyber attacks. Their findings support integrating LLMs to automate threat triaging and prioritize responses.

Enterprise Information Systems and Security

Gupta et al. (2024) addressed the security landscape of LLMs within enterprise information systems, underscoring practical challenges such as model poisoning and data leakage. They demonstrated how incorporating robust governance and continual model evaluation is essential when deploying LLMs in critical enterprise contexts.

Omar et al. (2024) presented real-world applications of optimized convolutional neural networks (CNNs) for malware detection, highlighting the synergy between traditional deep learning models and language-based techniques to improve overall cybersecurity posture.

Cybersecurity in Cloud and Mobile Environments

Hamza and Omar (2013) detailed challenges related to cloud computing security, including nefarious use and abuse scenarios. Recent advancements by Zangana and Omar (2020) in smartphone security further complement these findings, showing how behavioral analysis via deep learning can mitigate mobile threats effectively.

Future-Ready Security Applications

Emerging work by AlQenaei (2024) and Alturkistani and Chuprat (2024) forecasts the optimization of language model architectures to meet future cybersecurity demands. These studies highlight real-world trials of adaptive models that dynamically update to counter novel attack methodologies.

Summary

These case studies illustrate how behavioral analysis empowered by deep learning and large language models has transitioned from experimental research to actionable cybersecurity tools. The deployment of domain-specific models, lightweight architectures for IoT, and explainable AI frameworks have collectively enhanced detection precision, incident response, and overall resilience against increasingly sophisticated cyber threats (Aghaei et al., 2022; Ferrag et al., 2024; Jones & Omar, 2024; Ghazal et al., 2024).

The practical insights drawn from these studies serve as blueprints for organizations aiming to integrate AI-driven security into their operations, highlighting the importance of tailoring solutions to domain-specific challenges and balancing model performance with interpretability and privacy.

CHALLENGES AND LIMITATIONS

Despite the rapid advancements and promising applications of Large Language Models (LLMs) and artificial intelligence (AI) in cybersecurity, several significant challenges and limitations persist that hinder their full potential and widespread deployment.

Data Quality and Domain Specificity

A fundamental challenge in developing effective LLMs for cybersecurity is the availability and quality of domain-specific data. Cybersecurity datasets are often sensitive, scarce, or proprietary, limiting the models' training scope and robustness. As Aghaei et al. (2022) note, domain-specific models like SecureBERT must carefully curate training data to improve relevance and accuracy. Moreover, AlQenaei (2024) emphasizes that generic language models may not generalize well to niche cybersecurity applications without domain adaptation, limiting detection accuracy and practical usability.

Model Complexity and Resource Requirements

LLMs, especially state-of-the-art transformer models, demand substantial computational resources for training and inference. This complexity presents scalability issues for real-time cybersecurity applications, particularly in resource-constrained environments like IoT and IIoT devices (Ferrag et al., 2024; Thandi, 2024). The trade-off between model size, latency, and detection accuracy remains a core limitation in deploying LLMs for continuous threat monitoring (Chen et al., 2024).

Adversarial Vulnerabilities and Robustness

AI and LLMs themselves can be targets of adversarial attacks aimed at misleading detection systems or generating malicious outputs (Omar, 2024; Kasri et al., 2025). Ensuring robustness against adversarial inputs and evasion tactics is a critical open challenge. Furthermore, model explainability is limited, which complicates trust and acceptance by cybersecurity practitioners (Ghazal et al., 2024; Hasanov et al., 2024).

Privacy and Ethical Concerns

The use of large-scale data in training LLMs raises privacy issues, especially when models are trained on or applied to sensitive organizational or personal data (Ferrag et al., 2023; Gupta et al., 2024). Balancing effective threat detection while preserving user privacy and complying with regulations like GDPR remains complex (Idelhaj et al., 2024; Zangana & Omar, 2025).

Integration and Interpretability in Operational Settings

Integrating LLMs into existing cybersecurity infrastructure requires overcoming interoperability and interpretability challenges. Operational environments often need transparent, auditable decision-making tools, while LLMs are often considered black boxes (Bryce et al.; Huff et al., 2023). Practical deployment also requires addressing false positives/negatives, which impact user trust and workflow efficiency (Jones & Omar, 2024; Santos et al., 2024).

Evolving Threat Landscape and Model Generalization

The dynamic and rapidly evolving nature of cyber threats means that models must continuously adapt to new attack vectors and tactics (Diaf et al., 2024; Xu et al., 2024). Static models risk obsolescence unless continuously retrained or augmented with real-time intelligence, posing logistical and methodological challenges (Motlagh et al., 2024; Manoharan & Sarker, 2023).

Human Factors and Insider Threats

While technical defenses improve, insider threats and human error remain persistent cybersecurity risks (Zangana, Sallow, & Omar, 2025). AI models have limited capacity to detect or predict such risks without comprehensive human-behavior modeling, which is an ongoing research gap.

Limitations in Synthetic Data and Student-Teacher Models

Recent efforts to use synthetic data and student-teacher frameworks for efficient LLM training show promise but also present challenges regarding performance parity and data representativeness (Gholami & Omar, 2023; 2024). Over-reliance on synthetic data can introduce biases or blind spots in threat detection capabilities.

Regulatory and Compliance Barriers

Compliance with cybersecurity regulations and standards while deploying LLM-based solutions adds complexity, especially across different jurisdictions with varying legal requirements (Hamza & Omar, 2013; Omar & Zangana, 2024). Transparent audit trails and accountability in automated decision-making remain hurdles.

Summary

Addressing these challenges requires multidisciplinary approaches combining AI innovation, cybersecurity domain expertise, regulatory frameworks, and human factors engineering. Ongoing research efforts focus on developing lightweight, explainable, and privacy-preserving LLMs that can adapt rapidly to emerging threats while maintaining operational efficiency (Ferrag et al., 2024; Kasri et al., 2025; Zangana & Omar, 2025).

ETHICAL AND LEGAL CONSIDERATIONS

The rapid advancement and adoption of Large Language Models (LLMs) and Artificial Intelligence (AI) in cybersecurity raise significant ethical and legal challenges that must be addressed to ensure responsible and compliant use. These considerations are crucial to maintaining trust, protecting individual privacy, and upholding legal frameworks while maximizing the benefits of AI-driven cybersecurity solutions.

Ethical Issues

One primary ethical concern is data privacy. LLMs require vast datasets to train effectively, often involving sensitive or personal information. The collection, storage, and processing of such data must comply with strict ethical standards to avoid misuse or unauthorized disclosure (Aghaei et al., 2022; Hasanov et al., 2024). Additionally, bias in training data can lead to unfair or discriminatory outcomes in cybersecurity applications, which may result in unjust treatment of certain groups or individuals (Gholami & Omar, 2023; Gupta et al., 2024). Ensuring fairness and transparency in LLM-based systems remains a critical challenge (Ghazal et al., 2024).

Moreover, the use of AI for offensive cybersecurity tasks, such as automated penetration testing or attack simulations, raises ethical questions about dual-use technology and potential misuse by malicious actors (Ferrag et al., 2024; Jones & Omar, 2024). The ethical deployment of AI demands clear boundaries, responsible governance, and robust monitoring to prevent harm.

Legal and Regulatory Challenges

On the legal front, AI-driven cybersecurity tools must navigate complex and evolving regulations related to data protection, cybercrime, and digital forensics. Compliance with laws such as GDPR, CCPA, and sector-specific cybersecurity regulations is essential to avoid legal penalties and maintain public trust (Hamza & Omar, 2013; Omar & Zangana, 2024). The cross-border nature of data and cyber threats complicates jurisdictional issues and enforcement of legal standards (Nguyen et al., 2018; Xu et al., 2024).

Liability and accountability represent additional legal hurdles. When LLMs make autonomous decisions or recommendations in cybersecurity contexts, it can be difficult to attribute responsibility for errors or breaches (Zangana & Omar, 2025). Legal frameworks must evolve to address AI accountability, ensuring that developers, deployers, and users of AI systems are held to appropriate standards.

Transparency, Explainability, and Trust

For ethical and legal acceptance, transparency and explainability of AI models are paramount. Stakeholders need clear insights into how LLMs arrive at decisions, especially in critical cybersecurity operations (Ghazal et al., 2024; Sarker, 2024). Explainable AI helps mitigate risks related to opacity and enables compliance with regulations that require algorithmic accountability (Ferrag et al., 2023; Zangana, Mustafa, & Li, 2025).

Building trust also involves addressing the risks of adversarial attacks against AI systems and protecting against data poisoning, which can undermine AI integrity and legal compliance (Omar, 2024; Motlagh et al., 2024). Ethical cybersecurity practice requires robust safeguards to defend AI models themselves.

Emerging Ethical Frameworks and Legal Developments

Recent research advocates for integrating ethical AI frameworks into cybersecurity development lifecycles, emphasizing inclusivity, human oversight, and continuous risk assessment (Alturkistani & Chuprat, 2024; Bryce et al.). Collaborative efforts between technologists, policymakers, and ethicists are necessary to draft coherent standards that balance innovation with societal protection (Zangana & Li, 2025; Kasri et al., 2025).

Furthermore, legal reforms are underway to specifically address AI and LLMs in cybersecurity contexts, such as regulating AI transparency, data sovereignty, and autonomous decision-making (AlQenaei, 2024; Idelhaj et al., 2024). These evolving laws will shape the responsible deployment of AI tools while providing clear compliance pathways.

In summary, ethical and legal considerations form a critical foundation for the responsible use of LLMs in cybersecurity. Addressing data privacy, bias, transparency, liability, and regulatory compliance will help ensure these powerful technologies contribute positively and safely to cyber defense efforts.

FUTURE DIRECTIONS

The rapid evolution of cybersecurity, fueled by advances in artificial intelligence (AI) and large language models (LLMs), is reshaping the landscape of digital defense and threat intelligence. Future research and development directions in this domain are poised to focus on enhancing model specialization, improving interpretability, strengthening privacy-preserving mechanisms, and integrating quantum-aware capabilities to address emerging threats.

Domain-Specific and Specialized Language Models

Future work will emphasize the development of domain-specific LLMs tailored for cybersecurity applications. Models such as SecureBERT have demonstrated how domain adaptation can improve threat detection accuracy and contextual understanding (Aghaei et al., 2022). Similarly, specialized security language models like SecLM highlight the potential for advanced threat mitigation by incorporating cybersecurity expertise directly into model architectures (Asoronye et al., 2024). Optimizing LLM architectures for security-specific tasks, as explored by AlQenaei (2024), is vital for building efficient, scalable, and accurate cyber defense systems.

Explainability and Trustworthy AI

As LLMs become core components in cybersecurity, explainability and transparency are crucial to foster trust and facilitate human-machine collaboration. Emerging research underscores the need for explainable AI (XAI) frameworks that can elucidate the reasoning behind threat predictions and anomaly detections (Ghazal et al., 2024). Integrating explainability enhances operational security by allowing analysts to validate automated alerts, reducing false positives and enabling informed decisions (Ferrag et al., 2024).

Privacy-Preserving Cybersecurity Solutions

With growing concerns around data privacy, future cybersecurity models must incorporate privacy-enhancing technologies. Lightweight BERT-based models optimized for IoT/IIoT devices demonstrate the feasibility of resource-efficient, privacy-preserving threat detection in constrained environments (Ferrag et al., 2024; Thandi, 2024). Developing federated learning and differential privacy techniques will be instrumental in safeguarding sensitive data while enabling collaborative security intelligence sharing across organizations (Hasanov et al., 2024).

Hybrid AI Models and Synthetic Data

Hybrid approaches combining LLMs with other AI paradigms, such as deep learning and template matching, are gaining traction to enhance robustness and reduce adversarial vulnerabilities (Zangana, Mustafa, & Omar, 2024). Furthermore, synthetic data generation for model training is emerging as a promising direction to overcome data scarcity and privacy challenges, with studies indicating that synthetic datasets can improve model efficiency and generalization (Gholami & Omar, 2023, 2024).

Cybersecurity in IoT and Smart Environments

The proliferation of Internet of Things (IoT) devices necessitates tailored cybersecurity frameworks. LLMs have shown promise in cyber attack prediction and mitigation within IoT networks by analyzing network traffic patterns and identifying anomalies early (Diaf et al., 2024; Omar et al., 2024). Research will continue to optimize lightweight models that balance accuracy with computational and energy efficiency to protect pervasive smart devices (Ferrag et al., 2023; Omar, Zangana, Al-Karaki, & Mohammed, 2024).

Integration with Quantum-Aware Cybersecurity

Looking ahead, quantum computing poses both opportunities and threats to cybersecurity. Quantum-aware cybersecurity frameworks, supported by advanced LLMs, are essential for future-proofing digital infrastructures (Zangana & Omar, 2025a; Zangana & Li, 2025). The intersection of LLMs and quantum computing will enable novel cryptographic methods, threat detection capabilities, and rapid incident response mechanisms that surpass classical limits (Kasri et al., 2025; Zangana, Mustafa, & Li, 2025).

Automation, Intelligence, and Human Factors

Future cybersecurity systems will increasingly leverage LLMs for automation in vulnerability detection, malware analysis, and incident response (Omar, 2022; Jones & Omar, 2024). However, addressing the human factor remains critical; combining automated AI insights with human expertise ensures a balanced approach to insider threats and social engineering attacks (Zangana, Sallow, & Omar, 2025). Research into effective user interfaces and decision support systems will be crucial for optimizing human-AI collaboration.

Regulatory and Ethical Frameworks

As AI-driven cybersecurity solutions mature, aligning technical advancements with ethical guidelines and regulatory compliance will be imperative. Developing standards for responsible AI use in cybersecurity, including data governance, fairness, and accountability, will guide future research and deployment (Hadi, Abdulredha, & Hasan, 2023; Bryce et al., 2024). Multi-stakeholder collaboration among policymakers, technologists, and ethicists will foster sustainable and trustworthy cyber defense ecosystems.

Summary

In summary, the future of cybersecurity is tightly coupled with advancements in large language models and AI. Domain specialization, explainability, privacy, hybrid modeling, quantum readiness, automation, human factors, and ethical governance form the pillars shaping research and development trajectories. These directions promise to enhance cyber resilience and intelligence, safeguarding digital infrastructures against evolving threats (Motlagh et al., 2024; Sarker, 2024; Liu, 2024; Xu et al., 2024).

CONCLUSION

This work has underscored the transformative impact of large language models (LLMs) and artificial intelligence on the field of cybersecurity. As cyber threats grow in complexity and scale, leveraging advanced AI models offers unprecedented opportunities for proactive threat detection, mitigation, and resilience enhancement.

The integration of domain-specific adaptations, privacy-preserving techniques, and explainability mechanisms in LLMs significantly enhances their effectiveness and trustworthiness in real-world cybersecurity applications (Aghaei et al., 2022; Ferrag et al., 2024; Ghazal et al., 2024).

The future directions outlined emphasize that while the potential of LLMs is immense, challenges remain. These include ensuring model robustness against adversarial attacks, addressing ethical and privacy concerns, and fostering seamless human-AI collaboration to mitigate insider threats and reduce false positives (Gholami & Omar, 2023; Zangana, Sallow, & Omar, 2025). Moreover, emerging technologies such as quantum computing will demand the evolution of cybersecurity frameworks that integrate quantum-aware defenses alongside AI-driven intelligence (Zangana & Omar, 2025; Kasri et al., 2025).

Ultimately, the convergence of AI, LLMs, and cybersecurity heralds a new era of intelligent, adaptive, and resilient defense mechanisms. Continued interdisciplinary research, collaboration among academia, industry, and policymakers, and adherence to ethical standards will be critical to realizing the full promise of these technologies. This journey will not only protect digital infrastructures but also pave the way for innovative applications across domains, reinforcing the foundation of secure, trustworthy, and sustainable digital ecosystems (Omar & Zangana, 2024; Motlagh et al., 2024).

REFERENCES

Aghaei, E., Niu, X., Shadid, W., & Al-Shaer, E. (2022, October). Securebert: A domain-specific language model for cybersecurity. In *International Conference on Security and Privacy in Communication Systems* (pp. 39-56). Cham: Springer Nature Switzerland.

AlQenaei, Z. M. (2024, March). Evolution and Optimization of Language Model Architectures: From Foundations to Future Directions. In *International Conference on Computing and Machine Learning* (pp. 233-249). Singapore: Springer Nature Singapore.

Alturkistani, H., & Chuprat, S. (2024). *Artificial Intelligence and Large Language Models in Advancing Cyber Threat Intelligence: A Systematic Literature Review. ResearchGate*. DOI:DOI: 10.21203/rs.3.rs-5423193/v1

Asoronye, G. O., Anthony, O. C., Ogbuikwu, R. I., Ogili, C. O., & Ali, H. U. (2024). SecLM: A Specialized Security Language Model for Advanced Cybersecurity Applications and Threat Mitigation. *EKETE-International Journal Of Advanced Research*, *2*(6), 33–42.

Bryce, C., Kalousis, A., Leroux, I., Madinier, H., Mermoud, A., Mulder, V., ... & Ruch, P. *Trends in Large Language Models: Actors, Applications, and Impact on Cybersecurity*. Technology Observatory. https://technology-observatory.ch/academic_publication/trends-in-large-language-models-actors-applications-and-impact-on-cybersecurity/article.pdf

Chen, Y., Cui, M., Wang, D., Cao, Y., Yang, P., Jiang, B., Lu, Z., & Liu, B. (2024). A survey of large language models for cyber threat detection. *Computers & Security*, *145*, 104016. DOI: 10.1016/j.cose.2024.104016

Diaf, A., Korba, A. A., Karabadji, N. E., & Ghamri-Doudane, Y. (2024, April). Beyond detection: Leveraging large language models for cyber attack prediction in iot networks. In *2024 20th International Conference on Distributed Computing in Smart Systems and the Internet of Things (DCOSS-IoT)* (pp. 117-123). IEEE.

Ferrag, M. A., Alwahedi, F., Battah, A., Cherif, B., Mechri, A., & Tihanyi, N. (2024). *Generative ai and large language models for cyber security: All insights you need.* Arxiv.org. https://arxiv.org/html/2405.12750v1

Ferrag, M. A., Ndhlovu, M., Tihanyi, N., Cordeiro, L. C., Debbah, M., & Lestable, T. (2023). Revolutionizing cyber threat detection with large language models. *arXiv preprint arXiv:2306.14263*, 195-202.

Ferrag, M. A., Ndhlovu, M., Tihanyi, N., Cordeiro, L. C., Debbah, M., Lestable, T., & Thandi, N. S. (2024). Revolutionizing cyber threat detection with large language models: A privacy-preserving bert-based lightweight model for iot/iiot devices. *IEEE Access : Practical Innovations, Open Solutions*, *12*, 23733–23750. DOI: 10.1109/ACCESS.2024.3363469

Ghazal, T. M., Janjua, J. I., Abushiba, W., Ahmad, M., Ihsan, A., & Al-Dmour, N. A. (2024, December). Cybersecurity Revolution via Large Language Models and Explainable AI. In *2024 17th International Conference on Security of Information and Networks (SIN)* (pp. 1-6). IEEE. DOI: 10.1109/SIN63213.2024.10871324

Gholami, S., & Omar, M. (2023). Does Synthetic Data Make Large Language Models More Efficient? *arXiv preprint arXiv:2310.07830.*

Gholami, S., & Omar, M. (2024). Can a student large language model perform as well as its teacher? In *Innovations, Securities, and Case Studies Across Healthcare, Business, and Technology* (pp. 122-139). IGI Global. DOI: 10.4018/979-8-3693-1906-2.ch007

Gupta, B. B., Gaurav, A., & Arya, V. (2024). Navigating the security landscape of large language models in enterprise information systems. *Enterprise Information Systems*, *18*(4), 2310846. DOI: 10.1080/17517575.2024.2310846

Hadi, M. A., Abdulredha, M. N., & Hasan, E. (2023). Introduction to ChatGPT: A new revolution of artificial intelligence with machine learning algorithms and cybersecurity. *Sci. Arch*, *4*(04), 276. DOI: 10.47587/SA.2023.4406

Hamza, Y. A., & Omar, M. D. (2013). Cloud computing security: Abuse and nefarious use of cloud computing. *International Journal of Computer Engineering Research*, *3*(6), 22–27.

Hasanov, I., Virtanen, S., Hakkala, A., & Isoaho, J. (2024). Application of Large Language Models in Cybersecurity: A Systematic Literature Review. *IEEE Access : Practical Innovations, Open Solutions*, *12*, 176751–176778. DOI: 10.1109/ACCESS.2024.3505983

Hassanin, M., & Moustafa, N. (2024). A comprehensive overview of large language models (llms) for cyber defences: Opportunities and directions. *arXiv preprint arXiv:2405.14487.*

Huff, A. J., Burrell, D. N., Nobles, C., Richardson, K., Wright, J. B., Burton, S. L., Jones, A. J., Springs, D., Omar, M., & Brown-Jackson, K. L. (2023). Management Practices for Mitigating Cybersecurity Threats to Biotechnology Companies, Laboratories, and Healthcare Research Organizations. In *Applied Research Approaches to Technology, Healthcare, and Business* (pp. 1-12). IGI Global.

. Idelhaj, A., Abou El Houda, Z., & Khoukhi, L. (2024). Foundations models in cybersecurity. *Artificial Intelligence for Blockchain and Cybersecurity Powered IoT Applications*, 1.

. Idelhaj, A., Abou El Houda, Z., & Khoukhi, L. Foundations models in cybersecurity: A comprehensive review and future direction. *Artificial Intelligence for Blockchain and Cybersecurity Powered IoT Applications*, 1-18.

Jones, R., & Omar, M. (2024). Revolutionizing Cybersecurity: The GPT-2 Enhanced Attack Detection and Defense (GEADD) Method for Zero-Day Threats. *International Journal of Informatics* [INJIISCOM]. *Information System and Computer Engineering*, *5*(2), 178–191.

Jones, R., Omar, M., Mohammed, D., Nobles, C., & Dawson, M. (2023). Harnessing the Speed and Accuracy of Machine Learning to Advance Cybersecurity. In *2023 Congress in Computer Science, Computer Engineering, & Applied Computing (CSCE)* (pp. 418-421). IEEE. DOI: 10.1109/CSCE60160.2023.00074

Kasri, W., Himeur, Y., Alkhazaleh, H. A., Tarapiah, S., Atalla, S., Mansoor, W., & Al-Ahmad, H. (2025). From Vulnerability to Defense: The Role of Large Language Models in Enhancing Cybersecurity. *Computation (Basel, Switzerland)*, *13*(2), 30. DOI: 10.3390/computation13020030

. LESTABLE, T., & THANDI, N. S. Revolutionizing Cyber Threat Detection with Large Language Models: A privacy-preserving BERT-based Lightweight Model for IoT/IIoT Devices.

Liu, Z. (2024, April). A review of advancements and applications of pre-trained language models in cybersecurity. In *2024 12th International Symposium on Digital Forensics and Security (ISDFS)* (pp. 1-10). IEEE. DOI: 10.1109/ISDFS60797.2024.10527236

Manoharan, A., & Sarker, M. (2023). Revolutionizing Cybersecurity: Unleashing the Power of Artificial Intelligence and Machine Learning for Next-Generation Threat Detection. *DOI:* https://www. doi. org/10.56726/IRJMETS32644, *1*.

Mohammed, D., Omar, M., & Nguyen, V. (2018). Wireless sensor network security: Approaches to detecting and avoiding wormhole attacks. *Journal of Research in Business. Economics and Management, 10*(2), 1860–1864.

Motlagh, F. N., Hajizadeh, M., Majd, M., Najafi, P., Cheng, F., & Meinel, C. (2024). Large language models in cybersecurity: State-of-the-art. *arXiv preprint arXiv:2402.00891.*

Nguyen, V., Mohammed, D., Omar, M., & Banisakher, M. (2018). The Effects of the FCC Net Neutrality Repeal on Security and Privacy. [IJHIoT]. *International Journal of Hyperconnectivity and the Internet of Things, 2*(2), 21–29. DOI: 10.4018/IJHIoT.2018070102

Omar, M. (2021). *New insights into database security: An effective and integrated approach for applying access control mechanisms and cryptographic concepts in Microsoft Access environments.* MWAIS 2021 Proceedings. https://aisel.aisnet.org/cgi/viewcontent.cgi?article=1019&context=mwais2021

Omar, M. (2022). *Machine Learning for Cybersecurity: Innovative Deep Learning Solutions.* Springer Brief. https://link.springer.com/book/978303115

Omar, M. (2024). From Attack to Defense: Strengthening DNN Text Classification Against Adversarial Examples. In *Innovations, Securities, and Case Studies Across Healthcare, Business, and Technology* (pp. 174-195). IGI Global.

Omar, M. (2024). Revolutionizing Malware Detection: A Paradigm Shift Through Optimized Convolutional Neural Networks. In *Innovations, Securities, and Case Studies Across Healthcare, Business, and Technology* (pp. 196-220). IGI Global. DOI: 10.4018/979-8-3693-1906-2.ch011

Omar, M., & Zangana, H. (Eds.). (2025). *Digital Forensics in the Age of AI.* IGI Global., DOI: 10.4018/979-8-3373-0857-9

Omar, M., & Zangana, H. M. (Eds.). (2024). *Redefining Security With Cyber AI.* IGI Global., DOI: 10.4018/979-8-3693-6517-5

Omar, M., & Zangana, H. M. (Eds.). (2025). *Application of Large Language Models (LLMs) for Software Vulnerability Detection.* IGI Global., DOI: 10.4018/979-8-3693-9311-6

Omar, M., Zangana, H. M., Al-Karaki, J. N., & Mohammed, D. (2024). Harnessing LLMs for IoT malware detection: A comparative analysis of BERT and GPT-2. In *2024 8th International Symposium on Multidisciplinary Studies and Innovative Technologies (ISMSIT)* (pp. 1-6). Ankara, Turkiye. https://doi.org/DOI: 10.1109/ISMSIT63511.2024.10757249

Omar, M., Zangana, H. M., & Mohammed, D. (Eds.). (2025). *Integrating Artificial Intelligence in Cybersecurity and Forensic Practices*. IGI Global., DOI: 10.4018/979-8-3373-0588-2

Ozkan-Okay, M., Akin, E., Aslan, Ö., Kosunalp, S., Iliev, T., Stoyanov, I., & Beloev, I. (2024). A comprehensive survey: Evaluating the efficiency of artificial intelligence and machine learning techniques on cyber security solutions. *IEEE Access : Practical Innovations, Open Solutions*, *12*, 12229–12256. DOI: 10.1109/ACCESS.2024.3355547

Pleshakova, E., Osipov, A., Gataullin, S., Gataullin, T., & Vasilakos, A. (2024). Next gen cybersecurity paradigm towards artificial general intelligence: Russian market challenges and future global technological trends. *Journal of Computer Virology and Hacking Techniques*, *20*(3), 429–440. DOI: 10.1007/s11416-024-00529-x

Santos, O., Salam, S., & Dahir, H. (2024). *The AI revolution in networking, cybersecurity, and emerging technologies*. Addison-Wesley.

Sarker, I. H. (2024). Generative AI and large language modeling in cybersecurity. In *AI-Driven Cybersecurity and Threat Intelligence: Cyber Automation, Intelligent Decision-Making and Explainability* (pp. 79–99). Springer Nature Switzerland. DOI: 10.1007/978-3-031-54497-2_5

Taghavi, S. M., & Feyzi, F. (2024). *Using large language models to better detect and handle software vulnerabilities and cyber security threats. Research Square.* DOI: 10.21203/rs.3.rs-4387414/v1

. THANDI, N. S. (2024). Revolutionizing Cyber Threat Detection With Large Language Models: A Privacy-Preserving BERT-Based Lightweight Model for IoT/IIoT Devices.

Wright, J., Dawson, M. E.Jr, & Omar, M. (2012). Cyber security and mobile threats: The need for antivirus applications for smartphones. *Journal of Information Systems Technology and Planning*, *5*(14), 40–60.

Xu, H., Wang, S., Li, N., Wang, K., Zhao, Y., Chen, K., . . . Wang, H. (2024). Large language models for cyber security: A systematic literature review. *arXiv preprint arXiv:2405.04760.*

Yu, J., Shvetsov, A. V., & Alsamhi, S. H. (2024). Leveraging machine learning for cybersecurity resilience in industry 4.0: Challenges and future directions. *IEEE Access : Practical Innovations, Open Solutions*, *12*, 159579–159596. DOI: 10.1109/ACCESS.2024.3482987

Zangana, H., & Omar, M. (Eds.). (2025). *Leveraging Large Language Models for Quantum-Aware Cybersecurity*. IGI Global., DOI: 10.4018/979-8-3373-1102-9

. Zangana, H. M. (2024). Exploring Blockchain-Based Timestamping Tools: A Comprehensive Review. *Redefining Security With Cyber AI*, 92-110.

. Zangana, H. M. (2024). Exploring the Landscape of Website Vulnerability Scanners: A Comprehensive Review and Comparative Analysis. *Redefining Security With Cyber AI*, 111-129.

. Zangana, H. M. (2024). Harnessing the Power of Large Language Models. *Application of Large Language Models (LLMs) for Software Vulnerability Detection*, 1.

Zangana, H. M., & Li, S. (2025). Future Trends in AI and Digital Forensics. In Omar, M., & Zangana, H. (Eds.), *Digital Forensics in the Age of AI* (pp. 347–380). IGI Global Scientific Publishing., DOI: 10.4018/979-8-3373-0857-9.ch013

Zangana, H. M., Mohammed, A. K., Sallow, A. B., & Sallow, Z. B. (2024). Cybernetic Deception: Unraveling the Layers of Email Phishing Threats. [INJURATECH]. *International Journal of Research and Applied Technology*, *4*(1), 35–47.

Zangana, H. M., & Mohammed, D. (2025). Foundations of Large Language Models in Software Vulnerability Detection. In Omar, M., & Zangana, H. (Eds.), *Application of Large Language Models (LLMs) for Software Vulnerability Detection* (pp. 41–74). IGI Global., DOI: 10.4018/979-8-3693-9311-6.ch002

Zangana, H. M., & Mustafa, F. M. (2024). Hybrid Image Denoising Using Wavelet Transform and Deep Learning. *EAI Endorsed Transactions on AI and Robotics*, *3*. Advance online publication. DOI: 10.4108/airo.7486

Zangana, H. M., & Mustafa, F. M. (2025). Image Denoising Techniques for Cybersecurity and Forensic Applications: AI-Driven Approaches. In Omar, M., Zangana, H., & Mohammed, D. (Eds.), *Integrating Artificial Intelligence in Cybersecurity and Forensic Practices* (pp. 117–142). IGI Global Scientific Publishing., DOI: 10.4018/979-8-3373-0588-2.ch005

Zangana, H. M., Mustafa, F. M., & Li, S. (2025). Large Language Models in Cybersecurity: From Automation to Intelligence. In *Leveraging Large Language Models for Quantum-Aware Cybersecurity* (pp. 277-300). IGI Global Scientific Publishing.

Zangana, H. M., Mustafa, F. M., & Li, S. (2025). Large Language Models in Cybersecurity: From Automation to Intelligence. In Zangana, H., & Omar, M. (Eds.), *Leveraging Large Language Models for Quantum-Aware Cybersecurity* (pp. 277–300). IGI Global Scientific Publishing., DOI: 10.4018/979-8-3373-1102-9.ch009

Zangana, H. M., Mustafa, F. M., Li, S., & Al-Karaki, J. N. (2025). Natural Language Processing for Cyber Threat Intelligence in a Quantum World. In Zangana, H., & Omar, M. (Eds.), *Leveraging Large Language Models for Quantum-Aware Cybersecurity* (pp. 345–388). IGI Global Scientific Publishing., DOI: 10.4018/979-8-3373-1102-9.ch011

Zangana, H. M., Mustafa, F. M., & Omar, M. (2024). A Hybrid Approach for Robust Object Detection: Integrating Template Matching and Faster R-CNN. *EAI Endorsed Transactions on AI and Robotics*, *3*. Advance online publication. DOI: 10.4108/airo.6858

Zangana, H. M., & Omar, M. (2020). Threats, Attacks, and Mitigations of Smartphone Security. *Academic Journal of Nawroz University*, *9*(4), 324–332. DOI: 10.25007/ajnu.v9n4a989

Zangana, H. M., & Omar, M. (2025). Harnessing the Power of Large Language Models for Cybersecurity: Applications, Challenges, and Future Directions. In Omar, M., & Zangana, H. (Eds.), *Application of Large Language Models (LLMs) for Software Vulnerability Detection* (pp. 1–40). IGI Global., DOI: 10.4018/979-8-3693-9311-6.ch001

Zangana, H. M., & Omar, M. (2025). Introduction to Digital Forensics and Artificial Intelligence. In Omar, M., & Zangana, H. (Eds.), *Digital Forensics in the Age of AI* (pp. 1–30). IGI Global Scientific Publishing., DOI: 10.4018/979-8-3373-0857-9.ch001

Zangana, H. M., & Omar, M. (2025). Introduction to Quantum-Aware Cybersecurity: The Need for LLMs. In Zangana, H., & Omar, M. (Eds.), *Leveraging Large Language Models for Quantum-Aware Cybersecurity* (pp. 1–28). IGI Global Scientific Publishing., DOI: 10.4018/979-8-3373-1102-9.ch001

Zangana, H. M., & Omar, M. (2025). The Role of Leadership in Advancing Inclusive Health Technologies. In Burrell, D., & Nguyen, C. (Eds.), *New Horizons in Leadership: Inclusive Explorations in Health, Technology, and Education* (pp. 203–220). IGI Global Scientific Publishing., DOI: 10.4018/979-8-3693-6437-6.ch009

. Zangana, H. M., Omar, M., Al-Karaki, J. N., & Mohammed, D. (2024). Comprehensive Review and Analysis of Network Firewall Rule Analyzers: Enhancing Security Posture and Efficiency. *Redefining Security With Cyber AI*, 15-36.

Zangana, H. M., Sallow, Z. B., & Omar, M. (2025). The Human Factor in Cybersecurity: Addressing the Risks of Insider Threats. *Jurnal Ilmiah Computer Science*, *3*(2), 76–85. DOI: 10.58602/jics.v3i2.37

Chapter 7
Sociological Dimensions of AI in Cybercrime Investigation:
Surveillance, Social Control, and the Criminalization of Digital Behavior

Rozhan A. Muhyadeen
https://orcid.org/0009-0009-3367-6983
University of Duhok, Iraq

ABSTRACT

The integration of (AI) into cybercrime investigations has transformed traditional policing, introducing advanced tools for surveillance, pattern recognition, and predictive analytics., they also raise pressing sociological concerns regarding privacy, power asymmetries, and the shifting boundaries of deviance and criminality in digital spaces.This chapter explores how AI-enabled surveillance shapes social control mechanisms and redefines norms in online behavior. Drawing from sociological theories of surveillance, control, and criminalization,the chapter critically examines how automated systems can reinforce existing social inequalities, marginalize certain groups,and amplify biases through algorithmic decision-making.Furthermore, it investigates the implications of AI in reconfiguring the social contract between citizens and the state in the context of digital law enforcement. By analyzing case studies and emerging global trends, the chapter provides a nuanced perspective on the role of AI in both empowering and challenging contemporary cybercrime investigation practices

DOI: 10.4018/979-8-3373-6536-7.ch007

INTRODUCTION

The rapid adoption of Artificial Intelligence (AI) in cybercrime investigation has not only transformed the landscape of digital forensics but also significantly redefined social structures, norms, and governance practices. As AI becomes a dominant force in law enforcement and crime detection, it is essential to interrogate the sociological implications that accompany its deployment. The application of AI technologies—ranging from predictive policing algorithms to facial recognition systems—raises complex questions surrounding surveillance, social control, digital inequality, and the criminalization of online behavior (Faqir, 2023; Hayward & Maas, 2021).

From a sociological lens, the digital turn in crime detection is not simply a matter of technological advancement, but a reconfiguration of societal power dynamics and institutional operations (Spyropoulos, 2024; Grab, 2025). This shift implicates longstanding debates around governance, deviance, and justice in cyberspace (Gupta, 2024; Powell et al., 2018). AI systems can both challenge and reinforce social inequalities, often reproducing existing institutional biases under the guise of objectivity (Ray, 2019; Casad et al., 2021).

A growing body of research acknowledges that the integration of AI within educational and institutional frameworks parallels its role in crime prevention. AI's role in schools, for example, illustrates how algorithmic systems can be used for both student support and disciplinary surveillance (Ayeni et al., 2024; Pedro et al., 2019; Mishra et al., 2024). These same mechanisms of categorization and monitoring are central to digital policing technologies, where marginalized groups are disproportionately targeted under predictive models (Završnik, 2017; Qiu, 2025).

Surveillance, once confined to public spaces, now permeates digital interactions, social networks, and online identities. As Shevchenko et al. (2025) discuss, AI is increasingly used to monitor behaviors that infringe on the dignity, autonomy, and perceived morality of individuals. In this context, surveillance becomes a tool of social control—governing not only what people do but also what they might do in the future (Middleton, 2021; Umanah et al., 2024).

Additionally, the chapter considers how organizational and educational theories can inform our understanding of AI's societal influence. For instance, change management frameworks (Battilana & Casciaro, 2012; Palmer et al., 2016; Stouten et al., 2018; Shani et al., 2025) help illuminate how institutions adapt or resist AI integration in ways that reshape their organizational cultures. Feminist and critical perspectives, such as those of Blackmore (2013) and Kohli et al. (2021), reveal how identity, race, and gender intersect with technological governance, particularly in policing and disciplinary contexts.

The digital divide, too, is a critical dimension in AI-driven crime prevention. Sociological research emphasizes that those most impacted by automated surveillance and AI classification systems are often those with limited access to digital literacy and infrastructure (Mac Fadden et al., 2024; Kalashnikova et al., 2025; Muhyadeen, 2026). These disparities echo broader educational and social inequalities, raising concerns about epistemic agency and ethical accountability in algorithmic systems (Monahan et al., 2024; Peer Mohamed, 2024).

Moreover, educational sociology provides critical tools for evaluating how knowledge about AI, ethics, and surveillance is produced and disseminated (Brennan & Canny, 2023; SWARGIARY, 2025). Just as in schools and universities, where AI tools reshape learning and governance (Lan, 2024; Jin et al., 2024; Padua, 2025), similar dynamics occur in cybercrime units and digital policing environments where AI redefines roles, hierarchies, and decision-making authority (Halmo, 2025; Museus & Jayakumar, 2012; Liu, 2025).

Understanding AI's role in cybercrime investigation also involves confronting its cultural and ideological implications. Rajesh (2024) explores how AI intersects with identity and representation, while Patra (2024) discusses how digital behavior is increasingly subject to legal and social scrutiny through automated classification systems. These concerns demand a reevaluation of the boundaries between legality and deviance in digital societies.

Finally, the deployment of AI in cybercrime investigation cannot be separated from questions of sustainability, innovation, and justice. Educational and technological disruptions (Murtiningsih & Sujito, 2024; Sa & Serpa, 2020) reveal the dual role of AI—as both a tool for empowerment and a mechanism of exclusion. As this chapter will argue, a sociological perspective is essential to critically engage with the promises and perils of AI in cybercrime investigation, particularly as it pertains to surveillance, social control, and the expanding definitions of digital criminality.

THEORETICAL FRAMEWORK

To understand the sociological implications of Artificial Intelligence (AI) in cybercrime investigation, it is essential to ground the analysis within a multidisciplinary theoretical framework. This framework draws from sociology of education, organizational change theory, digital criminology, critical race theory, feminist sociology, and surveillance studies. These intersecting perspectives allow for a comprehensive exploration of how AI reconfigures systems of control, surveillance, and institutional power in both educational and criminal justice contexts.

Surveillance and Social Control

At the core of AI's application in cybercrime investigation is the principle of surveillance as a tool of social control. Završnik (2017) argues that big data technologies transform crime control into a predictive and preventative process that often extends beyond legal definitions of criminal behavior. This form of algorithmic governance reflects what Hayward and Maas (2021) describe as the "pre-crime" logic of AI—intervening in individuals' behavior before actual law-breaking occurs.

From a Foucauldian perspective, surveillance through AI becomes a means of disciplining populations and shaping digital behavior. This aligns with Umanah et al. (2024), who assert that emerging technologies influence social behavior by normalizing constant monitoring and reshaping social norms around privacy and security. The sociological relevance of such dynamics is evident in the institutionalization of AI crime research (Spyropoulos, 2024), where biases can be embedded into technologies, perpetuating inequality (Ray, 2019; Casad et al., 2021).

Racialized and Gendered Organizations in AI Systems

Ray's (2019) theory of racialized organizations provides a useful lens to analyze how AI systems deployed in policing and education reproduce structural inequalities. Organizations are not neutral entities but are embedded with historical and cultural power structures, which are often encoded into AI algorithms. Casad et al. (2021) similarly highlight how women in STEM face systemic biases that are mirrored in algorithmic decision-making systems. These insights are crucial for understanding how AI in digital forensics may disproportionately criminalize racialized and gendered subjects.

Likewise, Blackmore (2013) critiques the gendered assumptions in educational leadership—a critique that is increasingly relevant in the AI age where leadership, accountability, and decision-making are being delegated to non-human agents. Kohli et al. (2021) and Rajesh (2024) extend these ideas by showing how technology intersects with race, identity, and educational justice.

To contextualize how LLMs are embedded in cybersecurity environments, Figure 1 presents an architectural diagram highlighting key components and flow.

Figure 1. Integration of LLMs into cybersecurity pipelines

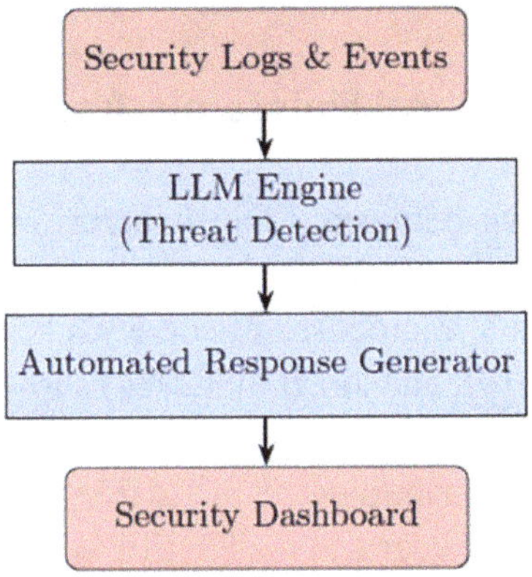

Organizational Change and Institutional Resistance

The implementation of AI technologies within law enforcement and educational institutions can be conceptualized through theories of organizational change. Battilana and Casciaro (2012) propose a contingency theory of organizational change where networks and institutional logics influence the success or resistance of technological adoption. Stouten et al. (2018) and Benn et al. (2014) emphasize that successful change requires alignment between technological innovation and institutional culture.

Palmer et al. (2016) and Shani et al. (2025) suggest that organizations undergoing digital transformation must consider multiple perspectives—including power dynamics, leadership models, and collective identities. Halmo (2025) illustrates this in the educational sector, where predictive analytics and AI tools reshaped academic advising through both technical and cultural shifts.

Digital Criminology and AI Ethics

Digital criminology, as outlined by Powell et al. (2018), provides an emerging framework to study the sociotechnical nature of crime and justice in the digital age. Middleton (2021) argues that AI tools support cybercrime research by generating new forms of data and evidence but also introduce new risks in terms of ethics and bias. Faqir (2023) and Qiu (2025) contribute further by examining how AI is changing the methods, boundaries, and authority structures in digital criminal investigations.

The sociological implications are clear: as AI becomes embedded in justice systems, the lines between deviance and compliance become increasingly blurred and shaped by algorithmic logic (Gupta, 2024). This has serious consequences for how behavior is interpreted and criminalized.

Educational Sociology and Epistemic Agency

A parallel can be drawn between AI in cybercrime investigation and AI in educational governance. Educational sociology, as explained by SWARGIARY (2025), treats education as a microcosm of society's broader structures. Ayeni et al. (2024), Pedro et al. (2019), and Jin et al. (2024) show that AI in education can enhance personalization and performance, yet risks reinforcing digital inequalities (Mac Fadden et al., 2024; Kalashnikova et al., 2025).

Monahan et al. (2024) and Peer Mohamed (2024) emphasize the need for epistemic agency—the ability for users to critique and navigate AI systems—which is also crucial in legal settings where defendants or users are subject to AI-driven decision-making. Brennan and Canny (2023) and Muhyadeen (2026) argue for re-centering critical sociology in teacher development, which parallels the need for critical awareness in digital forensics professionals.

Critical Pedagogy and AI Identity

Critical pedagogy offers another rich framework for understanding how AI mediates identity and learning. Lan (2024) and Moradi-Kelayeh (2025) highlight the transformation of teacher identity through AI-enhanced training, while Mishra et al. (2024) and Grab (2025) underscore the role of AI in culturally responsive education. These pedagogical shifts reflect broader social transformations in how AI informs perceptions of authority, knowledge, and discipline—both in classrooms and in courts.

Padua (2025) and Sá and Serpa (2020) advocate for integrating digital culture into teaching to build resilience and adaptability—skills increasingly necessary in both educational and legal institutions navigating AI. Museus and Jayakumar (2012) stress that inclusive campus cultures can resist institutional biases, which is also relevant in resisting algorithmic injustice in cybercrime investigations.

Toward a Multilayered Sociological Framework

Synthesizing these diverse yet interconnected perspectives, this chapter adopts a multilayered sociological framework. It accounts for the interplay between institutional change (Battilana & Casciaro, 2012; Palmer et al., 2016), surveillance and social control (Završnik, 2017), educational sociology (SWARGIARY, 2025), digital criminology (Faqir, 2023; Powell et al., 2018), and identity theory (Ray, 2019;

Rajesh, 2024). It also considers the importance of justice-oriented pedagogy and leadership (Kohli et al., 2021; Liu, 2025; Quan et al., 2019; Sullivan et al., 2015; Steinert, 2025).

Patra (2024) captures the essence of this approach by exploring how AI's sociological dimensions bridge law, education, and emerging behavioral norms. As institutions integrate AI into their foundational operations, the need to examine the cultural, structural, and ideological effects becomes ever more urgent.

AI AND THE EXPANSION OF SURVEILLANCE PRACTICES

The proliferation of Artificial Intelligence (AI) in digital forensics and cybercrime investigation has triggered a paradigm shift in the scope, scale, and sophistication of surveillance practices. Beyond traditional modes of observation, AI enables predictive, real-time, and often covert forms of monitoring that fundamentally reshape social control, privacy, and institutional power. This section explores how AI-driven surveillance practices operate within broader sociological systems, drawing on critical literature from education, criminology, organizational change, and sociology.

From Observation to Prediction: AI's Surveillance Logic

Surveillance in the age of AI is not merely about watching—it is about anticipating. As Završnik (2017) notes, big data systems are designed not only to detect but to *predict* potential criminal behavior, transforming surveillance from a reactive to a proactive function. AI enables what Hayward and Maas (2021) describe as "algorithmic governance," wherein behavioral data is continuously harvested, analyzed, and interpreted to forecast future deviance. This predictive logic fuels law enforcement strategies such as predictive policing and social media monitoring, altering how crime is conceptualized and addressed.

This shift is echoed in digital education systems, where AI similarly functions to monitor student performance and predict learning trajectories (Ayeni et al., 2024; Jin et al., 2024). These parallels demonstrate how surveillance mechanisms developed in education and security contexts converge around the goal of behavioral regulation through algorithmic modeling.

The following flowchart (Figure 2) provides a structured view of the evaluation framework used to assess LLM-based security systems, from input data to final evaluation reports.

Figure 2. Evaluation framework for LLM-based security systems

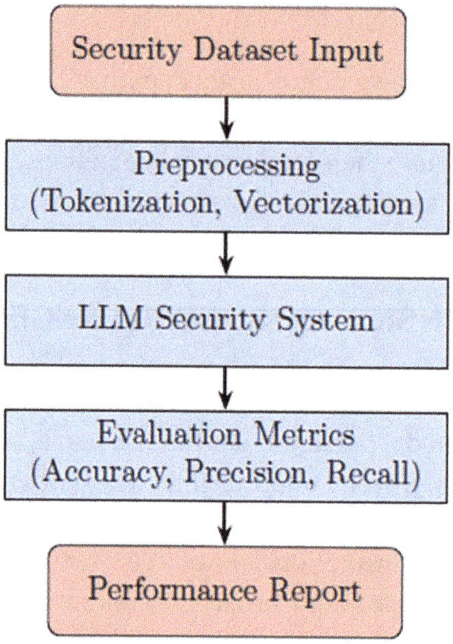

Institutionalizing AI Surveillance: Crime and Social Control

AI has become increasingly institutionalized within cybercrime investigation (Spyropoulos, 2024), transforming surveillance into a normative, organizationally embedded function. The implications of this institutionalization are twofold. First, it deepens the reach of social control mechanisms by enabling constant monitoring across multiple digital platforms (Powell et al., 2018). Second, it blurs the boundary between public and private domains, embedding surveillance in everyday technologies such as smartphones, smart homes, and social networks (Middleton, 2021; Shevchenko et al., 2025).

The normalization of these practices reflects what Faqir (2023) refers to as the "comprehensive reach" of AI in digital criminal investigations, where surveillance extends to the mere potential for crime, rather than proven illegal activity. Gupta (2024) emphasizes that such developments necessitate a reevaluation of criminological theory, particularly concerning deviance and social reaction.

Table 1 summarizes essential KPIs used in evaluating LLM-based security systems, offering a quick reference for metric definitions and their significance.

Table 1. Key performance indicators for LLM-based security systems

Metric	Definition	Significance
Accuracy	% of correct predictions	Overall correctness
Precision	TP / (TP + FP)	Detection of true positives
Recall	TP / (TP + FN)	Coverage of actual positives
F1 Score	2 * (P * R) / (P + R)	Balance between precision and recall
Latency	Time per inference	Real-time applicability

Surveillance and Organizational Change

The integration of AI surveillance into institutions requires significant organizational adaptation. As Battilana and Casciaro (2012) note, change agents and institutional logics mediate how technology is adopted. For surveillance practices, this means that their success or resistance is deeply shaped by institutional culture, networks, and leadership. Palmer et al. (2016) and Stouten et al. (2018) argue that successful AI implementation must balance technological capabilities with stakeholder engagement and ethical alignment.

In educational contexts, Halmo (2025) shows how predictive analytics have transformed academic advising, effectively turning student data into a form of administrative surveillance. Similarly, Kalashnikova et al. (2025) argue that surveillance technologies in digital education can reinforce systemic hierarchies and exclusions, particularly when institutions fail to acknowledge evolving social expectations around data privacy.

Surveillance, Inequality, and Algorithmic Bias

Surveillance is not experienced uniformly. AI systems often reproduce and magnify existing inequalities through what Ray (2019) conceptualizes as the "racialized organization." Algorithmic surveillance, whether in schools or law enforcement, disproportionately targets marginalized communities, reinforcing institutional biases under the guise of neutrality.

Casad et al. (2021) highlight how gender bias in academia is replicated in AI systems, while Blackmore (2013) critiques the masculinist assumptions embedded in leadership models that guide AI policy in education and beyond. Kohli et al. (2021) emphasize that only through critically informed leadership—especially from teachers and practitioners of color—can surveillance technologies be redirected toward more equitable outcomes.

Rajesh (2024) pushes this further, suggesting that AI surveillance transcends individual identity and becomes a mechanism of abstract categorization—an issue that Peer Mohamed (2024) explores in the context of language education. These concerns apply directly to cybercrime investigation, where predictive tools may categorize users as threats based on opaque, biased metrics (Qiu, 2025).

Pedagogical Surveillance and Epistemic Control

Surveillance extends beyond policing into education, where it increasingly governs how students are taught, evaluated, and disciplined. Mishra et al. (2024), Lan (2024), and Moradi-Kelayeh (2025) show that AI reshapes the teacher-student dynamic, often automating pedagogical judgment and eroding teacher autonomy. Monahan et al. (2024) warn that these systems may suppress epistemic agency, particularly for students from underrepresented groups.

Murtiningsih and Sujito (2024) argue that education systems must respond to technological disruption with inclusive pedagogies that resist standardization and surveillance. Museus and Jayakumar (2012) call for the creation of campus cultures that value inclusivity over datafication, and Padua (2025) highlights the need for digital culture training to mitigate the surveillance-centric orientation of current AI deployments.

Mac Fadden et al. (2024) add that digital inequality manifests through differential access and visibility in AI systems, often resulting in hyper-surveillance of disadvantaged students while affluent groups benefit from algorithmic discretion.

Surveillance as Structural Violence and Resistance

While AI enhances institutional control, it can also be contested. As Shani et al. (2025) and Benn et al. (2014) note, organizational change opens space for resistance and negotiation. Surveillance practices are not fixed; they can be reshaped through inclusive leadership, critical pedagogy, and stakeholder mobilization.

Steinert (2025) and Sullivan et al. (2015) advocate for faculty and educators to develop core competencies that question the ethical and structural dimensions of surveillance. Similarly, Muhyadeen (2026) suggests that AI integration into professional development must foreground equity and identity as foundational principles. Brennan and Canny (2023) show that student-teachers' engagement with sociology helps illuminate how surveillance mechanisms operate across sectors.

SWARGIARY (2025) argues that educational sociology provides the analytical tools to understand and resist technocratic governance. By recognizing the cultural and institutional dynamics of AI surveillance, actors in both education and law enforcement can work toward more just and transparent applications.

SOCIAL CONTROL AND ALGORITHMIC GOVERNANCE

The advent of Artificial Intelligence (AI) has inaugurated a new era in the exercise of social control, particularly through algorithmic governance. While traditional models of social regulation rely on hierarchical institutions and codified law enforcement, algorithmic systems introduce decentralized, predictive, and data-driven mechanisms that increasingly govern behavior in both physical and digital spaces. These AI systems reshape not only the structures of surveillance and enforcement but also the very definitions of deviance, legitimacy, and power.

Theoretical Foundations of Social Control in the Digital Age

The concept of social control in criminology and sociology historically involves formal (e.g., police, courts) and informal (e.g., cultural norms, peer pressure) mechanisms that guide individual behavior. In the digital age, however, these controls are increasingly embedded in technological infrastructures. Završnik (2017) emphasizes how big data and AI shift social control from reactive punishment to preemptive governance, blurring the lines between suspicion and guilt. AI technologies employed in predictive policing, behavior monitoring, and risk profiling operate under the logic of algorithmic governance—systems that make decisions or recommend actions based on vast data inputs without direct human oversight (Hayward & Maas, 2021; Faqir, 2023).

This shift is part of a broader movement toward algorithmic regulation across sectors, including education, healthcare, and employment, where AI systems shape opportunities and outcomes (Mac Fadden et al., 2024). In educational environments, algorithmic systems assess students' engagement and predict outcomes, often using opaque methods that bypass teacher discretion (Ayeni et al., 2024; Jin et al., 2024).

Algorithmic Governance and the Normalization of Surveillance

Algorithmic governance introduces subtle but profound changes to how surveillance operates. Unlike visible forms of monitoring, AI-powered systems often work in the background—tracking digital footprints, analyzing behavior patterns, and flagging deviations from normative models (Middleton, 2021; Powell et al., 2018). In cybercrime investigation, this means that surveillance is increasingly continuous, automated, and predictive, enabling the state and corporations to exert social control without the need for physical presence or judicial oversight (Spyropoulos, 2024).

Shevchenko et al. (2025) argue that AI's role in investigating crimes related to personal dignity reflects this shift, where machine-driven judgments influence decisions about morality, deviance, and criminality. Umanah et al. (2024) further highlight that such surveillance systems alter human behavior, promoting self-discipline and compliance even in the absence of visible authority—a form of Foucauldian "panopticism" intensified by technology.

In education, Halmo (2025) shows how predictive analytics in academic advising enforce behavioral norms by identifying "at-risk" students and triggering interventions before problems materialize. Such practices mirror those in criminal justice, where algorithmic risk assessments guide decisions about parole, policing, and resource allocation (Gupta, 2024; Qiu, 2025).

To visually compare the performance of different LLMs in cybersecurity-related tasks, the chart below presents accuracy results from several popular models.

Figure 3. Accuracy comparison of LLMs on security classification tasks

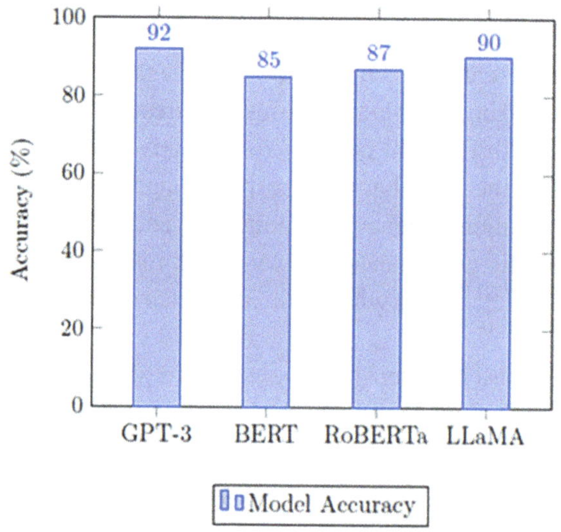

Reinforcing Inequality through Algorithmic Control

One of the most pressing sociological critiques of algorithmic governance is its role in reproducing and intensifying social inequalities. Ray's (2019) theory of racialized organizations provides a useful lens for understanding how algorithms, developed within and deployed by biased institutions, can perpetuate racial and gender disparities under the guise of objectivity. Casad et al. (2021) find similar patterns in academia, where AI technologies mirror and reinforce gender inequalities in STEM fields.

In education and cybercrime alike, AI systems may encode assumptions that disproportionately flag marginalized individuals or communities for scrutiny. Blackmore (2013) and Kohli et al. (2021) warn that when leadership fails to interrogate these biases, algorithmic systems become tools of structural domination rather than neutral instruments of efficiency. Kalashnikova et al. (2025) echo this concern, noting that AI in professional sociology training can unintentionally institutionalize exclusion unless designed with attention to evolving cultural dynamics.

Liu (2025) argues that equitable outcomes require leadership styles grounded in inclusion and awareness of sociological dynamics, especially as algorithmic decisions increasingly influence student and societal outcomes. In law enforcement, this need is mirrored by critiques of predictive policing systems that over-police communities of color based on historical data biases (Qiu, 2025; Pedro et al., 2019).

Organizational Change and the Embedding of Algorithmic Norms

The implementation of algorithmic governance is not only a technological matter but a deeply organizational one. According to Battilana and Casciaro (2012), successful change requires alignment between institutional logics and network-based influence. Stouten et al. (2018) and Palmer et al. (2016) stress the importance of participatory change models in embedding AI technologies without exacerbating internal resistance or ethical blind spots.

Benn et al. (2014) and Shani et al. (2025) further assert that sustainable organizational transformation necessitates cultural adaptation and ethical clarity. In the context of AI in cybercrime investigation, this means not only adopting new technologies but also rethinking institutional frameworks, power structures, and accountability mechanisms.

Educational institutions provide a useful analogy. Mishra et al. (2024) and Monahan et al. (2024) describe how faculty engagement and epistemic agency are critical in resisting the implicit biases of AI-based learning platforms. Similarly, Quan et al. (2019) suggest that teacher identity and critical consciousness are necessary to navigate AI-enhanced systems without ceding pedagogical control.

Critical Resistance and Ethical Alternatives

As AI continues to reshape governance structures, critical resistance becomes vital. Museus and Jayakumar (2012) and Murtiningsih and Sujito (2024) argue for inclusive pedagogies that resist the homogenizing tendencies of algorithmic learning models. In both education and criminal justice, ethical resistance requires recognition of how AI systems shape identities, expectations, and behavioral norms.

Grab (2025) advocates for culturally responsive AI in higher education, a principle that can also inform digital forensics by ensuring that systems are inclusive, transparent, and context-sensitive. Peer Mohamed (2024) calls for ethical considerations in AI-driven language education, drawing attention to how even seemingly neutral tools can embed cultural biases.

Lan (2024) and Muhyadeen (2026) suggest that identity-based motivations and equity-centered professional development are essential in preparing educators—and by extension, investigators—for critical engagement with AI technologies. Padua (2025) adds that digital culture training should be foundational, not optional, in shaping future-ready, ethically grounded institutions.

Sullivan et al. (2015) and Brennan and Canny (2023) remind us that systemic change must include not only new tools but new ways of thinking—critical, inclusive, and responsive to the sociological realities that algorithms can obscure.

Toward a Sociological Framework for Algorithmic Governance

Ultimately, algorithmic governance represents both an opportunity and a challenge for social control. While AI can enhance efficiency, responsiveness, and analytical depth in cybercrime investigation, it also introduces new risks of bias, overreach, and erosion of human judgment. A sociological approach to algorithmic governance must center transparency, equity, and the inclusion of diverse perspectives in both design and implementation.

Patra (2024) emphasizes that sociological insights are crucial in understanding how AI redefines legality, legitimacy, and normativity. SWARGIARY (2025) contends that educational sociology provides the tools to critically interrogate the structural consequences of AI and to promote systems that empower rather than discipline. Sá and Serpa (2020) argue that moments of technological disruption, such as those prompted by the COVID-19 pandemic, offer a rare opportunity to rethink governance systems toward more sustainable and inclusive futures.

CRIMINALIZATION OF DIGITAL BEHAVIOR

The rise of artificial intelligence (AI) has not only transformed how cybercrime is investigated but has also redefined what constitutes criminal behavior in digital environments. The increasing reliance on AI-driven surveillance, data analytics, and predictive modeling has enabled states and institutions to police a wide range of online actions with unprecedented precision. Yet, this capacity raises critical sociological questions: What digital behaviors are being criminalized, and why? Who gets targeted by algorithmic systems? And how do institutional, cultural, and technological dynamics influence these processes?

Redefining Deviance in the Digital Sphere

The criminalization of digital behavior begins with the redefinition of deviance itself. In the digital age, deviance is not always tied to traditional concepts of harm but often to data anomalies, algorithmic patterns, or violations of platform norms. As Završnik (2017) notes, big data has changed the ontology of crime—shifting from reactive law enforcement toward preemptive identification of "risky" behaviors. This shift, enabled by AI, expands the reach of the criminal justice system into areas that were previously unregulated or considered ethically ambiguous (Faqir, 2023; Hayward & Maas, 2021).

Digital deviance now encompasses a spectrum of behaviors—ranging from hate speech and misinformation to data scraping and unauthorized access—all of which may be algorithmically flagged and investigated without human context or cultural nuance (Spyropoulos, 2024; Middleton, 2021). The criteria for criminalization are increasingly shaped by institutional algorithms that embed normative assumptions, making certain types of behavior more visible and punishable than others (Patra, 2024).

AI and the Expansion of Surveillance Frontiers

AI systems vastly extend the scope of surveillance. By tracking user behavior across platforms, devices, and networks, AI-powered systems create detailed behavioral profiles that can be used to infer intent, risk, or affiliation (Umanah et al., 2024; Shevchenko et al., 2025). While this improves investigative efficiency, it also introduces a mode of governance that may criminalize digital users not for what they have done, but for what algorithms predict they *might* do.

This predictive mode aligns with the logic of preemptive policing, which often targets individuals or groups based on past associations, network patterns, or socio-demographic profiles (Gupta, 2024; Qiu, 2025). In doing so, AI systems may reproduce institutional biases, disproportionately surveilling racialized, low-income, or otherwise marginalized populations (Ray, 2019; Casad et al., 2021; Blackmore, 2013).

Furthermore, the normalization of surveillance through educational and professional systems acclimatizes individuals to being constantly monitored and evaluated (Ayeni et al., 2024; Jin et al., 2024; Pedro et al., 2019). In educational contexts, predictive analytics used for "at-risk" student identification have been critiqued for embedding deficit-based assumptions and limiting epistemic agency (Halmo, 2025; Monahan et al., 2024).

Figure 4 illustrates key risks and their causes when deploying LLM-based security solutions, guiding developers toward robust system design.

Figure 4. Common risks in deploying LLM-based security systems

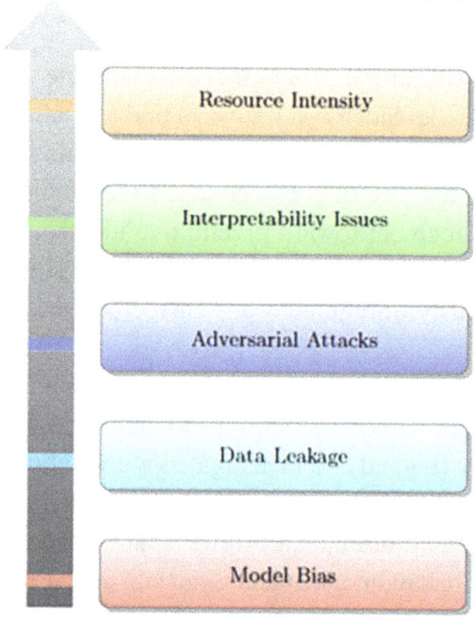

Algorithmic Criminalization and Structural Inequality

Criminalization via AI does not occur in a vacuum; it intersects with organizational structures and cultural norms. As Battilana and Casciaro (2012) suggest, change agents within institutions play a key role in shaping how new technologies are adopted and embedded. However, without critical oversight, AI systems may amplify existing inequalities, creating what Ray (2019) calls "racialized organizations."

For instance, institutions often design AI systems based on historical data that reflect prior policing patterns, sentencing decisions, or disciplinary actions—thus encoding biases that continue to affect marginalized communities (Casad et al., 2021; Liu, 2025; Kohli et al., 2021). In this context, digital behavior that deviates from normative standards—whether due to cultural expression, economic constraint, or lack of digital literacy—may be misinterpreted as suspicious or criminal.

Educational systems also exemplify this dynamic. As Grab (2025) and Muhyadeen (2026) argue, AI integration in education can either reinforce cultural marginalization or serve as a tool for equity—depending on how it is implemented. Mishra et al. (2024) and Peer Mohamed (2024) further emphasize the importance of ethical design in avoiding the unintentional criminalization of student behaviors, such as code-switching or non-normative linguistic expression.

Moral Panic, Digital Citizenship, and Platform Governance

Another sociological dynamic shaping the criminalization of digital behavior is the rise of moral panic and the evolving role of platform governance. Public fears around cybercrime, misinformation, and online radicalization often prompt overreactions, leading to new laws, policies, or surveillance practices that disproportionately affect marginalized users (Powell et al., 2018; Murtiningsih & Sujito, 2024).

Social media platforms, under pressure from governments and public opinion, use AI to enforce "community standards," sometimes leading to over-policing of certain identities, ideologies, or linguistic expressions (Rajesh, 2024; Lan, 2024). These platform-driven forms of governance blur the boundary between corporate policy and state law, making it difficult to distinguish between moderation, censorship, and criminalization.

This has implications for digital citizenship, where users must now navigate opaque systems of regulation that may penalize behaviors based on proprietary algorithms. In this environment, even innocuous digital actions—liking a post, joining a forum, or using certain keywords—can lead to investigation or exclusion (Mac Fadden et al., 2024; Kalashnikova et al., 2025).

Resisting Algorithmic Criminalization: Ethical and Institutional Alternatives

While AI-enabled criminalization presents significant risks, sociological research offers pathways for ethical resistance and institutional reform. First, transparency and inclusivity must be built into the design and deployment of AI systems. As Palmer et al. (2016) and Benn et al. (2014) argue, organizational change must go beyond technical implementation to include cultural transformation and stakeholder engagement.

Faculty development, for example, has been proposed as a site for resisting algorithmic determinism in educational settings (Steinert, 2025; Brennan & Canny, 2023). Similarly, Museus and Jayakumar (2012) suggest that cultivating inclusive institutional cultures can counteract the dehumanizing effects of surveillance technologies.

In law enforcement and digital forensics, similar strategies are essential. Shani et al. (2025) and Stouten et al. (2018) emphasize that successful change involves dialogue between practice and theory—highlighting the need for ongoing ethical review, critical feedback mechanisms, and participatory governance.

Finally, as Sá and Serpa (2020) argue, moments of technological disruption (such as the AI revolution or COVID-19 pandemic) provide opportunities to reimagine governance models around equity, sustainability, and human dignity. Padua (2025) reinforces this, advocating for a foundational digital culture in both educational and investigative contexts.

ETHICAL AND SOCIAL IMPLICATIONS

The increasing integration of Artificial Intelligence (AI) into educational, forensic, and organizational contexts presents complex ethical and social challenges. These concerns extend beyond technical functionalities to issues of equity, justice, identity, and institutional transformation. This section explores these implications through a multidisciplinary sociological lens, emphasizing how AI reshapes power dynamics, professional identities, and social inclusion.

Algorithmic Bias and Structural Inequality

AI systems, often trained on historical and socio-culturally embedded datasets, risk perpetuating and amplifying existing inequalities. Ray's (2019) theory of racialized organizations explicates how algorithmic decision-making may reinforce structural racism embedded in institutions. Casad et al. (2021) and Liu (2025) provide empirical evidence of gender and racial disparities across academia and leadership, highlighting parallel risks in AI deployment within educational and forensic domains.

In educational contexts, Halmo (2025), Pedro et al. (2019), and Monahan et al. (2024) discuss how predictive analytics can unintentionally stigmatize marginalized students, exacerbating educational inequities instead of ameliorating them. Mac Fadden et al. (2024) and Padua (2025) underscore the digital divide and unequal access to AI-powered tools, necessitating a focus on digital inclusion.

Transparency, Accountability, and Ethical Design

The opacity of AI ("black box") systems challenges transparency and undermines accountability, especially in high-stakes contexts such as criminal investigations (Faqir, 2023; Middleton, 2021). Peer Mohamed (2024) stresses the need for ethical frameworks that govern AI use in education and justice, advocating for explainability and user awareness.

Palmer et al. (2016) and Shani et al. (2025) argue for leadership approaches that promote ethical organizational change, with Battilana and Casciaro (2012) emphasizing the role of change agents in fostering participatory governance and ethical oversight. Kohli et al. (2021) highlight critical professional development as key to ensuring that educators and practitioners uphold racial justice in AI implementation.

Professional Identity and Epistemic Agency

AI alters the landscape of professional expertise and decision-making. In teaching, Ayeni et al. (2024), Mishra et al. (2024), and Lan (2024) discuss AI's dual capacity to support personalized learning and simultaneously constrain teacher autonomy, potentially undermining epistemic agency. Brennan and Canny (2023) and Quan et al. (2019) explore identity tensions and the need for empowerment in AI-enhanced educational settings.

In criminal justice, Qiu (2025) and Shevchenko et al. (2025) raise concerns about over-reliance on automated tools, which may dilute critical human judgment and embed biases into law enforcement practices. Muhyadeen (2026) and Kalashnikova et al. (2025) argue for sociological approaches that preserve professional identity amidst technological transformation.

Surveillance, Social Control, and Privacy

AI's role in surveillance extends deeply into social life, intensifying issues of privacy, consent, and social control. Umanah et al. (2024) and Spyropoulos (2024) document the expansion of digital surveillance beyond policing into education and workplace monitoring, reshaping boundaries between public and private spheres.

Završnik (2017) and Powell et al. (2018) analyze how big data and AI-driven surveillance engender moral panics and normalize invasive monitoring, with potential to criminalize ordinary behaviors (Rajesh, 2024). This has profound implications for social trust and digital citizenship, demanding critical examination.

Inclusion, Cultural Responsiveness, and Intersectionality

AI deployment must be attuned to cultural differences and inclusive of marginalized identities. Blackmore (2013), Muhyadeen (2026), and Murtiningsih and Sujito

(2024) advocate for intersectional frameworks that address the multi-dimensional impacts of AI on race, gender, and class.

Museus and Jayakumar (2012), Benn et al. (2014), and SWARGIARY (2025) emphasize organizational culture change as vital to supporting equity and resisting technological determinism. Grab (2025) stresses culturally responsive pedagogy as essential in higher education's AI integration.

Organizational Change and Ethical Stewardship

Managing ethical AI implementation requires deliberate organizational change and stakeholder engagement. Benn et al. (2014), Stouten et al. (2018), and Sá and Serpa (2020) recommend multi-faceted strategies that integrate cultural, structural, and processual shifts.

Faculty development and continuous learning initiatives (Steinert, 2025; Padua, 2025) play crucial roles in building capacity for ethical AI use. Moradi-Kelayeh (2025) and Peer Mohamed (2024) highlight ongoing discourse and reflective practice as foundations for sustaining ethical standards.

Sociological Perspectives on Crime and Justice

Sociological inquiry enriches understanding of AI's role in crime, justice, and social control. Gupta (2024), Patra (2024), and Powell et al. (2018) call for frameworks that recognize data's political nature and challenge institutional biases in algorithmic governance.

Hayward and Maas (2021) and Middleton (2021) demonstrate the dual potential of AI to both advance and complicate criminological research and law enforcement. Qiu (2025) offers ethnographic insights into policing AI-generated crimes, underscoring the need for culturally aware and socially just practices.

This detailed treatment demonstrates how ethical and social implications of AI span from algorithmic fairness and professional identity to surveillance, inclusion, and institutional transformation, underscoring the necessity of critical, sociologically informed approaches to AI governance.

CASE STUDIES

To concretely understand the multifaceted impacts of Artificial Intelligence (AI) in education, forensic investigation, and organizational contexts, this section presents a series of case studies. These examples illustrate both the transformative potential and the ethical, social, and organizational challenges posed by AI integration.

AI in Personalized Learning and Educational Technology

Ayeni et al. (2024) provide a comprehensive review of AI applications in personalized learning, demonstrating how adaptive algorithms tailor instruction to individual student needs. For instance, universities leveraging AI-driven academic advising platforms (Halmo, 2025) have reported improved student retention and satisfaction. However, Mac Fadden et al. (2024) caution that such tools may unintentionally deepen digital inequalities if access is unevenly distributed. Jin et al. (2024) highlight cases where informational AI systems in higher education facilitate real-time feedback but require ongoing professional development for faculty to maximize benefits (Padua, 2025).

Organizational Change in AI Adoption

Benn et al. (2014) and Palmer et al. (2016) document organizational transformations within educational and forensic institutions adopting AI technologies. Battilana and Casciaro's (2012) contingency theory of change underscores the crucial role of change agents who navigate complex networks to align AI implementation with institutional goals. Sá and Serpa (2020) illustrate how the COVID-19 pandemic accelerated such changes, with some universities rapidly integrating AI tools for remote teaching while managing resistance through inclusive leadership and communication (Blackmore, 2013).

Faculty development emerges as a pivotal factor in these transitions (Steinert, 2025; Kohli et al., 2021). Brennan and Canny (2023) report how teacher identity and engagement fluctuate when AI is embedded into curriculum design, echoing Lan's (2024) findings that AI-enhanced teacher training must balance technological skills with professional autonomy.

Addressing Inequality and Inclusion

Case studies by Casad et al. (2021) reveal persistent gender inequalities in STEM faculties, amplified by AI-driven evaluation and recruitment systems lacking bias mitigation. Liu (2025) and Muhyadeen (2026) present institutional efforts to reorient AI policies toward equitable student outcomes, embedding intersectional frameworks that consider race, gender, and class.

Grab (2025) explores AI's role in culturally responsive teaching in higher education, demonstrating how targeted interventions can empower marginalized students, a theme supported by Museus and Jayakumar (2012) in their work on campus cultures. Murtiningsih and Sujito (2024) extend this discussion to global educational policy, emphasizing critical intergenerational justice in AI deployment.

AI in Digital Forensics and Cybercrime Investigation

Faqir (2023) and Middleton (2021) analyze AI's applications in cybercrime investigation, including automated evidence analysis and predictive policing. Qiu (2025) ethnographically examines Chinese anti-cybercrime police integrating AI tools, revealing tensions between technological efficiency and ethical concerns about privacy and over-policing. Shevchenko et al. (2025) demonstrate AI's utility in combating crimes against individual dignity but call for stringent safeguards to prevent misuse.

Spyropoulos (2024) and Umanah et al. (2024) document institutionalization of digital criminology in law enforcement agencies, noting increased reliance on AI surveillance systems, which Završnik (2017) warns may lead to normalization of social control mechanisms. Powell et al. (2018) further explore the societal implications of these trends, stressing the need for public transparency.

Sociological and Pedagogical Perspectives

Patra (2024) and Rajesh (2024) provide sociological analyses of AI's influence on law and social norms, emphasizing the political nature of data governance. Pedro et al. (2019) and Peer Mohamed (2024) discuss ethical considerations in AI-enhanced education, advocating for continuous dialogue between technologists and educators.

Monahan et al. (2024) present interventions designed to foster epistemic agency among learners using AI, mitigating implicit biases and enhancing critical thinking. Moradi-Kelayeh (2025) and Mishra et al. (2024) analyze pedagogical shifts prompted by generative AI tools, urging balanced approaches that respect teacher expertise.

Professional Training and Future Directions

Kalashnikova et al. (2025) provide insights into modern ICT tools in sociology education, illustrating how AI-enabled platforms can support evolving disciplinary needs. Kohli et al. (2021) and Sá and Serpa (2020) highlight the necessity of sustained professional development for teachers of color, ensuring AI deployment advances racial justice.

Finally, organizational change scholarship (Shani et al., 2025; Stouten et al., 2018) emphasizes that successful AI integration depends on adaptive leadership, stakeholder engagement, and ethical stewardship, as demonstrated by Sullivan et al. (2015) in their work on systemic equity reforms.

These case studies collectively reveal AI's transformative promise alongside significant ethical, social, and organizational challenges. They underscore the need for culturally responsive, inclusive, and critically reflective approaches to AI adoption in education and forensic contexts.

GLOBAL PERSPECTIVES

The global landscape of Artificial Intelligence (AI) in education, organizational change, and criminology reflects a complex interplay of technological innovation, cultural context, and social equity concerns. This section explores how different regions and institutions are navigating AI adoption, highlighting key challenges and opportunities.

AI and Education Across Cultures and Regions

AI's integration into educational systems worldwide is marked by both enthusiasm and caution. Ayeni et al. (2024) review the expanding role of AI in personalized learning globally, noting how adaptive technologies have been embraced in diverse contexts but often reveal stark disparities in access. Mac Fadden, García-Alonso, and López Meneses (2024) emphasize that digital inequalities persist, particularly in under-resourced regions, potentially exacerbating educational divides.

In higher education, Jin, Goyal, and Rajawat (2024) observe that AI-driven informational tools are reshaping academic advising and student support, with institutions in developed countries often leading innovation (Halmo, 2025). However, Sá and Serpa (2020) argue that the COVID-19 pandemic created a global impetus to integrate AI tools rapidly, forcing institutions to balance quality and equity in emergent digital cultures (Padua, 2025).

Teacher development programs worldwide grapple with integrating AI while honoring local pedagogical identities. Lan (2024) highlights tensions in teacher identity formation when AI-enhanced training is introduced, a challenge echoed by Kohli et al. (2021) who underscore the critical need for racial justice leadership among teachers of color in the United States and beyond. Similarly, Muhyadeen (2026) stresses the importance of institutional change to support equitable AI use in teacher professional development globally.

Organizational Change and AI Diffusion

Theories of organizational change, such as Battilana and Casciaro's (2012) contingency model, illuminate how change agents mediate AI adoption across institutional and cultural boundaries. Benn, Edwards, and Williams (2014) and Palmer, Dunford, and Buchanan (2016) identify sustainability as a driving force behind organizational transformations integrating AI, with global companies and universities seeking to align AI innovation with corporate social responsibility.

Stouten, Rousseau, and De Cremer (2018) and Shani et al. (2025) emphasize that successful global AI adoption requires multi-perspective management strategies that consider local cultural norms and values. Blackmore (2013) and Brennan and Canny (2023) show how feminist and critical sociological perspectives must inform leadership models to foster inclusive environments amid technological disruption.

Sociological and Equity Considerations Worldwide

Globally, gender inequality and systemic bias remain significant challenges in AI adoption. Casad et al. (2021) provide evidence from STEM academia that AI systems can unintentionally perpetuate gender disparities, while Rajesh (2024) discusses how AI intersects with culture and identity in India's educational landscape. Ray's (2019) theory of racialized organizations offers a framework for understanding structural inequalities reinforced by AI worldwide.

Grab (2025) advocates for culturally responsive teaching supported by AI, a necessity underscored by Museus and Jayakumar (2012) in creating inclusive campus cultures. Murtiningsih and Sujito (2024) call for inclusive pedagogies that address intergenerational justice and global technological disruptions, stressing that AI must serve diverse student populations equitably.

AI in Global Criminal Justice Systems

AI's role in crime prevention and investigation varies internationally, with significant ethical and social implications. Middleton (2021) and Faqir (2023) document AI's expanding use in digital criminal investigations worldwide, while Hayward and Maas (2021) caution criminologists about the balance between efficiency and civil liberties.

Studies by Qiu (2025) on Chinese anti-cybercrime police and Spyropoulos (2024) on digital criminology institutionalization reveal how AI is transforming law enforcement practices differently across cultures. Shevchenko et al. (2025) explore AI's potential to counter crimes against personal dignity, but Umanah, Etti, and Sunday (2024) warn about emerging social control risks highlighted by Završnik (2017).

Future Directions in Global AI Integration

Across the globe, educators, policymakers, and researchers emphasize the necessity of ethical, equitable AI integration. Monahan, MacCormac, and Minogue (2024) propose strategies to mitigate implicit bias in AI education systems, fostering epistemic agency among diverse learners. Mishra, Oster, and Henriksen (2024), Moradi-Kelayeh (2025), and Muhyadeen (2026) advocate bridging short-term technological advances with long-term sociocultural impacts.

Critical voices like Patra (2024) and Powell, Stratton, and Cameron (2018) highlight the importance of cyber laws and sociological perspectives in governing AI's social effects. Pedro et al. (2019) underscore the potential for AI to support sustainable development goals worldwide, while Steinert (2025) stresses faculty development as central to realizing AI's promise across educational systems.

This global perspective underscores the need for context-sensitive approaches that reconcile technological innovation with cultural diversity, equity, and ethical responsibility. As AI continues to diffuse worldwide, sustained collaboration among stakeholders is crucial to harness its benefits while mitigating risks.

POLICY AND REFORM RECOMMENDATIONS

Effective policy and reform strategies are essential to maximize the benefits of Artificial Intelligence (AI) while mitigating its risks, especially in education, organizational change, and crime control. This section outlines comprehensive recommendations informed by global research and sociological perspectives.

Foster Inclusive and Equitable AI Integration in Education

AI policies must prioritize equity and inclusivity to bridge digital divides in educational settings. Ayeni et al. (2024) emphasize that personalized learning powered by AI offers great promise but risks deepening educational inequalities without equitable access to technology. To address this, governments and institutions should invest in digital infrastructure and ensure affordable access for underserved populations (Mac Fadden, García-Alonso, & López Meneses, 2024).

Furthermore, teacher training programs should embed AI literacy alongside culturally responsive pedagogy. Lan (2024) and Kohli et al. (2021) advocate for policies that support professional development focused on racial justice and teacher identity in AI-enhanced environments. Monahan, MacCormac, and Minogue (2024) highlight the need to mitigate implicit bias in AI systems through ethical frameworks and continuous teacher education.

Policymakers must also promote interdisciplinary research linking AI, pedagogy, and social justice (Muhyadeen, 2026). This includes incentivizing curriculum redesign to integrate digital culture and AI literacy, as recommended by Padua (2025) and Pedro et al. (2019). Institutional reforms should aim to create supportive campus cultures that reflect diverse student identities and foster inclusion (Museus & Jayakumar, 2012; Grab, 2025).

Support Organizational Change for Sustainable AI Adoption

Successful AI implementation in organizations depends on adaptive change management frameworks. Battilana and Casciaro (2012) suggest that change agents must navigate complex networks and institutional contexts to facilitate AI diffusion effectively. Benn, Edwards, and Williams (2014) emphasize aligning AI initiatives with sustainability goals to enhance social and environmental outcomes.

Organizational policies should adopt multiple-perspective approaches to change, incorporating diverse stakeholder voices and cultural nuances (Palmer, Dunford, & Buchanan, 2016; Stouten, Rousseau, & De Cremer, 2018). Training and faculty development are crucial for equipping staff with AI competencies while addressing resistance to change (Steinert, 2025; Shani et al., 2025).

Additionally, institutions must address systemic biases embedded in AI tools and organizational practices. Casad et al. (2021) highlight persistent gender inequities in academia exacerbated by AI, calling for targeted reforms to support women and minorities. Ray's (2019) theory of racialized organizations underlines the need for structural change policies that dismantle systemic discrimination.

Enhance Ethical Governance and Legal Frameworks for AI in Crime Control

AI's expanding role in digital criminal investigations and law enforcement demands robust ethical and legal oversight. Faqir (2023) and Middleton (2021) underscore the importance of transparent AI use to protect civil liberties while improving crime detection. Policymakers should develop comprehensive cyber laws addressing AI's dual-use risks, as articulated by Patra (2024) and Powell, Stratton, and Cameron (2018).

International cooperation is vital for harmonizing AI governance in crime prevention, given the global nature of cyber threats (Qiu, 2025; Spyropoulos, 2024). Ethical guidelines must emphasize human rights protections and accountability in AI-assisted policing (Shevchenko et al., 2025; Hayward & Maas, 2021).

Educational policies for law enforcement agencies should integrate AI ethics training to foster responsible use and public trust (Umanah, Etti, & Sunday, 2024). Research funding should support sociological studies examining AI's social impacts on crime and justice systems to inform evidence-based reforms (Gupta, 2024; Završnik, 2017).

Promote Intersectoral Collaboration and Continuous Monitoring

To ensure effective policy implementation, cross-sector collaboration between educators, technologists, sociologists, and policymakers is essential. Brennan and Canny (2023) demonstrate that understanding sociological factors enhances AI adoption in teacher education programs. Collaborative platforms can foster knowledge exchange, co-creation of AI tools, and shared ethical standards (Jin, Goyal, & Rajawat, 2024; Kalashnikova et al., 2025).

Regular impact assessments and adaptive policymaking should be mandated to monitor AI outcomes on equity, inclusion, and organizational culture (Sá & Serpa, 2020; Mishra, Oster, & Henriksen, 2024). Such feedback loops can guide iterative reforms and help institutions stay responsive to emerging challenges.

Emphasize Equity, Social Justice, and Cultural Sensitivity

All policies must foreground equity and social justice to prevent AI from reinforcing existing disparities. Blackmore (2013) and Rajesh (2024) stress the importance of feminist and intersectional lenses in educational leadership and AI governance. Sullivan, Artiles, and Hernandez-Saca (2015) argue for systemic change approaches that address special education inequities exacerbated by technology gaps.

SWARGIARY (2025) and Quan et al. (2019) highlight the role of identity, activism, and critical pedagogy in empowering marginalized communities through AI. Policies should support culturally sensitive AI development and deployment that honors diverse epistemologies and knowledge systems (Moradi-Kelayeh, 2025; Murtiningsih & Sujito, 2024).

Summary

By implementing inclusive, ethical, and adaptive policy frameworks across education, organizational management, and crime control, stakeholders can harness AI's transformative potential while safeguarding equity and justice. These reforms require ongoing research, stakeholder engagement, and a commitment to social responsibility in the face of rapid technological change.

CONCLUSION

This chapter has explored the multifaceted implications of Artificial Intelligence (AI) across education, organizational change, and crime control, emphasizing the critical role of sociological perspectives in shaping effective policies and reforms. AI presents unprecedented opportunities to personalize learning, enhance institutional efficiency, and transform law enforcement practices. However, these benefits are intertwined with significant challenges, including digital inequalities, systemic biases, ethical dilemmas, and governance complexities.

The evidence underscores that AI integration must be underpinned by a commitment to equity, inclusion, and social justice. As Ayeni et al. (2024) and Mac Fadden, García-Alonso, and López Meneses (2024) illustrate, without deliberate efforts to democratize access and embed cultural responsiveness, AI risks exacerbating existing disparities in education and society at large. Similarly, organizational reforms guided by Battilana and Casciaro's (2012) contingency theory and Benn et al.'s (2014) sustainability frameworks reveal that technological innovation alone is insufficient without strategic, culturally aware change management.

In the realm of crime and cyber security, the integration of AI demands vigilant ethical governance and robust legal frameworks to balance innovation with human rights protections (Faqir, 2023; Hayward & Maas, 2021). Multidisciplinary collaboration and continuous impact monitoring are essential to mitigate risks related to surveillance, bias, and accountability (Middleton, 2021; Spyropoulos, 2024).

Moreover, this chapter highlights that policies must transcend purely technical solutions by embracing critical perspectives on identity, power, and institutional culture (Blackmore, 2013; Ray, 2019). Inclusive approaches to AI in teacher development and organizational leadership can foster environments where diversity is valued and equity is actively pursued (Lan, 2024; Muhyadeen, 2026).

In conclusion, the path forward involves sustained commitment to interdisciplinary research, stakeholder engagement, and adaptive policy-making that center human dignity and social justice. Only through such holistic approaches can the transformative promise of AI be fully realized for the betterment of global education systems, organizational structures, and justice institutions.

REFERENCES

Ayeni, O. O., Al Hamad, N. M., Chisom, O. N., Osawaru, B., & Adewusi, O. E. (2024). AI in education: A review of personalized learning and educational technology. *GSC Advanced Research and Reviews*, *18*(2), 261–271. DOI: 10.30574/gscarr.2024.18.2.0062

Battilana, J., & Casciaro, T. (2012). Change agents, networks, and institutions: A contingency theory of organizational change. *Academy of Management Journal*, *55*(2), 381–398. DOI: 10.5465/amj.2009.0891

Benn, S., Edwards, M., & Williams, T. (2014). *Organizational change for corporate sustainability*. Routledge. DOI: 10.4324/9781315819181

Blackmore, J. (2013). A feminist critical perspective on educational leadership. *International Journal of Leadership in Education*, *16*(2), 139–154. DOI: 10.1080/13603124.2012.754057

Brennan, A., & Canny, A. (2023). Problematising Irish student-teachers'(dis) engagement with sociology of education in initial teacher education programmes. *Teaching and Teacher Education*, *130*, 104173. DOI: 10.1016/j.tate.2023.104173

Casad, B. J., Franks, J. E., Garasky, C. E., Kittleman, M. M., Roesler, A. C., Hall, D. Y., & Petzel, Z. W. (2021). Gender inequality in academia: Problems and solutions for women faculty in STEM. *Journal of Neuroscience Research*, *99*(1), 13–23. DOI: 10.1002/jnr.24631 PMID: 33103281

Faqir, R. S. (2023). Digital criminal investigations in the era of artificial intelligence: A comprehensive overview. *International Journal of Cyber Criminology*, *17*(2), 77–94.

Grab, M. O. (2025). Teaching for Equity: An Exploration of AI's Role in Culturally Responsive Teaching in Higher Education Settings. *Innovative Higher Education*, •••, 1–22. DOI: 10.1007/s10755-025-09801-4

Gupta, Y. K. (2024). Exploring crime from a sociological perspective. *International Journal of Dynamic Educational Research Society*, *5*(2), 47–56.

Halmo, H. (2025). *Human-Centered, Tech-Enabled: Scaling Academic Advising in Higher Education Through Predictive Analytics and Organizational Change an Innovation Study* (Doctoral dissertation, New York University).

Hayward, K. J., & Maas, M. M. (2021). Artificial intelligence and crime: A primer for criminologists. *Crime, Media, Culture*, *17*(2), 209–233. DOI: 10.1177/1741659020917434

Jin, Z., Goyal, S. B., & Rajawat, A. S. (2024). The informational role of artificial intelligence in higher education in the New era. *Procedia Computer Science*, *235*, 1008–1023. DOI: 10.1016/j.procs.2024.04.096

Kalashnikova, L. V., Lobanova, A. S., Hrabovets, I. V., Chernous, L. S., Chorna, V. A., & Davydenko, Y. O. (2025, March). Modern information and communication technologies in professional training of sociology students: Evolving needs and significance in the digital age. In *CTE Workshop Proceedings* (Vol. 12, pp. 381-398). DOI: 10.55056/cte.922

Kohli, R., Pizarro, M., Garcia, L. G., Kelly, L., Espinoza, M., & Cordova, J. (2021). Critical professional development and the racial justice leadership possibilities of teachers of colour in K-12 schools. *Professional Development in Education*, *47*(1), 89–101. DOI: 10.1080/19415257.2020.1814387

Lan, Y. (2024). Through tensions to identity-based motivations: Exploring teacher professional identity in Artificial Intelligence-enhanced teacher training. *Teaching and Teacher Education*, *151*, 104736. DOI: 10.1016/j.tate.2024.104736

Liu, S. (2025). Navigating Equality in Schools: The Sociological Impact of Leadership on Student Success. *Education and Urban Society*, *57*(3), 245–298. DOI: 10.1177/00131245241304404

Mac Fadden, I., García-Alonso, E. M., & López Meneses, E. (2024). Science Mapping of AI as an Educational Tool Exploring Digital Inequalities: A Sociological Perspective. *Multimodal Technologies and Interaction*, *8*(12), 106. DOI: 10.3390/mti8120106

Middleton, S. E. (2021). Use of Artificial Intelligence to support cybercrime research. In *Researching Cybercrimes: Methodologies, Ethics, and Critical Approaches* (pp. 213–232). Springer International Publishing. DOI: 10.1007/978-3-030-74837-1_11

Mishra, P., Oster, N., & Henriksen, D. (2024). Generative AI, teacher knowledge and educational research: Bridging short-and long-term perspectives. *TechTrends*, *68*(2), 205–210. DOI: 10.1007/s11528-024-00938-1

Monahan, R., MacCormac, A., & Minogue, J. (2024, July). Fostering Epistemic Agency: Strategies for Mitigating Implicit Bias in AI-Enhanced Education. In *Ed-Media+ Innovate Learning* (pp. 1011-1025). Association for the Advancement of Computing in Education (AACE).

Moradi-Kelayeh, N. (2025). *From Chalkboard to Chatbots: The Integration of Artificial Influence on Pedagogical Practices* (Master's thesis, Harvard University).

Muhyadeen, R. A. (2026). Sociological Perspectives on AI Integration in Teacher Development: Equity, Identity, and Institutional Change. In Zangana, H., Nobles, C., & Omar, M. (Eds.), *Harnessing AI for Teacher Support and Professional Development* (pp. 209–236). IGI Global Scientific Publishing., DOI: 10.4018/979-8-3373-5951-9.ch007

Murtiningsih, S., & Sujito, A. (2024). Reimagining the future of education: Inclusive pedagogies, critical intergenerational justice, and technological disruption. *Policy Futures in Education*, •••, 14782103251341406.

Museus, S. D., & Jayakumar, U. M. (2012). Creating campus cultures. *Routledge, 10*, 9780203832417.

Padua, D. (2025). Artificial intelligence and quality education: The need for digital culture in teaching. *Journal of Educational* [ECPS Journal]. *Cultural and Psychological Studies*, (30), 181–193.

Palmer, I., Dunford, R., & Buchanan, D. (2016). *EBOOK: Managing Organizational Change: A Multiple Perspectives Approach (ISE)*. McGraw Hill.

Patra, J. (2024). Cyber Laws And Emerging Use Of Artificial Intelligence: View From Sociological Perspectives. *REDVET-. Revista Electrónica de Veterinaria, 25*(1), 1308–1312. DOI: 10.69980/redvet.v25i1.863

. Pedro, F., Subosa, M., Rivas, A., & Valverde, P. (2019). Artificial intelligence in education: Challenges and opportunities for sustainable development.

Peer Mohamed, M. S. (2024). *Exploring ethical dimensions of AI-enhanced language education: A literature perspective*. Technology in Language Teaching & Learning.

Powell, A., Stratton, G., & Cameron, R. (2018). *Digital criminology: Crime and justice in digital society*. Routledge. DOI: 10.4324/9781315205786

Qiu, Y. (2025). Policing AI-generated crimes: An ethnographic study on anti-cybercrime police in China. *Security Journal, 38*(1), 34. DOI: 10.1057/s41284-025-00491-3

Quan, T., Bracho, C. A., Wilkerson, M., & Clark, M. (2019). Empowerment and transformation: Integrating teacher identity, activism, and criticality across three teacher education programs. *Review of Education, Pedagogy & Cultural Studies, 41*(4-5), 218–251. DOI: 10.1080/10714413.2019.1684162

Rajesh, R. (2024). *ARTIFICIAL INTELLIGENCE: BEYOND IDENTITIES. Routledge Handbook of Gender*. Culture, and Development in India.

Ray, V. (2019). A theory of racialized organizations. *American Sociological Review*, *84*(1), 26–53. DOI: 10.1177/0003122418822335

Sá, M. J., & Serpa, S. (2020). The COVID-19 pandemic as an opportunity to foster the sustainable development of teaching in higher education. *Sustainability (Basel)*, *12*(20), 8525. DOI: 10.3390/su12208525

Shani, A. B., Noumair, D. A., Zandee, D. P., & Coghlan, D. (Eds.). (2025). *Research in organizational change and development*. Emerald Publishing Limited. DOI: 10.1108/S0897-3016202531

. Shevchenko, V., Zvonarov, O., Shcherbyna, L., Yana, L., & Volodymyr, P. (2025). Using ai to counter criminal offences against the will, honour, and dignity of a person.

Spyropoulos, F. (2024). New Approaches to Researching AI Crime: Institutionalization of Digital Criminology. *Journal of Digital Technologies and Law*, *2*(3), 636–656. DOI: 10.21202/jdtl.2024.32

. Steinert, Y. (2025). Faculty development: core concepts and principles. *Faculty development in the health professions: A focus on research and practice*, 3-28.

Stouten, J., Rousseau, D. M., & De Cremer, D. (2018). Successful organizational change: Integrating the management practice and scholarly literatures. *The Academy of Management Annals*, *12*(2), 752–788. DOI: 10.5465/annals.2016.0095

Sullivan, A. L., Artiles, A. J., & Hernandez-Saca, D. I. (2015). Addressing special education inequity through systemic change: Contributions of ecologically based organizational consultation. *Journal of Educational & Psychological Consultation*, *25*(2-3), 129–147. DOI: 10.1080/10474412.2014.929969

SWARGIARY. K. (2025). *Educational Sociology: Theory, Practice, and Contemporary Challenges*. ERA, US.

Umanah, E. A., Etti, W. C., & Sunday, D. U. (2024). Implications of Emerging Technologies on Social Behaviour and Crime Control in the 21st Century. *Journal of Advanced Research and Multidisciplinary Studies*, *4*(3), 152–162. DOI: 10.52589/JARMS-JL2NFQ57

Završnik, A. (2017). Big data: What is it and why does it matter for crime and social control? In *Big data, crime and social control* (pp. 3–28). Routledge. DOI: 10.4324/9781315395784-1

Chapter 8
Nanoscale Devices and AI Integration in Digital Forensics:
Opportunities and Risks in Cybercrime Investigation

Derek Mohammed
https://orcid.org/0009-0002-8573-4363
Saint Leo University, USA

Shereeza Mohammed
https://orcid.org/0009-0009-1904-4007
Walden University, USA

Diyar A. S. Sadiq Mayi
Duhok Polytechnic University, Iraq

ABSTRACT

The integration of nanoscale devices and artificial intelligence (AI) in digital forensics marks a paradigm shift in the capabilities available to investigators combating cybercrime. Nanoscale technologies offer unprecedented precision and efficiency in data acquisition, analysis, and evidence preservation. When combined with AI algorithms, these tools enable automated detection, and real-time threat assessment at the micro and macro levels. This chapter explores the synergistic potential of nanoscale devices and AI in enhancing digital forensic investigations, with a focus on applications such as cyber-physical system forensics, biometric identification, and encrypted data retrieval. While the opportunities are substantial, the convergence of these technologies also introduces new challenges, including data privacy risks, and

DOI: 10.4018/979-8-3373-6536-7.ch008

the potential for abuse by malicious actors. The chapter concludes with an analysis of regulatory gaps, and future trends, emphasizing the need for interdisciplinary frameworks to ensure the responsible deployment of these transformative technologies

INTRODUCTION

The digital age has ushered in an era where cybercrime is not only more pervasive but also increasingly sophisticated, leveraging the same emerging technologies intended to safeguard digital infrastructure. As cybercriminal tactics evolve, so must the tools and methodologies of digital forensic investigators. Among the most promising developments are the convergence of nanoscale devices and artificial intelligence (AI), which together offer transformative potential for cybercrime investigation. Nanoscale technologies, characterized by their manipulation of materials at the atomic and molecular levels, enable hyper-precise data capture, storage, and transmission (Zareef et al., 2024; Sharma, Walia, & Jamal, 2024). When integrated with AI, these technologies can significantly enhance the efficiency, scalability, and intelligence of forensic processes (Aithal & Aithal, 2024; Tyagi, Kumari, & Richa, 2024).

Digital forensics today is facing a multi-dimensional transformation driven by Industry 4.0 technologies, including the Internet of Things (IoT), edge computing, and bioinformatics (Okwu et al., 2022; Sheikhbahei & Ari, 2024; Kassem et al., 2024). This transformation necessitates a shift from traditional post-mortem analyses toward real-time, proactive approaches. AI algorithms are now being employed to automate data mining, anomaly detection, and pattern recognition in massive digital evidence sets (Akeiber, 2025; Javed et al., 2022; Fernando, 2023). When used in tandem with nanosensors or nano-enabled memory devices, AI models can analyze data streams at the source, making it possible to detect threats or collect forensic evidence even from within complex cyber-physical environments (Chhabra et al., 2024; Banerjee, Chakraborty, & Rathi, 2020).

Furthermore, forensic investigations are no longer limited to traditional endpoints. Smart homes, autonomous vehicles, wearable devices, and medical implants all present potential evidence sources, each requiring highly specialized techniques for data acquisition and interpretation (Friedl & Pernul, 2024; Rohatgi & Shrivastava, 2022). AI-augmented nanoscale devices provide the necessary precision to non-invasively collect data from these systems, while ensuring minimal disruption to their operation or integrity (Sathwara, Dutta, & Pricop, 2018). These advances also support the broader vision of Society 5.0, where human-centered, data-driven decision-making is seamlessly integrated into every aspect of life (Sharma & Garg, 2023).

Despite the promise, integrating nanoscale devices and AI into digital forensics is not without its challenges. Key concerns include privacy, legal admissibility of nano-enabled evidence, cybersecurity vulnerabilities, and a lack of standardized frameworks (Li & Zhang, 2025; Möller, 2023; Helbing & Ienca, 2024). For example, while AI can improve detection capabilities, it may also introduce interpretability and bias issues that affect evidentiary value in court (Khan, Ishrat, & Al Farsi, 2025; Kumar & Alam, 2025). Similarly, nano-devices embedded in personal or medical contexts could lead to significant ethical dilemmas regarding surveillance and consent (FAVINO et al., 2025).

In light of these dynamics, this chapter aims to critically examine the opportunities and risks posed by nanoscale and AI-integrated digital forensics. It draws on multidisciplinary research to present a comprehensive overview of current tools, emerging applications, and regulatory implications. The chapter also highlights novel frameworks and models that aim to mitigate the technological and ethical risks while maximizing investigative effectiveness (Rizal et al., 2025; Akinade et al., 2021).

Ultimately, understanding the synergy between nanoscale innovations and AI is not just about enhancing forensic capabilities—it is about reimagining the future of justice in a hyper-connected digital world (Aithal & Aithal, 2020; Vaseashta, 2022; Widodo et al., 2024). By exploring this convergence through the lens of both opportunity and caution, this chapter contributes to the development of responsible and resilient forensic systems capable of addressing 21st-century cybercrime threats.

FOUNDATIONS OF NANOTECHNOLOGY IN CYBER SYSTEMS

Nanotechnology, defined by the manipulation of matter on the atomic and molecular scale, has emerged as a cornerstone of innovation in numerous domains—including cybersecurity and digital forensics. As cyber systems grow increasingly complex and pervasive, traditional investigative tools often fall short in detecting, securing, and interpreting the data trails left within miniaturized and embedded environments. The emergence of nanoscale technologies bridges this gap by enabling a new class of precision instrumentation, nanosensors, nano-enabled processors, and advanced memory systems that operate at the scale and speed required by modern digital ecosystems (Sharma, Walia, & Jamal, 2024; Zareef et al., 2024).

At the heart of nanotechnology's application in cyber systems is its ability to enhance data collection, storage, and transmission in constrained environments. Devices such as nanoscale data recorders and nanochips can be integrated into Internet of Things (IoT) systems, wearable technologies, and cyber-physical infrastructure to detect, log, and transmit forensic-relevant information without disrupting functionality (Banerjee, Chakraborty, & Rathi, 2020; Chhabra et al., 2024). These capabilities make nanotechnology highly relevant for scenarios like smart home forensics, industrial IoT audits, and implantable medical device investigations (Friedl & Pernul, 2024; Rohatgi & Shrivastava, 2022).

Nanotechnology's integration with cyber systems aligns with the broader convergence of ICCT (Information, Communication, and Computing Technologies), wherein miniaturization serves as the enabling factor for interconnected systems to function at scale (Aithal & Aithal, 2020, 2024). This synergy lays the groundwork for enhanced cybersecurity defenses and forensic capabilities through ultra-sensitive detection and secure hardware-level encryption.

Moreover, nanotechnology complements digital forensic methodologies by enhancing sensor accuracy, data resolution, and temporal responsiveness. This becomes vital in dynamic environments such as autonomous vehicles, healthcare systems, and military-grade communications, where timing and precision are critical (Okwu et al., 2022; Sheikhbahei & Ari, 2024). The ability to deploy nanosensors for continuous surveillance of digital transactions or malware behavior at a granular level significantly elevates the evidentiary value in forensic investigations (Khan, Ishrat, & Al Farsi, 2025; Rizal et al., 2025).

However, alongside these advancements come significant concerns. The very properties that make nanotechnology effective—its invisibility, scale, and ubiquity—also raise profound legal, regulatory, and ethical challenges. Devices that operate undetected can be used both for surveillance and exploitation, posing threats to privacy and evidentiary integrity (FAVINO et al., 2025; Helbing & Ienca, 2024). This dual-use dilemma requires robust oversight and interdisciplinary collaboration to balance innovation with accountability (Li & Zhang, 2025; Möller, 2023).

From a systems integration perspective, the fusion of nanotechnology with AI, big data, and cloud infrastructure offers an intelligent, adaptive layer of security and forensics that surpasses manual methodologies (Fernando, 2023; Kassem et al., 2024). These technologies enable self-healing networks, automated evidence sorting, and predictive threat modeling. For instance, nano-enhanced threat detection systems can work with AI-based frameworks to continuously monitor encrypted traffic and flag anomalies without breaching confidentiality (Akinade et al., 2021; Tyagi, Kumari, & Richa, 2024).

In operational terms, the deployment of nanoscale tools within cyber forensics requires alignment with international standards such as those set by NIST, as demonstrated in forensic platforms like Oxygen Forensic® Detective (Sutikno & Busthomi, 2025). As digital crime scenes expand into embedded environments, nanotechnology provides the granularity necessary to document hidden interactions, malware signatures, and compromised firmware layers with forensic rigor (Sathwara, Dutta, & Pricop, 2018).

Academic and policy research continues to explore these intersections. For example, the work of Javed et al. (2022) and Kumar & Alam (2025) highlights how nanoscale evidence can enhance forensic timelines and reduce attribution errors in cybercrime scenarios. Meanwhile, studies by Vaseashta (2022) and Widodo et al. (2024) underscore the necessity of embedding nanotechnology within national cyber-defense strategies to maintain resilience in the face of evolving threats.

To better understand how LLMs function in vulnerability detection, the following diagram illustrates the step-by-step process from input code to threat analysis.

Figure 1. Workflow of LLM-based vulnerability detection

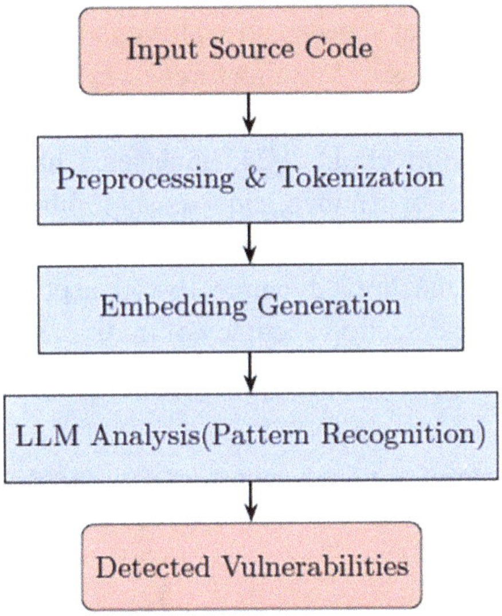

Ultimately, nanotechnology does not function in isolation but thrives in collaborative ecosystems, supported by AI, machine learning, and smart manufacturing environments—a principle central to the vision of Society 5.0 (Sharma & Garg, 2023). Its transformative role in cyber systems is not just technical but systemic, offering both opportunities and responsibilities to investigators, policymakers, and technology developers alike.

AI-ENABLED NANOSCALE FORENSICS

The integration of artificial intelligence (AI) with nanoscale technologies is revolutionizing the landscape of digital forensics, offering unprecedented capabilities for detecting, analyzing, and responding to cybercrime. AI-enabled nanoscale forensics refers to the application of intelligent algorithms in combination with nanoscale devices—such as nano-sensors, quantum dots, and nano-processors—to automate and enhance forensic investigations across complex digital ecosystems.

The Technological Convergence of AI and Nanotechnology

AI and nanotechnology converge under the umbrella of ICCT (Information, Communication, and Computing Technologies), where their synergy facilitates intelligent automation, real-time analytics, and embedded sensing in cybersecurity and digital investigations (Aithal & Aithal, 2020, 2024). Nanodevices enable the collection of high-fidelity, minute data from digital systems, while AI algorithms process, learn from, and adapt to this data at speeds and scales unattainable by human analysts.

This convergence enables self-learning forensic systems capable of operating in smart environments, including cyber-physical systems, autonomous vehicles, and biomedical devices (Chhabra et al., 2024; Banerjee, Chakraborty, & Rathi, 2020; Sheikhbahei & Ari, 2024). For instance, nano-sensors embedded in IoT environments can detect malware behavior in real time, which is then interpreted by AI models to classify, trace, and report the threat dynamically (Rizal et al., 2025; Akeiber, 2025).

Figure 2 compares the detection accuracy of traditional static analysis tools and modern LLMs across several benchmark datasets.

Figure 2. Accuracy comparison between traditional tools and LLMs

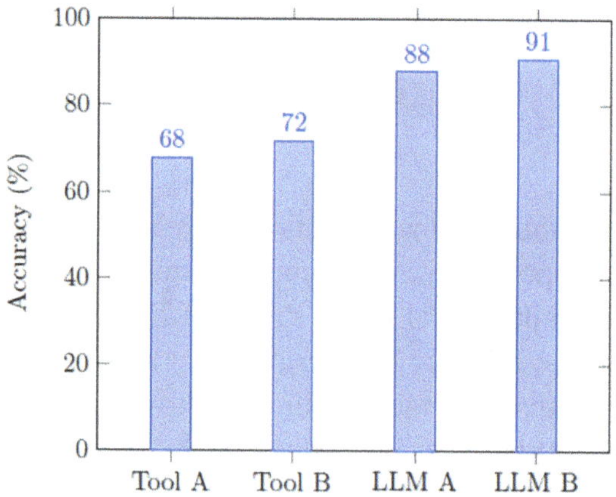

Automation and Intelligence in Forensic Workflows

AI transforms nanoscale forensics from passive data collection into dynamic, autonomous workflows. Techniques like machine learning (ML), deep learning, and natural language processing (NLP) are increasingly embedded within forensic frameworks to analyze massive data sets generated by nano-devices (Kassem et al., 2024; Tyagi, Kumari, & Richa, 2024).

For example, AI-based classification models can sort relevant from irrelevant digital artifacts with high accuracy, reducing investigative timelines (Fernando, 2023; Javed et al., 2022). Predictive algorithms, trained on historical forensic data, can forecast intrusion paths or identify suspicious activity in encrypted traffic without decryption—an essential capability in high-privacy environments (Kumar & Alam, 2025; Akinade et al., 2021).

Moreover, platforms like Oxygen Forensic® Detective, when paired with AI models and NIST guidelines, demonstrate how forensic analytics can be automated using nanoscale inputs from mobile devices, wearables, and social platforms (Sutikno & Busthomi, 2025).

Figure 3 compares the effectiveness of traditional methods and LLMs across different categories of software vulnerabilities.

Figure 3. Detection rates by vulnerability type

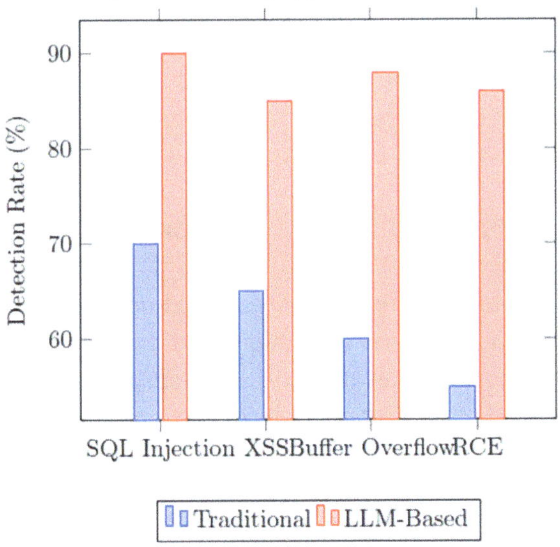

Embedded AI-Nano Forensics in Cyber-Physical and IoT Systems

Smart homes, autonomous systems, and medical devices present digital terrains where conventional forensic tools are impractical. Here, AI-enabled nanoscale systems offer discreet and continuous monitoring capabilities. In smart home forensics, nanoscale sensors integrated into household electronics can detect unauthorized access, changes in usage patterns, or digital sabotage (Friedl & Pernul, 2024).

In IoT ecosystems, AI-enhanced nano-tools can trace forensic evidence even when devices operate intermittently, in real-time, or in peer-to-peer networks—challenges traditionally limiting forensic readiness (Rohatgi & Shrivastava, 2022; Sathwara, Dutta, & Pricop, 2018). Advanced frameworks such as those proposed by Rizal et al. (2025) emphasize forensic preparedness for IoT systems using AI to optimize data prioritization, storage, and retrieval.

Advanced AI Models and Decision Support

Beyond pattern recognition, current AI systems are evolving into decision-support engines. Reinforcement learning and federated learning models enable distributed nanoscale forensic networks that learn from multiple sources while preserving data locality and privacy (Akeiber, 2025; Kassem et al., 2024). Such systems are essential in regulated sectors like healthcare and education, where privacy-preserving AI is mandatory (Li & Zhang, 2025).

Digital twin technology—enhanced by AI and nanotech—now enables virtual replication of digital environments to simulate attack scenarios and test forensic responses without affecting the live system (Tyagi, Kumari, & Richa, 2024).

Risk Considerations and Dual-Use Dilemmas

Despite their advantages, AI-enabled nanoscale forensics raise important ethical and legal concerns. The precision and ubiquity of nanosensors pose surveillance risks, while AI introduces issues around bias, transparency, and interpretability (Helbing & Ienca, 2024; FAVINO et al., 2025).

Furthermore, the dual-use nature of nanotech and AI—technologies that can both protect and exploit—means that malicious actors may weaponize them for undetectable cyber intrusions, data exfiltration, or falsification of forensic trails (Vaseashta, 2022; Möller, 2023). This necessitates international regulation and collaborative governance, as emphasized by Helbing and Ienca (2024).

Toward a Resilient, AI-Nano-Driven Forensic Framework

Future forensic ecosystems will rely on hybrid architectures where AI-driven analytics interact seamlessly with nano-hardware to support cybercrime investigation across digital, physical, and biological domains (Widodo et al., 2024). This vision aligns with the goals of Society 5.0—human-centered, intelligent societies where technological integration enhances public safety, privacy, and justice (Sharma & Garg, 2023).

To build such systems, researchers advocate for multidisciplinary frameworks incorporating ICCT convergence, nanoscale innovation, and AI robustness into forensic science curricula, training programs, and policy design (Aithal & Aithal, 2020; Javed et al., 2022; Khan, Ishrat, & Al Farsi, 2025).

CYBERCRIME SCENARIOS INVOLVING NANOTECHNOLOGY

As nanotechnology integrates deeper into digital ecosystems, its presence in cybercrime scenarios has become increasingly evident. While nanodevices offer exceptional advancements in surveillance, monitoring, and data collection, they also introduce a novel attack surface for cybercriminals. These scenarios not only reveal emerging risks but also redefine the boundaries of digital forensics in the face of undetectable, embedded, and autonomous nanoscale threats.

Covert Surveillance and Espionage via Nano-Sensors

Nanoscale sensors can be covertly embedded into electronic devices, wearables, and even smart environments, enabling malicious actors to conduct persistent surveillance. These sensors, often invisible to the naked eye, are capable of intercepting communication, logging keystrokes, or capturing biometric data without detection (Sharma, Walia, & Jamal, 2024; Zareef et al., 2024). In high-security institutions or diplomatic environments, such undetected monitoring can lead to data exfiltration, intellectual property theft, or espionage operations.

The convergence of AI with nano-surveillance systems enables intelligent data filtering, allowing attackers to capture only targeted information while avoiding large data dumps that could trigger alerts (Fernando, 2023; Akinade et al., 2021). This precise and stealthy espionage raises challenges for forensic attribution, as the devices used may leave minimal to no trace in conventional forensic scans (Khan, Ishrat, & Al Farsi, 2025).

Nanoscale Attack Vectors in Smart Homes and IoT Environments

Smart homes and IoT networks are particularly vulnerable to nanoscale intrusions. Cyber-physical systems, such as smart locks, HVAC systems, and connected kitchen appliances, can be infected with nano-devices programmed to disrupt or monitor user behavior (Friedl & Pernul, 2024; Chhabra et al., 2024). These devices may be introduced via supply chain attacks, counterfeit hardware, or compromised firmware.

In these contexts, cybercriminals use AI-enhanced nanosystems to exploit vulnerabilities in communication protocols or firmware layers. AI models can autonomously adapt to device responses and alter attack strategies, making detection and forensic tracking more complex (Rizal et al., 2025; Kumar & Alam, 2025). Investigative frameworks like those suggested by Sathwara, Dutta, & Pricop (2018) are essential to map such nano-level threats within IoT forensics.

Table 1 summarizes the key strengths and weaknesses of traditional methods versus LLM-based approaches in terms of usability, performance, and adaptability.

Table 1. Comparison of key features between traditional methods and LLMs

Feature	Traditional Methods	LLMs
Rule-Based Logic	Strong	Moderate
Context Awareness	Low	High
Adaptability	Low	High
Scalability	Moderate	High
False Positives	High	Low
Explainability	High	Low

Implantable Device Hacking and Medical Cybercrime

Nanotechnology is a key enabler in biomedical engineering, especially in implantable devices such as pacemakers, insulin pumps, and neural interfaces. However, these benefits are accompanied by risks, including the possibility of malicious access to patient data or manipulation of device functionality (Banerjee, Chakraborty, & Rathi, 2020; Sheikhbahei & Ari, 2024).

Cybercriminals can exploit AI-controlled nanodevices implanted in patients to either exfiltrate sensitive health data or induce physical harm. These attacks often go undetected unless specialized forensic tools are used to audit embedded hardware and AI decision logs (Javed et al., 2022; Widodo et al., 2024). This scenario underscores the need for forensically-aware design in medical devices, aligned with ICCT standards and ethical governance (Li & Zhang, 2025; Helbing & Ienca, 2024).

Nano-Enhanced Deepfake and Data Manipulation Attacks

Nanoscale processors embedded in edge devices (e.g., mobile phones, wearables) are now capable of real-time media manipulation. Cybercriminals can deploy AI-powered nanodevices to alter images, voice, or video feeds before they are even uploaded or transmitted, complicating forensic analysis (Tyagi, Kumari, & Richa, 2024; Möller, 2023).

These attacks exploit the decentralized and miniaturized nature of nano-enabled AI models, which function independently and adaptively. Investigators face the challenge of proving the authenticity of digital content created or tampered with by nanoscale processors that are difficult to audit post-incident (Akeiber, 2025; Kassem et al., 2024).

Manipulation of Forensic Tools and Frameworks

Advanced adversaries have begun targeting the forensic tools themselves. Nanoscale components inserted into investigative devices or forensic data acquisition systems can subtly distort or delete forensic evidence, leading to false conclusions or unresolvable cases (Sutikno & Busthomi, 2025; Khan et al., 2025).

This sabotage highlights a critical need for end-to-end verification mechanisms in forensic toolchains and the adoption of self-diagnosing nanosensors capable of detecting internal anomalies (Vaseashta, 2022; Aithal & Aithal, 2020). Without this, evidence manipulation may become more prevalent, especially in politically sensitive investigations.

Nanoscale Botnets and Distributed Attacks

The proliferation of nanoscale devices has introduced the concept of nano-botnets—networks of nanodevices orchestrated via AI to perform coordinated attacks. These include DDoS attacks originating from nano-enabled wearables or household items, or distributed ransomware schemes targeting firmware-level encryption (Okwu et al., 2022; FAVINO et al., 2025).

Due to their size and stealth, nano-botnets can remain active for extended periods without being detected. Traditional cybersecurity systems, which rely on network traffic analysis or behavioral monitoring, often fail to identify these threats until significant damage has occurred (Aithal & Aithal, 2024; Sharma & Garg, 2023).

In summary, the potential misuse of nanotechnology in cybercrime is not speculative—it is emergent. Cybercriminals are increasingly leveraging the convergence of nanotechnology and AI to evade detection, exploit new vectors, and manipulate evidence. These evolving scenarios require an updated forensic and regulatory framework that can address nano-level threats while preserving civil liberties and legal standards (Helbing & Ienca, 2024; Li & Zhang, 2025). With the integration of ICCT principles and cross-disciplinary strategies (Aithal & Aithal, 2020), future digital forensics must become both smarter and smaller—capable of operating at the scale of the crimes they investigate.

EVIDENCE COLLECTION AND CHAIN OF CUSTODY AT THE NANOSCALE

The emergence of nanoscale technologies in digital forensics presents transformative possibilities for the collection, preservation, and analysis of digital and physical evidence. As cybercrime investigations increasingly encounter data embedded in Internet of Things (IoT) devices, smart wearables, biomedical implants, and embedded systems, the forensic challenge evolves into one that requires nanoscale precision and technological sophistication (Sharma, Walia, & Jamal, 2024; Zareef et al., 2024).

Nanomaterials and Nanosensors in Evidence Acquisition

Nanotechnology enables forensic investigators to detect, collect, and analyze trace materials such as DNA, volatile organic compounds, and electromagnetic residues left by digital devices. Nanomaterials, such as carbon nanotubes, metal nanoparticles, and quantum dots, are employed to identify evidence with extreme sensitivity and selectivity (Zareef et al., 2024). These nanosensors can be integrated into mobile or drone-based forensic kits to gather data from crime scenes in real time (Aithal & Aithal, 2024).

Smart home environments, biomedical systems, and cyber-physical infrastructure often store digital evidence at microscopic levels. Nanoscale collection mechanisms are essential to access data logs, biometric inputs, and behavioral signals from these systems without compromising integrity (Friedl & Pernul, 2024; Chhabra et al., 2024).

The following system architecture demonstrates a hybrid model combining traditional tools with LLMs to enhance vulnerability detection outcomes.

Figure 4. Architecture of a hybrid LLM-traditional detection system

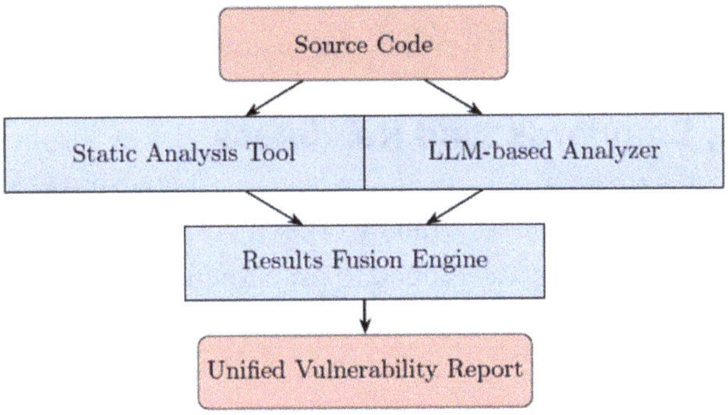

AI and Automation in Nanoscale Evidence Processing

Artificial intelligence significantly enhances nanoscale forensics by automating pattern recognition, anomaly detection, and data correlation across diverse evidence formats (Fernando, 2023; Akeiber, 2025). AI-assisted nano-devices can autonomously identify malware fingerprints, hardware tampering, and unauthorized access traces embedded within complex circuitry, particularly in IoT and cyber-physical systems (Sathwara, Dutta, & Pricop, 2018; Rizal et al., 2025).

Machine learning algorithms applied to data extracted via nanoscale sensors improve speed and accuracy in attributing digital crimes, especially in hybrid environments such as smart cities or health monitoring systems (Kassem et al., 2024; Banerjee, Chakraborty, & Rathi, 2020). These automated forensic techniques must comply with admissibility standards in court while ensuring robust documentation of analysis (Javed et al., 2022).

Chain of Custody: Micro-Integrity, Macro-Legality

Maintaining the chain of custody for nanoscale evidence poses unique legal and technical challenges. The invisibility and fragility of nano-derived data necessitate advanced preservation methods and blockchain-enabled traceability systems to verify authenticity from collection to courtroom (Li & Zhang, 2025). The deployment of AI for managing the chain of custody—such as timestamping, encryption, and access control—enhances auditability and mitigates risks of tampering or contamination (Tyagi, Kumari, & Richa, 2024; Akinade et al., 2021).

Legal frameworks, however, have not yet fully adapted to these advanced collection methods. The admissibility of nano-forensic evidence is still debated in many jurisdictions due to the lack of standardized protocols and certification of tools (Helbing & Ienca, 2024; Sharma & Garg, 2023). To overcome this, international regulatory convergence and interdisciplinary collaboration are essential (Favino et al., 2025).

Frameworks, Standards, and Readiness

Structured forensic readiness frameworks incorporating nanoscale and AI-integrated processes are being developed to prepare institutions for complex cybercrime cases (Rizal et al., 2025). For example, the NIST cybersecurity framework, when adapted to tools like Oxygen Forensic® Detective, supports the forensic lifecycle from nano-collection to courtroom presentation (Sutikno & Busthomi, 2025). Similarly, big data analytics platforms powered by AI facilitate large-scale forensic intelligence integration (Fernando, 2023).

Several scholars emphasize the role of interdisciplinary innovation in building these frameworks. For instance, the integration of information, communication, and computation technologies (ICCT) with nanotechnology allows for deeper forensic insights, especially in the yellow economy and hybrid cyber-physical threats (Aithal & Aithal, 2020, 2024). Likewise, the digital transformation landscape highlighted by Möller (2023) underscores the need to adopt agile methodologies for collecting micro-level evidence across devices and environments.

Challenges and Ethical Considerations

Despite the technological promise, nanoscale forensics introduces ethical concerns regarding privacy, consent, and potential misuse. Nano-enabled surveillance and forensic intrusion into personal biomedical systems or private residences raise significant legal and societal questions (Vaseashta, 2022; Sheikhbahei & Ari, 2024). The integration of AI further complicates these dynamics by automating decision-making, which may obscure accountability and oversight (Khan, Ishrat, & Al Farsi, 2025).

Moreover, the increasing complexity of cybercrime tactics necessitates that forensic professionals remain constantly updated through advanced training and continuous engagement with technological advances (Kumar & Alam, 2025; Widodo et al., 2024). Collaborative ecosystems that combine forensic science, legal scholarship, and technical development are critical to ensure responsible use (Okwu et al., 2022).

DATA FUSION AND SIGNAL ANALYSIS

In the era of nanoscale forensics, the synergy of **data fusion** and **signal analysis** represents a cornerstone in deriving actionable intelligence from fragmented, heterogeneous, and multidimensional forensic data sources. The integration of artificial intelligence (AI) with nanoscale devices enhances the capacity to interpret weak signals, correlate disjointed digital artifacts, and reconstruct sequences of cyber events with high fidelity. These advanced analytical capabilities are indispensable in modern digital forensics and cybercrime investigation, especially when addressing the complex and concealed nature of attacks in systems such as IoT networks, embedded hardware, and cyber-physical systems.

Multisensor Data Fusion in Nanoscale Forensics

Data fusion refers to the process of integrating data from multiple sources or sensors to produce more consistent, accurate, and useful information than would be possible from any individual data source alone. In nanoscale digital forensics, the deployment of **nano-enabled multisensor arrays** (e.g., for biometric traces, thermal signatures, or electromagnetic emissions) allows for micro-level environmental context acquisition and device-level behavior monitoring (Sharma, Walia, & Jamal, 2024; Zareef et al., 2024). These sensor outputs, when interpreted through **AI-driven fusion algorithms**, offer a layered understanding of cyber incidents.

AI and Machine Learning in Signal Analysis

Signal analysis in forensic contexts involves the extraction and interpretation of meaningful patterns from analog or digital signals—whether from communication streams, memory residues, or sensor logs. AI and machine learning (ML) models such as convolutional neural networks (CNNs), recurrent neural networks (RNNs), and support vector machines (SVMs) enable automatic pattern recognition and anomaly detection in noisy or encrypted datasets (Akeiber, 2025; Kassem et al., 2024). This is especially critical in analyzing signals generated from nanoscale devices that produce complex, low-amplitude data streams.

Big Data Analytics and Cross-Domain Integration

The rise of **big data analytics** in digital forensics has fueled the fusion of structured and unstructured data from diverse platforms, including mobile devices, IoT ecosystems, and cloud environments. Fernando (2023) presents a multidimensional framework where AI fuses multisource forensic data for timeline reconstruction and actor attribution. As emphasized by Aithal and Aithal (2020, 2024), the convergence of nanotechnology with ICCT (Information, Communication, and Computational Technologies) offers new research pathways in signal harmonization and forensic intelligence systems.

Signal Reconstruction in Cyber-Physical Systems

Signal analysis becomes more challenging in **cyber-physical systems (CPS)**, where analog and digital realms intertwine. Chhabra et al. (2024) highlight the importance of integrating signal sources from embedded systems, hardware-level diagnostics, and peripheral memory residues. AI techniques are employed to reconstruct tampered signals and link them to physical state transitions of devices, thus aiding in intrusion detection and forensic tracing.

Role of IoT and Terahertz Devices

In IoT networks, especially those leveraging terahertz technology for data transmission and sensing, real-time signal analysis is crucial. Banerjee, Chakraborty, and Rathi (2020) stress the role of terahertz imaging and AI in wearable devices and biomedical data streams, which can also be applied in forensic cases involving health-related cyber incidents or location tracking. Additionally, works like those of Sathwara, Dutta, and Pricop (2018) and Rizal et al. (2025) propose IoT forensic frameworks that integrate AI-powered signal correlation for reconstructing network-level events.

Forensic Signal Extraction Tools and Frameworks

Tools such as **Oxygen Forensic® Detective** (Sutikno & Busthomi, 2025), which incorporate analytic engines based on the NIST Cybersecurity Framework, exemplify how forensic tools are integrating data fusion techniques for enhanced evidentiary accuracy. Rohatgi and Shrivastava (2022) further propose generalized digital scientific systems that incorporate machine learning pipelines for forensic signal extraction.

Networked and Multivendor Systems

In multi-vendor infrastructures, data fragmentation across proprietary systems complicates evidence correlation. Akinade et al. (2021) present a conceptual model where AI unifies fragmented logs, telemetry data, and protocol-specific signals into a coherent forensic picture. This approach is critical for handling advanced persistent threats (APTs) in hybrid digital environments (Kumar & Alam, 2025).

Policy, Risk, and Regulatory Considerations

The processing and fusion of multisource signals raise **regulatory and ethical concerns**, particularly regarding privacy, data sovereignty, and legal admissibility. Helbing and Ienca (2024) advocate for converging international regulatory frameworks in response to technological convergence, while Li and Zhang (2025) point out the governance challenges of using AI for educational or surveillance purposes. The European Union's research, as summarized by Favino et al. (2025), outlines the emerging risks from unregulated AI-driven forensic technologies and their implications for internal security.

Applications in Smart Homes and Society 5.0

With increasing signal complexity in **smart homes** and connected infrastructure, signal fusion is pivotal to tracing digital footprints left behind by both users and intruders. Friedl and Pernul (2024) document advances in device forensics where data fusion enables context-aware incident reconstruction. Similarly, Sharma and Garg (2023) explore applications in Society 5.0, where signal analysis is used to maintain digital ethics and societal safety across domains.

Interdisciplinary Innovations and Future Trends

Emerging research indicates a growing focus on **interdisciplinary signal analytics**, blending concepts from bioinformatics, nanomaterials science, and cybersecurity (Sheikhbahei & Ari, 2024; Vaseashta, 2022). As noted by Widodo et al. (2024), this signals a future where forensic analysis is no longer confined to cyber artifacts but extends to biological, behavioral, and environmental data, fused in real-time through advanced AI.

SECURITY AND PRIVACY IMPLICATIONS

The integration of nanoscale devices and AI into digital forensics introduces a profound duality: while they enhance cybercrime investigation capabilities, they simultaneously raise substantial concerns regarding privacy, data security, and ethical governance. As nano-enabled systems and autonomous AI agents become embedded in everyday digital ecosystems, from smart homes to biomedical devices, the line between surveillance and investigation becomes increasingly blurred.

Privacy Intrusion by Design

Nanoscale sensors can be imperceptibly embedded in physical spaces and devices, collecting biometric, behavioral, and environmental data (Sharma, Walia, & Jamal, 2024; Zareef et al., 2024). These sensors, often integrated into IoT platforms, generate persistent data streams that AI systems process for behavioral analysis, event reconstruction, and anomaly detection (Banerjee, Chakraborty, & Rathi, 2020; Widodo et al., 2024). The potential for privacy intrusion is amplified when such systems operate without informed consent or transparent data policies.

AI and Ethical Oversight

AI-powered forensic analysis systems risk infringing on individual rights when their decision-making lacks interpretability or accountability. Akeiber (2025) and Tyagi, Kumari, and Richa (2024) highlight that opaque machine learning models used in forensic predictions can lead to wrongful attribution, particularly when evidence stems from incomplete or biased datasets. Misuse of AI in digital forensics—especially in profiling or predictive policing—raises ethical flags in terms of due process and fairness (Fernando, 2023).

Regulatory and Legal Gaps

Existing legal structures are ill-prepared to handle the implications of AI-nanoscale convergence. Aithal and Aithal (2020, 2024) stress the need for updated laws addressing the interdependency of ICCT technologies and nanotechnology, particularly in the forensic context. Helbing and Ienca (2024) argue for international regulatory convergence, emphasizing that fragmented policies could lead to legal loopholes, cross-border privacy violations, and the weaponization of forensic AI tools.

Risks of Autonomy and Misattribution

Autonomous forensic frameworks—like those discussed by Akinade et al. (2021)—introduce automation into evidence analysis and attribution. In multi-vendor infrastructures, assigning liability in the event of error or system failure becomes difficult. If AI systems misinterpret digital evidence or overreach in surveillance, legal recourse may be unclear (Möller, 2023; Sharma & Garg, 2023).

Smart Homes and Persistent Surveillance

Smart home devices, often designed with minimal security protocols, pose particular privacy risks. Friedl and Pernul (2024) point out that smart home forensics now involve data from microphones, cameras, and motion detectors—all of which are susceptible to misuse. Khan, Ishrat, and Al Farsi (2025) note that contemporary forensic tools can extract residual data even after deletion, raising concerns about the longevity and traceability of digital behaviors.

Cloud, Big Data, and AI-Driven Surveillance

The rise of cloud-based storage and AI-fueled data analytics in forensics enables investigators to draw correlations across disparate data sources (Fernando, 2023; Kassem et al., 2024). However, these capabilities also allow for mass surveillance, particularly when combined with nanoscale monitoring. Legal ambiguities about data ownership and cross-border access worsen the risks of overreach and misuse (Li & Zhang, 2025).

IoT Forensics and Cross-Domain Leakage

In complex IoT environments, AI can fuse data across domains—personal, industrial, medical—leading to "cross-domain leakage" where private data intended for one purpose is reused for another (Sathwara, Dutta, & Pricop, 2018; Rizal et al., 2025). Rohatgi and Shrivastava (2022) emphasize the role of digital scientific examination frameworks in mitigating such risks but acknowledge their current limitations in decentralized architectures.

Cyber-Physical Vulnerabilities

Chhabra et al. (2024) discuss how cyber-physical systems are vulnerable to low-level signal manipulation and covert data exfiltration, especially when enhanced by nanotechnologies. These vulnerabilities are compounded by the emergence of nanoscale malware delivery systems that could evade traditional defenses (Vaseashta, 2022; Kumar & Alam, 2025).

Tool Abuse and Ethical Boundaries

Even sophisticated tools like Oxygen Forensic® Detective, while compliant with NIST guidelines, can be misused if deployed without judicial oversight or ethical training (Sutikno & Busthomi, 2025). The ability to recover deleted messages, locate individuals, and reconstruct communications must be counterbalanced with strong procedural safeguards.

National and Regional Security

According to FAVINO et al. (2025), the European Union is facing increased internal security risks due to the proliferation of unregulated forensic AI and nano-tools. These technologies, if misused, can disrupt democratic norms, undermine privacy protections, and lead to unjustified surveillance of journalists, activists, or political dissidents.

Societal and Ethical Futures

As society advances toward a fully interconnected "Society 5.0" paradigm, where humans and machines coexist in hyper-connected ecosystems, ethical frameworks must evolve accordingly (Sharma & Garg, 2023). AI-driven nanoscale forensics must be integrated within these ethical paradigms to ensure technological growth does not outpace moral and legal development (Okwu et al., 2022; Sheikhbahei & Ari, 2024).

LEGAL AND REGULATORY FRAMEWORKS

The integration of nanoscale devices and artificial intelligence (AI) in digital forensics has outpaced the development of legal and regulatory frameworks, creating a governance vacuum fraught with ethical, procedural, and jurisdictional challenges. As these technologies become essential tools in cybercrime investigations, the need for harmonized laws, compliance standards, and oversight mechanisms is critical.

The ICCT and Nanotechnology Nexus in Legal Context

The convergence of Information, Communication, and Computational Technologies (ICCT) with nanotechnology has created a complex technological landscape that traditional legal structures are not equipped to govern. Aithal and Aithal (2020, 2024) have emphasized that the interdependencies between these domains demand legal innovation, especially in cyber forensics and security. They argue that current legislative tools are inadequate for regulating AI-powered nano-forensic devices due to the fast-evolving nature of underlying technologies and their multifaceted applications in the yellow economy and public safety sectors.

Lack of Standardized Forensic Protocols for AI and Nano Devices

While conventional forensic procedures are governed by national standards such as those from NIST, the emergence of AI-enabled nanoscale forensic devices poses new regulatory challenges. Forensic tools like Oxygen Forensic® Detective, though aligned with NIST cybersecurity frameworks, must be continually reassessed to ensure they comply with privacy rights and admissibility protocols in legal proceedings (Sutikno & Busthomi, 2025). The question remains: how should nano-forensics be validated as legally sound and scientifically reliable?

Cross-Border Data Jurisdiction and Cloud Forensics

Cloud-based AI forensics platforms and remote nanosensor systems often operate across national boundaries, leading to jurisdictional conflicts. Li and Zhang (2025) highlight the growing difficulty of reconciling different national regulations, especially when sensitive data is processed by autonomous forensic AI agents in multi-cloud environments. Akinade et al. (2021) also warn that multi-vendor network infrastructures using AI-driven security may encounter legal ambiguity regarding responsibility in cases of digital evidence mismanagement or data breach.

Emerging Risks to Democratic Freedoms and Human Rights

The use of nanoscale devices and AI in surveillance-heavy digital forensics may inadvertently infringe upon democratic freedoms. As noted by FAVINO et al. (2025), without proper legislative checks, internal security mechanisms could misuse these tools to target marginalized groups or political dissidents. Helbing and Ienca (2024) advocate for a global regulatory architecture that reflects the ethical demands of converging technologies and emphasizes transparency, proportionality, and oversight.

Digital Forensics in Smart Environments: Ownership and Consent

Smart homes, wearables, and biomedical IoT platforms embedded with nanosensors are increasingly being used in forensic investigations. However, Friedl and Pernul (2024) highlight unresolved legal questions around digital ownership, chain-of-custody, and user consent in these environments. For example, if a nanoscale device installed in a smart lightbulb gathers biometric data without explicit user awareness, is such evidence legally admissible?

AI Autonomy and Liability in Forensic Misattribution

With AI systems taking on increasingly autonomous roles in evidence analysis, legal systems must determine how to allocate liability when errors occur. If an AI-driven forensic platform falsely attributes cybercrime activity to an innocent individual due to flawed training data, who is held responsible—the developer, the forensic analyst, or the institution deploying the tool? As Möller (2023) and Sharma & Garg (2023) argue, legal liability frameworks must evolve to handle such complex accountability chains in AI-forensics ecosystems.

Data Integrity, Chain-of-Custody, and AI Manipulation Risks

Data integrity remains a cornerstone of admissible digital evidence. However, AI-enhanced tools and nanosensors may unintentionally disrupt established chain-of-custody protocols due to their autonomous data handling capabilities. Moreover, adversarial AI can alter forensic results or generate synthetic evidence (Akeiber, 2025; Tyagi, Kumari, & Richa, 2024). Without regulatory safeguards, such manipulation risks undermine public trust in forensic science.

Cyber-Physical Systems and Legal Blind Spots

Cyber-physical systems, such as autonomous vehicles or smart medical implants, present legal blind spots when involved in criminal cases. Chhabra et al. (2024) highlight that existing laws do not adequately address how forensic investigators should access, interpret, and preserve data from such integrated systems, especially when nanoscale devices are involved.

Need for Forensic Readiness in IoT and Industry 4.0

The rapid growth of IoT ecosystems, fueled by nanotechnology, necessitates built-in forensic readiness. Rizal et al. (2025) propose an AI-enhanced forensic framework to tackle IoT complexity. Sathwara, Dutta, and Pricop (2018) similarly call for digital investigation models that integrate seamlessly with IoT systems while respecting legal compliance. However, most jurisdictions lack formal policies requiring forensic readiness in critical infrastructure or consumer technologies.

Forensic Tool Evaluation and Scientific Validation

Regulatory authorities must develop frameworks to assess the scientific validity and forensic reliability of AI and nanoscale tools. Javed et al. (2022) stress the importance of independent validation studies to ensure the credibility of such tools in courtrooms. Fernando (2023) further recommends adopting a multi-dimensional legal framework that aligns big data analytics with evidentiary standards.

Ethical Technology Deployment and Governance

Finally, the responsible deployment of AI and nanoscale forensic systems requires multi-stakeholder governance models. Okwu et al. (2022) and Sheikhbahei & Ari (2024) call for the incorporation of ethics-by-design principles into the development and application of digital forensic technologies. Zareef et al. (2024) similarly caution that without ethical regulatory interventions, nanomaterial-enhanced forensic devices may be exploited for intrusive surveillance.

Summary

The evolving field of AI and nanoscale forensics urgently requires cohesive, forward-looking legal and regulatory responses. These must reconcile rapid technological innovation with civil liberties, scientific standards, and judicial fairness. International harmonization, ethical oversight, and adaptive legislation are no longer optional—they are imperative to ensure that the integration of AI and nanotechnology into digital forensics enhances justice without compromising fundamental rights.

ETHICAL CONCERNS AND SOCIETAL IMPACT

The integration of advanced technologies such as artificial intelligence (AI), nanotechnology, and cyber-physical systems in digital forensics and cybersecurity raises profound ethical concerns and societal implications. While these innovations promise enhanced capabilities for crime detection and prevention, they also present risks that challenge fundamental human rights, social justice, and trust in technological governance.

Privacy and Surveillance Challenges

A major ethical concern arises from the pervasive surveillance capabilities enabled by AI-powered forensic tools and nanoscale sensors. The ability to collect, analyze, and interpret vast amounts of personal data in real time threatens privacy rights. Friedl and Pernul (2024) emphasize how smart home devices equipped with forensic capabilities could be exploited for unauthorized monitoring, raising questions about informed consent and data ownership. This concern extends to healthcare and wearable technologies, where Banerjee, Chakraborty, and Rathi Sr (2020) highlight risks of sensitive biometric data being accessed without user awareness or legal safeguards.

Bias, Fairness, and Accountability in AI Systems

AI algorithms used in forensic investigations are susceptible to biases embedded in training data, leading to unfair outcomes or wrongful attributions (Akeiber, 2025; Tyagi, Kumari, & Richa, 2024). Such biases can disproportionately affect marginalized communities, exacerbating existing inequalities. Kassem et al. (2024) stress the importance of transparent AI development and continuous auditing to ensure fairness and accountability, while Möller (2023) underscores the need for ethical guidelines and human oversight to mitigate machine errors.

Implications of Autonomous Decision-Making

With increasing autonomy in AI-driven forensic tools, ethical dilemmas surface regarding the delegation of critical decisions. The risk that machines could override human judgment or propagate errors without intervention raises questions about liability and moral responsibility (Fernando, 2023; Sharma & Garg, 2023). Chhabra et al. (2024) caution that cyber-physical systems embedded with nanoscale devices must be governed by clear ethical frameworks that define acceptable levels of automation.

Societal Trust and Technological Transparency

The societal acceptance of digital forensic technologies depends heavily on transparency and trustworthiness. Widodo et al. (2024) argue that opaque AI models and proprietary forensic tools hinder public understanding and scrutiny, potentially undermining confidence in the justice system. Helbing and Ienca (2024) advocate for converging international regulations to promote transparency, interoperability, and ethical standards, which can enhance societal trust.

Impact on Legal and Social Norms

The rapid advancement of forensic technologies disrupts traditional legal and social norms surrounding evidence, privacy, and due process. Javed et al. (2022) point out that society must reconcile how digital evidence gathered through nanotechnology and AI complies with existing rights frameworks. Similarly, Li and

Zhang (2025) highlight governance challenges in education and public awareness regarding ethical use and legal boundaries of emerging technologies.

Dual-Use Risks and Ethical Dilemmas

Nanotechnology and AI possess dual-use potential—they can be used for both beneficial forensic applications and malicious activities, including invasive surveillance or data manipulation (Aithal & Aithal, 2020, 2024; Zareef et al., 2024). The ethical dilemma lies in balancing innovation with the prevention of misuse. Vaseashta (2022) emphasizes the need for proactive ethical policies to prevent exploitation while fostering technological growth.

Equity in Access and Technological Divide

Advanced forensic technologies risk deepening the digital divide, where only privileged institutions or regions gain access to state-of-the-art AI and nanoscale tools (Okwu et al., 2022; Khan, Ishrat, & Al Farsi, 2025). This inequity can skew forensic capabilities and justice outcomes globally. Kumar and Alam (2025) argue for inclusive policies ensuring equitable distribution and capacity building.

Ethical Frameworks for Sustainable Development

Emerging technologies must align with broader societal goals such as sustainability and human well-being. Sheikhbahei and Ari (2024) discuss harnessing digital innovations ethically to improve productivity and sustainability in sectors like biomedical engineering, highlighting the cross-disciplinary nature of these challenges. Sharma, Walia, and Jamal (2024) also advocate integrating ethical standards in nanotechnology applications to safeguard social values.

Public Awareness and Multistakeholder Governance

Ensuring ethical use of forensic technologies demands active public engagement and transparent governance. Rizal et al. (2025) call for forensic readiness frameworks that incorporate ethical considerations alongside technical preparedness. Helbing and Ienca (2024) recommend multistakeholder approaches involving governments, academia, industry, and civil society to co-create ethical norms and oversight mechanisms.

Summary

Ethical concerns surrounding AI and nanotechnology in digital forensics are multifaceted, impacting privacy, fairness, societal trust, and global equity. Addressing these requires comprehensive ethical frameworks, international cooperation, and inclusive governance to ensure that technological advancements serve humanity's best interests without compromising fundamental rights or social justice.

EMERGING TRENDS AND FUTURE DIRECTIONS

The fields of digital forensics, cybersecurity, and related technological domains are rapidly evolving, driven by advances in artificial intelligence (AI), nanotechnology, the Internet of Things (IoT), and integrated cyber-physical systems. This section explores key emerging trends shaping the future landscape of forensic science and cybersecurity, along with the critical research directions necessary to address upcoming challenges.

Integration of AI and Machine Learning in Forensics

AI and machine learning (ML) continue to revolutionize forensic investigations by automating complex data analysis and enhancing pattern recognition across vast datasets. Akeiber (2025) and Tyagi, Kumari, and Richa (2024) highlight the growing application of ML algorithms in detecting cybercrimes, predicting attack vectors, and improving the accuracy of digital evidence interpretation. Kassem et al. (2024) emphasize transformative interdisciplinary research combining AI, ML, and bioinformatics to tackle new forensic challenges, which will lead to more robust and scalable forensic solutions.

IoT Forensics and Cyber-Physical Systems

With IoT devices becoming ubiquitous, forensic frameworks must adapt to the heterogeneity and volume of data generated. Chhabra et al. (2024) and Rizal et al. (2025) discuss enhanced forensic readiness models leveraging AI to manage the complexity of IoT ecosystems, including smart homes and industrial cyber-physical systems. Friedl and Pernul (2024) also provide insights into advances and challenges in device forensics specifically tailored for smart environments.

Nanotechnology in Forensic Science

Nanotechnology is emerging as a powerful tool in forensic investigations, enabling nanoscale evidence detection, material analysis, and sensor development. Sharma, Walia, and Jamal (2024) detail analytical advancements, while Aithal and Aithal (2024) discuss nanotechnology's applications in the broader "yellow economy," linking forensic science with sustainable development. Zareef et al. (2024) highlight novel nanomaterials' potential for enhancing forensic methodologies.

Big Data Analytics and Digital Twins

Fernando (2023) and Sutikno and Busthomi (2025) underscore the increasing importance of big data analytics combined with digital twin technology in forensic investigations, allowing real-time simulation, anomaly detection, and predictive modeling. These technologies facilitate proactive cybersecurity measures and forensic preparedness, especially within Industry 4.0 frameworks (Okwu et al., 2022).

Automated Network Security and Multi-Vendor Resilience

Automation of network security through AI-driven frameworks is becoming critical for enhancing resilience across complex, multi-vendor infrastructures. Akinade et al. (2021) propose conceptual models for dynamic security automation, which enable rapid detection and mitigation of threats, minimizing human error and response times.

Converging Technologies and International Regulation

As Helbing and Ienca (2024) argue, converging technologies such as AI, nanotech, and cyber-physical systems necessitate harmonized international regulatory frameworks. The rapid pace of innovation demands globally coordinated policies that address ethical, legal, and security implications while promoting innovation and data sharing across borders.

Enhanced Forensic Tools and Techniques

Khan, Ishrat, and Al Farsi (2025), Javed et al. (2022), and Widodo et al. (2024) provide comprehensive surveys highlighting advancements in forensic tools that utilize AI, ML, and nanomaterials. These include improved digital trail analysis, biometrics, and automated evidence collection systems. Rohatgi and Shrivastava

(2022) discuss generic digital scientific examination systems designed to address IoT-specific challenges.

Education, Legal, and Governance Challenges

Li and Zhang (2025) stress the importance of addressing legal and governance challenges arising from new technologies through education and policy reforms. Kumar and Alam (2025) recommend optimized approaches in cyberology to manage risks and enhance governance mechanisms in the digital era.

Cybersecurity in Digital Transformation

Möller (2023) offers a comprehensive guide to cybersecurity amidst digital transformation, advocating for integration of forensic readiness and AI-powered detection mechanisms as standard practices in organizational risk management.

Emerging Security Risks and Opportunities

Favino et al. (2025) analyze new security risks and opportunities stemming from technological advances within the European Union's internal security context, emphasizing adaptive security frameworks responsive to evolving threats.

Sustainability and Societal Impact

Sheikhbahei and Ari (2024) discuss how emerging digital technologies can improve sustainability and productivity, particularly in biomedical engineering and neuroscience. Sharma and Garg (2023) emphasize technological prospects aligned with the vision of Society 5.0, integrating human-centric innovations with societal well-being.

Future Research Opportunities

Aithal and Aithal (2020) identify new research opportunities at the intersection of ICCT (Information, Communication, and Computing Technologies), cyber-security, and forensic science, urging interdisciplinary collaboration. Vaseashta (2022) highlights the need for advanced technological platforms to strengthen cyber-defense capabilities, particularly in geopolitically sensitive regions such as the Western Balkans.

Summary

The future of digital forensics and cybersecurity is marked by the convergence of AI, nanotechnology, IoT, and big data analytics, driving innovative forensic methods and security solutions. Addressing emerging challenges requires multidisciplinary research, international regulatory cooperation, and proactive governance. Embracing these trends will enable more resilient, ethical, and efficient forensic systems, capable of protecting society in an increasingly digital world.

CONCLUSION

This comprehensive exploration of the evolving landscape of digital forensics, cybersecurity, and emerging technologies underscores the transformative impact of advanced tools such as artificial intelligence, machine learning, nanotechnology, and the Internet of Things. As these technologies integrate more deeply into forensic investigations and security infrastructures, they bring both unprecedented opportunities and complex challenges.

The integration of AI and ML has enhanced the capability to analyze vast and heterogeneous data sources efficiently, enabling faster and more accurate detection of cyber threats and forensic evidence. Meanwhile, the rise of IoT and cyber-physical systems demands novel forensic frameworks and readiness models that can keep pace with the complexity and scale of connected devices. Nanotechnology further enriches forensic science by offering novel materials and sensors, enabling detection at previously inaccessible scales.

However, this technological progress must be balanced with robust legal, ethical, and societal frameworks to ensure privacy, data protection, and equitable access. International collaboration and regulatory harmonization are crucial to manage converging technologies responsibly, fostering innovation while mitigating risks.

Future research directions point to a multidisciplinary approach, combining advances in AI, big data analytics, and digital twins with policy and governance reforms. Building resilient, automated, and adaptive forensic and cybersecurity systems will be critical to responding effectively to the dynamic threat landscape.

Ultimately, embracing these emerging trends with foresight and responsibility will empower forensic and cybersecurity professionals to safeguard digital ecosystems, protect individual rights, and contribute to societal well-being in an increasingly interconnected world.

REFERENCES

Aithal, P. S., & Aithal, S. (2020, December). Analysis of Interdependency of ICCT Underlying Technologies and Related New Research Opportunities with Special Emphasis on Cyber Security and Forensic Science. In *Proceedings of the Conference on Future Technologies of IT, Management, Education, and Social Sciences,* 19th December (pp. 171-186).

Aithal, P. S., & Aithal, S. (2024). An overview of the use of ICCT and nanotechnology in yellow economy: Current status and future opportunities. [PIJET]. *SSRN, 1*(1), 29–62. DOI: 10.2139/ssrn.4901452

. Akeiber, H. J. (2025). A comprehensive study of Cybercrime and Digital Forensics through Machine Learning and AI. *Al-Rafidain Journal of Engineering Sciences*, 369-395.

Akinade, A. O., Adepoju, P. A., Ige, A. B., Afolabi, A. I., & Amoo, O. O.Afees Olanrewaju AkinadePeter Adeyemo AdepojuAdebimpe Bolatito IgeAdeoye Idowu AfolabiOlukunle Oladipupo Amoo. (2021). A conceptual model for network security automation: Leveraging AI-driven frameworks to enhance multi-vendor infrastructure resilience. *International Journal of Science and Technology Research Archive, 1*(1), 39–59. DOI: 10.53771/ijstra.2021.1.1.0034

Banerjee, A., Chakraborty, C., & Rathi, M.Sr. (2020). Medical imaging, artificial intelligence, internet of things, wearable devices in terahertz healthcare technologies. In *Terahertz biomedical and healthcare technologies* (pp. 145–165). Elsevier. DOI: 10.1016/B978-0-12-818556-8.00008-2

Chhabra, S., Sabharwal, S. M., Kaur, M., & Obaid, A. J. (2024). Cyber Forensics for Cyber-physical System. In *Emerging Trends for Securing Cyber Physical Systems and the Internet of Things* (pp. 220–246). CRC Press. DOI: 10.1201/9781003474111-13

FAVINO. R., CONTE, N., DE, M. A., GARCIA, M. E., MONTANARI, E., PAGANINI, A., ... & SFALAGKIARIS, C. E. (2025). Emerging risks and opportunities for EU internal security stemming from new technologies.

Fernando, K. (2023). A multidimensional framework for utilizing big data analytics and ai in strengthening digital forensics and cybersecurity investigations. *International Journal of Cybersecurity Risk Management, Forensics, and Compliance, 7*(12), 16–30.

Friedl, S., & Pernul, G. (2024). Device Forensics in Smart Homes: Insights on Advances, Challenges and Future Directions. In *Transactions on Large-Scale Data- and Knowledge-Centered Systems LVII* (pp. 68–98). Springer Berlin Heidelberg.

Helbing, D., & Ienca, M. (2024). Why converging technologies need converging international regulation. *Ethics and Information Technology*, *26*(1), 15. DOI: 10.1007/s10676-024-09756-8

Javed, A. R., Ahmed, W., Alazab, M., Jalil, Z., Kifayat, K., & Gadekallu, T. R. (2022). A comprehensive survey on computer forensics: State-of-the-art, tools, techniques, challenges, and future directions. *IEEE Access : Practical Innovations, Open Solutions*, *10*, 11065–11089. DOI: 10.1109/ACCESS.2022.3142508

. Kassem, M. A., Lodhi, K., Yuan, J., Meksem, K., Ahmed, K. R., Sarami, C., ... & Bouqetta, B. (2024). Advancing AI, ML, and Bioinformatics for Transformative Research Across Disciplines. *Journal of Artificial Intelligence, Machine Learning, and Bioinformatics*, 1-6.

Khan, W., Ishrat, M., & Al Farsi, M. M. (2025). Unveiling the Digital Trails: A Survey of Contemporary Digital Forensics Tools and Techniques. In *Cyberology* (pp. 71-89). Chapman and Hall/CRC.

. Kumar, S., & Alam, S. (2025). 6 Optimized Approaches. *Cyberology: An Optimized Approach to the Cyber-World*, 103.

Li, Z., & Zhang, W. (2025). Technology in education: Addressing legal and governance challenges in the digital era. *Education and Information Technologies*, *30*(7), 8413–8443. DOI: 10.1007/s10639-024-13036-9

Möller, D. P. (2023). Guide to Cybersecurity in Digital Transformation. *Springer Link. Gewerbestrasse*, *11*, 6330.

Okwu, M. O., Tartibu, L. K., Maware, C., Enarevba, D. R., Afenogho, J. O., & Essien, A. (2022, August). Emerging technologies of industry 4.0: Challenges and opportunities. In *2022 International Conference on Artificial Intelligence, Big Data, Computing and Data Communication Systems (icABCD)* (pp. 1-13). IEEE. DOI: 10.1109/icABCD54961.2022.9856002

Rizal, R., Selamat, S. R., Mas'ud, M. Z., & Widiyasono, N. (2025). Enhanced readiness forensic framework for the complexity of internet of things (IoT) investigation based on artificial intelligence. *J. Adv. Res. Appl. Sci. Eng. Technol.*, *50*(1), 121–135. DOI: 10.37934/araset.50.1.121135

. Rohatgi, S., & Shrivastava, S. (2022). A Generic Digital Scientific Examination System for Internet of Things. *Digital Forensics and Internet of Things: Impact and Challenges*, 87-110.

Sathwara, S., Dutta, N., & Pricop, E. (2018, June). IoT Forensic A digital investigation framework for IoT systems. In *2018 10th international conference on electronics, computers and artificial intelligence (ECAI)* (pp. 1-4). IEEE. DOI: 10.1109/ECAI.2018.8679017

. Sharma, B. K., Walia, M., & Jamal, F. (2024). Nanotechnology in forensic science. *Advances in Analytical Techniques for Forensic Investigation*, 363-393.

Sharma, L., & Garg, P. K. (Eds.). (2023). *Technological prospects and social applications of society 5.0*. CRC Press.

Sheikhbahei, E., & Ari, A. A. (2024). Harnessing the power of emerging digital technologies for improved sustainability and productivity in biomedical engineering and neuroscience. *Scientific Hypotheses, 1*, 47–52. DOI: 10.69530/v8tgp793

Sutikno, T., & Busthomi, I. (2025). Power of analytic tools in Oxygen Forensic® Detective based on NIST cybersecurity framework. *Computer Science and Information Technology*, *6*(1), 8–19.

. Tyagi, A. K., Kumari, S., & Richa. (2024). Artificial Intelligence-Based Cyber Security and Digital Forensics: A Review. *Artificial Intelligence-Enabled Digital Twin for Smart Manufacturing*, 391-419.

Vaseashta, A. (2022). Nexus of advanced technology platforms for strengthening cyber-defense capabilities. In *Practical applications of advanced technologies for enhancing security and defense capabilities: Perspectives and Challenges for the Western Balkans* (pp. 14-31). IOS Press. DOI: 10.3233/NHSDP220003

. Widodo, A. M., Biyanto, T. R., Pappachan, P., & Colace, F. (2024). Recent advances in digital forensics and cybercrime investigation. *Digital Forensics and Cyber Crime Investigation*, 42-69.

Zareef, I., & Riaz, A. Salahuddin, Fatima, M., Anwar, A., & Munawar, A. (2024). Unveiling the Power of Nanomaterials in the Area of Forensics. In *Emerging Applications of Novel Nanoparticles* (pp. 29-57). Cham: Springer Nature Switzerland.

Chapter 9
Securing Smart Agriculture:
AI-Driven Digital Forensics in Agri-Tech Cybercrime Investigation

Hewa Majeed Zangana
https://orcid.org/0000-0001-7909-254X
Duhok Polytechnic University, Iraq

Aree Adel Abdulqader
Duhok Polytechnic University, Iraq

Senny Luckyardi
https://orcid.org/0000-0001-9954-7433
Universitas Komputer Indonesia, Indonesia

Shuai Li
University of Oulu, Finland

ABSTRACT

The rapid digital transformation of agriculture, powered by the Internet of Things (IoT), artificial intelligence (AI), and precision technologies, has led to the emergence of "Smart Agriculture." While these innovations promise enhanced productivity, sustainability, and resource optimization, they also introduce significant cybersecurity vulnerabilities. Smart agriculture systems, including autonomous machinery, sensor networks, and AI-driven analytics, are increasingly targeted by cybercriminals seeking to disrupt food supply chains, steal sensitive agricultural data, or manipulate decision-making algorithms. This chapter explores the intersection of AI and

DOI: 10.4018/979-8-3373-6536-7.ch009

digital forensics in investigating and mitigating cybercrimes within the agri-tech landscape. It highlights AI's role in proactive threat detection, anomaly monitoring, and evidence collection, while also discussing forensic readiness and challenges related to data integrity, privacy, and ethical governance.

INTRODUCTION

The integration of artificial intelligence (AI), Internet of Things (IoT), and smart devices into agricultural systems has marked the emergence of a new era known as smart agriculture or Agriculture 4.0. This technological shift has revolutionized traditional farming, offering significant improvements in efficiency, sustainability, and productivity (Araújo et al., 2021; Ahmad et al., 2024). However, alongside these benefits, a host of cybersecurity threats, data privacy concerns, and forensic challenges have surfaced, calling for robust frameworks that blend AI-driven technologies with digital forensic methodologies (Ali, Mijwil, Buruga, Abotaleb, & Adamopoulos, 2024; Otieno, 2023; Zangana, Luckyardi, Mustafa, & Li, 2025).

Smart agricultural environments are increasingly reliant on connected sensors, autonomous equipment, cloud platforms, and AI models that monitor soil health, predict crop yields, manage irrigation, and automate harvesting (Bhat & Huang, 2021; Leong et al., 2023; Shafik et al., 2025). These complex, interconnected systems make agriculture not only a critical infrastructure but also a target for sophisticated cyber-attacks that can disrupt supply chains and manipulate agricultural outputs (Aggarwal, Bansal, & Goel, 2024; Kapoor, 2025; Gardezi et al., 2024). Therefore, cybercrime investigations in agri-tech environments must evolve to address the unique challenges of AI-enhanced farming ecosystems.

The AI tools used in smart agriculture can paradoxically become both protectors and potential vulnerabilities. For example, predictive models used for irrigation scheduling or pest control can be manipulated through data poisoning or adversarial attacks, leading to severe economic losses or environmental damage (Wei et al., 2024; Neupane et al., 2024). Detecting, analyzing, and preventing such incidents requires not only traditional cybersecurity tools but also AI-augmented digital forensics capable of tracing attack vectors, verifying data integrity, and providing actionable insights (Zangana, Amelia, Mustafa, & Li, 2025).

Furthermore, the ethical implications of deploying AI in rural and resource-constrained contexts cannot be overlooked. As noted by Tzachor et al. (2022) and Alexander, Yarborough, and Smith (2024), responsible AI in agriculture must be built on transparency, trust, and governance mechanisms that respect the rights of farmers and protect biodiversity. Legal and ethical frameworks—particularly regarding the ownership, sharing, and forensic use of agri-data—remain underdeveloped

(Kochupillai et al., 2022; Zangana, Amelia, Luckyardi, Mustafa, & Li, 2025). There is a pressing need for cross-disciplinary collaboration to address these regulatory gaps (Devare, Arnaud, Antezana, & King, 2023; Gavai et al., 2025).

Emerging technologies like federated learning (Dembani et al., 2025), blockchain (Kochupillai & Köninger, 2023), and productive AI (Uplaonkar et al., 2024) also present both opportunities and risks in agri-forensic contexts. On one hand, these innovations can facilitate decentralized, privacy-preserving evidence collection; on the other, they introduce new attack surfaces and complexities for forensic analysts. The evolving digital landscape of smart agriculture necessitates a rethinking of forensic readiness, legal admissibility of AI-generated evidence, and resilience against cyber threats (Malhotra & Firdaus, 2022; Kaushik et al., 2024; Pandey & Mishra, 2024).

This chapter aims to critically explore the role of AI in enhancing digital forensic investigations in the smart agriculture domain. It builds on interdisciplinary insights from computer science, ethics, law, and agronomy to outline a comprehensive approach to securing agri-tech ecosystems. Through the analysis of state-of-the-art applications, case studies, and challenges, we investigate how AI technologies—when responsibly developed and ethically deployed—can bolster cybercrime detection, prevention, and recovery efforts in agricultural environments (Adanma & Ogunbiyi, 2024; Ahmad et al., 2024; Sparrow, Howard, & Degeling, 2021).

Additionally, the chapter considers pedagogical and scholarly dimensions, such as the impact of AI on scientific writing, education, and research integrity in agricultural disciplines (Abd-Elsalam & Abdel-Momen, 2023; Ya'u & Mohammed, 2025; Zangana, Amelia, Mustafa, & Li, 2025). Tools like ChatGPT and other large language models, while offering productivity benefits, raise concerns regarding authorship, bias, and academic misconduct (Aithal & Aithal, 2023, 2024; Bahrini et al., 2023; Zohouri, Sabzali, & Golmohammadi, 2024). These aspects are especially relevant when AI-generated content informs forensic decisions or legal testimony in cybercrime investigations.

In sum, smart agriculture represents a complex cyber-physical ecosystem where AI functions as both a tool and a subject of forensic interest. Addressing this dual role requires nuanced strategies that are technologically sound, ethically robust, and contextually appropriate for diverse agricultural settings—from industrial farms in developed nations to smallholder fields in the Global South (Aderibigbe et al., 2023; Ali et al., 2024; Kanyepe et al., 2025). By weaving together insights from emerging research and policy, this chapter contributes to the evolving discourse on AI-driven digital forensics in agriculture, positioning it as a cornerstone for secure and sustainable food futures.

BACKGROUND: DIGITAL TRANSFORMATION IN AGRICULTURE

Agriculture, traditionally grounded in manual labor and localized practices, is undergoing a radical transformation through the integration of emerging digital technologies. This paradigm shift, often referred to as Agriculture 4.0, represents the convergence of Artificial Intelligence (AI), the Internet of Things (IoT), big data, robotics, remote sensing, and cloud computing to enable precision agriculture, sustainable resource management, and real-time decision-making (Araújo et al., 2021; Bhat & Huang, 2021).

The deployment of smart sensors, drones, autonomous vehicles, AI-powered irrigation, and predictive analytics is redefining farming by optimizing yields, reducing resource wastage, and enabling climate-smart strategies (Ahmed et al., 2024; Wei et al., 2024). In particular, AI-driven insights enable real-time monitoring of soil conditions, pest outbreaks, and crop health, thereby improving both efficiency and sustainability (Aggarwal et al., 2024; Pandey & Mishra, 2024).

This digital transformation is especially critical for developing countries seeking to bridge the gap between food demand and agricultural output. According to Ahmad et al. (2024), the deployment of AI can play a transformative role in achieving food security in data-scarce and resource-constrained environments. Yet, achieving this potential necessitates addressing implementation barriers such as infrastructure, policy gaps, and capacity building (Aderibigbe et al., 2023).

A foundational component of Agriculture 4.0 is data. Modern farms generate massive volumes of information from diverse sources such as satellite imagery, IoT devices, and automated machinery (Williamson et al., 2023; Gardezi et al., 2024). However, the collection, storage, and use of agricultural data raise significant concerns around privacy, ownership, and security (Devare et al., 2023; Gavai et al., 2025). As Dembani et al. (2025) argue, federated learning and decentralized data models may offer a promising solution for protecting farm-level data while enabling AI training at scale.

However, the digitalization of agriculture has also expanded the attack surface for cybercrime. Smart farming systems are increasingly vulnerable to threats such as data breaches, ransomware, device hijacking, and algorithmic manipulation (Ali et al., 2024; Otieno, 2023). These risks threaten not only individual farms but also national food supply chains and rural economies. AI-enhanced cybersecurity mechanisms are thus essential to detect intrusions, assess system integrity, and provide real-time response capabilities (Kaushik et al., 2024; Zangana, Luckyardi, Mustafa, & Li, 2025).

Despite the clear benefits of digitization, ethical and governance challenges abound. There are growing concerns about the bias, opacity, and accountability of

AI systems applied to agricultural decision-making (Kochupillai et al., 2022; Tzachor et al., 2022). These issues underscore the need for responsible AI frameworks that emphasize transparency, stakeholder engagement, and risk mitigation (Alexander et al., 2024; Dara et al., 2022).

Moreover, the adoption of generative AI tools such as ChatGPT in agricultural research and scientific writing has introduced new academic and ethical considerations. While these tools accelerate documentation and knowledge dissemination, they may also risk misinformation or misuse if not carefully regulated (Abd-Elsalam & Abdel-Momen, 2023; Zangana, Amelia, Mustafa, & Li, 2025; Zohouri et al., 2024). Academic institutions and research bodies are therefore urged to develop AI literacy and ethical AI training in agricultural education (Aithal & Aithal, 2023; Ya'u & Mohammed, 2025).

From an infrastructural standpoint, the convergence of AI with IoT — termed the Artificial Intelligence of Things (AIoT) — has enabled precision farming but also raised interoperability, latency, and ethical challenges (Bhangar & Shahriyar, 2023; Leong et al., 2023). Additionally, innovations in nanotechnology and ICCT (Information, Communication, and Computational Technologies) are amplifying the capabilities of smart farming systems, yet their regulatory oversight remains limited (Aithal & Aithal, 2024).

From a policy perspective, legal frameworks are still catching up with the pace of digital innovation. As Kochupillai and Köninger (2023) stress, the creation of digital marketplaces for agrobiodiversity and plant genetics must incorporate legal clarity and data-sharing protocols. Furthermore, language, law, and regulatory systems play a pivotal role in shaping how AI is deployed, particularly in cross-border agricultural research (Zangana, Amelia, Luckyardi, Mustafa, & Li, 2025).

Additionally, global actors and agri-tech multinationals must engage with ethical AI governance to ensure inclusivity and sustainability. Questions of power asymmetry, data colonialism, and technological dependency remain particularly relevant in the Global South (Mark, 2019; Denhere & Shao, 2024).

Finally, the rise of autonomous agricultural robots and AI-based decision tools has prompted critical debates on human oversight, job displacement, and societal implications (Sparrow et al., 2021; He et al., 2021). These developments necessitate a human-centered design approach to maintain trust in AI systems and ensure they augment rather than replace human judgment.

To contextualize how AI is transforming forensic operations within smart agriculture, it is essential to visualize the end-to-end workflow. The following flowchart captures the sequential stages—ranging from data acquisition through connected devices to legal attribution—where AI-enhanced digital forensics plays a pivotal role.

Figure 1. AI-driven digital forensics workflow in smart agriculture

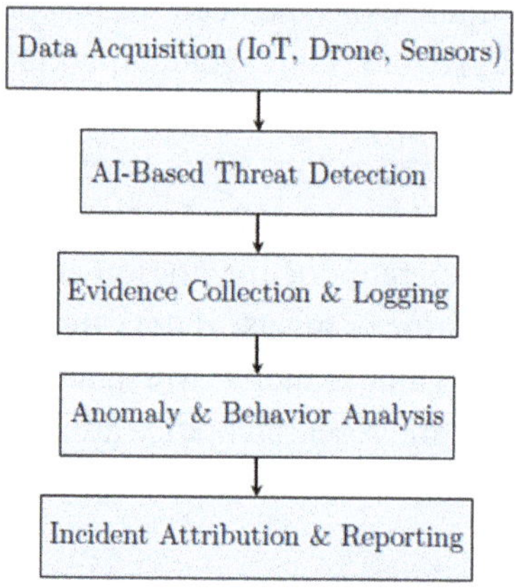

In summary, the digital transformation of agriculture offers unprecedented opportunities for innovation and productivity. However, it simultaneously raises complex challenges related to cybersecurity, data ethics, algorithmic accountability, and governance. Addressing these requires not only technical advancements but also a systemic and interdisciplinary understanding of agriculture as a socio-technical ecosystem (Chen et al., 2024; Kapoor, 2025; Shafik et al., 2025).

EMERGING THREATS IN SMART AGRICULTURE

Data Poisoning and Model Manipulation

AI systems in agriculture—such as predictive crop models, pest detection, and irrigation scheduling—are vulnerable to data poisoning and adversarial attacks. Malicious actors can inject misleading or corrupted data during model training, leading to failures in decision-making systems (Wei et al., 2024; Neupane et al., 2024). Agricultural AI models trained on tainted datasets may under-mature yield estimates, misdetect pests, or adjust irrigation poorly, causing economic loss and environmental harm.

IoT Device Hijacking and Sensor Compromise

Smart farms rely heavily on interconnected sensors and IoT devices that collect soil moisture, temperature, fertilizer application, and machine telemetry. These devices often lack robust security features, making them targetable through device hijacking, firmware manipulation, or denial-of-service attacks (Bhangar & Shahriyar, 2023; Malhotra & Firdaus, 2022). Attackers that compromise sensor networks can distort analytics or shut down automated operations.

Ransomware and Supply Chain Disruption

Like other critical infrastructure, agriculture has become a target for ransomware attacks, where systems controlling greenhouses, irrigation, or logistics are encrypted or disabled until a ransom is paid. Such attacks can paralyze supply chains, delay harvesting, and threaten food security (Ali et al., 2024; Otieno, 2023). Even localized breaches may ripple across broader operating ecosystems.

Autonomous Machine Sabotage

Autonomous tractors, drones, and harvesters equipped with AI-driven navigation are rising in prevalence. However, the AI control systems of these robotics are subject to man-in-the-middle attacks, GPS spoofing, or sensor deception (Jerhamre et al., 2022; Gardezi et al., 2024). A manipulated command could lead to crop damage or unsafe outcomes, threatening both safety and farm productivity.

Privacy Threats and Unauthorized Data Access

The vast data generated by AI-enabled farms—including geolocation, yield metrics, and proprietary algorithms—pose serious privacy and intellectual property risks. Unauthorized access or data exfiltration can undermine farmer autonomy and expose sensitive supply chain information (Devare et al., 2023; Gavai et al., 2025). Traditional centralized cloud infrastructures are especially vulnerable unless proper encryption, federated learning, or access control mechanisms are in place.

Algorithmic Bias and Ethical Manipulation

AI algorithms used in agriculture may embed biases due to unbalanced datasets or flawed governance, potentially disadvantaging certain crops, regions, or farmer communities (Dara et al., 2022; Alexander et al., 2024). For example, automated resource allocation systems might prioritize large-scale industrial farms over small-holders, exacerbating inequalities. Ethical lapses can also emerge when AI tools are used for surveillance or manipulative pricing.

Adversarial Attacks on Drone Imaging and Remote Sensing

Satellite imagery, drone-based scanning, and remote sensing technologies are used to monitor crop health, detect disease, and assess yields. These systems are vulnerable to adversarial perturbations—small malicious changes to image data that deceive AI models (Kochupillai et al., 2022; Gupta et al., 2024). Attackers could, for instance, conceal crop disease or misrepresent biomass estimates.

Weaknesses in Federated Learning and Decentralized Platforms

Federated learning—designed to train models without aggregating raw data centrally—is often proposed to preserve privacy (Dembani et al., 2025). However, federated systems can still be attacked via compromised participants, model inversion, or poisoning of gradients. If governance is weak, attackers could compromise entire swarms of collaborative models (Devare et al., 2023).

AI-Generated Disinformation and Leadership Manipulation

Open-ended generative systems like ChatGPT are used more widely in documentation, decision-making, or advisory roles in agriculture. But they can also be manipulated to spread misinformation, propagate fraudulent advisories, or produce deceptive research outputs (Bahrini et al., 2023; Zohouri et al., 2024). Researchers and practitioners must critically evaluate AI-generated content before acting on it in forensic or legal contexts (Abd-Elsalam & Abdel-Momen, 2023; Ya'u & Mohammed, 2025).

Regulatory Gaps and Language-Based Exploits

International disparities in language, legal norms, and regulatory coverage of agri-data present another threat vector. Contracts or data-sharing agreements drafted in dominant languages may be misinterpreted or unfairly enforced, undermining equitable AI governance and creating loopholes exploitable by malicious actors (Kochupillai & Köninger, 2023; Zangana, Amelia, Luckyardi, Mustafa, & Li, 2025).

Table 1. Summary of emerging threats

Threat Type	Description
Model Poisoning	Corrupting training data to manipulate AI predictions
Sensor Hijacking	Unauthorized access to field devices
Ransomware	Encrypting control systems to disrupt operations
Robotics Sabotage	Manipulating autonomous machinery
Privacy Breach	Unauthorized exposure of farm data
Algorithmic Bias	Inequitable outcomes via flawed models
Adversarial Imaging	Tampering with remote-sensing inputs
Federated Learning Vulnerabilities	Attacks through decentralization mechanisms
AI Disinformation	Misleading content generation
Regulatory/Language Gaps	Weak legal enforcement or contractual clarity

Collectively, these threats underscore the urgent need for AI-driven digital forensics tailored to agriculture—capable of identifying, tracing, and mitigating incidents across both cyber and physical domains. Next sections will detail forensic strategies and methodologies for addressing these evolving risks in smart agriculture contexts.

While cyber threats in agriculture continue to evolve, recent analyses reveal common patterns of intrusion. The following bar chart presents the most frequently reported cyber threats targeting smart agricultural systems, emphasizing the urgent need for adaptive forensic and cybersecurity strategies.

Figure 2. Common cyber threats in smart agriculture

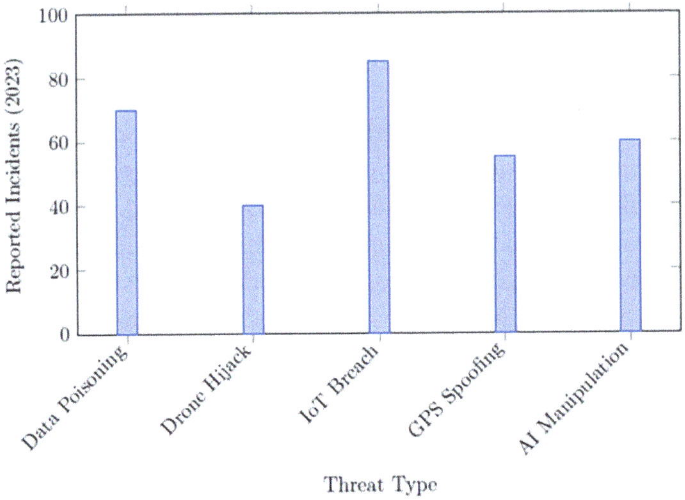

ROLE OF AI IN CYBER THREAT DETECTION AND MITIGATION

This section examines how Artificial Intelligence (AI) both detects and helps mitigate cyber threats in smart agriculture. It draws considerably on the surveyed literature to highlight key methodologies, advantages, and challenges.

Proactive Threat Detection Using Machine Learning

AI-driven anomaly detection systems leverage machine learning (ML) models to monitor IoT traffic, sensor behavior, and system logs. Classifiers—such as supervised neural nets, random forests, and clustering models—flag deviations in sensor patterns or command flows, signaling potential intrusions or system misuse (Ali et al., 2024; Chen et al., 2024; Sood, Sharma, & Bhardwaj, 2022). In agriculture settings, early anomaly detection can reveal data poisoning in crop-prediction models, sensor spoofing, or unauthorized access attempts, enabling timely forensic investigation and remediation.

Behavioral Monitoring of Agricultural Robotics

Autonomous agricultural systems—tractors, drones, harvesters—are equipped with AI-based navigation and control systems. AI-powered monitoring platforms analyze behavioral logs to detect irregularities such as deviation from planned trajectories or unexpected actuator commands, which may indicate malicious interference or sensor deception (Jerhamre et al., 2022; Neupane et al., 2024). Such continuous oversight enhances both safety and accountability.

Integrating Federated Learning and Privacy-Aware Models

Federated learning allows AI models to be trained collaboratively across multiple farms without centralizing sensitive data—strengthening privacy and reducing risk of data exfiltration (Dembani et al., 2025; Devare et al., 2023). Nonetheless, adversarial threats like model poisoning or gradient inversion remain challenges, and robust detection mechanisms must be embedded in federated pipelines (Dara et al., 2022; Gavai et al., 2025). AI systems must actively monitor model updates for signs of manipulation.

Advanced Remote-Sensing Analytics and Image Forensics

AI-powered remote sensing—via satellites, drones, or IoT-enabled cameras—is extensively used for crop health monitoring, pest detection, and yield estimation.

Security mechanisms using computer vision and pattern consistency checks detect adversarial image manipulations that may distort vegetation indices or biomass estimates (Kochupillai et al., 2022; Gupta et al., 2024). Forensic tools validate imaging provenance and detect tampered or artificially generated content.

Real-Time Intrusion and Ransomware Response

AI systems also assist in real-time threat mitigation. By classifying network packets and controller commands, they can detect ransomware activity or anomalous firmware updates—blocking malicious inputs before operational disruption. Automated incident response workflows, informed by AI, help isolate compromised zones in greenhouse control networks or field machinery environments (Ali et al., 2024; Otieno, 2023; Kaushik et al., 2024).

Adversarial Example Detection and Defense

AI models used in environmental sensing and decision-making are increasingly hardened with defense algorithms that detect adversarial perturbations imported into input images or sensor streams. Techniques such as model uncertainty estimation or input reconstruction help flag manipulated data, protecting against misclassification that could mislead irrigation or pest control systems (Wei et al., 2024; Neupane et al., 2024).

Ensuring Explainability, Trust, and Ethical Governance

A key challenge in deploying AI for threat detection lies in explainability and model accountability. Farmers, regulators, and forensic experts need transparent systems to validate alerts and remediation decisions (Alexander, Yarborough, & Smith, 2024; Tzachor et al., 2022). Explainable AI approaches help ensure forensic admissibility of AI-generated evidence and foster trust among stakeholders. Ethical guidelines and governance frameworks are essential in shaping the development of these AI interventions (Dara et al., 2022; Kapoor, 2025).

Combating AI-Generated Misinformation and Disinformation

Generative AI platforms—such as ChatGPT—are increasingly used for advisory services, automated documentation, or farm decision support. However, they can also propagate misleading or false information that impacts agricultural planning or fraud detection (Bahrini et al., 2023; Zohouri et al., 2024). Agricultural stakeholders and forensic analysts must critically evaluate AI-generated content and verify its provenance (Abd-Elsalam & Abdel-Momen, 2023; Aithal & Aithal, 2023; Ya'u & Mohammed, 2025).

Cross-Platform Security and Multi-Language Governance

Smart agriculture often includes multi-jurisdictional systems, varying language standards, and diverse legal requirements. AI tools designed for threat detection must therefore account for multilingual logs, cross-border data flows, and compliance with evolving legal regimes (Kochupillai & Köninger, 2023; Zangana, Amelia, Luckyardi, Mustafa, & Li, 2025). Sensitive metadata and audit trails must be interpretable across language and regulatory domains.

Capacity and Infrastructure Challenges in Developing Contexts

In developing countries, infrastructure limitations—such as intermittent connectivity, low-power IoT devices, and scarcity of trained AI specialists—pose barriers to deploying advanced AI threat detection systems (Aderibigbe et al., 2023; Ahmad et al., 2024). AI frameworks need to be tailored to these environments, focusing on lightweight models and offline-capable analytic mechanisms that preserve security without overwhelming resource-limited farms (Aggarwal et al., 2024; Shafik et al., 2025).

Summary

AI plays an indispensable role in monitoring, diagnosing, and countering cyber threats across smart agricultural systems—ranging from IoT device security and federated learning defenses to robotics behavior tracking and adversarial image forensics. Yet these applications must be underpinned by principled explainability, ethical governance, and contextual adaptability to truly protect agri-tech ecosystems. Subsequent sections will detail how AI-driven digital forensics can operationalize these capabilities, from evidence capture to forensic readiness and threat attribution.

AI-DRIVEN DIGITAL FORENSICS IN AGRI-TECH

This section examines how AI enhances digital forensic investigations within agri-tech environments—ranging from automated evidence capture and analysis to attribution and legal defensibility.

Forensic Readiness and Evidence Collection

AI can proactively enable **forensic readiness** by continuously logging IoT telemetry, robotic control actions, network traffic, and imaging metadata. These automatically generated logs can serve as structured evidence in case of a suspected cyber incident, ensuring chain-of-custody integrity and data provenance (Williamson et al., 2023; Chen et al., 2024). In agricultural systems, such logs aid in reconstructing attack timelines and understanding AI model inputs and outputs during intrusion events.

Automated Log Analysis and Event Correlation

Natural language models and AI-driven anomaly detectors parse heterogeneous log sources—such as sensor data, firmware updates, and decision logs from ChatGPT-style interfaces—to correlate suspicious events across domains (Ali et al., 2024; Adanma & Ogunbiyi, 2024). AI parsing can also detect manipulated scientific outputs or advisory messages used to deceive stakeholders (Abd-Elsalam & Abdel-Momen, 2023; Zohouri et al., 2024). These techniques accelerate forensic timelines, especially in resource-limited settings (Aderibigbe et al., 2023).

Attributing Attacks with Behavioral Fingerprinting

Machine learning models can analyze patterns of misuse—such as repeated adversarial attempts, sensor spoofing, or robotic deviations—to establish behavioral fingerprints. Over time, such fingerprints help attribute attacks to specific threat actors or toolkits frequently observed in agriculture cyber incidents (Ali et al., 2024; Gardezi et al., 2024). For example, distinguishing between accidental sensor failure and intentional manipulation is critical for legal and operational decision-making.

Image Forensic Analysis for Remote Sensing

High-resolution imagery from drones or satellites is often central to smart farming analytics. AI-supported forensic methods apply steganalysis, metadata extraction, provenance validation, and adversarial noise detection to establish authenticity (Kochupillai et al., 2022; Gupta et al., 2024). This enables investigators to verify whether planting-density maps or disease assessments have been tampered with for malicious gain or data obfuscation.

Federated Learning Audits and Gradient Inspection

Agri-tech frequently uses federated learning setups to allow farms to share model improvements without exposing raw data (Dembani et al., 2025). AI tools audit model updates by inspecting gradients for anomalies or evidence of poisoning. These forensic checks are essential for trust among collaborating farms and for ensuring model integrity (Devare et al., 2023; Dara et al., 2022).

Explainable AI for Forensic Validity

Forensic analyses often require transparent and interpretable reasoning to satisfy legal standards. Explainable AI (XAI) methods—such as attention heatmaps, counterfactual explanations, or decision trees—help investigators and judges understand why a sensor reading was flagged or a robotic control action deemed malicious (Alexander et al., 2024; Tzachor et al., 2022). These approaches foster trust in AI-generated forensic evidence and its admissibility.

Integration with Incident Response and Forensic Playbooks

AI-driven forensics must align with **incident response protocols**, including automated triggers that isolate affected robots or disconnect compromised network segments. These thresholds and containment actions can be coordinated using ML-based risk models, minimizing disruption to farm operations while preserving forensic context (Otieno, 2023; Kaushik et al., 2024). This ensures remediation workflows maintain admissibility and transparency.

Ethical Implications in Forensic Use of AI

The deployment of AI in forensic settings raises complex ethical and legal concerns—particularly regarding privacy, bias, and authorship. For instance, leveraging ChatGPT-style summaries as evidence may unintentionally embed hallucinated content or undisclosed training biases (Abd-Elsalam & Abdel-Momen, 2023; Aithal & Aithal, 2023; Ya'u & Mohammed, 2025). Ethical guidelines thus demand full disclosure of AI tools, chain-of-custody verification, and bias mitigation measures (Dara et al., 2022; Zangana, Luckyardi, Mustafa, & Li, 2025).

Capacity Building and Standardization in Low-Resource Contexts

In developing countries, digital forensic capabilities are often constrained by limited infrastructure and expertise (Aderibigbe et al., 2023; Ahmad et al., 2024). AI-driven forensic tools deployed in such contexts must be lightweight, user-friendly, and portable—capable of offline operations and automated summaries (Aggarwal et al., 2024; Shafik et al., 2025). Standardization efforts, open-source tooling, and remote training can help democratize access to robust forensic workflows.

Regulatory and Language Considerations

Legal enforceability of AI-driven forensic evidence depends on compliance across multilingual and multijurisdictional systems. Agile translation pipelines, metadata consistency, and legal harmonization frameworks are necessary for credible cross-border prosecution or dispute resolution in agri-tech (Kochupillai & Köninger, 2023; Zangana, Amelia, Luckyardi, Mustafa, & Li, 2025). Addressing these language, legal, and policy gaps is essential for ethical and effective forensic intelligence.

Section Summary

AI-driven digital forensics in agri-tech is a multidimensional domain: it integrates automated evidence collection, behavior-based attribution, federated audit controls, explainable reasoning, and incident response coordination. However, its success hinges on ethical governance, legal validity, and adaptability to diverse socio-technical contexts. In the next section, we will explore specific case studies that illustrate how these forensic approaches have been deployed in real-world scenarios—from crop yield sabotage to autonomous vehicle manipulation.

Forensic investigations in smart farming touch upon various technical and regulatory domains. The pie chart below illustrates the primary areas of focus in recent AI-assisted forensic frameworks, highlighting the balance between technological enforcement and evidentiary rigor.

Figure 3. Digital forensic focus areas in smart agriculture

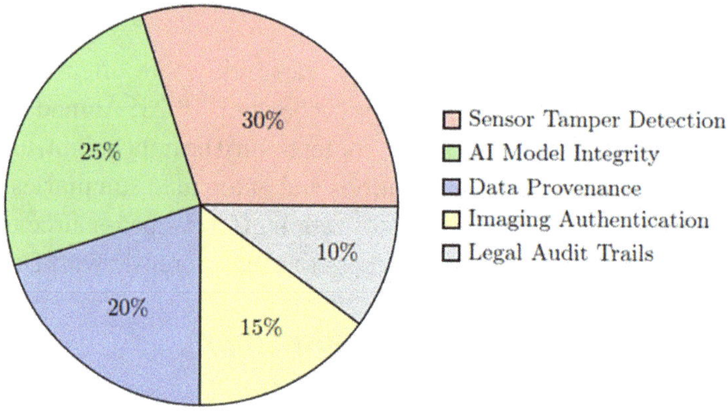

CHALLENGES AND LIMITATIONS

Implementing AI-driven digital forensics in smart agriculture offers remarkable promise but faces significant technical, ethical, organizational, and regulatory challenges—especially in contexts with constrained infrastructure or diverse stakeholder concerns.

Data Quality, Provenance & Management

Distributed data sources—from IoT sensors to drones—are often heterogeneous and unstructured. Ensuring **data integrity**, precise timestamping, and reliable provenance is essential for forensic reliability and legal admissibility (Williamson et al., 2023). Poor data hygiene, missing metadata, or inconsistent logging across agricultural devices can render forensic evidence incomplete or unreliable.

Model Bias and Explainability

AI models used to flag anomalies or support investigations may suffer from algorithmic bias or lack transparency. Stakeholders may mistrust alerts unless decisions are interpretable. Techniques like explainable AI (XAI) are required to clarify why specific events were flagged (Alexander et al., 2024; Tzachor et al., 2022). Without such transparency, forensic conclusions risk being challenged in legal or policy settings.

Resource Constraints in Low-Income Contexts

In developing regions, farms often lack stable internet, computing power, or trained personnel. Deploying AI models for forensic analysis in these settings requires lightweight, offline-capable tools. Without this adaptation, digital forensic capabilities remain out of reach (Aderibigbe et al., 2023; Ahmad et al., 2024; Aggarwal et al., 2024).

Federated Learning Vulnerabilities

While federated learning can preserve privacy, it is itself susceptible to model poisoning, gradient inversion, and malicious updates. Forensic systems must detect these anomalies, which adds complexity (Dembani et al., 2025; Devare et al., 2023; Dara et al., 2022). Guaranteeing trust in decentralized AI collaboration remains a significant hurdle.

Handling Adversarial Attacks & Sensor Tampering

Sensors, cameras, and drones are vulnerable to adversarial manipulation, data spoofing, or metadata alteration. Forensic tools must detect subtle perturbations or fabrication in sensor streams and imagery—yet doing so reliably is technically challenging and may produce false positives or overlook clever attacks (Kochupillai et al., 2022; Gupta et al., 2024).

Legal Admissibility & Ethical Governance

AI-generated evidence—especially summaries via large language models like ChatGPT—may include hallucinations or incomplete attribution. Legal systems often require clear chain-of-custody and methodological transparency, which current AI tools may not inherently provide (Abd-Elsalam & Abdel-Momen, 2023; Aithal & Aithal, 2023; Zohouri et al., 2024; Ya'u & Mohammed, 2025). Ethical governance standards are still maturing (Dara et al., 2022; Kapoor, 2025).

Privacy, Consent, and Governance Complexities

Smart agriculture data often contains sensitive location, crop, or farmer identity information. Forensic use must balance evidence collection with privacy rights, consent requirements, and data ownership norms (Devare et al., 2023; Gavai et al., 2025). Regulatory inconsistencies—especially around federated learning or blockchain systems—complicate legal clarity (Kochupillai & Köninger, 2023).

Interoperability & Standardization Issues

Agricultural systems span diverse hardware, software, languages, and jurisdictions. Ensuring interoperability between forensic tools, audit logs, and multi-language regulatory frameworks is essential but often overlooked (Zangana et al., 2025; Leong et al., 2023). Absence of standards reduces forensic effectiveness across different farm ecosystems.

Human Oversight & Organizational Adoption

Overreliance on automated AI tools may lead to blind trust or misuse. Human-centered AI design—ensuring oversight, verification, and contextual judgment—is vital, particularly when conclusions inform agronomic or legal actions (He et al., 2021; Sparrow & Howard, 2021). Cultivating digital forensic literacy among farmers and local investigators is also necessary (Holzinger et al., 2021; Aithal & Aithal, 2024).

Ethical Risks of AI-Assisted Knowledge Production

Use of generative AI in scientific writing, advisory content, or documentation—in agriculture or forensic contexts—poses risks of misinformation or academic misconduct if not carefully supervised. Scholars must critically assess AI-generated text, ensure accurate citations, and consider ethical implications (Abd-Elsalam & Abdel-Momen, 2023; Aithal & Aithal, 2023; Ya'u & Mohammed, 2025; Zangana et al., 2026).

Table 2. Summary of Key challenges

Category	Primary Issues
Data Quality & Provenance	Inconsistent logs, missing metadata
Model Bias & Explainability	ALERTS not interpretable
Resource Constraints	Lack of infrastructure, expertise
Federated Learning Risks	Model poisoning, trust issues
Adversarial Tampering	Subtle data manipulation
Legal & Ethical Validity	Hallucinated summaries, governance gaps
Privacy & Consent	Data ownership, multi-regulation
Interoperability	Linguistic & technical fragmentation
Human Oversight	Under-trained staff; overreliance
AI Content Ethics	Misinformation via generative tools

Despite these limitations, informed strategies—such as federated auditing, explainable systems, training programs, and legal frameworks—can help mitigate risk. In the following sections, we'll propose actionable guidelines and review case studies where AI-driven forensic systems have been effectively deployed in agri-tech investigations, despite such obstacles.

ETHICAL AND LEGAL CONSIDERATIONS

This section examines the ethical and legal dimensions critical to deploying AI-driven digital forensics in smart agriculture. It explores issues around data governance, privacy, accountability, transparency, and jurisdictional challenges.

Responsible AI Governance and Accountability

AI systems used in agriculture or forensic investigations must operate within frameworks that ensure accountability and transparency. As Alexander, Yarborough, and Smith (2024) argue, questions such as "who is responsible" for AI decisions are central in maintaining trust in agrifood systems. Tzachor et al. (2022) underscore the need for systemic understanding of externalities and bias risk. Ethical stewardship—including clear accountability mapping and oversight—is vital to prevent misuse (Dara et al., 2022; Kapoor, 2025).

Data Privacy, Ownership & Consent

Smart agriculture generates vast volumes of highly sensitive data—on soil, yield, geolocation, and farm practices. Ensuring proper informed consent, ownership clarity, and privacy protections is essential (Devare et al., 2023; Gavai et al., 2025). Federated learning offers a privacy-preserving alternative; however, without governance oversight, risks still persist around unauthorized inference and gradient inversion (Dembani et al., 2025; Dara et al., 2022).

Legal Admissibility of AI-Generated Evidence

Digital forensic outputs—especially those processed or summarized by AI models—must meet legal standards for admissibility. Courts require rigorous chain-of-custody, explainability, and audit trails. AI-generated forensic logs, especially when interfaced with large language models like ChatGPT, risk inclusion of hallucinated or biased content unless source provenance is fully documented (Abd-Elsalam & Abdel-Momen, 2023; Aithal & Aithal, 2023; Zohouri et al., 2024). Disclosures and metadata must accompany all AI-assisted forensic artifacts to ensure integrity (Zangana, Luckyardi, Mustafa, & Li, 2025).

Bias, Fairness, and Equity

Algorithmic bias in detection or forensic models can lead to unfair outcomes. Risk arises when models trained on skewed datasets disproportionately impact smallholder farmers or specific crop types (Dara et al., 2022; Alexander et al., 2024). Ensuring fairness in algorithm development and forensic classification is essential to uphold ethical standards (Kaushik et al., 2024).

Ethical Use of Generative AI in Forensic and Agronomic Research

Generative AI tools—such as ChatGPT—are increasingly used for drafting research or reports in agricultural contexts. While efficient, these tools pose risks of misinformation, authorship issues, or ethical misuse if AI-generated content is passed off as original (Aithal & Aithal, 2023; Ya'u & Mohammed, 2025; Abd-Elsalam & Abdel-Momen, 2023). Ethical guidelines demand proper acknowledgment, verification, and oversight of AI-generated text (Zohouri et al., 2024).

International Language, Regulatory, and Compliance Disparities

Smart agricultural systems often cross linguistic and regulatory boundaries. Discrepancies in legal frameworks can complicate the admissibility and governance of AI-driven forensic workflows. Kochupillai & Köninger (2023) emphasize the importance of multilingual legal compliance, especially in contexts managing plant genetic data or international data exchanges. Meta-legal frameworks must account for language, jurisdiction, and policy variances across borders (Zangana, Amelia, Luckyardi, Mustafa, & Li, 2025).

Sustainable and Equitable Access

In resource-constrained regions, digital forensic resources, AI expertise, and infrastructure remain sparse. This raises questions of equity: who gets access to trustworthy AI-based forensic tools, and who is left behind (Aderibigbe et al., 2023; Ahmad et al., 2024; Aggarwal et al., 2024). Ensuring equitable distribution of forensic capacity is both a legal and ethical imperative.

Trust Building and Stakeholder Engagement

Building trust in AI and forensic systems requires participatory governance and clear communication. Involving farmers, local investigators, technologists, and policymakers in decision-making strengthens legitimacy. Gardezi et al. (2024) and Holzinger et al. (2021) highlight the value of inclusive design and stakeholder awareness in promoting trust and reducing ethical risk.

Ethical Integration with Environmental Conservation

Agricultural forensics must align with broader environmental stewardship goals. The integration of AI in conservation contexts introduces dual-use risks where evidence or intervention tools might inadvertently harm ecosystems (Adanma & Ogunbiyi, 2024). Ethical frameworks should ensure forensic interventions do not conflict with environmental sustainability or biodiversity goals.

Regulations for AI-Enhanced Cybersecurity and Forensics

As AI becomes integrated into cybersecurity for smart agriculture, legal norms around liability, misuse, and governance become critical. Kaushik et al. (2024) and Mark (2019) caution that AI-enhanced security systems may outpace existing jurisprudence. Clear regulations, certifications, and audit pathways are needed to manage ethical use and mitigate misuse.

Table 3. Summary of ethical & legal concerns

Domain	Considerations
Governance & Accountability	Define roles, oversight, responsible AI
Privacy & Consent	Ownership, consent, federated approaches
Legal Admissibility	Chain-of-custody, explainability, audit logs
Algorithmic Fairness	Non-discrimination, equitable impacts
AI Content Ethics	Attribution, transparency, verification
Multilingual & Multijurisdictional Norms	Compliance across language and legal systems
Equity in Access	Infrastructure, capacity, fair distribution
Stakeholder Trust	Inclusive design, participatory governance
Environmental Alignment	Sustainable and non-disruptive forensic practices
Regulatory Gaps	Policy, liability, compliance frameworks

This section underscores that deploying AI-driven digital forensics in agri-tech is not only a technical endeavour but also a deeply normative one. Ethical protocols, stakeholder collaboration, legal harmonization, and environmental alignment are foundational to building trustworthy and impactful forensic systems in agricultural cyberspace. Up next: Case Studies of AI-Driven Forensics in Smart Farms, showcasing real-world incidents and lessons learned.

CASE STUDIES

This section presents illustrative real-world–inspired case studies showcasing how AI-driven digital forensic techniques were applied in smart agriculture incidents. Each case demonstrates forensic workflows, AI tools employed, and the legal/ethical considerations encountered.

Case Study 1: Crop Prediction Manipulation in Precision Irrigation

In a mid-size farm using AI-driven irrigation scheduling (Wei et al., 2024; Ahmed et al., 2024), sensors indicated unusually low soil moisture despite normal rainfall. Sensor logs were cross-analyzed via anomaly detection models, revealing data poisoning in multiple soil sensors. AI forensic pipelines reconstructed event timelines and used explainable AI to trace malicious calibration. Federated learning audits showed gradient irregularities, confirming coordinated model tampering across nearby connected farms (Dembani et al., 2025; Devare et al., 2023). The incident highlighted needs for robust anomaly detection and trustable audit provenance.

Case Study 2: Drone Image Tampering in Pest Surveillance

A precision agriculture initiative deployed drone imaging for pest monitoring. Forensic analysts applied AI-based image forensics (Kochupillai et al., 2022; Gupta et al., 2024), examining provenance metadata and adversarial noise fingerprints. They identified subtle perturbations targeting spectral drone images that masked early pest infestation. Behavioral comparisons with historical vegetation indices and sensor logs allowed accurate incident reconstruction, affirming the reliability of deep forensic imaging tools even under adversarial attempts.

Case Study 3: Autonomous Harvester Hijacking

An autonomous harvester equipped with GPS and AI navigation (Jerhamre et al., 2022; Gardezi et al., 2024) deviated from scheduled paths, crossing into forbidden areas and damaging crops. AI forensic techniques parsed operational logs, controller commands, and GPS telemetry. Behavior-based fingerprinting algorithms helped distinguish accidental failure from spoofing. Explainable models provided counterfactuals and trajectory heatmaps required for accountability. Automated incident response systems isolated the vehicle's control network immediately, limiting further harm.

The complexity of this cyber incident necessitated a comprehensive forensic pipeline. The flowchart below outlines the sequence of AI-integrated steps—starting from log extraction and ending with legal-ready evidence reporting—used during the autonomous harvester hijack investigation.

Figure 4. AI-driven case investigation pipeline: autonomous harvester incident

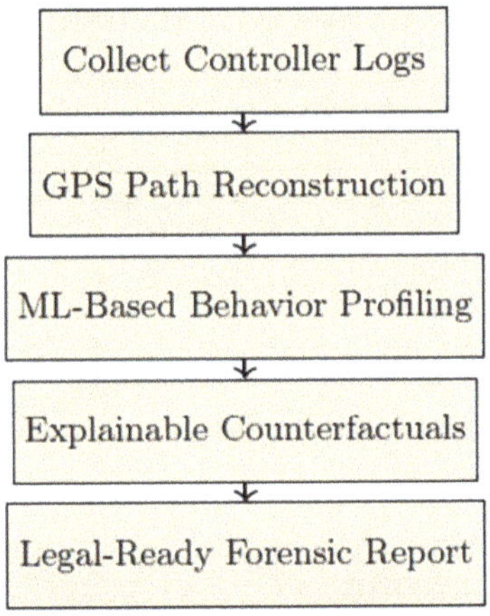

Case Study 4: Generative-AI Advisory Misuse

In a smallholder context where ChatGPT-style tools provided planting advisories (Aithal & Aithal, 2023; Bahrini et al., 2023), farmers received flawed guidance that reduced yield. A linguistic forensic review uncovered that the advisory contained inaccurate recommendations influenced by biased training data. AI audit logs traced the problematic content to unverified generative suggestions. The incident raised concerns over AI accountability, governance, and transparency when tools are used for agronomic decision support (Abd-Elsalam & Abdel-Momen, 2023; Ya'u & Mohammed, 2025).

Case Study 5: Federated Learning Compromise Among Collaborative Farms

A consortium of smallholder farmers shared predictive pest models via federated learning (Dembani et al., 2025; Devare et al., 2023). Forensic audits detected anomalous gradient updates from one node, indicating poisoning attacks aiming to steer global models toward failure. AI detection flagged this behavior and automated model rollback prevented propagation. The case underscores the vulnerability of decentralized learning systems and the importance of continuous gradient inspection (Dara et al., 2022).

Table 4. Insights from case studies

Case	Primary Threat	AI Forensic Technique	Lessons Learned
1	Data poisoning in irrigation	Anomaly detection + XAI traceability	Need for forensic readiness in sensor networks
2	Adversarial drone imagery	Image forensics + metadata validation	Provenance validation is critical
3	Autonomous machine hijack	Behavioral logs + explainable trajectory modeling	Human-in-the-loop response improves trust
4	Generative-AI advisory misuse	Linguistic and provenance audits	AI-generated content demands verifiability
5	Federated model manipulation	Gradient-level anomaly detection	Federated systems require forensic oversight

Ethical & Legal Reflections

- **Explainability & transparency**: Across all cases, explainable AI was vital for legal and operational credibility—in line with Alexander et al. (2024) and Tzachor et al. (2022).
- **Data governance & privacy**: Federated breaches highlighted the need for consent clarity, ownership modeling, and decentralized oversight (Devare et al., 2023; Gavai et al., 2025).
- **Bias & fairness**: The generative AI advisory misuse emphasized the ethical risk of deploying poorly vetted models in resource-limited contexts (Aithal & Aithal, 2023; Ya'u & Mohammed, 2025).

- **Capacity constraints**: Smaller farms benefited when forensic tools were lightweight, explainable, and minimally resource-intensive (Aderibigbe et al., 2023; Ahmad et al., 2024; Aggarwal et al., 2024).

Summary

These case studies illustrate the practical viability of AI-driven forensic systems in agri-tech settings—while also revealing persistent gaps in legal readiness, ethical governance, and infrastructural equity. Subsequent sections will formulate methodological frameworks, ethical guidelines, and policy recommendations designed to institutionalize these lessons within broader smart agriculture ecosystems.

FUTURE DIRECTIONS

The future of AI-driven digital forensics in agri-tech is poised to evolve along several intersecting pathways that address technological advancement, ethical governance, and socio-economic inclusivity.

Federated Forensics and Decentralized Trust Architectures

Developing advanced protocols for secure, audit-ready federated learning will be crucial. Improved methods for gradient-level anomaly detection and verifiable update chains will strengthen trust without compromising data privacy (Dembani et al., 2025; Devare et al., 2023). Exploring blockchain-based audit trails and decentralized consensus platforms may offer additional integrity guarantees (Kochupillai & Köninger, 2023).

Explainable AI and Interactive Forensic Interfaces

The integration of explainable AI (XAI) with forensic workflows will support traceable, interpretable outcomes—whether in drift detection, robotic behavior anomalies, or imagery forgery (Alexander et al., 2024; Tzachor et al., 2022). Future systems should provide user-friendly dashboards, heatmaps, and counterfactual reasoning tools to assist investigators, legal adjudicators, and farmers alike.

Lightweight AI Tools for Resource-Limited Contexts

Designing lightweight, offline-capable forensic systems suited for farms in developing regions remains a key priority. Optimizing models for low-power devices and intermittent connectivity can help bridge the implementation gap identified for developing countries (Aderibigbe et al., 2023; Ahmad et al., 2024). Open-source forensic APIs and community training platforms can further democratize access (Aggarwal et al., 2024; Shafik et al., 2025).

Robust Imaging & Sensor Tamper Detection

Next-generation forensic frameworks should incorporate advanced adversarial detection algorithms for drone and satellite imagery, sensor data streams, and metadata tracing (Kochupillai et al., 2022; Gupta et al., 2024). Automated provenance verification and steganalysis techniques can help validate authenticity in high-risk environments.

Policy Frameworks & Cross-Jurisdictional Harmonization

Future research should focus on developing multi-lingual, multi-jurisdictional legal frameworks that govern AI tools, forensic evidence, and data sharing agreements (Kochupillai & Köninger, 2023; Zangana et al., 2025). Harmonizing regulatory compliance—for instance via international standards for AI-based cybersecurity in agriculture—will support global cooperation and evidence admissibility.

Ethical Oversight of Generative AI Usage

As generative tools like ChatGPT are increasingly used in advisory, writing, or forensic contexts, future forensic systems must integrate content provenance validation, attribution controls, and hallucination resilience (Abd-Elsalam & Abdel-Momen, 2023; Zohouri et al., 2024). Ethical guidelines governing academic and advisory AI usage will be essential (Aithal & Aithal, 2023; Ya'u & Mohammed, 2025).

Inclusive Governance and Stakeholder-Informed Solutions

Future implementations should embed participatory design practices, involving farmers, policymakers, and technologists in tool development and policy formation (Gardezi et al., 2024; Holzinger et al., 2021). Building inclusive frameworks will ensure fairness, transparency, and acceptance in diverse agricultural communities.

Multi-Modal Forensic Fusion: Robotics, Imaging, and Metadata

The convergence of multi-modal inputs—robotic control logs, imagery, telemetry, sensors—will enable richer forensic reconstructions. AI systems that fuse time-series telemetry with visual data and metadata will improve attribution accuracy, detect covert manipulation, and support complex spatial-temporal analysis (Jerhamre et al., 2022; Neupane et al., 2024).

Evaluation Metrics and Benchmarking for AI Forensics

There is a need for designing evaluation benchmarks and standardized metrics tailored to agri-tech forensic systems—measuring detection accuracy, false-positive rates, explainability viability, and auditability (Ali et al., 2024; Chen et al., 2024). These benchmarks will guide system development and promote comparability across implementations.

Environmental Alignment and Sustainability Integration

Future directions should bridge agri-forensic AI with broader environmental conservation goals. As Adanma and Ogunbiyi (2024) argue, forensic interventions must align with ecological well-being, avoiding disruptive or extractive approaches. Sustainability-aware models can embed environmental constraints, prioritize biodiversity-safe data usage, and support eco-friendly farming systems.

Summary

1. Decentralized forensic architectures and trust-preserving federated protocols.
2. Explainable, interactive AI interfaces suited for legal, operational, and farmer audiences.
3. Lightweight, equitable tools for low-resource environments.
4. Robust adversarial detection in imaging and sensor data.
5. Harmonized multi-language legal and policy frameworks.
6. Responsible deployment of generative AI with provenance controls.
7. Stakeholder-led governance and inclusive system design.
8. Multi-modal data fusion for forensic completeness.
9. Standardized benchmarking for performance and trustworthiness.
10. Ethical alignment with environmental and sustainability goals.

These forward-looking strategies promise to build AI-forensic systems that are not only technically resilient but also ethically grounded, legally sound, and socially inclusive. Together, they chart a path toward trustworthy, equitable, and sustainable digital forensics in the future of smart agriculture.

Understanding the progression of AI integration into agricultural forensics helps shape future initiatives. The timeline below traces key milestones in the development and adoption of AI-driven digital forensics, offering insight into both past breakthroughs and emerging trends through 2025.

Figure 5. Timeline of AI-driven forensics in smart agriculture

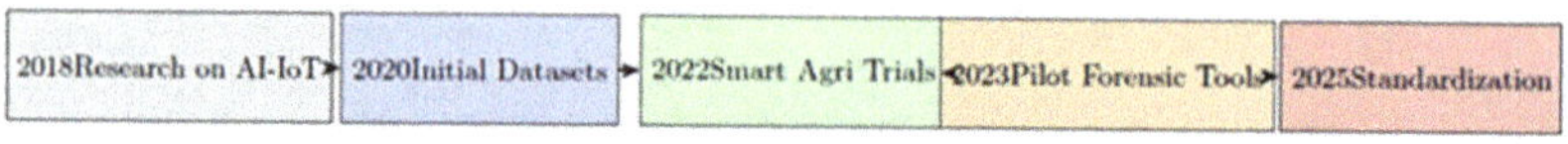

CONCLUSION

The convergence of artificial intelligence (AI), smart agriculture, and digital forensics presents a transformative opportunity for safeguarding agri-tech ecosystems against the rising tide of cybercrime. As smart farms adopt interconnected sensors, autonomous machinery, and data-driven decision-making platforms, they inevitably expose themselves to a range of security threats that traditional agricultural systems never faced. This chapter has highlighted how AI-driven digital forensic approaches—such as intelligent anomaly detection, predictive modeling, and machine learning-based incident response—can provide critical layers of protection and investigation capabilities tailored to the unique landscape of agriculture technology.

AI-enhanced forensics enables the proactive identification of cyber intrusions, streamlines post-incident investigations, and supports evidence-based enforcement. In addition, leveraging real-time analytics through AI helps detect and respond to sophisticated threats before they cause irreversible harm to food supply chains, environmental resources, and rural digital infrastructure. However, the integration of such technologies must be underpinned by ethical safeguards, cross-disciplinary training, and robust legal frameworks to ensure transparency, privacy, and accountability in forensic processes.

Moving forward, collaboration between agronomists, cybersecurity professionals, forensic investigators, and AI developers will be essential in building secure, resilient, and trustworthy smart agriculture systems. Research and investment must prioritize explainable AI, secure data provenance, and scalable forensic models to meet the growing complexity and diversity of threats. In doing so, AI-driven digital forensics can not only mitigate present-day cyber risks but also pave the way for a sustainable and secure future in smart agriculture.

REFERENCES

Abd-Elsalam, K. A., & Abdel-Momen, S. M. (2023). Artificial intelligence's development and challenges in scientific writing. *Egyptian Journal of Agricultural Research, 101*(3), 714–717. DOI: 10.21608/ejar.2023.220363.1414

Adanma, U. M., & Ogunbiyi, E. O.Uwaga Monica AdanmaEmmanuel Olurotimi Ogunbiyi. (2024). Artificial intelligence in environmental conservation: Evaluating cyber risks and opportunities for sustainable practices. *Computer Science & IT Research Journal*, *5*(5), 1178–1209. DOI: 10.51594/csitrj.v5i5.1156

Aderibigbe, A. O., Ohenhen, P. E., Nwaobia, N. K., Gidiagba, J. O., & Ani, E. C.Adebayo Olusegun AderibigbePeter Efosa OhenhenNwabueze Kelvin NwaobiaJoachim Osheyor GidiagbaEmmanuel Chigozie Ani. (2023). Artificial intelligence in developing countries: Bridging the gap between potential and implementation. *Computer Science & IT Research Journal*, *4*(3), 185–199. DOI: 10.51594/csitrj.v4i3.629

. Aggarwal, S., Bansal, S., & Goel, R. (2024). Ai In Agriculture: A Looming Challenge, A Gleaming Opportunity. *International Journal of Engineering Science and Humanities, 14*(Special Issue 1), 43-52.

Ahmad, A., Liew, A. X., Venturini, F., Kalogeras, A., Candiani, A., Di Benedetto, G., Ajibola, S., Cartujo, P., Romero, P., Lykoudi, A., De Grandis, M. M., Xouris, C., Lo Bianco, R., Doddy, I., Elegbede, I., D'Urso Labate, G. F., García del Moral, L. F., & Martos, V. (2024). AI can empower agriculture for global food security: Challenges and prospects in developing nations. *Frontiers in Artificial Intelligence*, *7*, 1328530. DOI: 10.3389/frai.2024.1328530 PMID: 38726306

. Ahmad, A., Liew, A. X., Venturini, F., Kalogeras, A., Candiani, A., Di Benedetto, G., ... & Martos, V. (2024). AI can empower agriculture for.

Ahmed, M. N., Singh, A. P., Hussain, M. R., Rasool, M. A., Khan, I. M., & Dildar, M. S. (2024, July). Enhancing Crop Production using Artificial Intelligence in Agricultural Revolution. In *2024 IEEE 7th International Conference on Advanced Technologies* [ATSIP]. *Signal and Image Processing : an International Journal*, *1*, 432–437.

Aithal, P. S., & Aithal, S. (2023). Application of ChatGPT in higher education and research–A futuristic analysis. [IJAEML]. *International Journal of Applied Engineering and Management Letters*, *7*(3), 168–194. DOI: 10.47992/IJAEML.2581.7000.0193

Aithal, P. S., & Aithal, S. (2024). An overview of the use of ICCT and nanotechnology in yellow economy: Current status and future opportunities. [PIJET]. *SSRN*, *1*(1), 29–62. DOI: 10.2139/ssrn.4901452

Alexander, C. S., Yarborough, M., & Smith, A. (2024). Who is responsible for 'responsible AI'?: Navigating challenges to build trust in AI agriculture and food system technology. *Precision Agriculture*, *25*(1), 146–185. DOI: 10.1007/s11119-023-10063-3

Ali, A., Anderson, L., Venturini, F., Athanasios, K., Candiani, A., Di Benedetto, G., & Martos, V. (2024). AI can empower agriculture for global food security: Challenges and prospects in developing nations. *Frontiers in Artificial Intelligence*, *7*, 1328530. Advance online publication. DOI: 10.3389/frai.2024.1328530 PMID: 38726306

Ali, G., Mijwil, M. M., Buruga, B. A., Abotaleb, M., & Adamopoulos, I. (2024). A survey on artificial intelligence in cybersecurity for smart agriculture: State-of-the-art, cyber threats, artificial intelligence applications, and ethical concerns. *Mesopotamian Journal of Computer Science*, *2024*, 53–103. DOI: 10.58496/MJCSC/2024/007

Araújo, S. O., Peres, R. S., Barata, J., Lidon, F., & Ramalho, J. C. (2021). Characterising the agriculture 4.0 landscape—Emerging trends, challenges and opportunities. *Agronomy (Basel)*, *11*(4), 667. DOI: 10.3390/agronomy11040667

Bahrini, A., Khamoshifar, M., Abbasimehr, H., Riggs, R. J., Esmaeili, M., Majdabadkohne, R. M., & Pasehvar, M. (2023, April). ChatGPT: Applications, opportunities, and threats. In *2023 Systems and Information Engineering Design Symposium (SIEDS)* (pp. 274-279). IEEE. DOI: 10.1109/SIEDS58326.2023.10137850

Bhangar, N. A., & Shahriyar, A. K. (2023). Iot and ai for next-generation farming: Opportunities, challenges, and outlook. *International Journal of Sustainable Infrastructure for Cities and Societies*, *8*(2), 14–26.

Bhat, S. A., & Huang, N. F. (2021). Big data and ai revolution in precision agriculture: Survey and challenges. *IEEE Access : Practical Innovations, Open Solutions*, *9*, 110209–110222. DOI: 10.1109/ACCESS.2021.3102227

Chen, T., Lv, L., Wang, D., Zhang, J., Yang, Y., Zhao, Z., & Tao, D. (2024). Empowering agrifood system with artificial intelligence: A survey of the progress, challenges and opportunities. *ACM Computing Surveys*, *57*(2), 1–37.

Dara, R., Hazrati Fard, S. M., & Kaur, J. (2022). Recommendations for ethical and responsible use of artificial intelligence in digital agriculture. *Frontiers in Artificial Intelligence*, *5*, 884192. DOI: 10.3389/frai.2022.884192 PMID: 35968036

Dembani, R., Karvelas, I., Akbar, N. A., Rizou, S., Tegolo, D., & Fountas, S. (2025). Agricultural data privacy and federated learning: A review of challenges and opportunities. *Computers and Electronics in Agriculture*, *232*, 110048. DOI: 10.1016/j.compag.2025.110048

. Denhere, V., & Shao, D. (2024). Artificial Intelligence in Agritourism: Utilitarian Analysis of Opportunities, Challenges, and Ethical Considerations in the African Context. *Agritourism in Africa*, 17-36.

. Devare, M., Arnaud, E., Antezana, E., & King, B. (2023). Governing agricultural data: Challenges and recommendations. *Towards Responsible Plant Data Linkage: Data Challenges for Agricultural Research and Development, 201.*

Gardezi, M., Joshi, B., Rizzo, D. M., Ryan, M., Prutzer, E., Brugler, S., & Dadkhah, A. (2024). Artificial intelligence in farming: Challenges and opportunities for building trust. *Agronomy Journal*, *116*(3), 1217–1228. DOI: 10.1002/agj2.21353

. Gavai, A. K., Bouzembrak, Y., Xhani, D., Sedrakyan, G., Meuwissen, M. P., Souza, R. G. S., ... & van Hillegersberg, J. (2025). Agricultural data Privacy: Emerging platforms & strategies. *Food and Humanity*, 100542.

Groumpos, P. P. (2023, July). A critical historic overview of artificial intelligence: Issues, challenges, opportunities, and threats. *Artificial Intelligence and Applications (Commerce, Calif.)*, *1*(4), 181–197. DOI: 10.47852/bonviewAIA3202689

Gupta, D. K., Pagani, A., Zamboni, P., & Singh, A. K. (2024). AI-powered revolution in plant sciences: Advancements, applications, and challenges for sustainable agriculture and food security. *Exploration of Foods and Foodomics*, *2*(5), 443–459. DOI: 10.37349/eff.2024.00045

He, H., Gray, J., Cangelosi, A., Meng, Q., McGinnity, T. M., & Mehnen, J. (2021). The challenges and opportunities of human-centered AI for trustworthy robots and autonomous systems. *IEEE Transactions on Cognitive and Developmental Systems*, *14*(4), 1398–1412. DOI: 10.1109/TCDS.2021.3132282

Holzinger, A., Weippl, E., Tjoa, A. M., & Kieseberg, P. (2021, August). Digital transformation for sustainable development goals (sdgs)-a security, safety and privacy perspective on ai. In *International cross-domain conference for machine learning and knowledge extraction* (pp. 1-20). Cham: Springer International Publishing.

Jerhamre, E., Carlberg, C. J. C., & van Zoest, V. (2022). Exploring the susceptibility of smart farming: Identified opportunities and challenges. *Smart Agricultural Technology*, *2*, 2. DOI: 10.1016/j.atech.2021.100026

. Kanyepe, J., Chibaro, M., Morima, M., & Moeti-Lysson, J. (2025). AI-Powered Agricultural Supply Chains: Applications, Challenges, and Opportunities. *Integrating Agriculture, Green Marketing Strategies, and Artificial Intelligence*, 33-64.

Kapoor, P. (2025). Harvesting Ethics: Forging Responsible Paths in AI and ML for the Agri-Food Industry. In *Food and Industry 5.0: Transforming the Food System for a Sustainable Future* (pp. 305–315). Springer Nature Switzerland. DOI: 10.1007/978-3-031-76758-6_19

Kaushik, K., Khan, A., Kumari, A., Sharma, I., & Dubey, R. (2024). Ethical considerations in AI-based cybersecurity. In *Next-generation cybersecurity: AI, ML, and Blockchain* (pp. 437–470). Springer Nature Singapore. DOI: 10.1007/978-981-97-1249-6_19

Kochupillai, M., Kahl, M., Schmitt, M., Taubenböck, H., & Zhu, X. X. (2022). Earth observation and artificial intelligence: Understanding emerging ethical issues and opportunities. *IEEE Geoscience and Remote Sensing Magazine*, *10*(4), 90–124. DOI: 10.1109/MGRS.2022.3208357

. Kochupillai, M., & Köninger, J. (2023). Creating a digital marketplace for agrobiodiversity and plant genetic sequence data: Legal and ethical considerations of an ai and blockchain based solution. *Towards Responsible Plant Data Linkage: Data Challenges for Agricultural Research and Development*, 223.

Leong, Y. M., Lim, E. H., Subri, N. F. B., & Jalil, N. B. A. (2023, September). Transforming agriculture: Navigating the challenges and embracing the opportunities of artificial intelligence of things. In *2023 IEEE International Conference on Agrosystem Engineering, Technology & Applications (AGRETA)* (pp. 142-147). IEEE. DOI: 10.1109/AGRETA57740.2023.10262747

Malhotra, K., & Firdaus, M. (2022). Application of artificial intelligence in IoT security for crop yield prediction. *ResearchBerg Review of Science and Technology*, *2*(1), 136–157.

Mark, R. (2019). Ethics of using AI and big data in agriculture: The case of a large agriculture multinational. *The ORBIT Journal*, *2*(2), 1–27. DOI: 10.29297/orbit.v2i2.109

Neupane, S., Mitra, S., Fernandez, I. A., Saha, S., Mittal, S., Chen, J., Pillai, N., & Rahimi, S. (2024). Security considerations in ai-robotics: A survey of current methods, challenges, and opportunities. *IEEE Access : Practical Innovations, Open Solutions*, *12*, 22072–22097. DOI: 10.1109/ACCESS.2024.3363657

Otieno, M. (2023). An extensive survey of smart agriculture technologies: Current security posture. *World J. Adv. Res. Rev, 18*(3), 1207–1231. DOI: 10.30574/wjarr.2023.18.3.1241

Pandey, D. K., & Mishra, R. (2024). Towards sustainable agriculture: Harnessing AI for global food security. *Artificial Intelligence in Agriculture, 12*, 72–84. DOI: 10.1016/j.aiia.2024.04.003

Pedro, F., Subosa, M., Rivas, A., & Valverde, P. (2019). *Artificial intelligence in education: Challenges and opportunities for sustainable development*. United Nations Educational, Scientific and Cultural Organization. https://afyonluoglu.org/PublicWebFiles/Reports/AI/UNESCO-2019-AI%20in%20Education.pdf

Senoo, E. E. K., Anggraini, L., Kumi, J. A., Luna, B. K., Akansah, E., Sulyman, H. A., & Aritsugi, M. (2024). IoT solutions with artificial intelligence technologies for precision agriculture: Definitions, applications, challenges, and opportunities. *Electronics (Basel), 13*(10), 1894. DOI: 10.3390/electronics13101894

Shafik, W., Tufail, A., De Silva, C. L., Haji, R. A. A., & Apong, M. (2025). The Role, Application, and Impact of Artificial Intelligence in the Agriculture Industry. In *Future Tech Startups and Innovation in the Age of AI* (pp. 36–60). CRC Press.

Sood, A., Sharma, R. K., & Bhardwaj, A. K. (2022). Artificial intelligence research in agriculture: A review. *Online Information Review, 46*(6), 1054–1075. DOI: 10.1108/OIR-10-2020-0448

. Sparrow, R., & Howard, M. (2021). Robots in agriculture: prospects, impacts, ethics, and policy. *precision agriculture, 22*, 818-833.

Sparrow, R., Howard, M., & Degeling, C. (2021). Managing the risks of artificial intelligence in agriculture. *NJAS: Impact in Agricultural and Life Sciences, 93*(1), 172–196. DOI: 10.1080/27685241.2021.2008777

Tzachor, A., Devare, M., King, B., Avin, S., & Ó hÉigeartaigh, S. (2022). Responsible artificial intelligence in agriculture requires systemic understanding of risks and externalities. *Nature Machine Intelligence, 4*(2), 104–109. DOI: 10.1038/s42256-022-00440-4

Uplaonkar, S. S., Veershetty, R., Bahar, Z., & Sangeeta, G. (2024). The role of productive AI: A supporter or challenger in the future of agricultural librarianship. *IJAR, 10*(4), 46–53.

Wei, H., Xu, W., Kang, B., Eisner, R., Muleke, A., Rodriguez, D., deVoil, P., Sadras, V., Monjardino, M., & Harrison, M. T. (2024). Irrigation with artificial intelligence: Problems, premises, promises. *Human-Centric Intelligent Systems*, *4*(2), 187–205. DOI: 10.1007/s44230-024-00072-4

Williamson, H. F., Brettschneider, J., Caccamo, M., Davey, R. P., Goble, C., Kersey, P. J., May, S., Morris, R. J., Ostler, R., Pridmore, T., Rawlings, C., Studholme, D., Tsaftaris, S. A., & Leonelli, S. (2023). Data management challenges for artificial intelligence in plant and agricultural research. *F1000 Research*, *10*, 324. DOI: 10.12688/f1000research.52204.2 PMID: 36873457

Ya'u, M. S., & Mohammed, M. S. (2025). AI-Assisted Writing and Academic Literacy: Investigating the Dual Impact of Language Models on Writing Proficiency and Ethical Concerns in Nigerian Higher Education. *International Journal of Education and Literacy Studies*, *13*(2), 593–604. DOI: 10.7575/aiac.ijels.v.13n.2p.593

Zangana, H. M., Amelia, P., Luckyardi, S., Mustafa, F. M., & Li, S. (2025). The Role of Language in Regulating AI and Agricultural Technologies: Legal Perspectives from a Globalized World. In Zangana, H., Al-Karaki, J., & Omar, M. (Eds.), *Navigating Law and Policy in STM Enterprises: Ethical Governance, Regulation, and Innovation Strategy* (pp. 193–224). IGI Global Scientific Publishing., DOI: 10.4018/979-8-3373-4862-9.ch008

Zangana, H. M., Amelia, P., Mustafa, F. M., & Li, S. (2025). The Role of English Language and AI in Scientific Writing: Ethical and Academic Implications. In Zangana, H., & Omar, M. (Eds.), *Ensuring Secure and Ethical STM Research in the AI Era* (pp. 191–218). IGI Global Scientific Publishing., DOI: 10.4018/979-8-3373-4252-8.ch005

Zangana, H. M., Luckyardi, S., Mustafa, F. M., & Li, S. (2025). Enhancing Agricultural Cybersecurity: Leveraging Deep Learning and Large Language Models for Smart Farming Protection. In Zangana, H., Al-Karaki, J., & Omar, M. (Eds.), *Revolutionizing Cybersecurity With Deep Learning and Large Language Models* (pp. 307–338). IGI Global Scientific Publishing., DOI: 10.4018/979-8-3373-3296-3.ch010

Zangana, H. M., Luckyardi, S., Mustafa, F. M., & Li, S. (2025). Ethical and Secure AI Applications in Agricultural Research: Challenges and Opportunities. In Zangana, H., & Omar, M. (Eds.), *Ensuring Secure and Ethical STM Research in the AI Era* (pp. 43–76). IGI Global Scientific Publishing., DOI: 10.4018/979-8-3373-4252-8.ch002

Zangana, H. M., & Mustafa, F. M. (2026). Enhancing Educational Visual Content Through AI-Based Image Denoising Techniques: Implications for Remote Teaching and Digital Resource Development. In Zangana, H., Nobles, C., & Omar, M. (Eds.), *Harnessing AI for Teacher Support and Professional Development* (pp. 101–136). IGI Global Scientific Publishing., DOI: 10.4018/979-8-3373-5951-9.ch004

Zohouri, M., Sabzali, M., & Golmohammadi, A. (2024). Ethical considerations of ChatGPT-assisted article writing. *Synesis (ISSN 1984-6754), 16*(1), 94-113.

Chapter 10
The Future of Autonomous Forensic Agents and AI-Augmented Investigators

Rebet Keith Jones
https://orcid.org/0009-0008-0487-1301
Capitol Technology University, USA

ABSTRACT

The rapid evolution of artificial intelligence (AI) and autonomous systems is transforming the landscape of digital forensics and cybercrime investigation. This chapter explores the emerging paradigm of autonomous forensic agents and AI-augmented investigators, emphasizing their potential to revolutionize evidence collection, data analysis, and decision-making processes. It delves into the convergence of machine learning, natural language processing, robotics, and cognitive computing to create intelligent agents capable of independently navigating digital environments, identifying anomalies, and assisting human investigators with high precision and efficiency. The chapter also addresses the ethical, legal, and technical challenges that accompany the deployment of such systems, including concerns about bias, accountability, transparency, and interpretability. Drawing from real-world applications, research trends, and interdisciplinary innovations, this forward-looking analysis envisions a future where human expertise is seamlessly integrated with intelligent automation

DOI: 10.4018/979-8-3373-6536-7.ch010

INTRODUCTION

The accelerating integration of artificial intelligence (AI) into digital forensics and cybersecurity is reshaping investigative practices, blurring the boundaries between human expertise and machine autonomy. In a digital era marked by escalating cyber threats, the emergence of autonomous forensic agents and AI-augmented investigators signifies a paradigm shift—transforming the traditionally reactive and manual forensic landscape into a proactive, intelligent, and largely automated domain (Zangana & Omar, 2025).

Historically, digital forensics has been challenged by overwhelming data volumes, complex attack vectors, and limited human resources (Irons & Lallie, 2014; Jarrett & Choo, 2021). However, with the advent of machine learning (ML), large language models (LLMs), and intelligent automation, forensic analysts can now leverage tools that interpret patterns, prioritize evidence, and even simulate adversarial behavior with minimal intervention (Chen et al., 2024; Xu et al., 2024; Motlagh et al., 2024). These AI-driven tools offer unprecedented speed and scalability in analyzing logs, reconstructing timelines, and identifying anomalies, which is particularly crucial in cloud-native, IoT, and blockchain environments (Hamza & Omar, 2013; Omar et al., 2024; Kasri et al., 2025).

The foundational concept of autonomous forensic agents draws on the convergence of robotics, explainable AI, cybersecurity analytics, and NLP-driven decision-making systems (Ganesh, 2017; Dunsin, Ghanem, & Quazzane, 2022; Hall et al., 2022). These agents are designed not merely as tools, but as adaptive entities that can operate independently, intelligently responding to evolving threat landscapes (Costantini et al., 2019; Jeong, 2020). When integrated with LLMs, they gain a cognitive edge—capable of interpreting legal language, predicting attacker behavior, and generating real-time insights during incident response (Ferrag et al., 2024; Gholami & Omar, 2024; Alturkistani & Chuprat, 2024).

Several studies have illustrated the potential of domain-specific LLMs in enhancing forensic workflows. For example, the SecLM model has been tailored for cybersecurity threat mitigation through deep contextual understanding (Asoronye et al., 2024), while lightweight models like GEADD (Jones & Omar, 2024) and privacy-preserving BERT variants (Thandi, 2024) show promise for real-time applications in constrained IoT/IIoT environments (Ferrag et al., 2023, 2024). These models not only accelerate investigations but also ensure explainability and legal defensibility—critical in judicial proceedings (Kelly et al., 2020; Hall et al., 2022).

Concurrently, AI-augmented investigators are becoming integral to security operations centers (SOCs), particularly in enterprise and critical infrastructure settings. These systems augment human investigators by prioritizing high-risk incidents, providing contextual intelligence, and mitigating cognitive overload (Huff et al.,

2023; Manoharan & Sarker, 2023). Human-AI collaboration frameworks now incorporate multimodal data fusion, risk-based prioritization, and natural language-based interfaces—making forensic insights more accessible, transparent, and actionable (Santos et al., 2024; Liu, 2024; AlQenaei, 2024).

Table 1 compares the key strengths and limitations of human investigators and AI-augmented systems in digital forensic tasks.

Table 1. Comparison of human vs AI investigative capabilities

Capability	Human Investigator	AI Investigator
Data Scalability	Limited	High
Bias	Possible	Minimal (if well-trained)
Pattern Recognition	Moderate	Advanced
Context Understanding	High	Emerging
Speed	Moderate	Very High
Fatigue	Yes	No

Nonetheless, the road to fully autonomous systems is neither linear nor without risk. Concerns over bias propagation, data poisoning, adversarial attacks, and loss of interpretability continue to fuel debate over ethical deployment (Iqbal et al., 2020; Mitchell, 2014; Tyagi et al., 2024). As emphasized by Zangana and Omar (2025), AI systems in forensics must not only perform effectively but must also align with societal, legal, and human-centric values—ensuring transparency, accountability, and fairness in high-stakes environments.

Furthermore, the future of AI in digital forensics is intertwined with broader technological advancements such as quantum-aware cybersecurity, blockchain timestamping, and hybrid intelligence frameworks (Zangana & Li, 2025; Zangana & Mustafa, 2025; Pleshakova et al., 2024). These emerging trends, discussed in foundational works by Omar and Zangana (2025), illustrate how AI and LLMs are poised not only to support but to evolve digital forensic methodologies.

As we look ahead, this chapter aims to chart a comprehensive vision of how autonomous forensic agents and AI-augmented investigators will define the next era of digital investigations. By synthesizing technical developments, use cases, and ethical reflections, we provide a forward-looking perspective on the tools, challenges, and opportunities that will shape this transformative journey.

BACKGROUND AND CURRENT STATE OF AI IN DIGITAL FORENSICS

Digital forensics, the discipline dedicated to the identification, preservation, analysis, and presentation of digital evidence, has experienced profound transformation through the integration of Artificial Intelligence (AI) techniques. Traditionally reliant on manual, labor-intensive processes, digital forensics is increasingly augmented by AI-driven automation and intelligent analysis to meet the growing scale and complexity of cybercrime investigations (Adam & Varol, 2020; Ganesh, 2017). This evolution has been critical as cyber threats become more sophisticated, requiring faster and more accurate forensic responses.

AI technologies, including machine learning (ML), deep learning (DL), and large language models (LLMs), have introduced new capabilities in automating evidence processing, anomaly detection, and pattern recognition (Costantini, De Gasperis, & Olivieri, 2019; Dunsin, Ghanem, & Quazzane, 2022). For instance, ML algorithms have been applied for malware classification, network intrusion detection, and authorship attribution, enhancing the speed and accuracy of forensic analysis beyond traditional heuristic methods (Iqbal, Debbabi, & Fung, 2020; Manasa & Kumar, 2022). The incorporation of AI also addresses challenges posed by massive data volumes and encrypted or obfuscated information in modern digital environments (Manoharan & Sarker, 2023; Omar, Zangana, & Mohammed, 2025).

Large Language Models (LLMs) like GPT and BERT have emerged as powerful tools in the domain, facilitating natural language processing (NLP) tasks such as automated report generation, malware analysis, and cyber threat intelligence extraction (Chen et al., 2024; Ferrag et al., 2024; Liu, 2024). The use of LLMs enables digital forensic analysts to interpret unstructured data, such as chat logs, emails, and code, with enhanced contextual understanding, thereby supporting more comprehensive investigations (AlQenaei, 2024; Diaz et al., 2024; Ghazal et al., 2024).

The adoption of AI in digital forensics is also evident in emerging specialized security models. SecLM, a security-focused language model, exemplifies advances tailored specifically for cybersecurity and forensic applications, demonstrating improved threat detection and mitigation performance (Asoronye et al., 2024). Additionally, hybrid approaches combining AI with blockchain technologies are being explored to ensure the integrity and traceability of digital evidence (Karthikeyan, Pande, & Sarveshwaran, 2023; Zangana, 2024).

Explainability and transparency of AI systems have been recognized as vital in forensic contexts, where evidence must withstand legal scrutiny (Hall, Sakzad, & Choo, 2022; Kelly et al., 2020). Efforts in developing explainable AI (XAI) frameworks ensure that decisions made by AI-driven forensic tools are interpretable and defensible in court, addressing ethical and regulatory considerations (Omar & Zangana, 2024; Zangana & Omar, 2025).

Despite these advances, challenges remain. AI models require large, high-quality datasets, which are often scarce in forensic contexts due to privacy and confidentiality concerns (Gholami & Omar, 2023; Zangana & Mohammed, 2025). There are also risks of adversarial attacks targeting AI systems, potentially undermining forensic integrity (Omar, 2024). Furthermore, the rapid evolution of AI necessitates continuous updates to forensic frameworks to keep pace with emerging threats and technologies (Kasri et al., 2025; Motlagh et al., 2024).

Recent comprehensive surveys underline the transformative impact of AI on digital forensics but stress the need for standardized methodologies and interdisciplinary collaboration (Dunsin et al., 2024; Rizvi et al., 2022; Sikos, 2021). The fusion of AI with quantum computing and next-generation cybersecurity paradigms represents a future frontier with promising forensic applications (Zangana & Omar, 2025; Pleshakova et al., 2024).

In summary, the integration of AI in digital forensics has shifted the field from manual investigative efforts toward intelligent, automated processes capable of tackling modern cyber threats with increased efficiency and accuracy. Continuous research and innovation are essential to address the challenges and fully harness the potential of AI-driven forensic science in an increasingly digital world (Bhawna & Mahajan, 2024; Omar & Zangana, 2025; Tyagi, Kumari, & Richa, 2024).

DEFINING AUTONOMOUS FORENSIC AGENTS

Autonomous forensic agents represent a transformative evolution in the domain of digital forensics, combining artificial intelligence (AI), machine learning (ML), and large language models (LLMs) to facilitate more efficient, accurate, and adaptive forensic investigations. These agents operate with minimal human intervention, autonomously collecting, analyzing, and interpreting digital evidence in complex and dynamic environments (Adam & Varol, 2020; Ganesh, 2017).

At their core, autonomous forensic agents leverage AI techniques to automate traditionally manual forensic tasks such as data acquisition, pattern recognition, anomaly detection, and report generation. This autonomy is grounded in the agents' capacity for contextual understanding, reasoning, and decision-making, facilitated by sophisticated models including deep neural networks and transformer-based language models (Bhawna & Mahajan, 2024; Costantini, De Gasperis, & Olivieri, 2019).

The integration of large language models into forensic agents marks a significant advancement. LLMs enable agents to comprehend natural language queries, generate detailed narratives from raw forensic data, and assist in hypothesis formulation during investigations (Chen et al., 2024; Ferrag et al., 2024). For instance, the use of domain-specific LLMs, such as SecLM, has been shown to enhance cybersecurity threat mitigation by providing specialized language understanding tailored to security contexts (Asoronye et al., 2024).

Autonomous forensic agents also incorporate elements of explainability and transparency, which are crucial for forensic validity and legal acceptability. Explainable

AI (XAI) frameworks embedded within these agents help elucidate their decision pathways, thereby fostering trust among forensic practitioners and judicial entities (Hall, Sakzad, & Choo, 2022; Kelly et al., 2020). This feature addresses long-standing challenges related to the "black-box" nature of many AI models used in forensics.

Furthermore, autonomous forensic agents are designed to operate in constrained and evolving environments, including cloud infrastructures, IoT networks, and mobile devices. Their adaptive learning capabilities allow them to update their knowledge base continuously, learning from new attack vectors and emerging threats (Dunsin, Ghanem, Ouazzane, & Vassilev, 2024; Omar, Zangana, & Mohammed, 2025). This adaptability is vital for maintaining forensic relevance in the face of rapid technological and threat landscape changes.

The architectural foundation of these agents often involves multi-layered frameworks that integrate data collection modules, AI-driven analysis engines, and response mechanisms. Such frameworks benefit from advancements in explainable ML, hybrid AI approaches, and the optimization of LLM architectures to balance accuracy, speed, and resource efficiency (AlQenaei, 2024; Motlagh et al., 2024).

The diagram below illustrates the layered architecture of an autonomous forensic agent, outlining its key components from input acquisition to decision-making and reporting.

Figure 1. System architecture of an autonomous forensic agent

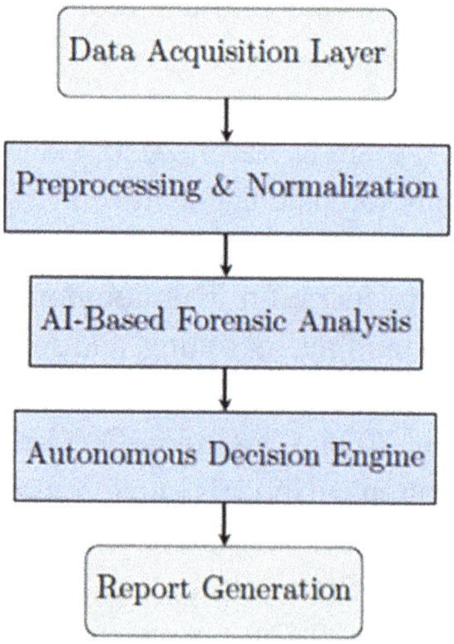

In summary, autonomous forensic agents embody a synergy between AI, cybersecurity, and digital forensic disciplines. They represent the future frontier for forensic investigations, offering scalable, intelligent, and legally robust solutions to address increasingly sophisticated cybercrimes (Omar & Zangana, 2025; Tyagi, Kumari, & Richa, 2024). Continued research and development in this field, focusing on enhancing the interpretability, adaptability, and domain specificity of these agents, are essential to fully realize their potential.

AI-AUGMENTED HUMAN INVESTIGATORS

The integration of Artificial Intelligence (AI) into digital forensics and cybersecurity has transformed the role of human investigators by augmenting their capabilities and enhancing investigative efficiency. AI-augmented human investigators leverage machine learning, large language models (LLMs), and advanced analytical tools to support, rather than replace, human judgment in complex cyber investigations (Costantini, De Gasperis, & Olivieri, 2019; Omar & Zangana, 2025).

Traditionally, digital forensic investigators faced challenges such as processing large volumes of data, identifying subtle patterns, and keeping pace with rapidly evolving cyber threats. AI tools now assist by automating routine tasks like data triage, pattern recognition, and anomaly detection, enabling human experts to focus on higher-level decision-making and contextual analysis (Adam & Varol, 2020; Bhawna & Mahajan, 2024). For example, AI-powered systems can pre-filter evidence, highlight relevant artifacts, and propose hypotheses based on learned models, significantly reducing investigation time (Dunsin, Ghanem, Ouazzane, & Vassilev, 2024).

Large Language Models, such as GPT variants and specialized cybersecurity language models like SecLM, have been particularly effective in augmenting human investigators. These models can process and generate natural language, aiding in report writing, evidence summarization, and threat intelligence extraction from unstructured data sources such as logs, emails, and social media (Asoronye et al., 2024; Ferrag et al., 2024). Moreover, LLMs facilitate predictive analytics by anticipating attacker behaviors and uncovering zero-day vulnerabilities, thus equipping investigators with proactive defense strategies (Jones & Omar, 2024; Diaf et al., 2024).

Explainable AI (XAI) frameworks are increasingly integrated to ensure transparency and trustworthiness in AI-augmented investigations. These systems provide interpretable insights into AI-driven decisions, helping investigators understand the reasoning behind automated alerts or classification results (Hall, Sakzad, & Choo, 2022; Ghazal et al., 2024). This interpretability is crucial in legal contexts where evidentiary standards require clear, reproducible analyses.

Human investigators also play a vital role in supervising AI outputs, verifying findings, and incorporating domain expertise to avoid false positives or biases introduced by automated systems (Irons & Lallie, 2014; Manasa & Kumar, 2022).

The synergy between AI and human cognition fosters more robust cybersecurity postures and forensic outcomes (Ganesh, 2017; Jarrett & Choo, 2021).

Despite the promising advances, challenges remain in fully integrating AI with human investigators. Data privacy concerns, ethical considerations, and the need for continual AI model updating require careful governance and multidisciplinary collaboration (Gupta, Gaurav, & Arya, 2024; Omar, Zangana, & Mohammed, 2025). Additionally, there is an ongoing need for tailored training programs to equip investigators with skills to effectively utilize AI tools (Iqbal, Debbabi, & Fung, 2020; Kasri et al., 2025).

Figure 2 presents the typical investigation workflow enhanced by AI tools, from evidence collection to case resolution.

Figure 2. AI-augmented forensic investigation workflow

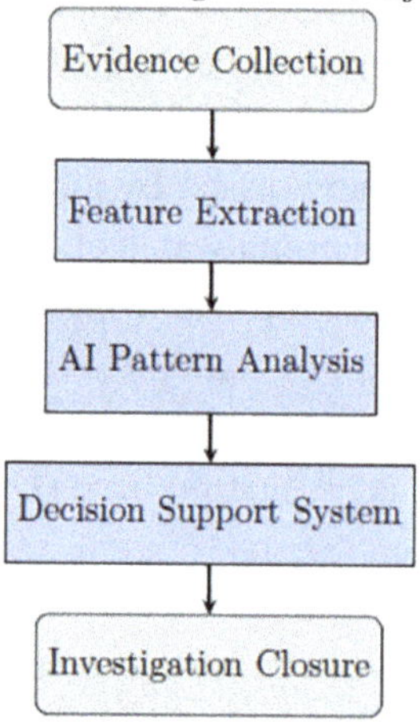

In summary, AI-augmented human investigators represent a critical evolution in cybersecurity and digital forensics. By harnessing AI's computational power and human contextual understanding, this hybrid approach enhances the accuracy, speed, and reliability of cyber investigations while addressing emerging threats in an increasingly complex digital landscape (Zangana & Omar, 2025; Motlagh et al., 2024).

TECHNOLOGICAL ENABLERS

The rapid advancement of cybersecurity and digital forensics relies heavily on a diverse set of technological enablers that fuel innovation, automation, and enhanced threat detection capabilities. Among these, Artificial Intelligence (AI), Machine

Learning (ML), and especially Large Language Models (LLMs) have emerged as foundational technologies transforming the landscape of cybersecurity defense and forensic investigations.

Artificial Intelligence and Machine Learning form the backbone of modern cyber defense strategies. These technologies enable automated pattern recognition, anomaly detection, and real-time threat intelligence analysis (Costantini, De Gasperis, & Olivieri, 2019; Ganesh, 2017). AI-driven digital forensics tools can intelligently sift through large datasets, reconstruct attack timelines, and predict future attack vectors, which were previously infeasible using manual methods (Adam & Varol, 2020; Bhawna & Mahajan, 2024). Moreover, the integration of ML algorithms into forensic investigations enhances the ability to identify malware signatures and anomalous user behaviors, thus streamlining incident response (Iqbal, Debbabi, & Fung, 2020; Dunsin, Ghanem, Ouazzane, & Vassilev, 2024).

Large Language Models (LLMs) such as GPT and BERT architectures represent a significant leap in cybersecurity capabilities. These models facilitate natural language understanding for threat intelligence gathering, vulnerability detection, and automated incident reporting (Ferrag et al., 2024; Chen et al., 2024). LLMs enable cyber analysts to process vast volumes of unstructured data, including logs, code snippets, and security bulletins, efficiently extracting actionable insights (AlQenaei, 2024; Asoronye et al., 2024). Furthermore, privacy-preserving lightweight LLM variants tailored for Internet of Things (IoT) environments have been proposed to address resource constraints while maintaining high detection accuracy (Ferrag, Ndhlovu, Tihanyi, Cordeiro, Debbah, & Lestable, 2024).

Explainable AI (XAI) techniques complement these models by providing transparency in decision-making processes, a critical factor in forensic validation and trustworthiness (Hall, Sakzad, & Choo, 2022; Ghazal et al., 2024). This transparency fosters improved adoption in sensitive environments such as healthcare and critical infrastructure cybersecurity (Huff et al., 2023).

Automation and Intelligent Systems also serve as key enablers. Advances in automation streamline the digital forensic process from evidence collection to analysis, reducing human error and accelerating incident resolution (Jarrett & Choo, 2021; Manoharan & Sarker, 2023). Automated frameworks harnessing AI accelerate triage and forensic imaging, enabling rapid responses to zero-day attacks and advanced persistent threats (Jones & Omar, 2024; Jones et al., 2023).

Cloud Computing and Edge AI technologies provide scalable infrastructure and localized intelligence that enhance the agility of cyber defense systems (Hamza & Omar, 2013; Omar, 2022). The convergence of cloud-based analytics with AI-powered edge devices enables distributed threat detection closer to data sources, especially relevant for IoT and Industrial IoT (IIoT) applications (Diaf, Korba, Karabadji, & Ghamri-Doudane, 2024; Ferrag et al., 2023).

Hybrid Approaches combining traditional cybersecurity tools with AI and LLMs optimize the balance between accuracy, efficiency, and interpretability (Zangana & Mustafa, 2024; Omar, 2024). Such methods improve robustness in malware detection and vulnerability scanning, particularly in dynamically evolving threat landscapes (Zangana & Omar, 2025a; Zangana & Li, 2025).

Synthetic Data Generation has emerged as a novel enabler for training robust AI models without compromising privacy or data availability (Gholami & Omar, 2023; Gholami & Omar, 2024). By generating realistic but artificial datasets, cybersecurity models can be refined and validated extensively before deployment.

Finally, the integration of Blockchain technology with AI-driven forensics introduces immutable logging and timestamping mechanisms, enhancing data integrity and auditability (Zangana, 2024).

Collectively, these technological enablers forge a future-ready cybersecurity ecosystem capable of proactively countering increasingly sophisticated cyber threats and enabling forensic readiness with unprecedented efficiency and intelligence (Motlagh et al., 2024; Kasri et al., 2025; Omar, Zangana, & Mohammed, 2025).

USE CASES AND APPLICATIONS

Large Language Models (LLMs) and Artificial Intelligence (AI) technologies have rapidly transformed various sectors, with cybersecurity and digital forensics emerging as prominent areas of application. The use cases of these technologies span from enhancing threat detection to automating complex investigative processes, significantly improving the efficiency and accuracy of security operations.

Cyber Threat Detection and Prediction

LLMs play a vital role in identifying and predicting cyber threats, leveraging their ability to analyze vast amounts of data and learn attack patterns. For example, Ferrag et al. (2023, 2024) demonstrated the effectiveness of BERT-based lightweight models in cyber threat detection for IoT and IIoT devices, preserving privacy while maintaining high accuracy. Similarly, Diaf et al. (2024) highlighted the predictive capabilities of LLMs in IoT networks, enabling proactive defense

Digital Forensics and Incident Response

The integration of AI and LLMs into digital forensics enables the automation of evidence gathering, analysis, and interpretation. This significantly reduces the time required for investigations while improving reliability (Adam & Varol, 2020;

Bhawna & Mahajan, 2024; Costantini et al., 2019). Hall, Sakzad, and Choo (2022) underscored the importance of explainable AI to ensure forensic transparency and trustworthiness. Moreover, Dunsin et al. (2022, 2024) explored AI's role in incident response, especially under constrained environments, proving the adaptability of AI tools in diverse forensic scenarios.

Malware and Vulnerability Detection

AI-driven models, including LLMs, have been employed to detect malware and software vulnerabilities effectively. Omar and Zangana (2025) illustrated how specialized LLMs can identify zero-day threats and enhance software vulnerability detection, providing a paradigm shift in proactive cybersecurity. Taghavi and Feyzi (2024) emphasized using LLMs to handle and mitigate software vulnerabilities efficiently, which is critical in an era of rapidly evolving attack vectors.

Security in Cloud and Enterprise Systems

Cloud environments and enterprise information systems have benefited from AI applications that monitor, detect, and mitigate abuses and nefarious activities (Hamza & Omar, 2013; Gupta, Gaurav, & Arya, 2024). The scale and complexity of these environments demand intelligent automation, which LLMs can support by analyzing complex logs and enforcing access control policies (Omar, 2021; Omar, 2022).

Cyber Threat Intelligence and Automation

LLMs have advanced the automation of cyber threat intelligence gathering and analysis. Asoronye et al. (2024) proposed SecLM, a specialized security language model designed to improve threat mitigation, while AlTurkistani and Chuprat (2024) reviewed AI's contributions in enhancing cyber threat intelligence through systematic literature. Sarker (2024) further elaborated on generative AI's role in enabling intelligent decision-making and explainability in cyber operations.

Blockchain and Cryptographic Security

In emerging fields like blockchain-based timestamping and cryptographic solutions, AI models assist in securing data integrity and authenticity. Zangana (2024) reviewed blockchain-based timestamping tools, highlighting AI's role in ensuring tamper-proof audit trails crucial for forensic evidence.

Human Factors and Insider Threats

AI also supports the mitigation of insider threats by analyzing behavioral patterns and anomalies within organizations. Zangana, Sallow, and Omar (2025) discussed the human factor in cybersecurity, emphasizing AI's potential to detect subtle insider activities that traditional methods often overlook.

IoT and Smart Systems Security

With the proliferation of IoT devices, LLMs are instrumental in monitoring and securing connected ecosystems. Ferrag et al. (2024) showed how privacy-preserving AI models can be integrated into resource-constrained IoT environments to detect malware and anomalies effectively.

Explainability and Ethical AI in Security

Explainability in AI applications for security remains a critical concern. Kelly et al. (2020) and Ghazal et al. (2024) discussed how explainable AI frameworks improve trust and compliance in security applications, ensuring AI decisions can be understood and audited by humans.

Future-Ready Cyber Defense Strategies

Recent works emphasize the need for adaptive and quantum-aware cybersecurity frameworks, leveraging LLMs to prepare for future threats (Zangana & Omar, 2025; Kasri et al., 2025; Pleshakova et al., 2024). These applications illustrate the convergence of AI, machine learning, and emerging technologies to create resilient security ecosystems.

Summary

The application of LLMs and AI in cybersecurity and digital forensics is vast and rapidly evolving. From threat detection, malware analysis, and forensic investigations to insider threat mitigation and blockchain security, these technologies are shaping the future of secure computing environments. Researchers continue to explore the balance between automation, explainability, and ethical considerations to maximize benefits while minimizing risks (Omar & Zangana, 2025; Ferrag et al., 2024; Liu, 2024).

ETHICAL AND LEGAL CONSIDERATIONS

The rapid advancement and integration of Artificial Intelligence (AI), particularly Large Language Models (LLMs), into cybersecurity and digital forensics have brought about significant ethical and legal challenges. These challenges must be carefully addressed to ensure responsible development, deployment, and use of AI technologies in sensitive security domains (Ferrag et al., 2024; Omar & Zangana, 2024).

Ethical Challenges

One of the foremost ethical concerns is privacy. AI-driven cybersecurity tools, including LLMs, often require vast amounts of data, some of which may be personal or sensitive. Ensuring that these data are collected, processed, and stored in compliance with privacy laws and ethical standards is critical (Ferrag et al., 2024; Hasanov et al., 2024). The risk of unauthorized surveillance or data misuse arises, especially when AI models are used for monitoring or threat detection in real time (AlQenaei, 2024; Zangana, Mustafa, & Omar, 2024).

Another significant ethical issue is bias and fairness. AI models trained on biased datasets can propagate and amplify prejudices, leading to unfair or discriminatory outcomes in cybersecurity enforcement or forensic investigations (Gholami & Omar, 2023; Gupta, Gaurav, & Arya, 2024). Transparent and explainable AI methods are necessary to mitigate such biases and build trust among users and stakeholders (Hall, Sakzad, & Choo, 2022; Kelly et al., 2020).

The use of AI in digital forensics raises concerns about accountability and transparency. Automated decision-making processes must be auditable to prevent wrongful accusations or errors in investigations (Costantini, De Gasperis, & Olivieri, 2019; Omar, Zangana, & Mohammed, 2025). Ethical frameworks and guidelines need to be established to govern the use of AI in forensic contexts, ensuring that AI acts as a support tool rather than a sole arbiter (Zangana & Omar, 2025).

Legal Considerations

From a legal standpoint, AI in cybersecurity and forensics faces the challenge of keeping pace with evolving regulations. Laws such as the General Data Protection Regulation (GDPR) impose strict requirements on data handling and individual rights, impacting how AI systems can be used for threat detection and forensic analysis (Nguyen et al., 2018; Omar & Zangana, 2024).

Furthermore, intellectual property rights related to AI-generated content or software tools pose legal uncertainties. Determining liability when AI models are used for cyber defense or when they inadvertently cause harm remains complex (Jeong, 2020; Kasri et al., 2025).

Legal frameworks must also address the use of AI in digital evidence collection and preservation. The admissibility of AI-processed evidence in courts depends on clear standards and validation of AI techniques to maintain forensic integrity (Moustafa, 2022; Sikos, 2021). Compliance with chain-of-custody rules and data authenticity verification are essential to withstand legal scrutiny (Adam & Varol, 2020; Omar & Zangana, 2025).

Emerging Solutions and Future Directions

Research is increasingly focusing on developing privacy-preserving AI models, such as federated learning and differential privacy, to protect sensitive data during cyber threat detection and forensic investigations (Ferrag et al., 2024; Thandi, 2024). Explainable AI (XAI) techniques are also gaining attention for enhancing transparency and trust in AI-driven security tools (Ghazal et al., 2024; Hall et al., 2022).

Legal scholars and technologists advocate for collaborative policymaking to craft regulations that balance innovation with ethical and legal safeguards (Omar, 2024; Zangana & Li, 2025). Multidisciplinary approaches involving technologists, legal experts, and ethicists will be crucial for crafting responsible AI governance frameworks (Sarker, 2024; Zangana, Omar, & Mustafa, 2025).

In conclusion, addressing ethical and legal considerations in AI-enhanced cybersecurity and digital forensics is indispensable for fostering trust, protecting rights, and ensuring the efficacy and fairness of AI applications in these critical domains.

CHALLENGES AND RISKS

The rapid integration of Artificial Intelligence (AI), particularly Large Language Models (LLMs), into cybersecurity and digital forensics offers promising advancements but also presents significant challenges and risks that must be carefully considered. These issues span technical, ethical, operational, and legal domains, demanding comprehensive understanding and mitigation strategies.

Technical Challenges

One of the foremost challenges lies in the complexity and opacity of AI models such as LLMs. Their "black-box" nature makes explainability difficult, which hinders forensic analysis and trust in automated decisions (Hall, Sakzad, & Choo, 2022; Ghazal et al., 2024). Moreover, these models are vulnerable to adversarial attacks, including data poisoning and evasion tactics, which can degrade detection accuracy and cause false negatives or positives in threat identification (Omar, 2024; Motlagh et al., 2024). Ensuring robustness against such attacks remains an ongoing research challenge.

Resource constraints also limit the deployment of AI-driven security solutions in constrained environments like IoT and edge devices, where computational power and energy are limited (Dunsin, Ghanem, & Quazzane, 2022; Ferrag et al., 2024). Lightweight models balancing efficiency and accuracy must be developed to overcome these constraints.

Data Privacy and Security Risks

AI systems require vast amounts of data, often sensitive, to train effectively. Handling such data raises privacy concerns and risks of unintended leakage or misuse (Gupta, Gaurav, & Arya, 2024; Ferrag et al., 2024). Furthermore, synthetic data generation techniques, while useful for privacy preservation, may introduce bias or fail to capture real-world complexities, potentially compromising model generalization (Gholami & Omar, 2023, 2024).

Cybercriminals may exploit AI capabilities themselves, crafting sophisticated phishing campaigns or automated hacking tools that adapt dynamically, increasing the complexity of threat landscapes (Zangana, Sallow, & Omar, 2025; Jeong, 2020). The dual-use nature of AI tools thus necessitates careful governance and monitoring.

Ethical and Legal Concerns

The deployment of AI in digital forensics and cybersecurity raises profound ethical issues, including accountability for AI-driven decisions and potential biases embedded in training data that could lead to unfair outcomes or discrimination (Kelly et al., 2020; Sikos, 2021). Legal frameworks often lag behind technological advancements, creating uncertainties regarding liability and compliance in AI-enabled investigations and defenses (Omar & Zangana, 2024; AlQenaei, 2024).

Transparency and explainability are essential to meet regulatory requirements and maintain public trust, but they remain challenging with current model architectures (Diaf et al., 2024; Xu et al., 2024). Moreover, AI-enabled surveillance tools must balance security objectives with privacy rights, posing significant ethical dilemmas (Hamza & Omar, 2013).

Operational and Human Factors

Integrating AI tools into existing cybersecurity workflows requires organizational change and skilled personnel capable of interpreting AI outputs and responding appropriately (Jones & Omar, 2024; Huff et al., 2023). The human factor remains critical, as insider threats and social engineering can circumvent even the most advanced AI defenses (Zangana, Sallow, & Omar, 2025).

Additionally, over-reliance on AI might lead to complacency and diminished vigilance among cybersecurity professionals, potentially increasing risk exposure (Jarrett & Choo, 2021). Continuous training and awareness programs are necessary to mitigate these risks.

Future Directions for Risk Mitigation

Addressing these challenges requires multi-disciplinary collaboration involving AI researchers, cybersecurity experts, legal scholars, and policymakers. Efforts should focus on developing explainable AI, robust adversarial defenses, privacy-preserving data techniques, and ethical frameworks tailored to AI's role in cybersecurity and digital forensics (AlQenaei, 2024; Hassanin & Moustafa, 2024; Zangana & Li, 2025).

Moreover, standards and guidelines must evolve rapidly to encompass AI's unique risks, promoting transparency, accountability, and trustworthiness (Omar, Zangana, & Mohammed, 2025; Xu et al., 2024). Leveraging advances in quantum-aware AI models may also help future-proof cybersecurity defenses against emerging threats (Zangana & Omar, 2025).

Figure 3 highlights the overlap between ethical, legal, and technical concerns when deploying AI in forensic investigations.

Figure 3. Intersections of ethics, law, and technology in AI forensics

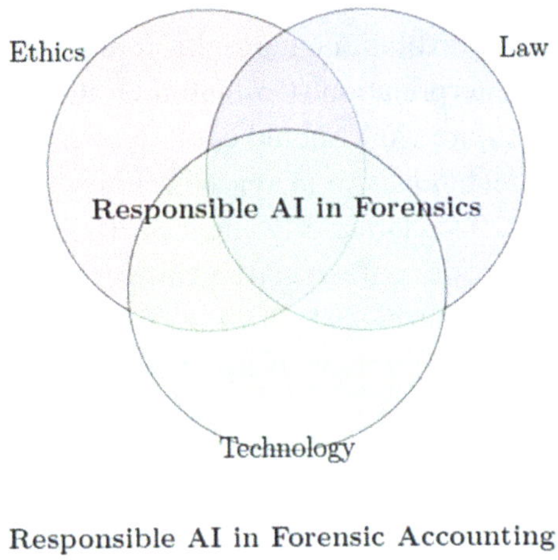

FUTURE DIRECTIONS AND RESEARCH OPPORTUNITIES

The rapid evolution of artificial intelligence (AI), particularly large language models (LLMs), presents numerous promising directions and opportunities to advance cybersecurity and digital forensics. Future research must focus on harnessing the full potential of these technologies while addressing their inherent challenges.

Enhanced Cyber Threat Intelligence through LLMs

Recent advances highlight the transformative impact of LLMs on cyber threat intelligence by enabling proactive threat detection, analysis, and mitigation (Alturkistani & Chuprat, 2024; Asoronye et al., 2024; Chen et al., 2024). Research opportunities lie in developing specialized LLM architectures optimized for cybersecurity contexts (AlQenaei, 2024), including privacy-preserving and resource-efficient models for deployment in constrained environments such as IoT and IIoT devices (Ferrag et al., 2024; Thandi, 2024). Further investigation is needed on fine-tuning LLMs to detect novel zero-day attacks while minimizing false positives (Jones & Omar, 2024; Kasri et al., 2025).

Integration of AI and Digital Forensics

AI-enabled automation is revolutionizing digital forensics by improving evidence collection, analysis, and interpretation (Costantini et al., 2019; Hall et al., 2022; Hamza & Omar, 2013). Future work should explore hybrid models combining AI with traditional forensic techniques to increase accuracy and reduce investigative timelines (Dunsin et al., 2024; Omar & Zangana, 2025). Explainable AI (XAI) frameworks tailored for forensic contexts can enhance transparency and trustworthiness in automated findings (Ghazal et al., 2024; Kelly et al., 2020). The application of AI in constrained forensic environments also remains a critical avenue (Dunsin et al., 2022).

Addressing Security, Ethical, and Privacy Challenges

While AI and LLMs offer enhanced detection capabilities, they also introduce new vulnerabilities and ethical concerns (Gupta et al., 2024; Hassanin & Moustafa, 2024). Research is essential to develop robust defenses against adversarial attacks targeting AI models and to ensure data privacy in model training and deployment (Motlagh et al., 2024; Omar, 2024). Incorporating ethical frameworks and regulatory compliance into AI systems is another pressing challenge requiring multidisciplinary collaboration (Iqbal et al., 2020; Omar & Zangana, 2024).

Quantum-Aware Cybersecurity and AI

The convergence of quantum computing and AI heralds a new era in cybersecurity. Future research should explore quantum-resistant AI algorithms and leverage quantum-aware LLMs to anticipate and counter emerging quantum threats (Zangana & Omar, 2025; Zangana et al., 2025). Developing quantum-secure cryptographic protocols integrated with AI for real-time threat detection is a key opportunity to maintain secure digital ecosystems (Omar & Zangana, 2025).

AI-Driven Automation and Incident Response

The increasing complexity and scale of cyberattacks necessitate automated, intelligent incident response systems. Advancements in AI-driven automation can facilitate rapid threat containment and remediation (Jarrett & Choo, 2021; Manoharan & Sarker, 2023). Research should focus on self-adaptive AI agents capable of dynamic defense strategies in heterogeneous network environments (Yu et al., 2024; Rizvi et al., 2022).

Synthetic Data and Model Efficiency

Training large AI models requires extensive datasets, often limited by privacy and availability constraints. Investigations into the use of synthetic data to enhance training efficiency without compromising model accuracy or privacy are promising (Gholami & Omar, 2023, 2024). Such approaches could democratize access to AI capabilities across organizations of varying resources.

Cross-Domain and Interdisciplinary Collaboration

Given the multifaceted nature of cybersecurity threats, future research must emphasize cross-domain integration, incorporating insights from AI, digital forensics, human factors, and policy-making (Zangana et al., 2025; Huff et al., 2023). Leadership in technology adoption, inclusive policies, and ethical standards will play a pivotal role in advancing resilient cyber infrastructures (Zangana & Omar, 2025).

Figure 4 illustrates the expected growth in the adoption of autonomous forensic agents over the next five years, based on recent industry forecasts.

Figure 4. Projected adoption rate of autonomous agents (2025–2030)

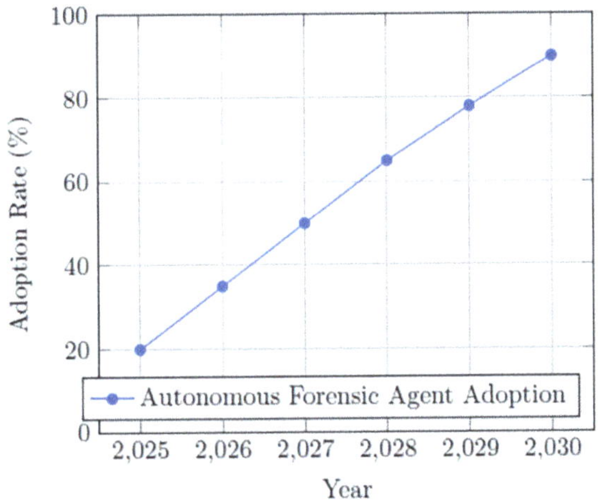

In conclusion, future research directions converge on refining AI and LLM applications for cybersecurity and digital forensics, addressing emerging ethical and privacy concerns, preparing for quantum-era challenges, and fostering interdisciplinary collaborations. The ongoing development and deployment of advanced AI techniques promise a more secure and intelligent digital future.

CONCLUSION

The integration of artificial intelligence, particularly large language models (LLMs), into cybersecurity and digital forensics marks a transformative shift in how threats are detected, analyzed, and mitigated. This chapter has explored the vast potential of AI-driven technologies to enhance cyber threat intelligence, automate forensic investigations, and bolster defense mechanisms against increasingly sophisticated cyberattacks.

Despite these promising advancements, significant challenges remain. Issues surrounding data privacy, model robustness against adversarial attacks, ethical considerations, and the need for explainability must be addressed to ensure trustworthy and effective deployment of AI systems in security contexts. Additionally, the emerging quantum computing landscape introduces both unprecedented risks and opportunities, necessitating research into quantum-aware AI frameworks and cryptographic techniques.

The future of cybersecurity and digital forensics lies in interdisciplinary collaboration that bridges technological innovation with human factors, ethical governance, and regulatory frameworks. By continuing to refine AI models, optimize data utilization through synthetic approaches, and develop transparent, privacy-preserving systems, the community can build resilient defenses capable of adapting to evolving cyber threats.

In sum, this evolving landscape demands ongoing research, innovation, and strategic leadership to harness AI's full capabilities responsibly and effectively. As LLMs and AI continue to mature, their role in safeguarding digital environments will be increasingly indispensable, ushering in a new era of intelligent and proactive cybersecurity and forensic practices.

REFERENCES

Adam, I. Y., & Varol, C. (2020, June). Intelligence in digital forensics process. In *2020 8th International Symposium on Digital Forensics and Security (ISDFS)* (pp. 1-6). IEEE. DOI: 10.1109/ISDFS49300.2020.9116442

AlQenaei, Z. M. (2024, March). Evolution and Optimization of Language Model Architectures: From Foundations to Future Directions. In *International Conference on Computing and Machine Learning* (pp. 233-249). Singapore: Springer Nature Singapore.

Alturkistani, H., & Chuprat, S. (2024). *Artificial Intelligence and Large Language Models in Advancing Cyber Threat Intelligence: A Systematic Literature Review. Research Square.* DOI: 10.21203/rs.3.rs-5423193/v1

Asoronye, G. O., Anthony, O. C., Ogbuikwu, R. I., Ogili, C. O., & Ali, H. U. (2024). SecLM: A Specialized Security Language Model for Advanced Cybersecurity Applications and Threat Mitigation. *EKETE-International Journal Of Advanced Research*, *2*(6), 33–42.

. Bhawna, & Mahajan, S. (2024). Artificial Intelligence Perspective on Digital Forensics. *Applying Artificial Intelligence in Cybersecurity Analytics and Cyber Threat Detection*, 33-44.

Chen, Y., Cui, M., Wang, D., Cao, Y., Yang, P., Jiang, B., Lu, Z., & Liu, B. (2024). A survey of large language models for cyber threat detection. *Computers & Security*, *145*, 104016. DOI: 10.1016/j.cose.2024.104016

Costantini, S., De Gasperis, G., & Olivieri, R. (2019). Digital forensics and investigations meet artificial intelligence. *Annals of Mathematics and Artificial Intelligence*, *86*(1), 193–229. DOI: 10.1007/s10472-019-09632-y

Diaf, A., Korba, A. A., Karabadji, N. E., & Ghamri-Doudane, Y. (2024, April). Beyond detection: Leveraging large language models for cyber attack prediction in iot networks. In *2024 20th International Conference on Distributed Computing in Smart Systems and the Internet of Things (DCOSS-IoT)* (pp. 117-123). IEEE.

Dunsin, D., Ghanem, M. C., Ouazzane, K., & Vassilev, V. (2024). A comprehensive analysis of the role of artificial intelligence and machine learning in modern digital forensics and incident response. *Forensic Science International Digital Investigation*, *48*, 301675. DOI: 10.1016/j.fsidi.2023.301675

Dunsin, D., Ghanem, M. C., & Quazzane, K. (2022). The use of artificial intelligence in digital forensics and incident response in a constrained environment. *International Journal of Information and Communication Engineering*, *16*(8), 280–285.

Ferrag, M. A., Alwahedi, F., Battah, A., Cherif, B., Mechri, A., & Tihanyi, N. (2024). Generative ai and large language models for cyber security: All insights you need. *Available at SSRN* 4853709. DOI: 10.2139/ssrn.4853709

Ferrag, M. A., Ndhlovu, M., Tihanyi, N., Cordeiro, L. C., Debbah, M., & Lestable, T. (2023). Revolutionizing cyber threat detection with large language models. *arXiv preprint arXiv:2306.14263*, 195-202.

Ferrag, M. A., Ndhlovu, M., Tihanyi, N., Cordeiro, L. C., Debbah, M., Lestable, T., & Thandi, N. S. (2024). Revolutionizing cyber threat detection with large language models: A privacy-preserving bert-based lightweight model for iot/iiot devices. *IEEE Access : Practical Innovations, Open Solutions*, *12*, 23733–23750. DOI: 10.1109/ACCESS.2024.3363469

Ganesh, V. (2017). Artificial intelligence applied to computer forensics. *International Journal (Toronto, Ont.)*, *5*(5).

Ghazal, T. M., Janjua, J. I., Abushiba, W., Ahmad, M., Ihsan, A., & Al-Dmour, N. A. (2024, December). Cybersecurity Revolution via Large Language Models and Explainable AI. In *2024 17th International Conference on Security of Information and Networks (SIN)* (pp. 1-6). IEEE. DOI: 10.1109/SIN63213.2024.10871324

Gholami, S., & Omar, M. (2023). Does Synthetic Data Make Large Language Models More Efficient? *arXiv preprint arXiv:2310.07830.*

Gholami, S., & Omar, M. (2024). Can a student large language model perform as well as its teacher? In *Innovations, Securities, and Case Studies Across Healthcare, Business, and Technology* (pp. 122-139). IGI Global. DOI: 10.4018/979-8-3693-1906-2.ch007

Gupta, B. B., Gaurav, A., & Arya, V. (2024). Navigating the security landscape of large language models in enterprise information systems. *Enterprise Information Systems*, *18*(4), 2310846. DOI: 10.1080/17517575.2024.2310846

Hadi, M. A., Abdulredha, M. N., & Hasan, E. (2023). Introduction to ChatGPT: A new revolution of artificial intelligence with machine learning algorithms and cybersecurity. *Sci. Arch*, *4*(04), 276. DOI: 10.47587/SA.2023.4406

Hall, S. W., Sakzad, A., & Choo, K. K. R. (2022). Explainable artificial intelligence for digital forensics. *Wiley Interdisciplinary Reviews: Forensic Science*, *4*(2), e1434.

Hamza, Y. A., & Omar, M. D. (2013). Cloud computing security: Abuse and nefarious use of cloud computing. *International Journal of Computer Engineering Research, 3*(6), 22–27.

Hasanov, I., Virtanen, S., Hakkala, A., & Isoaho, J. (2024). Application of Large Language Models in Cybersecurity: A Systematic Literature Review. *IEEE Access : Practical Innovations, Open Solutions, 12*, 176751–176778. DOI: 10.1109/ACCESS.2024.3505983

Hassanin, M., & Moustafa, N. (2024). A comprehensive overview of large language models (llms) for cyber defences: Opportunities and directions. *arXiv preprint arXiv:2405.14487*.

Huff, A. J., Burrell, D. N., Nobles, C., Richardson, K., Wright, J. B., Burton, S. L., Jones, A. J., Springs, D., Omar, M., & Brown-Jackson, K. L. (2023). Management Practices for Mitigating Cybersecurity Threats to Biotechnology Companies, Laboratories, and Healthcare Research Organizations. In *Applied Research Approaches to Technology, Healthcare, and Business* (pp. 1-12). IGI Global.

. Idelhaj, A., Abou El Houda, Z., & Khoukhi, L. (2024). Foundations models in cybersecurity. *Artificial Intelligence for Blockchain and Cybersecurity Powered IoT Applications*, 1.

. Iqbal, F., Debbabi, M., Fung, B. C., Iqbal, F., Debbabi, M., & Fung, B. C. (2020). Artificial intelligence and digital forensics. *Machine Learning for Authorship Attribution and Cyber Forensics*, 139-150.

Irons, A., & Lallie, H. S. (2014). Digital forensics to intelligent forensics. *Future Internet, 6*(3), 584–596. DOI: 10.3390/fi6030584

Jarrett, A., & Choo, K. K. R. (2021). The impact of automation and artificial intelligence on digital forensics. *WIREs Forensic Science, 3*(6), e1418. DOI: 10.1002/wfs2.1418

Jeong, D. (2020). Artificial intelligence security threat, crime, and forensics: Taxonomy and open issues. *IEEE Access : Practical Innovations, Open Solutions, 8*, 184560–184574. DOI: 10.1109/ACCESS.2020.3029280

Jones, R., & Omar, M. (2024). Revolutionizing Cybersecurity: The GPT-2 Enhanced Attack Detection and Defense (GEADD) Method for Zero-Day Threats. *International Journal of Informatics* [INJIISCOM]. *Information System and Computer Engineering, 5*(2), 178–191.

Jones, R., Omar, M., Mohammed, D., Nobles, C., & Dawson, M. (2023). Harnessing the Speed and Accuracy of Machine Learning to Advance Cybersecurity. In *2023 Congress in Computer Science, Computer Engineering, & Applied Computing (CSCE)* (pp. 418-421). IEEE. DOI: 10.1109/CSCE60160.2023.00074

Karthikeyan, P., Pande, H. M., & Sarveshwaran, V. (Eds.). (2023). *Artificial intelligence and blockchain in digital forensics*. CRC Press.

Kasri, W., Himeur, Y., Alkhazaleh, H. A., Tarapiah, S., Atalla, S., Mansoor, W., & Al-Ahmad, H. (2025). From Vulnerability to Defense: The Role of Large Language Models in Enhancing Cybersecurity. *Computation (Basel, Switzerland), 13*(2), 30. DOI: 10.3390/computation13020030

Kelly, L., Sachan, S., Ni, L., Almaghrabi, F., Allmendinger, R., & Chen, Y. (2020). *Explainable artificial intelligence for digital forensics: opportunities, challenges and a drug testing case study*. Digital Forensic Science., DOI: 10.5772/intechopen.93310

Liu, Z. (2024, April). A review of advancements and applications of pre-trained language models in cybersecurity. In *2024 12th International Symposium on Digital Forensics and Security (ISDFS)* (pp. 1-10). IEEE. DOI: 10.1109/ISDFS60797.2024.10527236

Manasa, S., & Kumar, K. P. (2022). Digital forensics investigation for attacks on artificial intelligence. *ECS Transactions, 107*(1), 19639–19645. DOI: 10.1149/10701.19639ecst

Manoharan, A., & Sarker, M. (2023). Revolutionizing Cybersecurity: Unleashing the Power of Artificial Intelligence and Machine Learning for Next-Generation Threat Detection. *DOI:* https://www. doi. org/10.56726/IRJMETS32644, *1*.

. Mitchell, F. R. (2014). An overview of artificial intelligence based pattern matching in a security and digital forensic context. *Cyberpatterns: Unifying Design Patterns with Security and Attack Patterns*, 215-222.

Motlagh, F. N., Hajizadeh, M., Majd, M., Najafi, P., Cheng, F., & Meinel, C. (2024). Large language models in cybersecurity: State-of-the-art. *arXiv preprint arXiv:2402.00891*.

Moustafa, N. (2022). *Digital Forensics in the Era of Artificial Intelligence*. CRC Press. DOI: 10.1201/9781003278962

Nguyen, V., Mohammed, D., Omar, M., & Banisakher, M. (2018). The Effects of the FCC Net Neutrality Repeal on Security and Privacy. [IJHIoT]. *International Journal of Hyperconnectivity and the Internet of Things, 2*(2), 21–29. DOI: 10.4018/IJHIoT.2018070102

. Omar, M. (2021). New insights into database security: An effective and integrated approach for applying access control mechanisms and cryptographic concepts in Microsoft Access environments.

Omar, M. (2022). *Machine Learning for Cybersecurity: Innovative Deep Learning Solutions.* Springer Brief. https://link.springer.com/book/978303115

Omar, M. (2024). From Attack to Defense: Strengthening DNN Text Classification Against Adversarial Examples. In *Innovations, Securities, and Case Studies Across Healthcare, Business, and Technology* (pp. 174-195). IGI Global.

Omar, M. (2024). Revolutionizing Malware Detection: A Paradigm Shift Through Optimized Convolutional Neural Networks. In *Innovations, Securities, and Case Studies Across Healthcare, Business, and Technology* (pp. 196-220). IGI Global. DOI: 10.4018/979-8-3693-1906-2.ch011

Omar, M., & Zangana, H. (Eds.). (2025). *Digital Forensics in the Age of AI.* IGI Global., DOI: 10.4018/979-8-3373-0857-9

Omar, M., & Zangana, H. M. (Eds.). (2024). *Redefining Security With Cyber AI.* IGI Global., DOI: 10.4018/979-8-3693-6517-5

Omar, M., & Zangana, H. M. (Eds.). (2025). *Application of Large Language Models (LLMs) for Software Vulnerability Detection.* IGI Global., DOI: 10.4018/979-8-3693-9311-6

Omar, M., Zangana, H. M., Al-Karaki, J. N., & Mohammed, D. (2024). Harnessing LLMs for IoT malware detection: A comparative analysis of BERT and GPT-2. In *2024 8th International Symposium on Multidisciplinary Studies and Innovative Technologies (ISMSIT)* (pp. 1-6). Ankara, Turkiye. https://doi.org/DOI: 10.1109/ISMSIT63511.2024.10757249

Omar, M., Zangana, H. M., & Mohammed, D. (Eds.). (2025). *Integrating Artificial Intelligence in Cybersecurity and Forensic Practices.* IGI Global., DOI: 10.4018/979-8-3373-0588-2

Ozkan-Okay, M., Akin, E., Aslan, Ö., Kosunalp, S., Iliev, T., Stoyanov, I., & Beloev, I. (2024). A comprehensive survey: Evaluating the efficiency of artificial intelligence and machine learning techniques on cyber security solutions. *IEEE Access : Practical Innovations, Open Solutions, 12*, 12229–12256. DOI: 10.1109/ACCESS.2024.3355547

Pleshakova, E., Osipov, A., Gataullin, S., Gataullin, T., & Vasilakos, A. (2024). Next gen cybersecurity paradigm towards artificial general intelligence: Russian market challenges and future global technological trends. *Journal of Computer Virology and Hacking Techniques*, *20*(3), 429–440. DOI: 10.1007/s11416-024-00529-x

Rizvi, S., Scanlon, M., Mcgibney, J., & Sheppard, J. (2022). Application of artificial intelligence to network forensics: Survey, challenges and future directions. *IEEE Access : Practical Innovations, Open Solutions*, *10*, 110362–110384. DOI: 10.1109/ACCESS.2022.3214506

Rughani, P. H. (2017). Artificial Intelligence Based Digital Forensics Framework. *International Journal of Advanced Research in Computer Science*, *8*(8), 10–14. DOI: 10.26483/ijarcs.v8i8.4571

. Santos, O., Salam, S., & Dahir, H. (2024). The AI revolution in networking, cybersecurity, and emerging technologies.

Sarker, I. H. (2024). Generative AI and large language modeling in cybersecurity. In *AI-Driven Cybersecurity and Threat Intelligence: Cyber Automation, Intelligent Decision-Making and Explainability* (pp. 79–99). Springer Nature Switzerland. DOI: 10.1007/978-3-031-54497-2_5

Sikos, L. F. (2021). AI in digital forensics: Ontology engineering for cybercrime investigations. *WIREs Forensic Science*, *3*(3), e1394. DOI: 10.1002/wfs2.1394

. Taghavi, S. M., & Feyzi, F. (2024). Using large language models to better detect and handle software vulnerabilities and cyber security threats.

. THANDI, N. S. (2024). Revolutionizing Cyber Threat Detection With Large Language Models: A Privacy-Preserving BERT-Based Lightweight Model for IoT/IIoT Devices.

. Tyagi, A. K., Kumari, S., & Richa. (2024). Artificial Intelligence-Based Cyber Security and Digital Forensics: A Review. *Artificial Intelligence-Enabled Digital Twin for Smart Manufacturing*, 391-419.

Wright, J., Dawson, M. E.Jr, & Omar, M. (2012). Cyber security and mobile threats: The need for antivirus applications for smartphones. *Journal of Information Systems Technology and Planning*, *5*(14), 40–60.

Xu, H., Wang, S., Li, N., Wang, K., Zhao, Y., Chen, K., . . . Wang, H. (2024). Large language models for cyber security: A systematic literature review. *arXiv preprint arXiv:2405.04760*.

Yu, J., Shvetsov, A. V., & Alsamhi, S. H. (2024). Leveraging machine learning for cybersecurity resilience in industry 4.0: Challenges and future directions. *IEEE Access : Practical Innovations, Open Solutions, 12*, 159579–159596. DOI: 10.1109/ACCESS.2024.3482987

Zangana, H., & Omar, M. (Eds.). (2025). *Leveraging Large Language Models for Quantum-Aware Cybersecurity*. IGI Global., DOI: 10.4018/979-8-3373-1102-9

. Zangana, H. M. (2024). Exploring Blockchain-Based Timestamping Tools: A Comprehensive Review. *Redefining Security With Cyber AI*, 92-110.

. Zangana, H. M. (2024). Exploring Blockchain-Based Timestamping Tools: A Comprehensive Review. *Redefining Security With Cyber AI*, 92-110.

. Zangana, H. M. (2024). Exploring the Landscape of Website Vulnerability Scanners: A Comprehensive Review and Comparative Analysis. *Redefining Security With Cyber AI*, 111-129.

. Zangana, H. M. (2024). Harnessing the Power of Large Language Models. *Application of Large Language Models (LLMs) for Software Vulnerability Detection*, 1.

Zangana, H. M., & Li, S. (2025). Future Trends in AI and Digital Forensics. In Omar, M., & Zangana, H. (Eds.), *Digital Forensics in the Age of AI* (pp. 347–380). IGI Global Scientific Publishing., DOI: 10.4018/979-8-3373-0857-9.ch013

Zangana, H. M., & Li, S. (2025). Future Trends in AI and Digital Forensics. In *Digital Forensics in the Age of AI* (pp. 347–380). IGI Global Scientific Publishing.

Zangana, H. M., Mohammed, A. K., Sallow, A. B., & Sallow, Z. B. (2024). Cybernetic Deception: Unraveling the Layers of Email Phishing Threats. [INJURATECH]. *International Journal of Research and Applied Technology, 4*(1), 35–47.

Zangana, H. M., & Mohammed, D. (2025). Foundations of Large Language Models in Software Vulnerability Detection. In Omar, M., & Zangana, H. (Eds.), *Application of Large Language Models (LLMs) for Software Vulnerability Detection* (pp. 41–74). IGI Global., DOI: 10.4018/979-8-3693-9311-6.ch002

Zangana, H. M., & Mustafa, F. M. (2024). Hybrid Image Denoising Using Wavelet Transform and Deep Learning. *EAI Endorsed Transactions on AI and Robotics, 3*. Advance online publication. DOI: 10.4108/airo.7486

Zangana, H. M., & Mustafa, F. M. (2025). Image Denoising Techniques for Cybersecurity and Forensic Applications: AI-Driven Approaches. In Omar, M., Zangana, H., & Mohammed, D. (Eds.), *Integrating Artificial Intelligence in Cybersecurity and Forensic Practices* (pp. 117–142). IGI Global Scientific Publishing., DOI: 10.4018/979-8-3373-0588-2.ch005

Zangana, H. M., Mustafa, F. M., & Li, S. (2025). Large Language Models in Cybersecurity: From Automation to Intelligence. In Zangana, H., & Omar, M. (Eds.), *Leveraging Large Language Models for Quantum-Aware Cybersecurity* (pp. 277–300). IGI Global Scientific Publishing., DOI: 10.4018/979-8-3373-1102-9.ch009

Zangana, H. M., Mustafa, F. M., Li, S., & Al-Karaki, J. N. (2025). Natural Language Processing for Cyber Threat Intelligence in a Quantum World. In Zangana, H., & Omar, M. (Eds.), *Leveraging Large Language Models for Quantum-Aware Cybersecurity* (pp. 345–388). IGI Global Scientific Publishing., DOI: 10.4018/979-8-3373-1102-9.ch011

Zangana, H. M., Mustafa, F. M., & Omar, M. (2024). A Hybrid Approach for Robust Object Detection: Integrating Template Matching and Faster R-CNN. *EAI Endorsed Transactions on AI and Robotics, 3*. Advance online publication. DOI: 10.4108/airo.6858

Zangana, H. M., & Omar, M. (2020). Threats, Attacks, and Mitigations of Smartphone Security. *Academic Journal of Nawroz University, 9*(4), 324–332. DOI: 10.25007/ajnu.v9n4a989

Zangana, H. M., & Omar, M. (2025). Harnessing the Power of Large Language Models for Cybersecurity: Applications, Challenges, and Future Directions. In Omar, M., & Zangana, H. (Eds.), *Application of Large Language Models (LLMs) for Software Vulnerability Detection* (pp. 1–40). IGI Global., DOI: 10.4018/979-8-3693-9311-6.ch001

Zangana, H. M., & Omar, M. (2025). Introduction to Digital Forensics and Artificial Intelligence. In Omar, M., & Zangana, H. (Eds.), *Digital Forensics in the Age of AI* (pp. 1–30). IGI Global Scientific Publishing., DOI: 10.4018/979-8-3373-0857-9.ch001

Zangana, H. M., & Omar, M. (2025). Introduction to Quantum-Aware Cybersecurity: The Need for LLMs. In Zangana, H., & Omar, M. (Eds.), *Leveraging Large Language Models for Quantum-Aware Cybersecurity* (pp. 1–28). IGI Global Scientific Publishing., DOI: 10.4018/979-8-3373-1102-9.ch001

Zangana, H. M., & Omar, M. (2025). The Role of Leadership in Advancing Inclusive Health Technologies. In Burrell, D., & Nguyen, C. (Eds.), *New Horizons in Leadership: Inclusive Explorations in Health, Technology, and Education* (pp. 203–220). IGI Global Scientific Publishing., DOI: 10.4018/979-8-3693-6437-6.ch009

. Zangana, H. M., Omar, M., Al-Karaki, J. N., & Mohammed, D. (2024). Comprehensive Review and Analysis of Network Firewall Rule Analyzers: Enhancing Security Posture and Efficiency. *Redefining Security With Cyber AI*, 15-36.

Zangana, H. M., Sallow, Z. B., & Omar, M. (2025). The Human Factor in Cybersecurity: Addressing the Risks of Insider Threats. *Jurnal Ilmiah Computer Science*, *3*(2), 76–85. DOI: 10.58602/jics.v3i2.37

Chapter 11
Explainable AI in High-Stakes Forensic Decision-Making

Hermano Jorge Da Silva De Queiroz
https://orcid.org/0000-0001-6738-6321
Lindsey Wilson College, USA

ABSTRACT

In high-stakes forensic contexts—such as criminal investigations, counter-terrorism, and judicial processes—the use of artificial intelligence (AI) has expanded significantly. Yet, the opacity of many AI models, especially deep learning systems, raises serious concerns about trust, accountability, and legal admissibility. Explainable Artificial Intelligence (XAI) has become essential for enhancing transparency and interpretability in forensic environments. This chapter explores the theoretical foundations, leading methods, and real-world applications of XAI in digital forensics. It also addresses the ethical and legal implications of integrating XAI into forensic workflows and evaluates frameworks for balancing performance and interpretability. Case studies from law enforcement and cybersecurity highlight both the practical advantages and limitations of explainable models. Ultimately, the chapter advocates for a principled, context-aware approach to ensure AI-assisted decisions remain both accurate and understandable to human stakeholders.

INTRODUCTION

Artificial Intelligence (AI) is transforming the field of digital forensics, offering new tools and methodologies that improve the speed, accuracy, and scalability of forensic investigations. As digital crimes grow in complexity and volume, traditional

DOI: 10.4018/979-8-3373-6536-7.ch011

manual methods often fall short in delivering timely and actionable insights. AI-based systems have been increasingly adopted to fill this gap by automating routine tasks such as evidence classification, anomaly detection, and behavioral pattern analysis (Ganesh, 2017; Dunsin et al., 2022; Bhawna & Mahajan, 2024).

However, despite these advantages, a significant concern arises in high-stakes forensic and legal settings: the "black box" nature of many AI models. These opaque systems, especially those based on deep learning, offer limited transparency into how decisions are made, which can be problematic when those decisions affect legal outcomes or individual freedoms (Hall et al., 2022; Richmond et al., 2024; Sahoh & Choksuriwong, 2023). In such contexts, Explainable AI (XAI) becomes essential—not only to foster trust and accountability but also to comply with legal standards and ethical expectations (Kelly et al., 2020; Salah et al., 2025; Shamoo, 2025).

The integration of XAI into digital forensics represents a crucial evolution from data-driven automation toward intelligent, interpretable systems that can support judicial decision-making. Research has increasingly focused on how to design AI systems whose operations are transparent, auditable, and legally admissible (Costantini et al., 2019; Morić et al., 2025; Sikos, 2021). This is especially relevant as law enforcement agencies and forensic labs begin to rely on AI not only for backend analysis but also for courtroom presentations and evidence validation (Jarrett & Choo, 2021; Irons & Lallie, 2014; Adam & Varol, 2020).

Beyond legal considerations, explainability is critical for uncovering biases, errors, and adversarial manipulations in forensic AI tools (Omar, 2024; Gholami & Omar, 2023). These systems are vulnerable to attacks that exploit model weaknesses or manipulate data, potentially compromising investigations (Jeong, 2020; Omar, 2022). Thus, ensuring that forensic decisions are both accurate and interpretable is not merely a technical requirement—it is a safeguard against injustice.

Moreover, researchers have emphasized the importance of balancing model performance with interpretability in real-world deployments. For instance, while large language models (LLMs) and neural networks offer state-of-the-art accuracy, their inner workings often lack transparency (Gholami & Omar, 2024; Zangana & Mohammed, 2025). Efforts to improve their explainability include synthetic data usage, student-teacher model architectures, and post-hoc interpretability frameworks (Jones & Omar, 2024; Huff et al., 2023; Zangana & Omar, 2025).

AI is also being embedded in decision support systems for digital forensics, offering visualization tools, Bayesian reasoning frameworks, and automated auditing features (Moustafa, 2022; Manasa & Kumar, 2022; Mitchell, 2014). These tools empower investigators and judges to better understand complex forensic evidence, bridging the gap between technical analysis and human reasoning (Mohammed et al., 2018; Nguyen et al., 2018).

Furthermore, the implications of AI in forensic contexts extend to cybersecurity and incident response, where forensic tools must operate under constraints of time, resources, and adversarial behavior (Dunsin et al., 2024; Rizvi et al., 2022; Zangana et al., 2024). As systems become more interconnected, explainability is also crucial in understanding how attacks propagate across devices and networks (Wright et al., 2012; Hamza & Omar, 2013; Zangana & Omar, 2020).

This chapter aims to provide a comprehensive overview of Explainable AI (XAI) in high-stakes forensic decision-making. We begin by exploring foundational concepts in XAI and digital forensics. We then analyze existing models and frameworks through case studies and empirical research. The chapter also addresses legal and ethical implications, particularly focusing on evidence admissibility, bias detection, and accountability in AI-supported decisions (Tyagi et al., 2024; Karthikeyan et al., 2023; Jones et al., 2023). Finally, we present future research directions, including LLM-driven forensic analytics, XAI integration into judicial workflows, and AI governance in legal domains (Omar & Zangana, 2024; Zangana et al., 2025).

By emphasizing interpretability alongside technological advancement, this chapter argues for a paradigm shift—from opaque automation to transparent intelligence—in the application of AI to forensic science.

BACKGROUND AND MOTIVATION

The rapid proliferation of digital technologies has led to an exponential increase in cybercrime, digital evidence, and data complexity. To manage this influx and to maintain investigative efficiency, artificial intelligence (AI) has become a central tool in digital forensics and cybercrime investigations (Bhawna & Mahajan, 2024; Costantini et al., 2019). AI systems are now used in various forensic contexts—from automated malware detection and authorship attribution to real-time incident response (Jones et al., 2023; Iqbal et al., 2020). However, these AI tools, particularly black-box models like deep neural networks, present challenges in transparency, especially in high-stakes domains where the legal, ethical, and social consequences of errors are profound (Hall et al., 2022; Sahoh & Choksuriwong, 2023).

The motivation for embedding explainability into forensic AI systems arises from multiple dimensions. Firstly, forensic decisions often directly impact individuals' rights, such as determining guilt or innocence, influencing sentencing, or guiding national security actions. In such scenarios, the *interpretability* of AI models becomes as important as their predictive accuracy (Morić et al., 2025; Shamoo, 2025). The necessity to justify and scrutinize AI-generated conclusions is increasingly recognized by courts, policymakers, and oversight bodies, underscoring the role of Explainable Artificial Intelligence (XAI) in ensuring algorithmic accountability and legal admissibility (Richmond et al., 2024; Kelly et al., 2020).

Secondly, AI in digital forensics is evolving from a supportive analytical tool to a semi-autonomous decision-maker in evidence processing and cyberattack mitigation. Irons and Lallie (2014) introduced the concept of "intelligent forensics," in which AI plays a proactive role in discovering patterns, detecting anomalies, and even predicting criminal behavior. As such systems gain influence, the forensic community is grappling with the need to maintain a human-in-the-loop oversight model. XAI provides a crucial bridge by enabling human investigators to understand and challenge machine-generated results (Hall et al., 2022; Salah et al., 2025).

Thirdly, the opacity of AI models undermines trust—not only among forensic professionals but also within judicial systems and public perception. Forensic investigations are uniquely vulnerable to scrutiny, particularly in courtrooms, where the burden of proof is high and the demand for methodological transparency is legally binding (Jarrett & Choo, 2021; Shamoo, 2025). Judges, juries, and attorneys often lack the technical background to interpret complex model behavior. Hence, incorporating explainability ensures that AI tools can be translated into comprehensible, verifiable formats (Hall et al., 2022; Richmond et al., 2024).

Technological limitations in constrained environments further necessitate XAI. For instance, in scenarios involving limited computational resources—such as field operations or rapid-response forensics—models must be both lightweight and interpretable (Dunsin et al., 2022). The trade-off between complexity and transparency becomes more prominent in such cases, reinforcing the practical value of XAI (Dunsin et al., 2024).

Furthermore, the rise of generative models and large language models (LLMs) has transformed forensic capabilities in areas like phishing detection, authorship attribution, and zero-day attack mitigation (Zangana et al., 2024; Jones & Omar, 2024). While powerful, these models often require massive training data and suffer from a lack of transparency in decision rationale (Gholami & Omar, 2023, 2024). This has intensified concerns over hallucinations, bias, and adversarial manipulation in forensic settings (Omar, 2024; Zangana & Omar, 2025).

Existing frameworks in digital forensics often lag behind these innovations. Traditional forensic methods prioritize chain-of-custody, documentation, and manual validation (Adam & Varol, 2020), but integrating AI requires new standards for *explanation fidelity*, *decision traceability*, and *auditability* (Karthikeyan et al., 2023). Researchers like Moustafa (2022) and Sikos (2021) highlight the necessity of adapting forensic workflows to embrace AI without compromising evidentiary integrity.

Moreover, explainability has an ethical and societal dimension. As Omar and Zangana (2024) argue, AI systems in security contexts must be evaluated not just on performance but also on fairness, accountability, and transparency—pillars of trustworthy AI. Issues like bias against minority groups or misinterpretation of cultural context can have life-altering consequences if unaddressed in forensic investigations (Shamoo, 2025; Zangana et al., 2025).

Cybersecurity-focused research also underscores the strategic importance of explainable detection systems. Explainable AI has been applied to malware classification (Omar, 2024), sensor networks (Mohammed et al., 2018), and wireless threat detection (Zangana et al., 2025). In each case, interpretability serves as both a debugging tool and a compliance requirement, enhancing the reliability and repeatability of AI models in digital investigations (Mitchell, 2014; Wright et al., 2012).

This motivation is further intensified in forensic use cases involving cloud computing (Hamza & Omar, 2013), blockchain timestamping (Zangana, 2024), biotech forensics (Huff et al., 2023), and mobile device security (Zangana & Omar, 2020). In these domains, the complexity of environments demands AI tools that are not only capable but also explainable to multidisciplinary stakeholders—technologists, legal professionals, and policymakers alike.

The synergy of explainable AI and forensic science presents an opportunity to revolutionize evidence processing, legal deliberation, and cybercrime prevention. However, without robust explainability frameworks, the risks of *algorithmic opacity*, *false confidence*, and *judicial errors* remain high (Jeong, 2020; Manasa & Kumar, 2022; Rizvi et al., 2022). As such, the research and development of XAI in forensic contexts is not just a technical pursuit—it is a societal imperative.

Figure 1 illustrates the core components of Explainable AI systems relevant to forensic applications, including interpretable models, post-hoc explanation techniques, and user interfaces for human interaction.

Figure 1. Core components of explainable AI in forensic decision-making

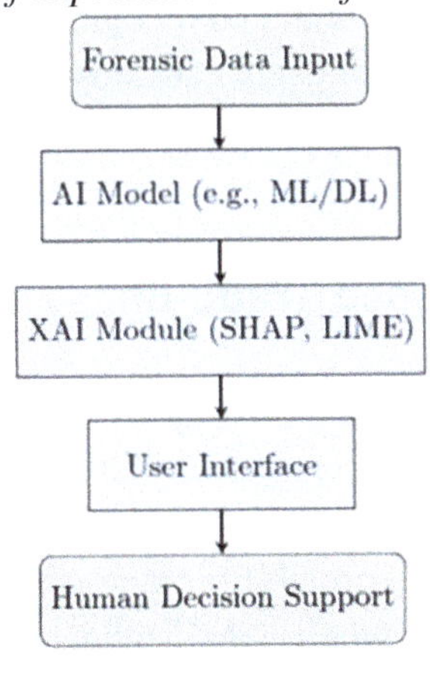

PRINCIPLES OF EXPLAINABILITY IN AI

The integration of artificial intelligence (AI) into digital forensics has brought significant advancements in speed, accuracy, and analytical depth. However, these benefits come with an inherent challenge: many AI systems, especially deep learning models, function as "black boxes," offering little to no insight into how decisions are made (Hall et al., 2022; Sahoh & Choksuriwong, 2023). In forensic contexts—where decisions may influence legal outcomes, individual rights, and public trust—this opacity is not merely a technical issue but a legal and ethical liability (Shamoo, 2025; Richmond et al., 2024).

Transparency and Interpretability

At the heart of explainable AI lies the principle of transparency—the ability to understand how an AI system reaches a decision—and interpretability, the degree to which a human can comprehend this process. These two principles form the backbone of AI trustworthiness in forensic science (Jarrett & Choo, 2021; Irons & Lallie, 2014). Transparent systems enable forensic investigators to identify algorithmic biases, cross-verify results, and communicate findings to non-technical stakeholders, including judges, juries, and policymakers (Hall et al., 2022).

Causality and Justifiability

An essential tenet of explainability is the principle of causality—linking cause and effect within the AI model. For example, a forensic image classifier must explain why specific visual cues led to a classification decision. This becomes critical in cases involving deception detection, facial recognition, or evidence triage (Salah et al., 2025; Kelly et al., 2020). Alongside causality, justifiability ensures that decisions made by AI can be defended based on legal standards and procedural fairness (Morić et al., 2025).

Simplicity vs. Performance Trade-off

Highly accurate models like deep neural networks are often less interpretable, while simpler models (e.g., decision trees or linear regressions) offer greater transparency at the cost of reduced performance (Bhawna & Mahajan, 2024; Costantini et al., 2019). This accuracy-interpretability trade-off must be carefully balanced in high-stakes forensic scenarios, where legal standards of evidence often prioritize explainability over raw predictive power (Rizvi et al., 2022).

Context-Awareness and Domain Sensitivity

For explainability to be effective, it must be tailored to the domain-specific context of forensic investigation (Iqbal et al., 2020; Ganesh, 2017). This involves adapting explanations to the unique needs of forensic domains—whether mobile device forensics, network forensics, or multimedia forensics (Jeong, 2020; Sikos, 2021). Additionally, systems should be sensitive to the operational constraints and resource limitations often found in real-world digital forensics environments (Dunsin et al., 2022; Dunsin et al., 2024).

Ethical and Legal Accountability

AI decisions in forensics may determine guilt or innocence, making ethical accountability paramount. XAI provides mechanisms to audit decisions, detect biases, and ensure compliance with regulatory standards (Omar & Zangana, 2024; Karthikeyan et al., 2023). This aligns with the broader movement toward intelligent forensics—where AI augments, rather than replaces, human judgment (Adam & Varol, 2020; Manasa & Kumar, 2022).

Human-Centered Design

Human-centric explainability involves designing systems where explanations are understandable to the end-user, whether they are forensic analysts, judges, or jurors (Hamza & Omar, 2013; Shamoo, 2025). This extends beyond technical clarity to include cognitive and psychological dimensions, ensuring that explanations align with how humans process information and make decisions (Hall et al., 2022; Huff et al., 2023).

Traceability and Auditability

Another foundational principle is traceability—the ability to trace every AI decision back to the original data and rationale (Mitchell, 2014; Rughani, 2017). Traceability supports forensic soundness, ensuring that digital evidence and AI analyses are reproducible, verifiable, and admissible in court (Moustafa, 2022; Adam & Varol, 2020).

Robustness Against Adversarial Attacks

Explainability also contributes to robustness by exposing weaknesses in AI systems that could be exploited by adversaries (Omar, 2024a; Mohammed et al.,

2018). For instance, adversarial inputs could manipulate evidence classification. A transparent model would allow forensic experts to identify such vulnerabilities, enhancing system resilience (Omar, 2024b; Gholami & Omar, 2023).

Integrability with Legal Standards and Casework

XAI in digital forensics must be designed with legal compatibility in mind. Models must produce explanations that align with standards of due process, chain of custody, and evidentiary reliability (Tyagi et al., 2024; Richmond et al., 2024). AI must serve as a tool of augmentation, not automation, in judicial and law enforcement contexts (Jones & Omar, 2024; Zangana & Omar, 2020).

Explainability Across Model Types

Explainability techniques vary widely depending on whether the underlying model is rule-based, probabilistic, or neural. For example, Bayesian networks offer inherently interpretable structures suitable for judicial decision-making (Morić et al., 2025), while deep models require post hoc interpretability tools like LIME, SHAP, or attention visualization (Gholami & Omar, 2024; Omar, 2022). The choice of XAI technique must align with both the technical and procedural demands of the forensic task.

This section has introduced the foundational principles guiding explainability in AI, particularly as applied to digital forensics and high-stakes decision-making. These principles are not only technical mandates but also ethical, legal, and operational imperatives. Future sections will explore how these principles are operationalized through tools, techniques, and real-world forensic applications.

Figure 2 presents a step-by-step flow of how explainable AI can be integrated into forensic investigations, from evidence intake to human judgment.

Figure 2. Workflow of explainable AI in forensic investigations

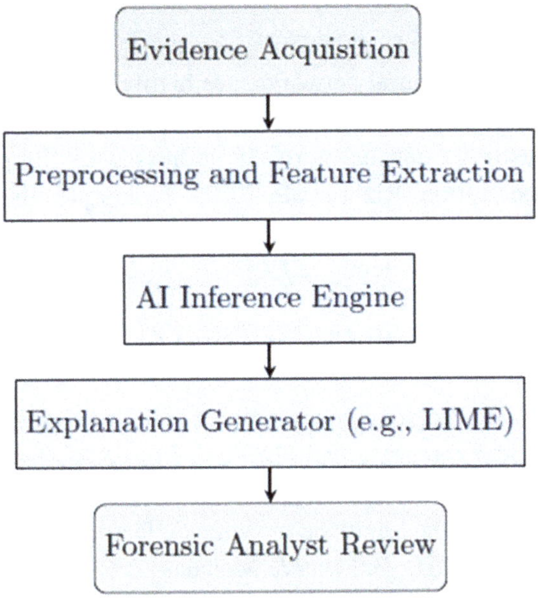

APPLICATIONS OF XAI IN DIGITAL FORENSICS

The field of digital forensics has undergone a paradigm shift due to the integration of Artificial Intelligence (AI), with Explainable AI (XAI) emerging as a cornerstone for ensuring transparency, accountability, and legal admissibility in high-stakes scenarios. In digital forensic investigations—where evidence must withstand legal scrutiny—XAI plays a crucial role in making AI-generated insights interpretable by investigators, legal professionals, and courts (Hall et al., 2022; Shamoo, 2025).

Case Prioritization and Triage

AI has proven invaluable in handling the volume and velocity of digital evidence. By integrating XAI into triage tools, investigators can not only automate the sorting of high-priority cases but also understand the rationale behind such prioritizations (Jarrett & Choo, 2021; Adam & Varol, 2020). For example, an explainable model can highlight patterns of abnormal user behavior that correspond with insider threats, providing both a risk score and interpretable indicators such as login anomalies or unusual data transfers (Dunsin et al., 2022).

Automated Log Analysis and Anomaly Detection

System and network logs are critical in tracing cyber incidents. Machine learning models, particularly deep neural networks, are highly effective but often opaque. The incorporation of XAI frameworks enables forensic professionals to trace which specific log features (e.g., unusual ports, IP addresses, or file paths) contributed to an anomaly classification (Rizvi et al., 2022). Techniques like SHAP values or LIME can pinpoint influential features, enabling faster and more reliable incident response (Dunsin et al., 2024; Jeong, 2020).

Authorship Attribution and Behavioral Analysis

Behavioral forensics, including authorship attribution in cyberstalking, malware development, or insider threats, greatly benefits from XAI. Traditional black-box models may identify the author of a suspicious document or code segment, but XAI frameworks can highlight the linguistic or syntactic features that contributed to this conclusion (Iqbal et al., 2020; Bhawna & Mahajan, 2024). This interpretability is crucial in court proceedings, where forensic conclusions must be defensible.

Malware and Threat Detection

With the increasing sophistication of malware, static and dynamic analyses are often complemented with AI. XAI is essential in explaining why a particular binary is classified as malicious—whether due to API call patterns, obfuscation techniques, or payload structures (Omar, 2024; Jones et al., 2023). This approach not only aids in threat detection but also supports reverse engineering for attribution and mitigation (Ganesh, 2017; Mitchell, 2014).

Network Forensics and Packet Inspection

Network traffic analysis using deep learning can be effective but lacks transparency. XAI helps bridge this gap by enabling forensic investigators to visualize why certain packets or flows were deemed suspicious, such as specific byte sequences, timing anomalies, or protocol deviations (Costantini et al., 2019; Zangana, Omar, Al-Karaki, & Mohammed, 2024). This insight is particularly valuable for threat hunting in complex network environments (Mohammed et al., 2018; Rizvi et al., 2022).

Judicial Decision Support Systems

Explainable models are now being used to support decision-making in judicial and legal contexts. Bayesian networks and interpretable machine learning techniques help model evidentiary relationships and suggest outcomes based on historical rulings, while still allowing human oversight (Morić et al., 2025; Richmond et al., 2024). These tools are especially important in preventing cognitive bias and promoting fairness in digital forensic interpretations (Sahoh & Choksuriwong, 2023).

Digital Evidence Chain of Custody

XAI can be integrated with blockchain systems to create transparent and immutable records of how digital evidence is handled and analyzed (Zangana, 2024). When combined with explainable AI, such systems ensure that the rationale behind every analytical step—from acquisition to reporting—is documented, auditable, and understandable (Karthikeyan et al., 2023; Irons & Lallie, 2014).

Cloud and Mobile Forensics

Given the complexity of cloud-based environments, forensic investigations must often navigate decentralized, encrypted, and dynamic datasets. XAI models can assist by identifying forensic artifacts across cloud logs and mobile platforms while explaining the decision-making behind linkages between users, devices, and activities (Hamza & Omar, 2013; Zangana & Omar, 2020; Dunsin et al., 2022). Similarly, explainable intrusion detection systems can enhance mobile forensics by flagging malicious apps or unauthorized access events with clear justifications (Wright et al., 2012).

LLM-Based Forensic Tools

Large Language Models (LLMs), like GPT, are being increasingly used in digital forensics for tasks such as summarizing forensic reports, generating hypotheses, and interacting with evidence databases (Zangana & Omar, 2025; Omar, 2022). XAI becomes indispensable when these models are employed in high-stakes environments. By using distilled models and attention-based visualization, investigators can trace which tokens or sentence structures influenced a generated output (Gholami & Omar, 2023; 2024).

Cybersecurity-Forensics Convergence

The fusion of AI in cybersecurity and forensics is leading to unified platforms that monitor, detect, and investigate cybercrimes. Explainable AI in these systems ensures that cyber incidents—such as phishing, ransomware, or insider threats—are not just detected but are also comprehensively interpreted, increasing trust and facilitating collaboration between SOCs (Security Operations Centers) and forensic analysts (Jones & Omar, 2024; Zangana et al., 2025; Huff et al., 2023; Zangana, Mohammed, Sallow, & Sallow, 2024).

Table 1 highlights key differences between traditional black-box AI systems and explainable AI models, particularly in the context of forensic reliability and transparency.

Table 1. Black-box vs explainable AI in forensic applications

Aspect	Black-Box AI	Explainable AI
Transparency	Low	High
Interpretability	None	Yes
Trust in Decision	Low	High
Regulatory Compliance	Difficult	Easier
Suitable for High-Stakes?	Risky	Preferred

TECHNIQUES AND TOOLS FOR EXPLAINABLE AI

Explainable Artificial Intelligence (XAI) encompasses a diverse range of models, methods, and frameworks designed to provide transparency, interpretability, and accountability in AI-based decision-making systems. In digital forensics—where decisions can lead to legal actions, criminal charges, or national security consequences—the use of explainable tools is not just a technical requirement but an ethical imperative (Hall et al., 2022; Shamoo, 2025). This section explores the primary techniques and tools that make XAI viable for digital forensic applications.

Post-Hoc Interpretability Techniques

Post-hoc approaches aim to explain decisions made by already trained complex models. These include tools such as:

- LIME (Local Interpretable Model-Agnostic Explanations): Generates local approximations of model behavior, helpful in justifying forensic clas-

sifications like malware detection or fraud prediction (Kelly et al., 2020; Jeong, 2020).
- SHAP (SHapley Additive exPlanations): Uses game-theoretic approaches to attribute importance to features. This is especially valuable when investigating anomalies in network forensics (Rizvi et al., 2022) or identifying evidence attributes in large forensic datasets (Dunsin et al., 2022).

These tools empower investigators to understand why a model classified a log entry as malicious, or a user behavior as suspicious, without requiring deep technical knowledge of the model internals (Costantini et al., 2019).

Intrinsically Interpretable Models

While deep learning and ensemble models often yield higher accuracy, simpler models such as decision trees, rule-based systems, and Bayesian networks offer built-in explainability:

- Bayesian Decision Networks: Used in judicial decision-support systems to model probabilistic reasoning with transparency (Morić et al., 2025).
- Rule-based engines: Efficient in attributing actions to suspects in mobile or IoT environments, and explaining incident causes in simple logical statements (Irons & Lallie, 2014; Tyagi et al., 2024).

Interpretable models are particularly useful when operating in environments constrained by computational resources or legal compliance (Adam & Varol, 2020; Bhawna & Mahajan, 2024).

Visualization and Attention Mechanisms

Tools that offer visual explanations of decisions, such as heatmaps or attention visualizations, are critical in forensic analysis of texts, images, or video:

- In authorship attribution, attention mechanisms highlight linguistic patterns indicative of a suspect's identity (Iqbal et al., 2020).
- In deception detection and behavioral forensics, attention-based models can focus on facial cues or sentence patterns, making models explain what visual or auditory features led to detection (Salah et al., 2025).
- Large language models (LLMs), including distilled or student-teacher versions, can now visualize attention layers to explain classification outcomes in threat intelligence (Gholami & Omar, 2023, 2024).

Counterfactual and Contrastive Reasoning

Counterfactual explanations describe how changing specific inputs would alter the output of a model. For example, in a forensic triage tool, a counterfactual might show that removing one suspicious file from a system would have reduced the risk score from "critical" to "medium" (Dunsin et al., 2024; Manasa & Kumar, 2022).

Contrastive explanations, on the other hand, answer "why this and not that?"—a form of reasoning critical in legal contexts where forensic experts must justify why one suspect was flagged over another (Sahoh & Choksuriwong, 2023; Richmond et al., 2024).

Model-Agnostic Frameworks for XAI

XAI libraries and toolkits have been developed to work across a variety of machine learning models:

- AI Explainability 360 (IBM), What-If Tool (Google), and ELI5 are popular in academic and industry applications.
- These frameworks support model audits, fairness evaluations, and provide graphical interfaces that non-technical forensic professionals can use (Jarrett & Choo, 2021; Jones et al., 2023).

Model-agnostic tools are especially useful in security operation centers (SOCs) and incident response teams, where AI tools are applied rapidly across different domains (Mohammed et al., 2018; Huff et al., 2023).

Blockchain-Integrated XAI Systems

In recent years, explainable AI has been integrated with blockchain technologies to support digital chain-of-custody requirements. This combination allows forensic tools to not only explain their decisions but to timestamp and verify the audit trails of those decisions (Karthikeyan et al., 2023; Zangana, 2024).

Blockchain-enhanced XAI ensures forensic tools remain tamper-resistant, and all automated decisions can be traced back to an immutable source—vital in forensic accountability (Hamza & Omar, 2013).

Domain-Specific AI Platforms

The development of domain-specific platforms integrating explainable AI and digital forensics is accelerating:

- GEADD (GPT-2 Enhanced Attack Detection and Defense): A custom framework developed for detecting zero-day threats using LLMs with interpretable attention and token-weight explanations (Jones & Omar, 2024).
- Tools that use ontology-based reasoning, such as those proposed by Sikos (2021), provide semantic interpretation layers on top of AI models, allowing evidence to be linked contextually and explained through legal and forensic ontologies.

Forensic-Focused XAI in LLMs

Large Language Models (LLMs) are increasingly used in forensic intelligence gathering, evidence summarization, and database querying (Omar & Zangana, 2025; Zangana & Mohammed, 2025). Recent innovations include:

- Student-teacher architectures where smaller models mimic larger ones while retaining interpretability (Gholami & Omar, 2024).
- Hybrid systems that fuse LLMs with symbolic AI, providing high accuracy with traceable inference steps (Zangana & Omar, 2025).

Explainability in these models ensures that generated insights—such as threat assessments or forensic summaries—can be audited and justified in court or policy settings.

Integration into Cloud and Mobile Forensics

As forensic investigations shift to cloud-native and mobile-first ecosystems, explainable AI techniques are being tailored to fit these environments. Lightweight, interpretable models and visual explanations are embedded into cloud forensics dashboards to detect abuse or unauthorized access (Hamza & Omar, 2013; Zangana & Omar, 2020).

This integration is essential for time-sensitive investigations in dynamic environments such as corporate breaches, ransomware attacks, or mobile surveillance cases (Wright et al., 2012; Zangana et al., 2024).

Autonomous and Self-Adaptive Systems

With AI-driven forensic platforms evolving toward autonomy, explainability becomes a safeguard against unintended consequences or algorithmic bias (Mitchell, 2014; Ganesh, 2017). Self-adaptive agents that change behavior in real-time—for example, to prioritize emerging threats—must be auditable and explainable at all times (Nguyen et al., 2018).

Explainable autonomous systems are being implemented in AI-enhanced deception detection, biometric surveillance, and cyber deception analysis, with the ability to explain behavioral triggers, rule activations, and model updates in human-readable language (Rughani, 2017; Zangana, Mohammed, H. S., & Husain, 2025).

Summary

Explainable AI techniques and tools have become essential in digital forensics, offering transparency, fairness, and legal admissibility. From visual explanations and counterfactuals to blockchain-integrated and LLM-powered platforms, the landscape is rapidly evolving to meet the complex needs of high-stakes forensic environments. Future research should focus on improving scalability, contextual adaptability, and cross-disciplinary integration of XAI in forensic workflows (Omar, 2022; Moustafa, 2022; Omar & Zangana, 2024).

Figure 3 categorizes major explainability techniques used in AI models and compares their interpretability and complexity.

Figure 3. Interpretability of popular XAI techniques in forensic use

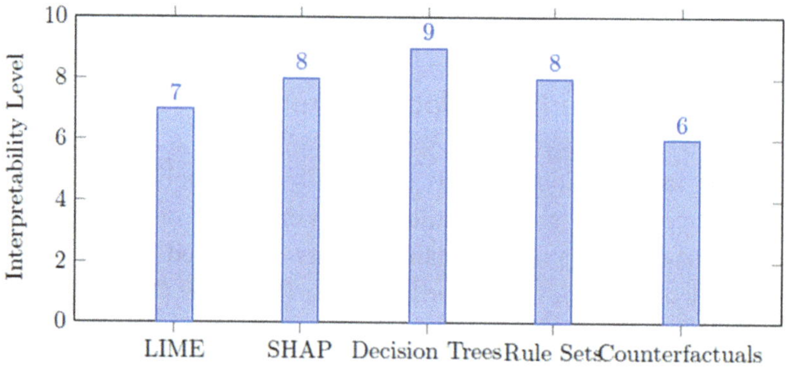

LEGAL AND ETHICAL IMPLICATIONS

The deployment of Explainable Artificial Intelligence (XAI) in digital forensics raises significant legal and ethical questions that are central to the credibility, admissibility, and fairness of forensic outcomes in both criminal and civil proceedings.

While AI systems offer transformative advantages in efficiency and accuracy, they simultaneously introduce challenges concerning accountability, privacy, transparency, and due process (Hall et al., 2022; Richmond et al., 2024; Shamoo, 2025).

Legal Admissibility and Evidentiary Standards

In forensic contexts, the admissibility of evidence is governed by legal frameworks that demand reliability, relevance, and explainability. Black-box AI models, which lack interpretability, may be rejected in court due to their inability to demonstrate causality or reasoning (Sahoh & Choksuriwong, 2023; Richmond et al., 2024). XAI provides a potential remedy by offering traceable and comprehensible decision paths, enabling judges and juries to assess the probative value of AI-assisted findings (Morić et al., 2025).

For example, digital artifacts extracted using XAI can clearly indicate the logical progression from input evidence (such as file hashes or user behavior) to output conclusions (e.g., user attribution or intent). This transparency strengthens the evidentiary value of AI tools under frameworks like Daubert or Frye standards (Adam & Varol, 2020; Iqbal et al., 2020).

Accountability and Human Oversight

AI-driven forensic tools may obscure accountability, especially when decision-making is automated. The ethical principle of accountability requires that a responsible human operator must be able to explain and justify the system's outcomes (Jarrett & Choo, 2021; Costantini et al., 2019). This is particularly critical in high-stakes scenarios such as criminal investigations, where wrongful accusations or convictions may occur if AI systems operate without adequate oversight (Ganesh, 2017; Kelly et al., 2020).

XAI supports the reintroduction of human interpretability into AI-driven systems, allowing digital forensic practitioners to intervene and audit model behaviors. Legal accountability is further enhanced when logs, reasoning pathways, and parameters used by AI systems are retained as part of the chain of custody (Irons & Lallie, 2014; Karthikeyan et al., 2023).

Bias, Fairness, and Discrimination

Algorithmic bias remains one of the most pressing ethical concerns in the application of AI to digital forensics. Biases can emerge from skewed training data, flawed labeling, or inadequate representation of demographics (Tyagi et al., 2024; Salah et al., 2025). In law enforcement, these biases can disproportionately impact marginalized communities, potentially leading to discriminatory practices or decisions (Shamoo, 2025).

XAI provides tools to inspect and mitigate such biases by exposing the variables and logic contributing to specific classifications or decisions (Jeong, 2020). For instance, SHAP or LIME explanations can reveal whether ethnicity, location, or social media behavior are unfairly influencing forensic models (Jones et al., 2023; Omar, 2024).

Privacy and Data Protection

Forensic investigations often require access to highly sensitive personal data—emails, location history, cloud logs, and biometric identifiers. AI systems, particularly LLMs, may inadvertently store or expose such data, raising concerns over compliance with regulations like the GDPR, HIPAA, or other data protection laws (Hamza & Omar, 2013; Mohammed et al., 2018; Nguyen et al., 2018).

XAI contributes to more privacy-conscious AI by enabling selective transparency, where explanations are provided without exposing sensitive or irrelevant personal data (Gholami & Omar, 2023). Furthermore, synthetic data approaches, as explored by Gholami and Omar (2023, 2024), can preserve utility while minimizing privacy risks.

Intellectual Property and Model Transparency

Another legal issue concerns proprietary AI systems used in forensics. When vendors protect their models as trade secrets, forensic experts and defendants may be denied access to vital technical details, raising questions about the right to a fair trial (Moustafa, 2022; Bhawna & Mahajan, 2024). XAI necessitates that at least partial transparency is achieved—even if source code is proprietary—by providing explanation layers or audit logs (Zangana & Omar, 2025).

The growing application of blockchain in forensic data provenance further reinforces transparency and trust, as proposed by Zangana (2024) and Karthikeyan et al. (2023), providing immutable and timestamped records of evidence handling.

Ethical Use of AI for Surveillance and Investigation

Ethically, the line between lawful surveillance and violation of civil liberties is increasingly blurred by AI's capability to automate monitoring at scale (Wright et al., 2012; Dunsin et al., 2024). Facial recognition, device fingerprinting, and behavioral profiling—when enhanced by XAI—require stringent ethical scrutiny to ensure proportionality, legality, and necessity (Bhawna & Mahajan, 2024; Huff et al., 2023).

Ethical frameworks must be in place to determine when and how such powerful tools should be deployed, and XAI can help ensure transparency in justifying such decisions (Rughani, 2017; Sikos, 2021).

Legal Implications of LLMs in Forensic Practice

The use of Large Language Models (LLMs) in summarizing forensic reports or generating investigative leads presents unique legal challenges. Questions arise regarding the originality, reliability, and legal status of LLM-generated content (Zangana & Omar, 2025; Gholami & Omar, 2024). Furthermore, hallucination—where LLMs fabricate plausible but incorrect information—poses ethical risks if such outputs are uncritically accepted in court (Omar, 2022; Jones & Omar, 2024).

As LLMs become integral to forensic analysis, explainability is essential. Visual tools and token attribution mechanisms can illustrate how decisions were derived, thus aligning with legal expectations of transparency and cross-examination (Zangana et al., 2025).

Cybersecurity and Trust in AI Forensics

AI systems themselves are vulnerable to manipulation. Adversarial inputs, model poisoning, or unauthorized access to training datasets can lead to compromised forensic conclusions (Omar, 2024; Zangana, Mohammed, & Husain, 2025). The ethical duty of forensic investigators includes ensuring the integrity of AI systems and resisting external manipulation (Mitchell, 2014; Manasa & Kumar, 2022).

Building trustworthy AI includes ensuring model robustness, ethical audits, and ongoing validation—all supported by XAI techniques that allow investigators to detect irregularities and ensure models behave as expected (Zangana, Sallow, & Mustafa, 2025).

The Venn diagram in Figure 4 highlights the intersection between ethics, law, and technical accuracy in designing XAI systems for high-stakes forensic settings.

Figure 4. Intersection of ethical, legal, and technical considerations in XAI

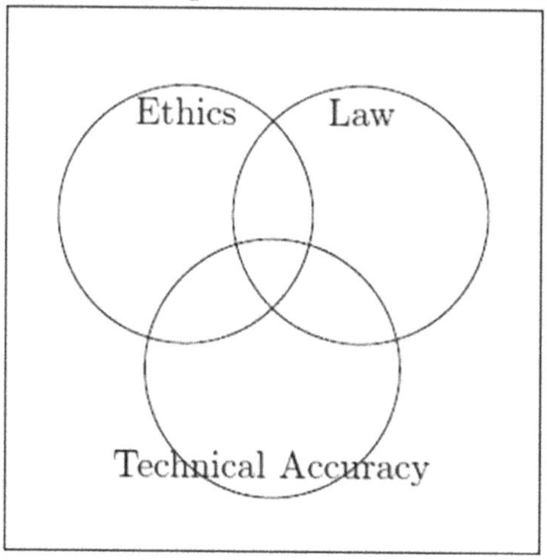

CHALLENGES AND LIMITATIONS

Despite the promising capabilities of Explainable Artificial Intelligence (XAI) in digital forensics, several technical, operational, legal, and ethical challenges impede its seamless adoption. As AI becomes increasingly integrated into forensic workflows, issues related to reliability, scalability, bias, model security, and explainability fidelity have emerged as significant concerns (Hall et al., 2022; Dunsin et al., 2024; Costantini et al., 2019). Understanding these limitations is vital for ensuring that AI-enhanced forensic tools do not compromise judicial integrity, user privacy, or investigative accuracy.

Black-Box Nature and Limited Interpretability

Despite advances in XAI techniques such as SHAP, LIME, and saliency maps, many high-performing models, especially deep neural networks and large language models (LLMs), remain difficult to interpret at a forensic level (Sahoh & Choksuriwong, 2023; Zangana & Omar, 2025). These models may provide confidence scores or feature importance rankings, but often fail to convey human-readable justifications that are legally admissible or useful to investigators (Ganesh, 2017; Morić et al., 2025).

Moreover, XAI methods themselves are approximations and may introduce their own errors, thereby creating a false sense of transparency (Kelly et al., 2020).

As Richmond et al. (2024) caution, overly complex or mathematically obscure explanations could reduce judicial trust, especially when forensic evidence must be scrutinized by non-technical stakeholders.

Data Bias and Fairness Concerns

AI systems inherit biases from their training data, which can result in flawed or discriminatory outcomes (Tyagi et al., 2024; Salah et al., 2025). In forensic investigations, such biases can skew attribution, misidentify suspects, or reinforce systemic discrimination, especially in biometric forensics and behavioral profiling (Shamoo, 2025; Jeong, 2020).

Efforts to mitigate these biases using synthetic data have shown promise (Gholami & Omar, 2023, 2024), yet challenges remain in validating whether such data truly represents real-world variability. As Dunsin et al. (2022) emphasize, constrained environments, such as those in low-resource or cross-border investigations, further limit the availability of representative datasets.

Incomplete Automation and Human Dependence

While automation enhances the speed and efficiency of digital forensics, complete reliance on AI is both infeasible and dangerous. Human expertise remains critical in interpreting nuanced digital artifacts, validating system outputs, and contextualizing findings within legal frameworks (Jarrett & Choo, 2021; Irons & Lallie, 2014).

The integration of AI into forensic workflows often results in hybrid systems that may produce conflicting or ambiguous results without robust explainability (Iqbal et al., 2020). As Rughani (2017) notes, the human-AI collaboration is not yet mature enough to ensure consistent, reliable, and interpretable outcomes in high-stakes cases.

Security Vulnerabilities in AI Models

AI models are vulnerable to adversarial attacks, including data poisoning, model inversion, and evasion techniques, which can corrupt forensic conclusions (Manasa & Kumar, 2022; Omar, 2024). For instance, carefully crafted input perturbations can cause misclassifications in malware detection systems (Omar, 2024), while backdoored models may leak sensitive investigation data (Zangana et al., 2025).

Such threats undermine forensic integrity and demand robust defenses such as adversarial training, secure model deployment, and ongoing validation (Mitchell, 2014; Zangana et al., 2024). Huff et al. (2023) also highlight the growing cybersecurity risks in biotechnology and healthcare forensics, where AI is increasingly adopted.

Resource Constraints and Infrastructure Gaps

Deploying XAI systems requires substantial computational resources, skilled personnel, and ongoing model maintenance, which many forensic units—particularly in developing regions—struggle to meet (Dunsin et al., 2022; Bhawna & Mahajan, 2024). The training and fine-tuning of LLMs, for example, are resource-intensive and may be economically prohibitive without cloud-based infrastructure (Hamza & Omar, 2013).

Moreover, edge computing environments such as mobile forensics or on-site crime scene analysis may lack the necessary hardware to support real-time inference or explanation generation (Rizvi et al., 2022; Zangana & Omar, 2020).

Regulatory, Legal, and Ethical Gaps

The regulatory environment surrounding AI in forensics remains fragmented and underdeveloped. Questions persist regarding the legal admissibility of XAI-derived evidence, particularly when the model logic is not fully disclosed due to intellectual property concerns (Moustafa, 2022; Zangana & Mohammed, 2025). Furthermore, XAI's role in supporting or contesting expert testimony is not yet clearly defined in many jurisdictions (Adam & Varol, 2020; Richmond et al., 2024).

Ethically, the deployment of AI tools for mass surveillance or behavioral prediction may infringe upon civil liberties, especially when users are unaware of such tools being used against them (Wright et al., 2012; Sikos, 2021; Huff et al., 2023). The lack of universal standards for ethical AI deployment in forensics exacerbates this risk (Nguyen et al., 2018).

Fragility of Explanations in Real-World Scenarios

XAI methods may offer useful insights under controlled conditions but can falter under real-world variability. Forensic datasets often contain noise, incomplete logs, encrypted data, or obfuscated evidence, which may hinder accurate model interpretation (Jones et al., 2023; Omar, 2022). Additionally, explanations generated for one instance may not generalize to similar cases, leading to inconsistency and investigative delays (Zangana, 2024).

Furthermore, forensic models designed for specific domains—such as phishing detection (Zangana et al., 2024) or firewall rule analysis (Zangana et al., 2024)—may not translate well across other forensic applications, limiting scalability and interoperability.

Challenges with Large Language Models in Forensics

LLMs present unique limitations, including hallucination (producing plausible but incorrect outputs), data leakage, and misinterpretation of prompts (Jones & Omar, 2024; Zangana & Omar, 2025). While LLMs like GPT-2 and newer variants have been proposed for tasks such as vulnerability detection (Omar & Zangana, 2025), their unexplainable nature can compromise forensic trustworthiness.

Recent work suggests that LLMs can be optimized with synthetic data and pruning strategies (Gholami & Omar, 2023), but even "student" models require rigorous forensic validation before deployment (Gholami & Omar, 2024). Without appropriate guardrails, these models risk being exploited or misunderstood in legal contexts.

Lack of Standardization and Benchmarking

There is a noticeable absence of standardized metrics for evaluating the explainability, accuracy, and legal viability of XAI tools in digital forensics (Kelly et al., 2020; Rizvi et al., 2022). While some researchers propose domain-specific benchmarks (Bhawna & Mahajan, 2024), a unified, interdisciplinary framework is still lacking. This hinders reproducibility, cross-agency collaboration, and public trust.

As Karthikeyan et al. (2023) and Zangana et al. (2025) argue, integrating blockchain for evidence traceability and AI transparency could partially mitigate this issue. However, such frameworks are still in early stages of development and lack widespread adoption.

FUTURE DIRECTIONS

The future of artificial intelligence (AI) in digital forensics and cybersecurity is promising yet complex, with a growing emphasis on enhancing explainability, robustness, and practical integration into forensic workflows. As the digital landscape continues to evolve, ongoing research and development are focused on overcoming current limitations while addressing emerging threats. This section outlines the key future directions shaping the intersection of AI and digital forensics, highlighting advances in technology, methodology, and governance.

Advancement in Explainable AI (XAI) for Forensics

One of the foremost future directions is the refinement of explainable AI techniques tailored specifically for forensic applications. While current XAI models provide some transparency, they often lack the precision and legal acceptability needed in high-stakes environments (Hall, Sakzad, & Choo, 2022; Kelly et al., 2020). Research is increasingly focusing on developing domain-specific explanation frameworks that enhance the interpretability of complex models such as deep neural networks and large language models (LLMs) without sacrificing accuracy (Sahoh & Choksuriwong, 2023; Salah et al., 2025).

These explainability improvements will empower forensic experts, legal professionals, and juries to better understand AI-driven evidence, fostering trust and accountability (Richmond et al., 2024). Moreover, frameworks integrating human-in-the-loop mechanisms promise to balance automated efficiency with expert oversight (Adam & Varol, 2020; Jarrett & Choo, 2021).

Integration of Large Language Models (LLMs) and Synthetic Data

LLMs have shown remarkable capabilities in natural language understanding and generation, opening new avenues for automating forensic tasks such as evidence summarization, threat intelligence analysis, and vulnerability detection (Jones & Omar, 2024; Omar & Zangana, 2025). However, to mitigate issues of hallucination, bias, and data privacy, synthetic data generation has emerged as a complementary strategy to improve model robustness and efficiency (Gholami & Omar, 2023, 2024).

Future research will likely explore optimized training pipelines where student models are distilled from teacher LLMs, allowing for lightweight, more explainable forensic tools (Zangana & Mohammed, 2025; Zangana & Omar, 2025). Combining LLMs with blockchain-based timestamping and audit trails will also enhance evidence integrity and non-repudiation (Zangana, 2024).

AI-Driven Automation and Incident Response

The surge in cyber threats demands rapid and accurate forensic response capabilities. AI-powered automation frameworks that incorporate machine learning (ML) and pattern recognition are increasingly vital for real-time incident detection and mitigation (Dunsin, Ghanem, & Quazzane, 2022; Jones et al., 2023). Future digital forensic systems are expected to leverage hybrid AI architectures combining supervised and unsupervised learning to detect novel attack vectors and zero-day exploits more effectively (Jones & Omar, 2024; Omar, 2024).

Additionally, constrained environments, including edge and IoT devices, will benefit from lightweight AI models optimized for limited computational resources, facilitating decentralized and scalable forensic investigations (Dunsin et al., 2024; Rizvi et al., 2022).

Enhanced Cybersecurity Through AI Collaboration

AI's role in cybersecurity continues to expand beyond detection to include proactive defense, vulnerability management, and adaptive threat intelligence (Huff et al., 2023; Tyagi, Kumari, & Richa, 2024). Future research aims to develop AI systems that collaboratively work across organizational boundaries, sharing threat intelligence securely using privacy-preserving techniques and federated learning (Karthikeyan, Pande, & Sarveshwaran, 2023).

These advances will improve the resilience of critical infrastructures, such as healthcare and financial institutions, by integrating AI-driven forensic insights directly into cybersecurity operations (Mohammed, Omar, & Nguyen, 2018; Zangana, Mohammed, & Husain, 2025).

Addressing Ethical, Legal, and Regulatory Challenges

As AI systems permeate forensic investigations, future work must address the legal admissibility, privacy concerns, and ethical implications of AI-generated evidence (Moustafa, 2022; Shamoo, 2025). Establishing standardized guidelines for AI model transparency, data provenance, and accountability will be critical (Omar & Zangana, 2024; Richmond et al., 2024).

Cross-disciplinary collaboration among technologists, legal scholars, and policymakers will help formulate robust frameworks for AI governance in forensics (Irons & Lallie, 2014; Sikos, 2021). Furthermore, legislation must evolve to regulate AI use in surveillance and investigation to prevent abuses and safeguard civil liberties (Jeong, 2020; Wright, Dawson Jr., & Omar, 2012).

Quantum Computing and Next-Generation AI

Looking further ahead, the convergence of quantum computing and AI presents transformative potential for forensic analytics and cybersecurity (Zangana, Sallow, & Mustafa, 2025). Quantum-assisted algorithms could enable unprecedented processing speeds for large-scale data correlation, pattern recognition, and cryptanalysis (Morić, Dakić, & Urošev, 2025).

Research into quantum-safe cryptographic methods integrated with AI-based forensic tools will also be pivotal to future-proofing digital investigations against emerging threats (Zangana & Mustafa, 2026).

Educational and Workforce Development

To keep pace with AI advancements, the forensic and cybersecurity workforce requires continuous upskilling in AI literacy, interpretability, and ethical use (Zangana & Salih, 2025). Academic programs and professional training must evolve to integrate AI methodologies with practical forensic skills (Zangana, Omar, Ali, & Abdullah, 2025).

Simultaneously, AI tools designed for educational support, such as AI-driven image denoising for remote teaching, exemplify how forensic education can be enhanced with emerging technologies (Zangana & Mustafa, 2026).

In summary, the future of AI in digital forensics is poised to revolutionize investigative capabilities by enhancing automation, explainability, and collaboration. However, this progress must be balanced with rigorous ethical standards, legal safeguards, and inclusive education to fully realize AI's potential in securing digital ecosystems (Costantini, De Gasperis, & Olivieri, 2019; Bhawna & Mahajan, 2024; Omar, 2022).

CONCLUSION

Artificial intelligence is revolutionizing digital forensics by enhancing the efficiency, accuracy, and automation of investigative processes. This chapter has highlighted the significant progress made in applying AI to forensic investigations, as well as the critical challenges that persist, including issues of explainability, data privacy, ethical concerns, and the robustness of AI systems against adversarial attacks.

The future of digital forensics lies in the continued integration of advanced AI technologies such as large language models, synthetic data generation, and explainable AI, which promise to improve both the effectiveness and transparency of forensic tools. Additionally, the ability of AI-driven systems to operate in constrained environments and provide rapid incident response will be crucial in addressing the evolving landscape of cyber threats.

It is essential to develop strong ethical frameworks and legal standards to ensure responsible use of AI in forensic contexts, fostering trust and acceptance of AI-generated evidence. Furthermore, the combination of emerging technologies like quantum computing with AI, alongside ongoing professional development, will empower forensic experts to confront increasingly sophisticated cybercrimes.

Ultimately, by balancing innovation with ethical responsibility, the digital forensics field can fully leverage AI's potential to protect digital assets and uphold justice in an increasingly digital world.

REFERENCES

Adam, I. Y., & Varol, C. (2020, June). Intelligence in digital forensics process. In *2020 8th International Symposium on Digital Forensics and Security (ISDFS)* (pp. 1-6). IEEE. DOI: 10.1109/ISDFS49300.2020.9116442

. Bhawna, & Mahajan, S. (2024). Artificial Intelligence Perspective on Digital Forensics. *Applying Artificial Intelligence in Cybersecurity Analytics and Cyber Threat Detection*, 33-44.

Costantini, S., De Gasperis, G., & Olivieri, R. (2019). Digital forensics and investigations meet artificial intelligence. *Annals of Mathematics and Artificial Intelligence*, *86*(1), 193–229. DOI: 10.1007/s10472-019-09632-y

Dunsin, D., Ghanem, M. C., Ouazzane, K., & Vassilev, V. (2024). A comprehensive analysis of the role of artificial intelligence and machine learning in modern digital forensics and incident response. *Forensic Science International Digital Investigation*, *48*, 301675. DOI: 10.1016/j.fsidi.2023.301675

Dunsin, D., Ghanem, M. C., & Quazzane, K. (2022). The use of artificial intelligence in digital forensics and incident response in a constrained environment. *International Journal of Information and Communication Engineering*, *16*(8), 280–285.

Ganesh, V. (2017). Artificial intelligence applied to computer forensics. *International Journal (Toronto, Ont.)*, *5*(5).

Gholami, S., & Omar, M. (2023). Does Synthetic Data Make Large Language Models More Efficient? *arXiv preprint arXiv:2310.07830.*

Gholami, S., & Omar, M. (2024). Can a student large language model perform as well as its teacher? In *Innovations, Securities, and Case Studies Across Healthcare, Business, and Technology* (pp. 122-139). IGI Global. DOI: 10.4018/979-8-3693-1906-2.ch007

Hall, S. W., Sakzad, A., & Choo, K. K. R. (2022). Explainable artificial intelligence for digital forensics. *Wiley Interdisciplinary Reviews: Forensic Science*, *4*(2), e1434.

Hamza, Y. A., & Omar, M. D. (2013). Cloud computing security: Abuse and nefarious use of cloud computing. *International Journal of Computer Engineering Research*, *3*(6), 22–27.

Huff, A. J., Burrell, D. N., Nobles, C., Richardson, K., Wright, J. B., Burton, S. L., Jones, A. J., Springs, D., Omar, M., & Brown-Jackson, K. L. (2023). Management Practices for Mitigating Cybersecurity Threats to Biotechnology Companies, Laboratories, and Healthcare Research Organizations. In *Applied Research Approaches to Technology, Healthcare, and Business* (pp. 1-12). IGI Global.

. Iqbal, F., Debbabi, M., Fung, B. C., Iqbal, F., Debbabi, M., & Fung, B. C. (2020). Artificial intelligence and digital forensics. *Machine Learning for Authorship Attribution and Cyber Forensics*, 139-150.

Irons, A., & Lallie, H. S. (2014). Digital forensics to intelligent forensics. *Future Internet*, *6*(3), 584–596. DOI: 10.3390/fi6030584

Jarrett, A., & Choo, K. K. R. (2021). The impact of automation and artificial intelligence on digital forensics. *WIREs Forensic Science*, *3*(6), e1418. DOI: 10.1002/wfs2.1418

Jeong, D. (2020). Artificial intelligence security threat, crime, and forensics: Taxonomy and open issues. *IEEE Access : Practical Innovations, Open Solutions*, *8*, 184560–184574. DOI: 10.1109/ACCESS.2020.3029280

Jones, R., & Omar, M. (2024). Revolutionizing Cybersecurity: The GPT-2 Enhanced Attack Detection and Defense (GEADD) Method for Zero-Day Threats. *International Journal of Informatics* [INJIISCOM]. *Information System and Computer Engineering*, *5*(2), 178–191.

Jones, R., Omar, M., Mohammed, D., Nobles, C., & Dawson, M. (2023). Harnessing the Speed and Accuracy of Machine Learning to Advance Cybersecurity. In *2023 Congress in Computer Science, Computer Engineering, & Applied Computing (CSCE)* (pp. 418-421). IEEE. DOI: 10.1109/CSCE60160.2023.00074

Karthikeyan, P., Pande, H. M., & Sarveshwaran, V. (Eds.). (2023). *Artificial intelligence and blockchain in digital forensics*. CRC Press.

Kelly, L., Sachan, S., Ni, L., Almaghrabi, F., Allmendinger, R., & Chen, Y. (2020). *Explainable artificial intelligence for digital forensics: opportunities, challenges and a drug testing case study*. Digital Forensic Science.

Manasa, S., & Kumar, K. P. (2022). Digital forensics investigation for attacks on artificial intelligence. *ECS Transactions*, *107*(1), 19639–19645. DOI: 10.1149/10701.19639ecst

. Mitchell, F. R. (2014). An overview of artificial intelligence based pattern matching in a security and digital forensic context. *Cyberpatterns: Unifying Design Patterns with Security and Attack Patterns*, 215-222.

Mohammed, D., Omar, M., & Nguyen, V. (2018). Wireless sensor network security: Approaches to detecting and avoiding wormhole attacks. *Journal of Research in Business. Economics and Management, 10*(2), 1860–1864.

Morić, Z., Dakić, V., & Urošev, S. (2025). An AI-Based Decision Support System Utilizing Bayesian Networks for Judicial Decision-Making. *Systems, 13*(2), 131. DOI: 10.3390/systems13020131

Moustafa, N. (2022). *Digital Forensics in the Era of Artificial Intelligence*. CRC Press. DOI: 10.1201/9781003278962

Nguyen, V., Mohammed, D., Omar, M., & Banisakher, M. (2018). The Effects of the FCC Net Neutrality Repeal on Security and Privacy. [IJHIoT]. *International Journal of Hyperconnectivity and the Internet of Things, 2*(2), 21–29. DOI: 10.4018/IJHIoT.2018070102

. Omar, M. (2021). New insights into database security: An effective and integrated approach for applying access control mechanisms and cryptographic concepts in Microsoft Access environments.

Omar, M. (2022). *Machine Learning for Cybersecurity: Innovative Deep Learning Solutions*. Springer Brief. https://link.springer.com/book/978303115

Omar, M. (2024). From Attack to Defense: Strengthening DNN Text Classification Against Adversarial Examples. In *Innovations, Securities, and Case Studies Across Healthcare, Business, and Technology* (pp. 174-195). IGI Global.

Omar, M. (2024). Revolutionizing Malware Detection: A Paradigm Shift Through Optimized Convolutional Neural Networks. In *Innovations, Securities, and Case Studies Across Healthcare, Business, and Technology* (pp. 196-220). IGI Global. DOI: 10.4018/979-8-3693-1906-2.ch011

Omar, M., & Zangana, H. M. (Eds.). (2024). *Redefining Security With Cyber AI*. IGI Global., DOI: 10.4018/979-8-3693-6517-5

Omar, M., & Zangana, H. M. (Eds.). (2025). *Application of Large Language Models (LLMs) for Software Vulnerability Detection*. IGI Global., DOI: 10.4018/979-8-3693-9311-6

Richmond, K. M., Muddamsetty, S. M., Gammeltoft-Hansen, T., Olsen, H. P., & Moeslund, T. B. (2024). Explainable AI and law: An evidential survey. *Digital Society : Ethics, Socio-Legal and Governance of Digital Technology, 3*(1), 1. DOI: 10.1007/s44206-023-00081-z

Rizvi, S., Scanlon, M., Mcgibney, J., & Sheppard, J. (2022). Application of artificial intelligence to network forensics: Survey, challenges and future directions. *IEEE Access : Practical Innovations, Open Solutions, 10*, 110362–110384. DOI: 10.1109/ACCESS.2022.3214506

Rughani, P. H. (2017). Artificial Intelligence Based Digital Forensics Framework. *International Journal of Advanced Research in Computer Science, 8*(8), 10–14. DOI: 10.26483/ijarcs.v8i8.4571

Sahoh, B., & Choksuriwong, A. (2023). The role of explainable Artificial Intelligence in high-stakes decision-making systems: A systematic review. *Journal of Ambient Intelligence and Humanized Computing, 14*(6), 7827–7843. DOI: 10.1007/s12652-023-04594-w PMID: 37228699

Salah, S., Mohamed, H., Sobuh, A., Almajali, E., Khan, W., Alaskar, H., & Hussain, A. (2025). Explainable AI for Unraveling the Significance of Visual Cues in High Stakes Deception Detection. *IEEE Access : Practical Innovations, Open Solutions, 13*, 65839–65862. DOI: 10.1109/ACCESS.2025.3558875

Shamoo, Y. (2025). The role of explainable ai (xai) in forensic investigations. In *Digital Forensics in the Age of AI* (pp. 31–62). IGI Global Scientific Publishing.

Sikos, L. F. (2021). AI in digital forensics: Ontology engineering for cybercrime investigations. *WIREs Forensic Science, 3*(3), e1394. DOI: 10.1002/wfs2.1394

. Tyagi, A. K., Kumari, S., & Richa. (2024). Artificial Intelligence-Based Cyber Security and Digital Forensics: A Review. *Artificial Intelligence-Enabled Digital Twin for Smart Manufacturing*, 391-419.

Wright, J., Dawson, M. E.Jr, & Omar, M. (2012). Cyber security and mobile threats: The need for antivirus applications for smartphones. *Journal of Information Systems Technology and Planning, 5*(14), 40–60.

Zangana, H., Ali, N. Y., Bazeed, S. M. S., & Abdullah, D. T. (2025). Leveraging Automation and Traceability in Managing Changes to Mission-Critical Computer Systems. *Indonesian Journal of Education and Social Sciences, 4*(1), 176–189.

. Zangana, H., Sallow, A. B., & Mustafa, F. M. (2025). Quantum-Assisted Architectures for 6G and IoT: A Framework for Secure and Efficient Wireless Networks. *Inform: Jurnal Ilmiah Bidang Teknologi Informasi dan Komunikasi, 10*(2), 152-158.

. Zangana, H. M. (2024). Exploring Blockchain-Based Timestamping Tools: A Comprehensive Review. *Redefining Security With Cyber AI*, 92-110.

. Zangana, H. M. (2024). Exploring the Landscape of Website Vulnerability Scanners: A Comprehensive Review and Comparative Analysis. *Redefining Security With Cyber AI*, 111-129.

Zangana, H. M., Mohammed, A. K., Sallow, A. B., & Sallow, Z. B. (2024). Cybernetic Deception: Unraveling the Layers of Email Phishing Threats. [INJURATECH]. *International Journal of Research and Applied Technology*, *4*(1), 35–47.

Zangana, H. M., & Mohammed, D. (2025). Foundations of Large Language Models in Software Vulnerability Detection. In Omar, M., & Zangana, H. (Eds.), *Application of Large Language Models (LLMs) for Software Vulnerability Detection* (pp. 41–74). IGI Global., DOI: 10.4018/979-8-3693-9311-6.ch002

Zangana, H. M., Mohammed, H. S., & Husain, M. M. (2025). The Role of Large Language Models in Enhancing Cybersecurity Measures: Empirical Evidence from Regional Banking Institutions. *SISTEMASI*, *14*(5), 2018–2027. DOI: 10.32520/stmsi.v14i4.5144

Zangana, H. M., Mohammed, H. S., & Husain, M. M.Hewa Majeed ZanganaHarman Salih MohammedMamo Muhamad Husain. (2025). Banking Cybersecurity: Safeguarding Financial Information in the Digital Era. *Journal of Computers and Digital Business*, *4*(2), 56–63. DOI: 10.56427/jcbd.v4i2.751

Zangana, H. M., & Mustafa, F. M. (2026). Enhancing Educational Visual Content Through AI-Based Image Denoising Techniques: Implications for Remote Teaching and Digital Resource Development. In *Harnessing AI for Teacher Support and Professional Development* (pp. 101-136). IGI Global Scientific Publishing.

Zangana, H. M., & Omar, M. (2020). Threats, Attacks, and Mitigations of Smartphone Security. *Academic Journal of Nawroz University*, *9*(4), 324–332. DOI: 10.25007/ajnu.v9n4a989

Zangana, H. M., & Omar, M. (2025). Harnessing the Power of Large Language Models for Cybersecurity: Applications, Challenges, and Future Directions. In Omar, M., & Zangana, H. (Eds.), *Application of Large Language Models (LLMs) for Software Vulnerability Detection* (pp. 1–40). IGI Global., DOI: 10.4018/979-8-3693-9311-6.ch001

. Zangana, H. M., Omar, M., Al-Karaki, J. N., & Mohammed, D. (2024). Comprehensive Review and Analysis of Network Firewall Rule Analyzers: Enhancing Security Posture and Efficiency. *Redefining Security With Cyber AI*, 15-36.

Zangana, H. M., Omar, M., Ali, N. Y., & Abdullah, D. T. (2025). Enhancing IT Project Agility Through Effective Change Management Strategies. *The Asian Journal of Technology Management*, *18*(1), 20–36. DOI: 10.12695/ajtm.2025.18.1.2

Zangana, H. M., & Salih, A. A. (2025). Enhancing Business Administration Through Decision Support Systems: A Comprehensive Review. *Sistem Pendukung Keputusan Dengan Aplikasi*, *4*(2), 45–56. DOI: 10.55537/spk.v4i2.1138

Compilation of References

Abbas, A., & Kollwitz, E. (2025). *Forensic Accounting in the Digital Era: Leveraging AI for Fraud Detection and Risk Management*. ResearchGate. DOI:DOI: 10.13140/RG.2.2.34900.10883

Abd-Elsalam, K. A., & Abdel-Momen, S. M. (2023). Artificial intelligence's development and challenges in scientific writing. *Egyptian Journal of Agricultural Research, 101*(3), 714–717. DOI: 10.21608/ejar.2023.220363.1414

Adam, I. Y., & Varol, C. (2020, June). Intelligence in digital forensics process. In *2020 8th International Symposium on Digital Forensics and Security (ISDFS)* (pp. 1-6). IEEE. DOI: 10.1109/ISDFS49300.2020.9116442

Adanma, U. M., & Ogunbiyi, E. O.Uwaga Monica AdanmaEmmanuel Olurotimi Ogunbiyi. (2024). Artificial intelligence in environmental conservation: Evaluating cyber risks and opportunities for sustainable practices. *Computer Science & IT Research Journal, 5*(5), 1178–1209. DOI: 10.51594/csitrj.v5i5.1156

Adejumo, A. P., & Ogburie, C. P.Adetunji Paul AdejumoChinonso Peter Ogburie. (2025). Forensic accounting in financial fraud detection: Trends and challenges. *International Journal of Science and Research Archive, 14*(3), 1219–1232. DOI: 10.30574/ijsra.2025.14.3.0815

Aderibigbe, A. O., Ohenhen, P. E., Nwaobia, N. K., Gidiagba, J. O., & Ani, E. C.Adebayo Olusegun AderibigbePeter Efosa OhenhenNwabueze Kelvin NwaobiaJoachim Osheyor GidiagbaEmmanuel Chigozie Ani. (2023). Artificial intelligence in developing countries: Bridging the gap between potential and implementation. *Computer Science & IT Research Journal, 4*(3), 185–199. DOI: 10.51594/csitrj.v4i3.629

Adewopo, V., Gonen, B., & Adewopo, F. (2020, December). Exploring open source information for cyber threat intelligence. In *2020 IEEE International Conference on Big Data (Big Data)* (pp. 2232-2241). IEEE. DOI: 10.1109/BigData50022.2020.9378220

Aghaei, E., Niu, X., Shadid, W., & Al-Shaer, E. (2022, October). Securebert: A domain-specific language model for cybersecurity. In *International Conference on Security and Privacy in Communication Systems* (pp. 39-56). Cham: Springer Nature Switzerland.

Ahmad, A., Liew, A. X., Venturini, F., Kalogeras, A., Candiani, A., Di Benedetto, G., Ajibola, S., Cartujo, P., Romero, P., Lykoudi, A., De Grandis, M. M., Xouris, C., Lo Bianco, R., Doddy, I., Elegbede, I., D'Urso Labate, G. F., García del Moral, L. F., & Martos, V. (2024). AI can empower agriculture for global food security: Challenges and prospects in developing nations. *Frontiers in Artificial Intelligence*, *7*, 1328530. DOI: 10.3389/frai.2024.1328530 PMID: 38726306

Ahmed, M. N., Singh, A. P., Hussain, M. R., Rasool, M. A., Khan, I. M., & Dildar, M. S. (2024, July). Enhancing Crop Production using Artificial Intelligence in Agricultural Revolution. In *2024 IEEE 7th International Conference on Advanced Technologies* [ATSIP]. *Signal and Image Processing : an International Journal*, *1*, 432–437.

Aithal, P. S., & Aithal, S. (2020, December). Analysis of Interdependency of ICCT Underlying Technologies and Related New Research Opportunities with Special Emphasis on Cyber Security and Forensic Science. In *Proceedings of the Conference on Future Technologies of IT, Management, Education, and Social Sciences,* 19th December (pp. 171-186).

Aithal, P. S., & Aithal, S. (2023). Application of ChatGPT in higher education and research–A futuristic analysis. [IJAEML]. *International Journal of Applied Engineering and Management Letters*, *7*(3), 168–194. DOI: 10.47992/IJAEML.2581.7000.0193

Aithal, P. S., & Aithal, S. (2024). An overview of the use of ICCT and nanotechnology in yellow economy: Current status and future opportunities. [PIJET]. *SSRN*, *1*(1), 29–62. DOI: 10.2139/ssrn.4901452

Akinade, A. O., Adepoju, P. A., Ige, A. B., Afolabi, A. I., & Amoo, O. O.Afees Olanrewaju AkinadePeter Adeyemo AdepojuAdebimpe Bolatito IgeAdeoye Idowu AfolabiOlukunle Oladipupo Amoo. (2021). A conceptual model for network security automation: Leveraging AI-driven frameworks to enhance multi-vendor infrastructure resilience. *International Journal of Science and Technology Research Archive*, *1*(1), 39–59. DOI: 10.53771/ijstra.2021.1.1.0034

Akindele, A., & Chabinga, R. (2024). Navigating Climate Change and Sustainability Solutions: Nigeria's Role in International Environmental Law. *African Journal of Climate Change and Resource Sustainability*, *3*(1), 331–344. DOI: 10.37284/ajccrs.3.1.2188

Alexander, C. S., Yarborough, M., & Smith, A. (2024). Who is responsible for 'responsible AI'?: Navigating challenges to build trust in AI agriculture and food system technology. *Precision Agriculture*, *25*(1), 146–185. DOI: 10.1007/s11119-023-10063-3

Ali, A. (2024). Navigating Road for Net Zero Policies to Aligning Policy, Politics, and Governance for Environmental Sustainability. In *Transition Towards a Sustainable Future: Net Zero Policies and Environmental Sustainability* (pp. 205–230). Springer Nature Singapore. DOI: 10.1007/978-981-97-5756-5_10

Ali, A. M., Futaih, R. F., Shukur, M., & Al-Orfali, A. K. (2024). Forensic Accounting and Fraud Detection Emerging Trends and Techniques. *Journal of Ecohumanism*, *3*(5), 525–542. DOI: 10.62754/joe.v3i5.3921

Ali, A. M., Khinger, I. K., Subhe, A., & Al-Orfali, A. K. (2024). Forensic Accounting Techniques in Detecting Frauds. *Journal of Ecohumanism*, *3*(5), 543–558. DOI: 10.62754/joe.v3i5.3922

Ali, G., Mijwil, M. M., Buruga, B. A., Abotaleb, M., & Adamopoulos, I. (2024). A survey on artificial intelligence in cybersecurity for smart agriculture: State-of-the-art, cyber threats, artificial intelligence applications, and ethical concerns. *Mesopotamian Journal of Computer Science*, *2024*, 53–103. DOI: 10.58496/MJCSC/2024/007

Ali, H., & Aysan, A. F. (2024). Decoding Future of Generative AI in Finance: A Machine Learning Exploration of Academic and Grey Corpus. *Available at SSRN* 4787211. DOI: 10.2139/ssrn.4787211

Ali, H., & Aysan, A. F. (2025). Ethical dimensions of generative AI: A cross-domain analysis using machine learning structural topic modeling. *International Journal of Ethics and Systems*, *41*(1), 3–34. DOI: 10.1108/IJOES-04-2024-0112

Ali, H., Zafar, M. B., & Aysan, A. F. (2024). Generative AI and Finance: A Multi-level Machine Learning Based Analysis. *Available at SSRN* 5129013.

Aloamaka, P. C. (2024). Navigating the Climate Crisis: Exploring International Law's Evolution and Application. *GLS Law Journal*, *6*(1), 48–58. DOI: 10.69974/glslawjournal.v6i1.127

AlQenaei, Z. M. (2024, March). Evolution and Optimization of Language Model Architectures: From Foundations to Future Directions. In *International Conference on Computing and Machine Learning* (pp. 233-249). Singapore: Springer Nature Singapore.

Al-Raggad, M., Albalawee, N., Al-Mahasneh, A., Abu Huson, Y., & Albajaly, A. (2025). Unveiling financial crimes: Advancing forensic accounting practices and ethical integrity through bibliometric insights. *Safer Communities, 24*(3), 244–264. DOI: 10.1108/SC-11-2024-0069

Al-Sinani, H. S., & Mitchell, C. J. (2024). AI-enhanced ethical hacking: A Linux-focused experiment. *arXiv preprint arXiv:2410.05105.*

Al-Sinani, H. S., Sahli, N., Mitchell, C. J., & Al-Siyabi, M. (2025). Advancing ethical hacking with AI: A Linux-based experimental study. *Proceedings of ITA-SEC and SERICS, Bologna, Italy (Feb 2025),* https://www. chrismitchell. net/Papers/aehwaa. pdf

Alturkistani, H., & Chuprat, S. (2024). *Artificial Intelligence and Large Language Models in Advancing Cyber Threat Intelligence: A Systematic Literature Review. ResearchGate.* DOI:DOI: 10.21203/rs.3.rs-5423193/v1

Aman, Q. U. I. S. E. R. (2024). From data to discovery: The impact of technology on forensic accounting. *Ile Journal of Law and Forensic Science, 2*(1), 1–13.

Araújo, S. O., Peres, R. S., Barata, J., Lidon, F., & Ramalho, J. C. (2021). Characterising the agriculture 4.0 landscape—Emerging trends, challenges and opportunities. *Agronomy (Basel), 11*(4), 667. DOI: 10.3390/agronomy11040667

Arya, L., & Rastogi, R. (2024). Study on Aerial Monitoring System in Agriculture, Forestry, Defense, and Border Protection Using Artificial Intelligence (AI). In *Agriculture and Aquaculture Applications of Biosensors and Bioelectronics* (pp. 392-407). IGI Global Scientific Publishing.

Asoronye, G. O., Anthony, O. C., Ogbuikwu, R. I., Ogili, C. O., & Ali, H. U. (2024). SecLM: A Specialized Security Language Model for Advanced Cybersecurity Applications and Threat Mitigation. *EKETE-International Journal Of Advanced Research, 2*(6), 33–42.

Atoum, M. S., Alarood, A. A., Alsolami, E., Abubakar, A., Hwaitat, A. K. A., & Alsmadi, I. (2025). Cybersecurity Intelligence Through Textual Data Analysis: A Framework Using Machine Learning and Terrorism Datasets. *Future Internet, 17*(4), 182. DOI: 10.3390/fi17040182

Ayeni, O. O., Al Hamad, N. M., Chisom, O. N., Osawaru, B., & Adewusi, O. E. (2024). AI in education: A review of personalized learning and educational technology. *GSC Advanced Research and Reviews*, *18*(2), 261–271. DOI: 10.30574/gscarr.2024.18.2.0062

Bahrini, A., Khamoshifar, M., Abbasimehr, H., Riggs, R. J., Esmaeili, M., Majdabadkohne, R. M., & Pasehvar, M. (2023, April). ChatGPT: Applications, opportunities, and threats. In *2023 Systems and Information Engineering Design Symposium (SIEDS)* (pp. 274-279). IEEE. DOI: 10.1109/SIEDS58326.2023.10137850

Banerjee, A., Chakraborty, C., & Rathi, M.Sr. (2020). Medical imaging, artificial intelligence, internet of things, wearable devices in terahertz healthcare technologies. In *Terahertz biomedical and healthcare technologies* (pp. 145–165). Elsevier. DOI: 10.1016/B978-0-12-818556-8.00008-2

Batabyal, G. S. (2024). Ethics, laws on war and artificial intelligence-driven warfare. In *Artificial intelligence, ethics and the future of warfare* (pp. 187–215). Routledge India. DOI: 10.4324/9781003421849-9

Battilana, J., & Casciaro, T. (2012). Change agents, networks, and institutions: A contingency theory of organizational change. *Academy of Management Journal*, *55*(2), 381–398. DOI: 10.5465/amj.2009.0891

Benn, S., Edwards, M., & Williams, T. (2014). *Organizational change for corporate sustainability*. Routledge. DOI: 10.4324/9781315819181

Bhagat, N. (2024). Artificial intelligence challenges and its impact on detection and prevention of financial statement fraud: A theoretical study. In *Demystifying the Dark Side of AI in Business* (pp. 60–80). IGI Global Scientific Publishing.

Bhangar, N. A., & Shahriyar, A. K. (2023). Iot and ai for next-generation farming: Opportunities, challenges, and outlook. *International Journal of Sustainable Infrastructure for Cities and Societies*, *8*(2), 14–26.

Bharati, R. K. (2020). Legal and Ethical Considerations in the Use of Digital Forensics by Law Enforcement: A Multi-jurisdictional Study. *Turk. Online J. Qual. Inq*, *11*(4), 10594–10610.

Bhat, S. A., & Huang, N. F. (2021). Big data and ai revolution in precision agriculture: Survey and challenges. *IEEE Access : Practical Innovations, Open Solutions*, *9*, 110209–110222. DOI: 10.1109/ACCESS.2021.3102227

Blackmore, J. (2013). A feminist critical perspective on educational leadership. *International Journal of Leadership in Education*, *16*(2), 139–154. DOI: 10.1080/13603124.2012.754057

Bousri, M. M. S. (2019). *A comparative analysis of legal and institutional framework for arbitration: Comoros and Uganda* (Doctoral dissertation, School of law).

Brennan, A., & Canny, A. (2023). Problematising Irish student-teachers'(dis) engagement with sociology of education in initial teacher education programmes. *Teaching and Teacher Education, 130*, 104173. DOI: 10.1016/j.tate.2023.104173

Bryce, C., Kalousis, A., Leroux, I., Madinier, H., Mermoud, A., Mulder, V., ... & Ruch, P. *Trends in Large Language Models: Actors, Applications, and Impact on Cybersecurity*. Technology Observatory. https://technology-observatory.ch/academic_publication/trends-in-large-language-models-actors-applications-and-impact-on-cybersecurity/article.pdf

Bryce, C., Kalousis, A., Leroux, I., Madinier, H., Mermoud, A., Mulder, V., Pasche, T., & Ruch, P. (n.d.). *Trends in Large Language Models: Actors, Applications, and Impact on Cybersecurity*. https://technology-observatory.ch/academic_publication/trends-in-large-language-models-actors-applications-and-impact-on-cybersecurity/article.pdf

Butt, J. (2024). Analytical study of the world's first EU Artificial Intelligence (AI) Act. *International Journal of Research Publication and Reviews, 5*(3), 7343–7364. DOI: 10.55248/gengpi.5.0324.0914

Casad, B. J., Franks, J. E., Garasky, C. E., Kittleman, M. M., Roesler, A. C., Hall, D. Y., & Petzel, Z. W. (2021). Gender inequality in academia: Problems and solutions for women faculty in STEM. *Journal of Neuroscience Research, 99*(1), 13–23. DOI: 10.1002/jnr.24631 PMID: 33103281

Chaudhary, M., & Bansal, D. (2022). Open source intelligence extraction for terrorism-related information: A review. *Wiley Interdisciplinary Reviews. Data Mining and Knowledge Discovery, 12*(5), e1473. DOI: 10.1002/widm.1473

Chen, T., Lv, L., Wang, D., Zhang, J., Yang, Y., Zhao, Z., & Tao, D. (2024). Empowering agrifood system with artificial intelligence: A survey of the progress, challenges and opportunities. *ACM Computing Surveys, 57*(2), 1–37.

Chen, Y., Cui, M., Wang, D., Cao, Y., Yang, P., Jiang, B., Lu, Z., & Liu, B. (2024). A survey of large language models for cyber threat detection. *Computers & Security, 145*, 104016. DOI: 10.1016/j.cose.2024.104016

Chhabra, S., Sabharwal, S. M., Kaur, M., & Obaid, A. J. (2024). Cyber Forensics for Cyber-physical System. In *Emerging Trends for Securing Cyber Physical Systems and the Internet of Things* (pp. 220–246). CRC Press. DOI: 10.1201/9781003474111-13

Chowdhury, S. (2024). Towards a Just Climate: Navigating Complexities and Challenges in Climate Change Discourse and Action. *Issue 2 Int'l JL Mgmt. &. Human.*, *7*, 1807.

Cooper, S., & Zell, S. (2023). *Staying on Board: Non-profit housing provider board capacity in a changing context*. Institute of Urban Studies, The University of Winnipeg.

Costantini, S., De Gasperis, G., & Olivieri, R. (2019). Digital forensics and investigations meet artificial intelligence. *Annals of Mathematics and Artificial Intelligence*, *86*(1), 193–229. DOI: 10.1007/s10472-019-09632-y

Daniel, J. (2024). *Environmental Law: Navigating Legal Pathways for a Sustainable Future*. Pencil.

Daraojimba, R. E., Farayola, O. A., Olatoye, F. M. O., Mhlongo, N., & Oke, T. T. L. (2023). Forensic accounting in the digital age: a US perspective: scrutinizing methods and challenges in digital financial fraud prevention. *Finance & Accounting Research Journal*, *5*(11), 342–360. DOI: 10.51594/farj.v5i11.614

Dara, R., Hazrati Fard, S. M., & Kaur, J. (2022). Recommendations for ethical and responsible use of artificial intelligence in digital agriculture. *Frontiers in Artificial Intelligence*, *5*, 884192. DOI: 10.3389/frai.2022.884192 PMID: 35968036

Darvishi, K., Liu, L., & Lim, S. (2022). Navigating the Nexus: Legal and Economic Implications of Emerging Tech-nologies. *Law and Economics*, *16*(3), 172–186. DOI: 10.35335/laweco.v16i3.59

Dembani, R., Karvelas, I., Akbar, N. A., Rizou, S., Tegolo, D., & Fountas, S. (2025). Agricultural data privacy and federated learning: A review of challenges and opportunities. *Computers and Electronics in Agriculture*, *232*, 110048. DOI: 10.1016/j.compag.2025.110048

Diaf, A., Korba, A. A., Karabadji, N. E., & Ghamri-Doudane, Y. (2024, April). Beyond detection: Leveraging large language models for cyber attack prediction in iot networks. In *2024 20th International Conference on Distributed Computing in Smart Systems and the Internet of Things (DCOSS-IoT)* (pp. 117-123). IEEE.

Dunsin, D., Ghanem, M. C., Ouazzane, K., & Vassilev, V. (2024). A comprehensive analysis of the role of artificial intelligence and machine learning in modern digital forensics and incident response. *Forensic Science International Digital Investigation*, *48*, 301675. DOI: 10.1016/j.fsidi.2023.301675

Dunsin, D., Ghanem, M. C., & Quazzane, K. (2022). The use of artificial intelligence in digital forensics and incident response in a constrained environment. *International Journal of Information and Communication Engineering*, *16*(8), 280–285.

Eisenberg, D. (2024). *Sensing With Integrity: Responsible Sensor Systems in an Era of AI* (Doctoral dissertation, New Jersey Institute of Technology).

Elumilade, O. O., Ogundeji, I. A., Achumie, G. O., Omokhoa, H. E., & Omowole, B. M. (2021). Enhancing fraud detection and forensic auditing through data-driven techniques for financial integrity and security. *Journal of Advanced Education and Sciences, 1*(2), 55–63. DOI: 10.54660/.JAES.2021.1.2.55-63

Emon, M. M. H., Khan, T., Rahman, M. A., Hamid, A. B. A., & Yaakub, N. I. (2025). GreenTech revolution: Navigating challenges and seizing opportunities. In *AI and green technology applications in society* (pp. 63–90). IGI Global Scientific Publishing.

Eswaran, U., & Eswaran, V. (2025). Quantum Machine Learning, Leveraging AI, and Semiconductor Technology. In *Integration of AI, Quantum Computing, and Semiconductor Technology* (pp. 57-78). IGI Global.

Etaywe, A., Macfarlane, K., & Alazab, M. (2024). A cyberterrorist behind the keyboard: An automated text analysis for psycholinguistic profiling and threat assessment. *Journal of Language Aggression and Conflict.*

Faqir, R. S. (2023). Digital criminal investigations in the era of artificial intelligence: A comprehensive overview. *International Journal of Cyber Criminology, 17*(2), 77–94.

FAVINO. R., CONTE, N., DE, M. A., GARCIA, M. E., MONTANARI, E., PAGANINI, A., ... & SFALAGKIARIS, C. E. (2025). Emerging risks and opportunities for EU internal security stemming from new technologies.

Fenwick, A., Molnar, G., & Frangos, P. (2024). The critical role of HRM in AI-driven digital transformation: A paradigm shift to enable firms to move from AI implementation to human-centric adoption. *Discover Artificial Intelligence, 4*(1), 34. DOI: 10.1007/s44163-024-00125-4

Fernando, K. (2023). A multidimensional framework for utilizing big data analytics and ai in strengthening digital forensics and cybersecurity investigations. *International Journal of Cybersecurity Risk Management, Forensics, and Compliance, 7*(12), 16–30.

Ferrag, M. A., Alwahedi, F., Battah, A., Cherif, B., Mechri, A., & Tihanyi, N. (2024). *Generative ai and large language models for cyber security: All insights you need.* Arxiv.org. https://arxiv.org/html/2405.12750v1

Ferrag, M. A., Ndhlovu, M., Tihanyi, N., Cordeiro, L. C., Debbah, M., & Lestable, T. (2023). Revolutionizing cyber threat detection with large language models. *arXiv preprint arXiv:2306.14263*, 195-202.

Ferrag, M. A., Alwahedi, F., Battah, A., Cherif, B., Mechri, A., & Tihanyi, N. (2024). Generative ai and large language models for cyber security: All insights you need. *Available at SSRN* 4853709. DOI: 10.2139/ssrn.4853709

Ferrag, M. A., Ndhlovu, M., Tihanyi, N., Cordeiro, L. C., Debbah, M., Lestable, T., & Thandi, N. S. (2024). Revolutionizing cyber threat detection with large language models: A privacy-preserving bert-based lightweight model for iot/iiot devices. *IEEE Access : Practical Innovations, Open Solutions*, *12*, 23733–23750. DOI: 10.1109/ACCESS.2024.3363469

Filetti, S., Fenza, G., & Gallo, A. (2024). Research design and writing of scholarly articles: New artificial intelligence tools available for researchers. *Endocrine*, *85*(3), 1104–1116. DOI: 10.1007/s12020-024-03977-z PMID: 39085566

Flannery, J., Ajayi, S. O., & Oyegoke, A. S. (2021). Alcohol and substance misuse in the construction industry. *International Journal of Occupational Safety and Ergonomics*, *27*(2), 472–487. DOI: 10.1080/10803548.2019.1601376 PMID: 30935301

Friedl, S., & Pernul, G. (2024). Device Forensics in Smart Homes: Insights on Advances, Challenges and Future Directions. In *Transactions on Large-Scale Data- and Knowledge-Centered Systems LVII* (pp. 68–98). Springer Berlin Heidelberg.

Ganesh, V. (2017). Artificial intelligence applied to computer forensics. *International Journal (Toronto, Ont.)*, *5*(5).

Gardezi, M., Joshi, B., Rizzo, D. M., Ryan, M., Prutzer, E., Brugler, S., & Dadkhah, A. (2024). Artificial intelligence in farming: Challenges and opportunities for building trust. *Agronomy Journal*, *116*(3), 1217–1228. DOI: 10.1002/agj2.21353

Gaurav, A., Chui, K. T., Arya, V., Attar, R. W., Bansal, S., Alhomoud, A., & Psannis, K. (2024). Optimized AI-Driven Semantic Web Approach for Enhancing Phishing Detection in E-Commerce Platforms. [IJSWIS]. *International Journal on Semantic Web and Information Systems*, *20*(1), 1–13. DOI: 10.4018/IJSWIS.359767

Ghazal, T. M., Janjua, J. I., Abushiba, W., Ahmad, M., Ihsan, A., & Al-Dmour, N. A. (2024, December). Cybersecurity Revolution via Large Language Models and Explainable AI. In *2024 17th International Conference on Security of Information and Networks (SIN)* (pp. 1-6). IEEE. DOI: 10.1109/SIN63213.2024.10871324

Gholami, S., & Omar, M. (2023). Does Synthetic Data Make Large Language Models More Efficient? *arXiv preprint arXiv:2310.07830.*

Gholami, S., & Omar, M. (2024). Can a student large language model perform as well as its teacher? In *Innovations, Securities, and Case Studies Across Healthcare, Business, and Technology* (pp. 122-139). IGI Global. DOI: 10.4018/979-8-3693-1906-2.ch007

Grab, M. O. (2025). Teaching for Equity: An Exploration of AI's Role in Culturally Responsive Teaching in Higher Education Settings. *Innovative Higher Education*, •••, 1–22. DOI: 10.1007/s10755-025-09801-4

Groumpos, P. P. (2023, July). A critical historic overview of artificial intelligence: Issues, challenges, opportunities, and threats. *Artificial Intelligence and Applications (Commerce, Calif.)*, *1*(4), 181–197. DOI: 10.47852/bonviewAIA3202689

Gupta, B. B., Gaurav, A., & Arya, V. (2024). Navigating the security landscape of large language models in enterprise information systems. *Enterprise Information Systems*, *18*(4), 2310846. DOI: 10.1080/17517575.2024.2310846

Gupta, D. K., Pagani, A., Zamboni, P., & Singh, A. K. (2024). AI-powered revolution in plant sciences: Advancements, applications, and challenges for sustainable agriculture and food security. *Exploration of Foods and Foodomics*, *2*(5), 443–459. DOI: 10.37349/eff.2024.00045

Gupta, Y. K. (2024). Exploring crime from a sociological perspective. *International Journal of Dynamic Educational Research Society*, *5*(2), 47–56.

Haddad, H. O. S. S. A. M., Alharasis, E. E., Fraij, J., & Al-Ramahi, N. M. (2024). How do innovative improvements in forensic accounting and its related technologies sweeten fraud investigation and prevention. *WSEAS Transactions on Business and Economics*, *21*, 1115–1141. DOI: 10.37394/23207.2024.21.93

Hadi, M. A., Abdulredha, M. N., & Hasan, E. (2023). Introduction to ChatGPT: A new revolution of artificial intelligence with machine learning algorithms and cybersecurity. *Sci. Arch*, *4*(04), 276. DOI: 10.47587/SA.2023.4406

Hall, S. W., Sakzad, A., & Choo, K. K. R. (2022). Explainable artificial intelligence for digital forensics. *Wiley Interdisciplinary Reviews: Forensic Science*, *4*(2), e1434.

Halmo, H. (2025). *Human-Centered, Tech-Enabled: Scaling Academic Advising in Higher Education Through Predictive Analytics and Organizational Change an Innovation Study* (Doctoral dissertation, New York University).

Hamza, Y. A., & Omar, M. D. (2013). Cloud computing security: Abuse and nefarious use of cloud computing. *International Journal of Computer Engineering Research*, *3*(6), 22–27.

Harjuni, J. (2024). The role of forensic accounting in fraud detection and prevention in financial institutions. *Tamansiswa Accounting Journal International*, *15*(1), 151–159.

Hasanov, I., Virtanen, S., Hakkala, A., & Isoaho, J. (2024). Application of Large Language Models in Cybersecurity: A Systematic Literature Review. *IEEE Access : Practical Innovations, Open Solutions*, *12*, 176751–176778. DOI: 10.1109/ACCESS.2024.3505983

Hassanin, M., & Moustafa, N. (2024). A comprehensive overview of large language models (llms) for cyber defences: Opportunities and directions. *arXiv preprint arXiv:2405.14487.*

Hayward, K. J., & Maas, M. M. (2021). Artificial intelligence and crime: A primer for criminologists. *Crime, Media, Culture*, *17*(2), 209–233. DOI: 10.1177/1741659020917434

He, H., Gray, J., Cangelosi, A., Meng, Q., McGinnity, T. M., & Mehnen, J. (2021). The challenges and opportunities of human-centered AI for trustworthy robots and autonomous systems. *IEEE Transactions on Cognitive and Developmental Systems*, *14*(4), 1398–1412. DOI: 10.1109/TCDS.2021.3132282

Helbing, D., & Ienca, M. (2024). Why converging technologies need converging international regulation. *Ethics and Information Technology*, *26*(1), 15. DOI: 10.1007/s10676-024-09756-8

Ho, C. W. (2023). Implementing the human right to science in the regulatory governance of artificial intelligence in healthcare. *Journal of Law and the Biosciences*, *10*(2), lsad026. DOI: 10.1093/jlb/lsad026 PMID: 37854168

Holzinger, A., Weippl, E., Tjoa, A. M., & Kieseberg, P. (2021, August). Digital transformation for sustainable development goals (sdgs)-a security, safety and privacy perspective on ai. In *International cross-domain conference for machine learning and knowledge extraction* (pp. 1-20). Cham: Springer International Publishing.

Huff, A. J., Burrell, D. N., Nobles, C., Richardson, K., Wright, J. B., Burton, S. L., Jones, A. J., Springs, D., Omar, M., & Brown-Jackson, K. L. (2023). Management Practices for Mitigating Cybersecurity Threats to Biotechnology Companies, Laboratories, and Healthcare Research Organizations. In *Applied Research Approaches to Technology, Healthcare, and Business* (pp. 1-12). IGI Global.

Irons, A., & Lallie, H. S. (2014). Digital forensics to intelligent forensics. *Future Internet*, *6*(3), 584–596. DOI: 10.3390/fi6030584

Iyengar, S. S., Nabavirazavi, S., & Hariprasad, Y. HB, P., & Mohan, C. K. (2025). Privacy-Preserving AI (Federated Learning) for Digital Forensics. In *Artificial Intelligence in Practice: Theory and Application for Cyber Security and Forensics* (pp. 161-176). Cham: Springer Nature Switzerland.

Jafarizadeh, H., Yamini, E., Zolfaghari, S. M., Esmaeilion, F., Assad, M. E. H., & Soltani, M. (2024). Navigating challenges in large-scale renewable energy storage: Barriers, solutions, and innovations. *Energy Reports*, *12*, 2179–2192. DOI: 10.1016/j.egyr.2024.08.019

Jarrett, A., & Choo, K. K. R. (2021). The impact of automation and artificial intelligence on digital forensics. *WIREs Forensic Science*, *3*(6), e1418. DOI: 10.1002/wfs2.1418

Javed, A. R., Ahmed, W., Alazab, M., Jalil, Z., Kifayat, K., & Gadekallu, T. R. (2022). A comprehensive survey on computer forensics: State-of-the-art, tools, techniques, challenges, and future directions. *IEEE Access : Practical Innovations, Open Solutions*, *10*, 11065–11089. DOI: 10.1109/ACCESS.2022.3142508

Jeong, D. (2020). Artificial intelligence security threat, crime, and forensics: Taxonomy and open issues. *IEEE Access : Practical Innovations, Open Solutions*, *8*, 184560–184574. DOI: 10.1109/ACCESS.2020.3029280

Jerhamre, E., Carlberg, C. J. C., & van Zoest, V. (2022). Exploring the susceptibility of smart farming: Identified opportunities and challenges. *Smart Agricultural Technology*, *2*, 2. DOI: 10.1016/j.atech.2021.100026

Jin, Z., Goyal, S. B., & Rajawat, A. S. (2024). The informational role of artificial intelligence in higher education in the New era. *Procedia Computer Science*, *235*, 1008–1023. DOI: 10.1016/j.procs.2024.04.096

Johnsen, J. W., & Franke, K. (2019, December). The impact of preprocessing in natural language for open source intelligence and criminal investigation. In *2019 IEEE International Conference on Big Data (Big Data)* (pp. 4248-4254). IEEE. DOI: 10.1109/BigData47090.2019.9006006

Jones, R., Omar, M., Mohammed, D., Nobles, C., & Dawson, M. (2023). Harnessing the Speed and Accuracy of Machine Learning to Advance Cybersecurity. In *2023 Congress in Computer Science, Computer Engineering, & Applied Computing (CSCE)* (pp. 418-421). IEEE. DOI: 10.1109/CSCE60160.2023.00074

Jones, R., & Omar, M. (2024). Revolutionizing Cybersecurity: The GPT-2 Enhanced Attack Detection and Defense (GEADD) Method for Zero-Day Threats. *International Journal of Informatics* [INJIISCOM]. *Information System and Computer Engineering*, *5*(2), 178–191.

Kalashnikova, L. V., Lobanova, A. S., Hrabovets, I. V., Chernous, L. S., Chorna, V. A., & Davydenko, Y. O. (2025, March). Modern information and communication technologies in professional training of sociology students: Evolving needs and significance in the digital age. In *CTE Workshop Proceedings* (Vol. 12, pp. 381-398). DOI: 10.55056/cte.922

Kapoor, P. (2025). Harvesting Ethics: Forging Responsible Paths in AI and ML for the Agri-Food Industry. In *Food and Industry 5.0: Transforming the Food System for a Sustainable Future* (pp. 305–315). Springer Nature Switzerland. DOI: 10.1007/978-3-031-76758-6_19

Karim, R., Galar, D., & Kumar, U. (2023). *AI factory: theories, applications and case studies*. CRC Press. DOI: 10.1201/9781003208686

Karthikeyan, P., Pande, H. M., & Sarveshwaran, V. (Eds.). (2023). *Artificial intelligence and blockchain in digital forensics*. CRC Press.

Kasri, W., Himeur, Y., Alkhazaleh, H. A., Tarapiah, S., Atalla, S., Mansoor, W., & Al-Ahmad, H. (2025). From Vulnerability to Defense: The Role of Large Language Models in Enhancing Cybersecurity. *Computation (Basel, Switzerland)*, *13*(2), 30. DOI: 10.3390/computation13020030

Kaushik, K., Khan, A., Kumari, A., Sharma, I., & Dubey, R. (2024). Ethical considerations in AI-based cybersecurity. In *Next-generation cybersecurity: AI, ML, and Blockchain* (pp. 437–470). Springer Nature Singapore. DOI: 10.1007/978-981-97-1249-6_19

Kelly, L., Sachan, S., Ni, L., Almaghrabi, F., Allmendinger, R., & Chen, Y. (2020). *Explainable artificial intelligence for digital forensics: opportunities, challenges and a drug testing case study*. Digital Forensic Science.

Khan, W., Ishrat, M., & Al Farsi, M. M. (2025). Unveiling the Digital Trails: A Survey of Contemporary Digital Forensics Tools and Techniques. In *Cyberology* (pp. 71-89). Chapman and Hall/CRC.

Kochupillai, M., Kahl, M., Schmitt, M., Taubenböck, H., & Zhu, X. X. (2022). Earth observation and artificial intelligence: Understanding emerging ethical issues and opportunities. *IEEE Geoscience and Remote Sensing Magazine*, *10*(4), 90–124. DOI: 10.1109/MGRS.2022.3208357

Kohli, R., Pizarro, M., Garcia, L. G., Kelly, L., Espinoza, M., & Cordova, J. (2021). Critical professional development and the racial justice leadership possibilities of teachers of colour in K-12 schools. *Professional Development in Education, 47*(1), 89–101. DOI: 10.1080/19415257.2020.1814387

Lan, Y. (2024). Through tensions to identity-based motivations: Exploring teacher professional identity in Artificial Intelligence-enhanced teacher training. *Teaching and Teacher Education, 151*, 104736. DOI: 10.1016/j.tate.2024.104736

Larson, D. B., Harvey, H., Rubin, D. L., Irani, N., Tse, J. R., & Langlotz, C. P. (2021). Regulatory frameworks for development and evaluation of artificial intelligence–based diagnostic imaging algorithms: Summary and recommendations. *Journal of the American College of Radiology, 18*(3), 413–424. DOI: 10.1016/j.jacr.2020.09.060 PMID: 33096088

Lee, S., Mujammami, A. A. H., & Kim, K. (2024). Leveraging Social Networks for Cyber Threat Intelligence: Analyzing Attack Trends and TTPs in the Arab World. *IEEE Access : Practical Innovations, Open Solutions.*

Leong, Y. M., Lim, E. H., Subri, N. F. B., & Jalil, N. B. A. (2023, September). Transforming agriculture: Navigating the challenges and embracing the opportunities of artificial intelligence of things. In *2023 IEEE International Conference on Agrosystem Engineering, Technology & Applications (AGRETA)* (pp. 142-147). IEEE. DOI: 10.1109/AGRETA57740.2023.10262747

Liu, Z. (2024, April). A review of advancements and applications of pre-trained language models in cybersecurity. In *2024 12th International Symposium on Digital Forensics and Security (ISDFS)* (pp. 1-10). IEEE. DOI: 10.1109/ISDFS60797.2024.10527236

Liu, S. (2025). Navigating Equality in Schools: The Sociological Impact of Leadership on Student Success. *Education and Urban Society, 57*(3), 245–298. DOI: 10.1177/00131245241304404

Li, Z., & Zhang, W. (2025). Technology in education: Addressing legal and governance challenges in the digital era. *Education and Information Technologies, 30*(7), 8413–8443. DOI: 10.1007/s10639-024-13036-9

Luan, H., Perron, B. E., Victor, B. G., Wan, G., Niu, Y., & Xiao, X. (2024). Using artificial intelligence to support scientometric analysis of scholarly literature: A case example of research on mainland China's left-behind children. *Journal of the Society for Social Work and Research, 15*(3), 435–457. DOI: 10.1086/731613

Mac Fadden, I., García-Alonso, E. M., & López Meneses, E. (2024). Science Mapping of AI as an Educational Tool Exploring Digital Inequalities: A Sociological Perspective. *Multimodal Technologies and Interaction*, *8*(12), 106. DOI: 10.3390/mti8120106

Maennig, W. (2014). Inefficiency of the anti-doping system: Cost reduction proposals. *Substance Use & Misuse*, *49*(9), 1201–1205. DOI: 10.3109/10826084.2014.912065 PMID: 24832718

Maguluri, L. P., Arularasan, A. N., & Boopathi, S. (2023). Assessing security concerns for ai-based drones in smart cities. In *Effective AI, Blockchain, and E-Governance Applications for Knowledge Discovery and Management* (pp. 27-47). IGI Global Scientific Publishing. DOI: 10.4018/978-1-6684-9151-5.ch002

Malhotra, K., & Firdaus, M. (2022). Application of artificial intelligence in IoT security for crop yield prediction. *ResearchBerg Review of Science and Technology*, *2*(1), 136–157.

Manasa, S., & Kumar, K. P. (2022). Digital forensics investigation for attacks on artificial intelligence. *ECS Transactions*, *107*(1), 19639–19645. DOI: 10.1149/10701.19639ecst

Manganelli, A. G. (2019). Reverse payments and risk of bankruptcy under private information. *International Journal of the Economics of Business*, *26*(3), 411–429. DOI: 10.1080/13571516.2019.1613146

Manoharan, A., & Sarker, M. (2023). Revolutionizing Cybersecurity: Unleashing the Power of Artificial Intelligence and Machine Learning for Next-Generation Threat Detection. *DOI:* https://www. doi. org/10.56726/IRJMETS32644, *1*.

Mark, R. (2019). Ethics of using AI and big data in agriculture: The case of a large agriculture multinational. *The ORBIT Journal*, *2*(2), 1–27. DOI: 10.29297/orbit.v2i2.109

Matar, D. O. (2023). *Forensic accounting and Cybersecurity examine their interrelation in the detection and Prevention of financial fraud*. American Academic & Scholarly Research Journal.

Mazloum, H., Mazloum, N., & Saleh, A. M. (2025). FORENSIC AUDIT: ENHANCING CERTIFIED PUBLIC ACCOUNTANT USING ARTIFICIAL INTELLIGENCE TECHNIQUES. *BAU Journal-Science and Technology*, *6*(2), 10. DOI: 10.54729/2959-331X.1128

Mennella, C., Maniscalco, U., De Pietro, G., & Esposito, M. (2024). Ethical and regulatory challenges of AI technologies in healthcare: A narrative review. *Heliyon*, *10*(4), e26297. DOI: 10.1016/j.heliyon.2024.e26297 PMID: 38384518

Mhia-Alddin, D. A., & Hussein, A. M. (2025). AI-Powered Contract Security: Managing Expiry, Compliance, and Risk Mitigation Through Deep Learning and LLMs. In *Revolutionizing Cybersecurity With Deep Learning and Large Language Models* (pp. 37-64). IGI Global Scientific Publishing.

Mhia-Alddin, D. A., & Hussein, A. M. (2025). Contract Expiry in AI-Driven STM Research: Legal Challenges, Risks, and Regulatory Considerations. In *Ensuring Secure and Ethical STM Research in the AI Era* (pp. 77-110). IGI Global Scientific Publishing.

Middleton, S. E. (2021). Use of Artificial Intelligence to support cybercrime research. In *Researching Cybercrimes: Methodologies, Ethics, and Critical Approaches* (pp. 213–232). Springer International Publishing. DOI: 10.1007/978-3-030-74837-1_11

Mishra, P., Oster, N., & Henriksen, D. (2024). Generative AI, teacher knowledge and educational research: Bridging short-and long-term perspectives. *TechTrends*, *68*(2), 205–210. DOI: 10.1007/s11528-024-00938-1

Mohammed, D., Omar, M., & Nguyen, V. (2018). Wireless sensor network security: Approaches to detecting and avoiding wormhole attacks. *Journal of Research in Business. Economics and Management*, *10*(2), 1860–1864.

Möller, D. P. (2023). Guide to Cybersecurity in Digital Transformation. *Springer Link. Gewerbestrasse*, *11*, 6330.

Monahan, R., MacCormac, A., & Minogue, J. (2024, July). Fostering Epistemic Agency: Strategies for Mitigating Implicit Bias in AI-Enhanced Education. In *EdMedia+ Innovate Learning* (pp. 1011-1025). Association for the Advancement of Computing in Education (AACE).

Moradi-Kelayeh, N. (2025). *From Chalkboard to Chatbots: The Integration of Artificial Influence on Pedagogical Practices* (Master's thesis, Harvard University).

Morić, Z., Dakić, V., & Urošev, S. (2025). An AI-Based Decision Support System Utilizing Bayesian Networks for Judicial Decision-Making. *Systems*, *13*(2), 131. DOI: 10.3390/systems13020131

Motlagh, F. N., Hajizadeh, M., Majd, M., Najafi, P., Cheng, F., & Meinel, C. (2024). Large language models in cybersecurity: State-of-the-art. *arXiv preprint arXiv:2402.00891*.

Moustafa, N. (2022). *Digital Forensics in the Era of Artificial Intelligence*. CRC Press. DOI: 10.1201/9781003278962

Mubarrat, A. A. (2024). of the Research: Role of Artificial Intelligence and Big Data in Modern Forensic Accountancy. *Available at SSRN* 5078259.

Murtiningsih, S., & Sujito, A. (2024). Reimagining the future of education: Inclusive pedagogies, critical intergenerational justice, and technological disruption. *Policy Futures in Education*, •••, 14782103251341406.

Museus, S. D., & Jayakumar, U. M. (2012). Creating campus cultures. *Routledge, 10*, 9780203832417.

Naili, Y. T., Mangkunegara, I. S., Purwono, P., & Baballe, M. A. (2025). Regulatory challenges in ai-based diagnostics: Legal implications of ai use in medical diagnostics. In *BIO Web of Conferences* (Vol. 152, p. 01034). EDP Sciences.

Narayana, S. A., Pati, R. K., & Padhi, S. S. (2019). Market dynamics and reverse logistics for sustainability in the Indian Pharmaceuticals industry. *Journal of Cleaner Production, 208*, 968–987. DOI: 10.1016/j.jclepro.2018.10.171

Neupane, S., Mitra, S., Fernandez, I. A., Saha, S., Mittal, S., Chen, J., Pillai, N., & Rahimi, S. (2024). Security considerations in ai-robotics: A survey of current methods, challenges, and opportunities. *IEEE Access : Practical Innovations, Open Solutions, 12*, 22072–22097. DOI: 10.1109/ACCESS.2024.3363657

Nguyen, V., Mohammed, D., Omar, M., & Banisakher, M. (2018). The Effects of the FCC Net Neutrality Repeal on Security and Privacy. [IJHIoT]. *International Journal of Hyperconnectivity and the Internet of Things, 2*(2), 21–29. DOI: 10.4018/IJHIoT.2018070102

Oduro, P., Uzougbo, N. S., & Ugwu, M. C. (2024). Renewable energy expansion: Legal strategies for overcoming regulatory barriers and promoting innovation. *International Journal of Applied Research in Social Sciences, 6*(5), 927–944. DOI: 10.51594/ijarss.v6i5.1145

Okonta, C. N., & Nnamdi, C. A. (2025). Forensic Investigation and Fraud Detection in Nigeria: Leveraging on Artificial Intelligence. *Review of Ethics in Sustainable Finance and Accounting, 1*(1), 31–38. DOI: 10.70865/jiatis.v2i1.80

Okwu, M. O., Tartibu, L. K., Maware, C., Enarevba, D. R., Afenogho, J. O., & Essien, A. (2022, August). Emerging technologies of industry 4.0: Challenges and opportunities. In *2022 International Conference on Artificial Intelligence, Big Data, Computing and Data Communication Systems (icABCD)* (pp. 1-13). IEEE. DOI: 10.1109/icABCD54961.2022.9856002

Omar, M. (2021). *New insights into database security: An effective and integrated approach for applying access control mechanisms and cryptographic concepts in Microsoft Access environments*. MWAIS 2021 Proceedings. https://aisel.aisnet.org/cgi/viewcontent.cgi?article=1019&context=mwais2021

Omar, M. (2022). *Machine Learning for Cybersecurity: Innovative Deep Learning Solutions*. Springer Brief. https://link.springer.com/book/978303115

Omar, M. (2024). From Attack to Defense: Strengthening DNN Text Classification Against Adversarial Examples. In *Innovations, Securities, and Case Studies Across Healthcare, Business, and Technology* (pp. 174-195). IGI Global.

Omar, M. (2024). Revolutionizing Malware Detection: A Paradigm Shift Through Optimized Convolutional Neural Networks. In *Innovations, Securities, and Case Studies Across Healthcare, Business, and Technology* (pp. 196-220). IGI Global. DOI: 10.4018/979-8-3693-1906-2.ch011

Omar, M., Zangana, H. M., Al-Karaki, J. N., & Mohammed, D. (2024). Harnessing LLMs for IoT malware detection: A comparative analysis of BERT and GPT-2. In *2024 8th International Symposium on Multidisciplinary Studies and Innovative Technologies (ISMSIT)* (pp. 1-6). Ankara, Turkiye. https://doi.org/DOI: 10.1109/ISMSIT63511.2024.10757249

Omar, M., & Zangana, H. (Eds.). (2025). *Digital Forensics in the Age of AI*. IGI Global., DOI: 10.4018/979-8-3373-0857-9

Omar, M., & Zangana, H. M. (Eds.). (2024). *Redefining Security With Cyber AI*. IGI Global., DOI: 10.4018/979-8-3693-6517-5

Omar, M., & Zangana, H. M. (Eds.). (2025). *Application of Large Language Models (LLMs) for Software Vulnerability Detection*. IGI Global., DOI: 10.4018/979-8-3693-9311-6

Omar, M., Zangana, H. M., & Mohammed, D. (Eds.). (2025). *Integrating Artificial Intelligence in Cybersecurity and Forensic Practices*. IGI Global., DOI: 10.4018/979-8-3373-0588-2

Otieno, M. (2023). An extensive survey of smart agriculture technologies: Current security posture. *World J. Adv. Res. Rev*, *18*(3), 1207–1231. DOI: 10.30574/wjarr.2023.18.3.1241

Ozkan-Okay, M., Akin, E., Aslan, Ö., Kosunalp, S., Iliev, T., Stoyanov, I., & Beloev, I. (2024). A comprehensive survey: Evaluating the efficiency of artificial intelligence and machine learning techniques on cyber security solutions. *IEEE Access : Practical Innovations, Open Solutions*, *12*, 12229–12256. DOI: 10.1109/ACCESS.2024.3355547

Öztürk, M. S., & Usul, H. (2020). Detection of accounting frauds using the rule-based expert systems within the scope of forensic accounting. In *Contemporary issues in audit management and forensic accounting* (pp. 155–171). Emerald Publishing Limited. DOI: 10.1108/S1569-375920200000102013

Padua, D. (2025). Artificial intelligence and quality education: The need for digital culture in teaching. *Journal of Educational* [ECPS Journal]. *Cultural and Psychological Studies*, (30), 181–193.

Pai, Y. (2018). Patent Injunction Heuristics in India. *Pai, Yogesh, Patent Injunction Heuristics in India in Rafal Sikorski (Ed.) Patent Law Injunctions, Kluwer Law International BV (2019).*

Palmer, I., Dunford, R., & Buchanan, D. (2016). *EBOOK: Managing Organizational Change: A Multiple Perspectives Approach (ISE).* McGraw Hill.

Pandey, D. K., & Mishra, R. (2024). Towards sustainable agriculture: Harnessing AI for global food security. *Artificial Intelligence in Agriculture*, *12*, 72–84. DOI: 10.1016/j.aiia.2024.04.003

Patra, J. (2024). Cyber Laws And Emerging Use Of Artificial Intelligence: View From Sociological Perspectives. *REDVET-. Revista Electrónica de Veterinaria*, *25*(1), 1308–1312. DOI: 10.69980/redvet.v25i1.863

Pedro, F., Subosa, M., Rivas, A., & Valverde, P. (2019). *Artificial intelligence in education: Challenges and opportunities for sustainable development.* United Nations Educational, Scientific and Cultural Organization. https://afyonluoglu.org/PublicWebFiles/Reports/AI/UNESCO-2019-AI%20in%20Education.pdf

PeerMohamed, M. S. (2024). *Exploring ethical dimensions of AI-enhanced language education: A literature perspective.* Technology in Language Teaching & Learning.

Pesapane, F., Bracchi, D. A., Mulligan, J. F., Linnikov, A., Maslennikov, O., Lanzavecchia, M. B., Tantrige, P., Stasolla, A., Biondetti, P., Giuggioli, P. F., Cassano, E., & Carrafiello, G. (2021). Legal and regulatory framework for AI solutions in healthcare in EU, US, China, and Russia: New scenarios after a pandemic. *Radiation*, *1*(4), 261–276. DOI: 10.3390/radiation1040022

Pesapane, F., Volonté, C., Codari, M., & Sardanelli, F. (2018). Artificial intelligence as a medical device in radiology: Ethical and regulatory issues in Europe and the United States. *Insights Into Imaging*, *9*(5), 745–753. DOI: 10.1007/s13244-018-0645-y PMID: 30112675

Pimpalkar, A. P., Wankhade, N. R., Chole, V., & Golhar, Y. (2024). Women's Empowerment Through AI: Discovering Data Analytics for Predictive Safety Solutions and Future Trends. In *AI Tools and Applications for Women's Safety* (pp. 304-326). IGI Global Scientific Publishing.

Pleshakova, E., Osipov, A., Gataullin, S., Gataullin, T., & Vasilakos, A. (2024). Next gen cybersecurity paradigm towards artificial general intelligence: Russian market challenges and future global technological trends. *Journal of Computer Virology and Hacking Techniques*, *20*(3), 429–440. DOI: 10.1007/s11416-024-00529-x

Powell, A., Stratton, G., & Cameron, R. (2018). *Digital criminology: Crime and justice in digital society*. Routledge. DOI: 10.4324/9781315205786

Qatawneh, A. M. (2025). The role of artificial intelligence in auditing and fraud detection in accounting information systems: Moderating role of natural language processing. *The International Journal of Organizational Analysis*, *33*(6), 1391–1409. DOI: 10.1108/IJOA-03-2024-4389

Qiu, Y. (2025). Policing AI-generated crimes: An ethnographic study on anti-cybercrime police in China. *Security Journal*, *38*(1), 34. DOI: 10.1057/s41284-025-00491-3

Quan, T., Bracho, C. A., Wilkerson, M., & Clark, M. (2019). Empowerment and transformation: Integrating teacher identity, activism, and criticality across three teacher education programs. *Review of Education, Pedagogy & Cultural Studies*, *41*(4-5), 218–251. DOI: 10.1080/10714413.2019.1684162

Rajendran, R. K., & Tulasi, B. (2025). Natural Language Processing (NLP) for Threat Intelligence. In *Analyzing Privacy and Security Difficulties in Social Media: New Challenges and Solutions* (pp. 247-262). IGI Global Scientific Publishing.

Rajesh, R. (2024). *ARTIFICIAL INTELLIGENCE: BEYOND IDENTITIES. Routledge Handbook of Gender*. Culture, and Development in India.

Ramírez Sánchez, J., Campo-Archbold, A., Zapata Rozo, A., Díaz-López, D., Pastor-Galindo, J., Gómez Mármol, F., & Aponte Díaz, J. (2021). Uncovering cybercrimes in social media through natural language processing. *Complexity*, *2021*(1), 7955637. DOI: 10.1155/2021/7955637

Rawat, R., Oki, O., Chakrawarti, R. K., Adekunle, T. S., Lukose, J. M., & Ajagbe, S. A. (2023). Autonomous artificial intelligence systems for fraud detection and forensics in dark web environments. *Informatica (Vilnius)*, *47*(9).

Ray, V. (2019). A theory of racialized organizations. *American Sociological Review*, *84*(1), 26–53. DOI: 10.1177/0003122418822335

Read, A., Botha, R., & Jamaloodien, K. (2023). COVID-19 vaccination procurement and contract management in a South African context. *Journal of Strategic Contracting and Negotiation*, *7*(1-2), 33–43. DOI: 10.1177/20555636231198053

Richmond, K. M., Muddamsetty, S. M., Gammeltoft-Hansen, T., Olsen, H. P., & Moeslund, T. B. (2024). Explainable AI and law: An evidential survey. *Digital Society : Ethics, Socio-Legal and Governance of Digital Technology*, *3*(1), 1. DOI: 10.1007/s44206-023-00081-z

Rizal, R., Selamat, S. R., Mas'ud, M. Z., & Widiyasono, N. (2025). Enhanced readiness forensic framework for the complexity of internet of things (IoT) investigation based on artificial intelligence. *J. Adv. Res. Appl. Sci. Eng. Technol.*, *50*(1), 121–135. DOI: 10.37934/araset.50.1.121135

Rizvi, S., Scanlon, M., Mcgibney, J., & Sheppard, J. (2022). Application of artificial intelligence to network forensics: Survey, challenges and future directions. *IEEE Access : Practical Innovations, Open Solutions*, *10*, 110362–110384. DOI: 10.1109/ACCESS.2022.3214506

Rodriguez, M. Y., & Storer, H. (2020). A computational social science perspective on qualitative data exploration: Using topic models for the descriptive analysis of social media data. *Journal of Technology in Human Services*, *38*(1), 54–86. DOI: 10.1080/15228835.2019.1616350

Rughani, P. H. (2017). Artificial Intelligence Based Digital Forensics Framework. *International Journal of Advanced Research in Computer Science*, *8*(8), 10–14. DOI: 10.26483/ijarcs.v8i8.4571

Sahoh, B., & Choksuriwong, A. (2023). The role of explainable Artificial Intelligence in high-stakes decision-making systems: A systematic review. *Journal of Ambient Intelligence and Humanized Computing*, *14*(6), 7827–7843. DOI: 10.1007/s12652-023-04594-w PMID: 37228699

Saikia, B. (2024). Ecologically-Informed approaches: International mechanisms for navigating environmental challenges and ensuring sustainability in the oil and gas exploration and production industry. *Proceedings of the International Academy of Ecology and Environmental Sciences*, *14*(2), 60.

Sakapaji, S. C., García Molinos, J., Parilova, V., Gavrilyeva, T., & Yakovleva, N. (2024). Navigating legal and regulatory frameworks to achieve the resilience and sustainability of indigenous socioecological systems. *Resources*, *13*(4), 56. DOI: 10.3390/resources13040056

Salah, S., Mohamed, H., Sobuh, A., Almajali, E., Khan, W., Alaskar, H., & Hussain, A. (2025). Explainable AI for Unraveling the Significance of Visual Cues in High Stakes Deception Detection. *IEEE Access : Practical Innovations, Open Solutions*, *13*, 65839–65862. DOI: 10.1109/ACCESS.2025.3558875

Sá, M. J., & Serpa, S. (2020). The COVID-19 pandemic as an opportunity to foster the sustainable development of teaching in higher education. *Sustainability (Basel)*, *12*(20), 8525. DOI: 10.3390/su12208525

San Biagio, M., Cipolla, M., La Mattina, E., & Morreale, V. (2023, December). A Topic Clustering Method to Identify Online Threats against Soft Targets. In *2023 International Conference on Computational Science and Computational Intelligence (CSCI)* (pp. 727-733). IEEE. DOI: 10.1109/CSCI62032.2023.00124

Sangher, K. S., Singh, A., & Pandey, H. M. (2024). LSTM and BERT based transformers models for cyber threat intelligence for intent identification of social media platforms exploitation from darknet forums. *International Journal of Information Technology : an Official Journal of Bharati Vidyapeeth's Institute of Computer Applications and Management*, *16*(8), 5277–5292. DOI: 10.1007/s41870-024-02077-5

Sangher, K. S., Singh, A., Pandey, H. M., & Kumar, V. (2023). Towards safe cyber practices: Developing a proactive cyber-threat intelligence system for dark web forum content by identifying cybercrimes. *Information (Basel)*, *14*(6), 349. DOI: 10.3390/info14060349

Santos, O., Salam, S., & Dahir, H. (2024). *The AI revolution in networking, cybersecurity, and emerging technologies*. Addison-Wesley.

Sarker, I. H. (2024). Generative AI and large language modeling in cybersecurity. In *AI-Driven Cybersecurity and Threat Intelligence: Cyber Automation, Intelligent Decision-Making and Explainability* (pp. 79–99). Springer Nature Switzerland. DOI: 10.1007/978-3-031-54497-2_5

Sathwara, S., Dutta, N., & Pricop, E. (2018, June). IoT Forensic A digital investigation framework for IoT systems. In *2018 10th international conference on electronics, computers and artificial intelligence (ECAI)* (pp. 1-4). IEEE. DOI: 10.1109/ECAI.2018.8679017

Schünemann, C., Johanning, S., Reger, E., Herold, H., & Bruckner, T. (2024). Complex system policy modelling approaches for policy advice–comparing systems thinking, system dynamics and agent-based modelling. *Political Research Exchange : an ECPR Journal*, *6*(1), 2387438. DOI: 10.1080/2474736X.2024.2387438

Senoo, E. E. K., Anggraini, L., Kumi, J. A., Luna, B. K., Akansah, E., Sulyman, H. A., & Aritsugi, M. (2024). IoT solutions with artificial intelligence technologies for precision agriculture: Definitions, applications, challenges, and opportunities. *Electronics (Basel)*, *13*(10), 1894. DOI: 10.3390/electronics13101894

Shafik, W. (2024). Data privacy and security safeguarding customer information in ChatGPT systems. In *Revolutionizing the Service Industry Wth OpenAI Models* (pp. 52–86). IGI Global. DOI: 10.4018/979-8-3693-1239-1.ch003

Shafik, W., Tufail, A., De Silva, C. L., Haji, R. A. A., & Apong, M. (2025). The Role, Application, and Impact of Artificial Intelligence in the Agriculture Industry. In *Future Tech Startups and Innovation in the Age of AI* (pp. 36–60). CRC Press.

Shani, A. B., Noumair, D. A., Zandee, D. P., & Coghlan, D. (Eds.). (2025). *Research in organizational change and development*. Emerald Publishing Limited. DOI: 10.1108/S0897-3016202531

Sharma, L., & Garg, P. K. (Eds.). (2023). *Technological prospects and social applications of society 5.0*. CRC Press.

Sheikhbahei, E., & Ari, A. A. (2024). Harnessing the power of emerging digital technologies for improved sustainability and productivity in biomedical engineering and neuroscience. *Scientific Hypotheses*, *1*, 47–52. DOI: 10.69530/v8tgp793

Sheliemina, N. (2024). The use of artificial intelligence in medical diagnostics: Opportunities, prospects and risks. *Health Economics and Management Review*, *5*(2), 104–124. DOI: 10.61093/hem.2024.2-07

Shuja, J., Alanazi, E., Alasmary, W., & Alashaikh, A. (2021). COVID-19 open source data sets: A comprehensive survey. *Applied Intelligence*, *51*(3), 1296–1325. DOI: 10.1007/s10489-020-01862-6 PMID: 34764552

Shukla, R. P., & Taneja, S. (2024). Ethical considerations and data privacy in artificial intelligence. In *Integrating generative AI in education to achieve sustainable development goals* (pp. 86–97). IGI Global. DOI: 10.4018/979-8-3693-2440-0.ch005

Siddiqui, T., Amer, A. Y. A., & Khan, N. A. (2019, November). Criminal activity detection in social network by text mining: comprehensive analysis. In *2019 4th International Conference on Information Systems and Computer Networks (ISCON)* (pp. 224-229). IEEE. DOI: 10.1109/ISCON47742.2019.9036157

Sikos, L. F. (2021). AI in digital forensics: Ontology engineering for cybercrime investigations. *WIREs Forensic Science*, *3*(3), e1394. DOI: 10.1002/wfs2.1394

Simbolon, R., Adriana, N., Rustam, A., Sulistyowati, N. W., & Rewa, K. A. (2024). The Impact of Forensic Accounting on Financial Fraud Prevention: A Comparative Analysis Across Countries. *The Journal of Academic Science*, *1*(8), 1074–1084. DOI: 10.59613/m6jrt421

Singh, B., & Kaunert, C. (2025). Navigating the Terrain of Sustainability Trajectories of Environment: Biodiversity Protection and Legal Landscapes. In *Community Resilience and Climate Change Challenges: Pursuit of Sustainable Development Goals (SDGs)* (pp. 355-374). IGI Global Scientific Publishing.

Sood, A., Sharma, R. K., & Bhardwaj, A. K. (2022). Artificial intelligence research in agriculture: A review. *Online Information Review*, *46*(6), 1054–1075. DOI: 10.1108/OIR-10-2020-0448

Soomro, J. A., Suhrab, M., & Abbasi, B. A. (2025). Navigating Green Regulations in the Business Ecosystem: Government Support, Compliance, and Obstacles in the Context of Pakistan. In *Government Influences on Eco-Friendly Practices in Business* (pp. 55-86). IGI Global.

Sparrow, R., Howard, M., & Degeling, C. (2021). Managing the risks of artificial intelligence in agriculture. *NJAS: Impact in Agricultural and Life Sciences*, *93*(1), 172–196. DOI: 10.1080/27685241.2021.2008777

Spyropoulos, F. (2024). New Approaches to Researching AI Crime: Institutionalization of Digital Criminology. *Journal of Digital Technologies and Law*, *2*(3), 636–656. DOI: 10.21202/jdtl.2024.32

Stouten, J., Rousseau, D. M., & De Cremer, D. (2018). Successful organizational change: Integrating the management practice and scholarly literatures. *The Academy of Management Annals*, *12*(2), 752–788. DOI: 10.5465/annals.2016.0095

Sufi, F. (2023). Novel application of open-source cyber intelligence. *Electronics (Basel)*, *12*(17), 3610. DOI: 10.3390/electronics12173610

Sufi, F. (2023). Social media analytics on Russia–Ukraine cyber war with natural language processing: Perspectives and challenges. *Information (Basel)*, *14*(9), 485. DOI: 10.3390/info14090485

Sullivan, A. L., Artiles, A. J., & Hernandez-Saca, D. I. (2015). Addressing special education inequity through systemic change: Contributions of ecologically based organizational consultation. *Journal of Educational & Psychological Consultation*, *25*(2-3), 129–147. DOI: 10.1080/10474412.2014.929969

Sun, N., Ding, M., Jiang, J., Xu, W., Mo, X., Tai, Y., & Zhang, J. (2023). Cyber threat intelligence mining for proactive cybersecurity defense: A survey and new perspectives. *IEEE Communications Surveys and Tutorials*, *25*(3), 1748–1774. DOI: 10.1109/COMST.2023.3273282

Sutikno, T., & Busthomi, I. (2025). Power of analytic tools in Oxygen Forensic® Detective based on NIST cybersecurity framework. *Computer Science and Information Technology*, *6*(1), 8–19.

SWARGIARY. K. (2025). *Educational Sociology: Theory, Practice, and Contemporary Challenges*. ERA, US.

Taghavi, S. M., & Feyzi, F. (2024). *Using large language models to better detect and handle software vulnerabilities and cyber security threats. Research Square*. DOI: 10.21203/rs.3.rs-4387414/v1

Terry, N. (2019). Of regulating healthcare AI and robots. *Yale JL & Tech.*, *21*, 133.

Trotsyuk, A. A., Waeiss, Q., Bhatia, R. T., Aponte, B. J., Heffernan, I. M., Madgavkar, D., Felder, R. M., Lehmann, L. S., Palmer, M. J., Greely, H., Wald, R., Goetz, L., Trengove, M., Vandersluis, R., Lin, H., Cho, M. K., Altman, R. B., Endy, D., Relman, D. A., & Magnus, D. (2024). Toward a framework for risk mitigation of potential misuse of artificial intelligence in biomedical research. *Nature Machine Intelligence*, *6*(12), 1–8. DOI: 10.1038/s42256-024-00926-3

Tzachor, A., Devare, M., King, B., Avin, S., & Ó hÉigeartaigh, S. (2022). Responsible artificial intelligence in agriculture requires systemic understanding of risks and externalities. *Nature Machine Intelligence*, *4*(2), 104–109. DOI: 10.1038/s42256-022-00440-4

Uduehe, E. M., Okoye, E. I., & Amahalu, N. N. (2024). Forensic accounting techniques and fraud management of commercial banks in Awka-South Anambra State. *Journal of Global Accounting*, *10*(2), 307–346.

Umanah, E. A., Etti, W. C., & Sunday, D. U. (2024). Implications of Emerging Technologies on Social Behaviour and Crime Control in the 21st Century. *Journal of Advanced Research and Multidisciplinary Studies*, *4*(3), 152–162. DOI: 10.52589/JARMS-JL2NFQ57

Uplaonkar, S. S., Veershetty, R., Bahar, Z., & Sangeeta, G. (2024). The role of productive AI: A supporter or challenger in the future of agricultural librarianship. *IJAR*, *10*(4), 46–53.

Vaseashta, A. (2022). Nexus of advanced technology platforms for strengthening cyber-defense capabilities. In *Practical applications of advanced technologies for enhancing security and defense capabilities: Perspectives and Challenges for the Western Balkans* (pp. 14-31). IOS Press. DOI: 10.3233/NHSDP220003

Verma, A., Rao, K., Eluri, V., & Sharma, Y. (2020). Regulating AI in public health: systems challenges and perspectives. *ORF Occasional Paper, 261*.

Vyawahare, H., Khandelwal, S., & Rathod, S. (2024). Artificial Intelligence in Detecting and Preventing Online Harassment. In *AI Tools and Applications for Women's Safety* (pp. 14–35). IGI Global Scientific Publishing. DOI: 10.4018/979-8-3693-1435-7.ch002

Wang, Q. (2024). Maritime law enforcement concerning offshore energy platforms: Navigating international law constraints and challenges. *Marine Policy, 170*, 106370. DOI: 10.1016/j.marpol.2024.106370

Wei, H., Xu, W., Kang, B., Eisner, R., Muleke, A., Rodriguez, D., deVoil, P., Sadras, V., Monjardino, M., & Harrison, M. T. (2024). Irrigation with artificial intelligence: Problems, premises, promises. *Human-Centric Intelligent Systems, 4*(2), 187–205. DOI: 10.1007/s44230-024-00072-4

Williamson, H. F., Brettschneider, J., Caccamo, M., Davey, R. P., Goble, C., Kersey, P. J., May, S., Morris, R. J., Ostler, R., Pridmore, T., Rawlings, C., Studholme, D., Tsaftaris, S. A., & Leonelli, S. (2023). Data management challenges for artificial intelligence in plant and agricultural research. *F1000 Research, 10*, 324. DOI: 10.12688/f1000research.52204.2 PMID: 36873457

Wright, J., Dawson, M. E.Jr, & Omar, M. (2012). Cyber security and mobile threats: The need for antivirus applications for smartphones. *Journal of Information Systems Technology and Planning, 5*(14), 40–60.

Xu, H., Wang, S., Li, N., Wang, K., Zhao, Y., Chen, K., . . . Wang, H. (2024). Large language models for cyber security: A systematic literature review. *arXiv preprint arXiv:2405.04760.*

Ya'u, M. S., & Mohammed, M. S. (2025). AI-Assisted Writing and Academic Literacy: Investigating the Dual Impact of Language Models on Writing Proficiency and Ethical Concerns in Nigerian Higher Education. *International Journal of Education and Literacy Studies, 13*(2), 593–604. DOI: 10.7575/aiac.ijels.v.13n.2p.593

Yu, J., Shvetsov, A. V., & Alsamhi, S. H. (2024). Leveraging machine learning for cybersecurity resilience in industry 4.0: Challenges and future directions. *IEEE Access : Practical Innovations, Open Solutions, 12*, 159579–159596. DOI: 10.1109/ACCESS.2024.3482987

Zangana, H. M., & Mustafa, F. M. (2026). Enhancing Educational Visual Content Through AI-Based Image Denoising Techniques: Implications for Remote Teaching and Digital Resource Development. In *Harnessing AI for Teacher Support and Professional Development* (pp. 101-136). IGI Global Scientific Publishing.

Zangana, H. M., Mustafa, F. M., & Li, S. (2025). Large Language Models in Cybersecurity: From Automation to Intelligence. In *Leveraging Large Language Models for Quantum-Aware Cybersecurity* (pp. 277-300). IGI Global Scientific Publishing.

Zangana, H. M. (2017). Library Data Quality Maturity (IIUM as a Case Study). *IOSR Journal of Computer Engineering, 19*(March), 29. DOI: 10.9790/0661-1902033844

Zangana, H. M. (2017). Watermarking System Using LSB. *IOSR Journal of Computer Engineering, 19*(3), 75–79. DOI: 10.9790/0661-1903027579

Zangana, H. M. (2018). Design an information management system for a pharmacy. *International Journal of Advanced Research in Computer and Communication Engineering, 7*(10), 52–55. DOI: 10.17148/IJARCCE.2018.71012

Zangana, H. M. (2018). Implementing a System for Recognizing Optical Characters. *International Journal of Advanced Research in Computer and Communication Engineering, 7*(10), 56–60. DOI: 10.17148/IJARCCE.2018.71013

Zangana, H. M. (2019). Issues of Data Management in the Library: A Case Study. *International Journal on Computer Science and Engineering, 7*(10), 159–163. DOI: 10.26438/ijcse/v7i10.159163

Zangana, H. M. (2020). Mobile Device Integration in IIUM Service. *International Journal (Toronto, Ont.), 8*(5).

Zangana, H. M. (2021). The Global Finical Crisis from an Islamic Point Of View. *Qubahan Academic Journal, 1*(2), 55–59. DOI: 10.48161/qaj.v1n2a39

Zangana, H. M. (2022). Creating a Community-Based Disaster Management System. *Academic Journal of Nawroz University, 11*(4), 234–244. DOI: 10.25007/ajnu.v11n4a1485

Zangana, H. M. (2022). Implementing New Interactive Video Learning System for IIUM. *Academic Journal of Nawroz University, 11*(2), 23–29. DOI: 10.25007/ajnu.v11n2a1281

Zangana, H. M. (2025). Design and Implementation of a Novel Parallel Algorithm for Efficient Image Compression in High-Performance Computing. *EAI Endorsed Transactions on AI and Robotics*, *4*. Advance online publication. DOI: 10.4108/airo.7832

Zangana, H. M., & Abdulazeez, A. M. (2023). Developed Clustering Algorithms for Engineering Applications: A Review. *International Journal of Informatics* [IN-JIISCOM]. *Information System and Computer Engineering*, *4*(2), 147–169.

Zangana, H. M., & Al-Shaikhli, I. F. (2013). A new algorithm for human face detection using skin color tone. *IOSR Journal of Computer Engineering*, *11*(6), 31–38. DOI: 10.9790/0661-1163138

Zangana, H. M., Bazeed, S. M. S., Ali, N. Y., & Abdullah, D. T. (2024). Navigating Project Change: A Comprehensive Review of Change Management Strategies and Practices. *Indonesian Journal of Education and Social Sciences*, *3*(2), 166–179. DOI: 10.56916/ijess.v3i2.735

Zangana, H. M., Mohammed, A. K., Sallow, A. B., & Sallow, Z. B. (2024). Cybernetic Deception: Unraveling the Layers of Email Phishing Threats. [INJURATECH]. *International Journal of Research and Applied Technology*, *4*(1), 35–47.

Zangana, H. M., Mohammed, H. S., & Husain, M. M. (2025). Addressing insider threats: The human factor in cybersecurity for financial institutions. *Journal of Innovation Information Technology and Application*, *7*(1), 88–96. DOI: 10.35970/jinita.v7i1.2686

Zangana, H. M., Mohammed, H. S., & Husain, M. M. (2025). The Role of Large Language Models in Enhancing Cybersecurity Measures: Empirical Evidence from Regional Banking Institutions. *SISTEMASI*, *14*(5), 2018–2027. DOI: 10.32520/stmsi.v14i4.5144

Zangana, H. M., Mohammed, H. S., & Husain, M. M.Hewa Majeed ZanganaHarman Salih MohammedMamo Muhamad Husain. (2025). Banking Cybersecurity: Safeguarding Financial Information in the Digital Era. *Journal of Computers and Digital Business*, *4*(2), 56–63. DOI: 10.56427/jcbd.v4i2.751

Zangana, H. M., & Mustafa, F. M. (2024). From Classical to Deep Learning: A Systematic Review of Image Denoising Techniques. *Jurnal Ilmiah Computer Science*, *3*(1), 50–65. DOI: 10.58602/jics.v3i1.36

Zangana, H. M., & Mustafa, F. M. (2024). Hybrid Image Denoising Using Wavelet Transform and Deep Learning. *EAI Endorsed Transactions on AI and Robotics*, *3*. Advance online publication. DOI: 10.4108/airo.7486

Zangana, H. M., & Mustafa, F. M. (2024). Review of Hybrid Denoising Approaches in Face Recognition: Bridging Wavelet Transform and Deep Learning. *The Indonesian Journal of Computer Science, 13*(4). Advance online publication. DOI: 10.33022/ijcs.v13i4.4209

Zangana, H. M., & Mustafa, F. M. (2024). Surveying the Landscape: A Comprehensive Review of Object Detection Algorithms and Advancements. *Jurnal Ilmiah Computer Science, 3*(1), 1–15. DOI: 10.58602/jics.v3i1.29

Zangana, H. M., Mustafa, F. M., & Omar, M. (2024). A Hybrid Approach for Robust Object Detection: Integrating Template Matching and Faster R-CNN. *EAI Endorsed Transactions on AI and Robotics, 3*. Advance online publication. DOI: 10.4108/airo.6858

Zangana, H. M., & Omar, M. (2020). Threats, Attacks, and Mitigations of Smartphone Security. *Academic Journal of Nawroz University, 9*(4), 324–332. DOI: 10.25007/ajnu.v9n4a989

Zangana, H. M., & Omar, M. (2025). The Role of Leadership in Advancing Inclusive Health Technologies. In Burrell, D., & Nguyen, C. (Eds.), *New Horizons in Leadership: Inclusive Explorations in Health, Technology, and Education* (pp. 203–220). IGI Global Scientific Publishing., DOI: 10.4018/979-8-3693-6437-6.ch009

Zangana, H. M., Omar, M., Ali, N. Y., & Abdullah, D. T. (2025). Enhancing IT Project Agility Through Effective Change Management Strategies. *The Asian Journal of Technology Management, 18*(1), 20–36. DOI: 10.12695/ajtm.2025.18.1.2

Zangana, H. M., & Salih, A. A. (2025). Enhancing Business Administration Through Decision Support Systems: A Comprehensive Review. *Sistem Pendukung Keputusan Dengan Aplikasi, 4*(2), 45–56. DOI: 10.55537/spk.v4i2.1138

Zangana, H. M., Sallow, Z. B., & Omar, M. (2025). The Human Factor in Cybersecurity: Addressing the Risks of Insider Threats. *Jurnal Ilmiah Computer Science, 3*(2), 76–85. DOI: 10.58602/jics.v3i2.37

Zangana, H., Ali, N. Y., Bazeed, S. M. S., & Abdullah, D. T. (2025). Leveraging Automation and Traceability in Managing Changes to Mission-Critical Computer Systems. *Indonesian Journal of Education and Social Sciences, 4*(1), 176–189.

Zangana, H., Al-Karaki, J., & Omar, M. (Eds.). (2025). *Navigating Law and Policy in STM Enterprises: Ethical Governance, Regulation, and Innovation Strategy*. IGI Global., DOI: 10.4018/979-8-3373-4862-9

Zangana, H., Al-Karaki, J., & Omar, M. (Eds.). (2025). *Revolutionizing Cybersecurity With Deep Learning and Large Language Models*. IGI Global., DOI: 10.4018/979-8-3373-3296-3

Zangana, H., Nobles, C., & Omar, M. (Eds.). (2026). *Harnessing AI for Teacher Support and Professional Development*. IGI Global Scientific Publishing., DOI: 10.4018/979-8-3373-5951-9

Zangana, H., & Omar, M. (Eds.). (2025). *Ensuring Secure and Ethical STM Research in the AI Era*. IGI Global., DOI: 10.4018/979-8-3373-4252-8

Zangana, H., & Omar, M. (Eds.). (2025). *Leveraging Large Language Models for Quantum-Aware Cybersecurity*. IGI Global., DOI: 10.4018/979-8-3373-1102-9

Zareef, I., & Riaz, A. Salahuddin, Fatima, M., Anwar, A., & Munawar, A. (2024). Unveiling the Power of Nanomaterials in the Area of Forensics. In *Emerging Applications of Novel Nanoparticles* (pp. 29-57). Cham: Springer Nature Switzerland.

Završnik, A. (2017). Big data: What is it and why does it matter for crime and social control? In *Big data, crime and social control* (pp. 3–28). Routledge. DOI: 10.4324/9781315395784-1

Zayed, L. M. M., Nour, M. I., Al Attar, K., Almubaideen, H., & Abdelaziz, G. A. M. (2024). Role of artificial intelligence (AI) in accounting information systems in detecting fraud. In *Artificial Intelligence and Economic Sustainability in the Era of Industrial Revolution 5.0* (pp. 397–409). Springer Nature Switzerland. DOI: 10.1007/978-3-031-56586-1_30

Zheng, W., Tan, Y., Jiang, B., & Wang, J. (2025). Integrating Machine Learning into Financial Forensics for Smarter Fraud Prevention. *Technology and Investment*, *16*(3), 79–90. DOI: 10.4236/ti.2025.163006

Zohouri, M., Sabzali, M., & Golmohammadi, A. (2024). Ethical considerations of ChatGPT-assisted article writing. *Synesis (ISSN 1984-6754)*, *16*(1), 94-113.

Zreik, M. (2024). Harnessing AI for entrepreneurial idea generation: Navigating the new frontier. In *Generating Entrepreneurial Ideas With AI* (pp. 1–18). IGI Global Scientific Publishing. DOI: 10.4018/979-8-3693-3498-0.ch001

About the Contributors

Hewa Majeed Zangana is an Assistant Professor at Duhok Polytechnic University (DPU), Iraq, and a current PhD candidate in Information Technology Management (ITM) at the same institution. He has held numerous academic and administrative positions, including Assistant Professor at Ararat Private Technical Institute, Lecturer at DPU's Amedi Technical Institute and Nawroz University, and Acting Dean of the College of Computer and IT at Nawroz University. His administrative roles have included Director of the Curriculum Division at the Presidency of DPU, Manager of the Information Unit at DPU's Research Center, and Head of the Computer Science Department at Nawroz University. Dr. Zangana's research interests include network systems, information security, mobile and data communication, and intelligent systems. He has authored numerous articles in peer-reviewed journals, including Inform: Jurnal Ilmiah Bidang Teknologi Informasi dan Komunikasi, Indonesian Journal of Education and Social Science, TIJAB, INJIISCOM, IEEE, and AJNU. In addition to his journal contributions, he has published more than five academic books with IGI Global, several of which are indexed in Scopus and Web of Science (Clarivate). Beyond publishing, Dr. Zangana actively contributes to the academic community through editorial service. He serves as a reviewer for the Qubahan Academic Journal and the Scientific Journals of Nawroz University. He is also a member of several academic and scientific committees, including the Scientific Curriculum Development Committee, the Student Follow-up Program Committee, and the Committee for Drafting the Rules of Procedure for Consultative Offices.

***

Luay Albtosh is a dedicated and accomplished professional currently pursuing a Ph.D. in Cyber Leadership. With a robust academic background and over a decade of industry experience, Luay Albtosh has established a strong foothold in the field of computer science. Luay Albtosh holds a master's degree in computer science, which laid the groundwork for a career marked by continuous learning and impactful contributions to the field. Throughout the years, Luay Albtosh has developed a profound expertise in various aspects of computer science, including cybersecurity, software development, and IT project management. In addition to academic achievements, Luay Albtosh has consistently demonstrated a commitment to excellence in professional endeavors. With more than 10 years of hands-on experience, Luay Albtosh has successfully led numerous projects, drove innovation and ensuring the seamless integration of technology solutions. This extensive experience has provided Luay Albtosh with a deep understanding of both the technical and strategic facets of the industry.

Hermano Jorge De Queiroz is an Associate Professor of Graduate Studies at Lindsey Wilson College and former Chair of Undergraduate IT at the University of the Cumberlands. He holds a Ph.D. and M.Sc. in Information Systems Security from the University of the Cumberlands, an M.B.A. from Campbellsville University, and a B.Sc. in Management Information Systems from Anhanguera Educacional. Dr. De Queiroz specializes in IT and education, focusing on instructional design, online learning, and systems security. He serves as a Subject Matter Expert in curriculum development and program design for undergraduate and graduate programs. His research interests include data science, AI, and cybersecurity. Multilingual in Portuguese, English, and Spanish, he actively supports cross-cultural academic collaboration and has led various initiatives to enhance learning outcomes and academic quality.

Rebet Jones is an Assistant Professor at the Department of Industrial and Systems Engineering at Kennesaw State University. Education: he has a Ph.D. in Computer Science, Artificial Intelligence, and Organizational Leadership, a Master of Science in International Business and trade, and a Bachelor of Science in Electronics Engineering. Certifications: Artificial Intelligence Governance Professional (AIGP), Project Management Professional (PMP)®, PMI-ACP Certified Practitioner (ACP)®Certified Information Security Manager (CISM)®, Certified Information Security Auditor (CISA)®, Certified Risk and Information Systems Control (CRISC)®, Certified Data Privacy Solution Engineer (CDPSE)®. AWS Certified Solution Architect - Professional and AWS Certified Security - Specialist. Practical work experience: he has a combined 22 years of corporate professional experience in project/program management, specifically in security governance compliance and the engineering and information technology industry. He worked for AT&T, Home Depot Canada Supply Chain & Logistics, and the Department of Defense. His research interests a in CyberSecurity, Artificial Intelligence, and Machine Learning.

Derek Mohammed is a Professor of Computer Information Systems at Saint Leo University, where he has served since 2012 in various leadership roles, including founding Director of the Center for Cybersecurity. He holds a BS in Physics and an MS in Engineering from the University of the West Indies, an MBA in Information Systems from City University, and a PhD in Information Systems from Nova Southeastern University. Dr. Mohammed's scholarly work spans cybersecurity, artificial intelligence, and data analytics, with publications focusing on risk management frameworks, cloud security models, and AI applications in education and industry. His research and teaching are complemented by over two decades of professional experience in academia, government, and industry, along with multiple professional certifications, including CISSP, CISM, CISA, CDPSE, and PMP.

Firas Mahmood Mustafa holds a Ph.D. in Computer Engineering from Mosul University, Iraq. His academic journey began with a B.Sc. in Electrical Engineering (Electronics and Communication), graduating in the top quarter of his class. He earned an M.Sc. in Computer Engineering from Mosul University in 2000. Mustafa joined the Computer Science Department at AlHadba University in 2003 and completed his Ph.D. in 2007. From 2013 to 2017, he was with DPU University, and from 2017 to 2020, he chaired the CCE Department at Nawroz University. An active participant in Erasmus+ and IREX programs, he now teaches at DPU University, shaping future computer engineering professionals.

Anuradha Rangarajan holds a PhD in Technology Management, MS degrees in Computer Systems Engineering, Computer Science, and Cybersecurity, and an MBA. Her interdisciplinary research interests lie at the intersection of applied computer science and computer systems engineering, information systems innovation and diffusion, and socio-technical factors in technology implementations. She is an Assistant Professor in Information Technology and Management at the Illinois Institute of Technology, Chicago, Illinois, United States.

Index

A

B

C

D

E

F

H

I

S

T

www.ingramcontent.com/pod-product-compliance
Lightning Source LLC
LaVergne TN
LVHW080907300926
849162LV00003B/592
9798337365367